CLOSE CALL

RAF Close Air Support in the Mediterranean

Volume I

Defeat in France to el Hamma 1939-1943

This volume is dedicated to all unit scribes, diarists, autobiographers, curators, archivists, researchers, historians, photographers and fellow writers who over the years have made it possible to shed light on past events.

Close Call

RAF Close Air Support in the Mediterranean

Vic Flintham

First published in 2020 by Crécy Publishing

ISBN 9781902109640

Printed in Bulgaria by Multiprint

Crécy Publishing Limited
1a Ringway Trading Estate, Shadowmoss Rd, Manchester M22 5LH
www.crecy.co.uk

Front cover top: The RAF commitment to provision of cab-ranks for the first time was given to the Kittyhawk squadrons with Spitfire and Hurricane cover. 112 Sqn with its distinctive sharks-teeth nose was one of several involved. *Author's collection*

Front cover bottom: A1924 is at a UK aerodrome, possibly Larkhill, with F.E.2bs and an R.E.8 in the background. *Author's collection*

Front flap: SBD-3 Dauntlesses of VGS-26 and F4F-4 Wildcats of VGF-26 on the flight deck of USS *Sangamon. USN Official*

Back cover top: In June 1941 the Curtiss Tomahawk began replacing the Gladiators of 112 Sqn, as seen here with Tomahawk IIb AK461/A etc. at Sidi Haneish in July 1941. *AST collection*

Back cover middle left: One of the most important aircraft in providing support to the Army was the Albacore of the Fleet Air Arm. *Author's collection*

Back cover middle right: Blenheims of 2 Group Bomber Command flew numerous interdiction missions during May and early June in France and the Low Countries. *Author's collection*

Back cover bottom: Two squadrons of light bombers, 88 and 226. One of the former's aircraft is Boston IIIA BZ377 RH-F. *AST collection*

Title page profile: Blenheim I L8376/UQ-D 211 Sqn. *Luca G. Canossa*

Page 3 top: The Sopwith T.F.2 Salamander was a dedicated trench fighter design based on the Snipe fighter but with an armoured 'box' around the pilot and protection for the fuel tank. *Author's collection*

Page 3 bottom: In this obviously posed photograph Beaufighter VIf V8748/ZJ-R was caught at Drem in September 1943 with six WAAFs forming a human chain taking ammunition boxes to the tail of the aircraft! *Author's collection*

Page 3 profile: Spitfire Vb JK112/WU-A 225 Sqn. *Luca G. Canossa*

Contents

Preface

My uncle, Captain Aubrey Cuthbert Young, DFC, had an interesting war, busy and brave in equal measure. Commissioned as a gunner officer, he resented having to contribute to his colonel's pack of hounds and sought fresh pastures. He spotted a requirement for Royal Artillery officers to train as pilots, volunteered and was accepted – to the annoyance of his CO.

He trained with 22 Elementary Flying Training School (EFTS) at Cambridge between 13 February and 4 May 1942, crashing Tiger Moth T7306 on his first solo at 14hr 25mins total air time. On passing through to 43 Operational Training Unit (OTU), having crashed T7266, this time on take-off he was marked 'average', with the comment 'His flying should be carefully watched'! Graduating from the OTU, he completed the Air Observation Post (AOP) course on 28 June with a total of seventy hours dual and seventy-six solo on Tiger Moth and Auster I.

After a short time with 659 Sqn, he was posted to 657 Sqn at Clifton, embarking immediately for North Africa where he flew training and communications sorties and air tests until moving to Italy in January 1944. With A Flight he then directed guns from the Cassino battles up to the Gothic line, earning a DFC directing a shoot south of Ravenna.

In March 1945 the squadron moved to the Netherlands, then Germany, returning to the UK in November. Aubrey made his last flight, from Andover, on 16 January 1946, and with 773 hours solo in his logbook; he never flew again. At the height of the fighting in Italy he was airborne for up to five one-hour sorties a day, flying on most days apart from during a brief period of leave. This was when fighter and bomber units were grounded for days, or even weeks on end, due to appalling weather and strong winds.

Before he died, my uncle typed up his handwritten war diary and gave me a copy; I also had access to his logbook and photographs. One thing that intrigued me was the occasional reference to 'Rover David'. Aubrey explained that this was the call sign for a system that allowed him to direct RAF fighter-bombers on to appropriate targets. I decided that one day I would try to find out more.

With other projects around I put research on the back-burner until, out of the blue, I had an email from the Museum of Army Flying. An American lady had identified photos held by the museum that had me as the donor and she wished to make contact: would it be OK for the museum to pass on my details? The photos were among some that Aubrey had given me and I was more than happy for her to get in touch.

Cathy Murray is the niece of Arrol Macfarlane, also an AOP pilot during the war. Arrol had typed up his war story for his sons in 1955 and it was her intention to edit (corrections of fact only), add more photos and to self-publish for the wider family. Remarkably, it transpired that Arrol ('Mac') had served in A Flight with Aubrey throughout 1944 and 1945. Because a flight had four pilots and there were four flights to a squadron and then fourteen operational AOP squadrons during the Second World War, it was remarkable that two veterans, having served together, should commit their memories to paper and that, independently, members of their families should be striving to make their exploits more accessible.

I was sent a draft of the book, *Warlike Sketches*, by Cathy and the contents were of more than passing interest. Not only did 'Rover David' crop up again, it became clear that in A Flight of 657 Sqn at least, AOP pilots did a lot more than direct artillery shoots. So started the quest in earnest for the who, what and why of Rover David.

At an early stage in planning I asked my pal Ray Hankin, once of *The Aeroplane and Flying Review International* and highly competent editor of my most recent book, if he would be interested in helping. He took the bait and we started a scoping exercise, visiting The National Archive (TNA). From documents there it quickly became clear that a book around AOP in Italy, with a bit of forward air control thrown in, would overlook some very important issues. Thus, the emphasis turned to close air support in relation to artillery actions.

Late in the writing process, in October 2018, I had an email from Adrian Rigby. He had bought

Warlike Sketches because his father, Tony, had also been an AOP pilot in Italy – serving with none other than A Flight of 657 Sqn! Adrian was able to furnish logbook and photos which have added to the sum of knowledge.

Trying to determine how the book might evolve eventually has proved difficult. The war in North Africa and Italy has been well-researched and written up and there are numerous scholarly treatises on close air support, directed predominantly at an academic or military audience. There are, though, problems with many of these works.

First, they are based on formal documents written by authors holding medium- to high-level rank and describing either intentions, or being lengthy and generalised summaries recalled after the event. I decided to review the command documents, but also to test assertions against what actually happened on the day as recorded in squadron operational records, individual logbooks, diaries and autobiographies. The results were surprising and showed that analysis sometimes ignored evidence and, unsurprisingly, that personal accounts, sometimes years later, understandably displayed lapses of memory.

The other problem was that although standard texts refer to systems, they rarely describe how those systems actually worked. Communications are critical for artillery support and for close air support, so how they were *intended* to operate and how they *actually* operated are of considerable interest. With material from The National Archive and a great deal of help from staff at the RAF Museum, I believe that I have been able to piece together how air support for the Army really evolved and matured, from intentions in the early Western Desert battles to refinement in Italy when approaching the war's end.

I had intended to start the narrative at the Battle of El Alamein and work forward, with a catch-all opening chapter describing how air support had, or had not, worked from the end of the First World War onwards. In the event this preliminary canter proved to be compelling stuff and essential in understanding what underpinned the later systems. Thus, the introductory scene-setting ended up as not one chapter but five, working through the pre-war years, defeat in France and Norway, formal changes in the UK including the establishment of Army Co-operation Command, and events in East Africa and the Western Desert.

The only references I could find initially for Rover David were to a control system, involving solely the RAF, and described by several writers as having been invented by one David Heysham. Clearly one author had lifted from another, because the originator turned out to be South African-born Wg Cdr Geoffrey David Haysom, RAF. Basically, a system of using specialist personnel right at the forward edge of the battlefield, able to communicate with ground attack units, Rover David evolved to enable immediate attack on targets beyond the range or scope of artillery. And with air supremacy won, AOP pilots were flying over the front line with impunity and calling in fighter-bombers the moment they spotted a likely target.

In writing this book I have tried to use the terms, and thus the thinking, applying at the time. For instance, although the Commonwealth of Nations was a term applied to the British Empire from 1926, it was not widely used and I have preferred Dominions. In respect of the air forces, it was often the Dominions that provided many of the squadrons in the Mediterranean theatre, and indeed many of the pilots of notionally RAF squadrons. So, by going back to the terminology and ideas of the day, I have tried to secure a better understanding of the way in which the war was fought. With hindsight, it is all too easy for historians to draw false conclusions or apply unjust criticism, but at the time participants had no idea of when and how the war would end – only hopes and aspirations.

One idiosyncrasy retained is the use in a number of quotes of the alternative 'straffe' for 'strafe'. This is not a misquote but the intrusion of '*sic*' throughout would spoil the flow of significant quotes.

I have avoided trying to think in terms of *doctrine*. Although the proposition may have been applied earlier, the first use I have found so far of doctrine in relation to RAF processes is in the AHB Narrative,[1] dated 1955. Staff colleges and learned journals now routinely apply acronyms like ALI (Air Land Integration) and C³I (Command, Control, Communications and Intelligence) retrospectively to air support during the Second World War. But although the ideas are helpful in analysis, they were not applied during the Second World War and I don't find it helpful to shoehorn contemporaneous thinking and relatively immature or spontaneous systems into modern and sophisticated constructs.

The scope of the book eventually and inevitably extended to embrace wider support for the Army, including interdiction of the lines of communication and supplies. I have mainly confined my descriptions and analysis to the Mediterranean theatre for it was here, far from oversight from Whitehall, that immediacy of action was more important than protocol and smart uniforms, and that trial and innovation thrived. The fact that so many of the key players were from the Dominions, or were reservists, probably ensured also that practical demands were more important than compliance with approved procedure.

To make sense of developments in the Mediterranean theatre it seemed important to me to gain some understanding of the wider context within which the regional battles were played out. I hope that my narrative reflects that.

As my research and writing progressed, so did the word count until it overran significantly the limit for a manageable book. The decision was therefore taken to split it into two volumes, the first covering the period from the tail-end of the First World War to the final battles in North Africa. The second volume, already written, will cover the war in Italy.

The British Army and the relevant air force units and constructs are described in an appendix for those not immediately familiar with the finer points of military formations. Other appendices describe the main types of aircraft, artillery pieces and tanks involved, the code letters carried by relevant squadrons and abbreviations. A bibliography relevant to each volume is also included.

The wider and fluent application of air power in support not only of the Army, but the Navy also, has not, I believe, received due recognition. This is reflected typically in the Army and Navy view of the RAF's part in the Dunkirk withdrawal (as I have noted in Chapter 3 and where I have also, hopefully, set the record straight) which resonated for some years after the event. The contribution of the Allied air forces is fittingly and modestly described in the Official History of the War in the Mediterranean:[2]

> 'Many of a multitude of operations took place far out of sight and hearing of the forces on land and sea yet were an indispensable condition of those forces' accomplishments.'

Copyright and Photographs

Over the years I have acquired through private purchase, auction or gift several hundreds of thousands of photographs, in each case guaranteeing copyright. However, it has become clear that in a few cases copyright lives elsewhere. With so many images available on the internet – some official ones from the war clearly without restriction on their use in publications – the ownership of images has become blurred.

I have taken as much care as possible to ensure that photographs are properly credited. If I have inadvertently used images without due recognition then I apologise without reservation in the hope that their use will at least be seen to enhance appreciation of an important part of modern history.

The photographs vary considerably in quality. It should be appreciated that many were taken on box brownie cameras using dated film that then remained in the camera for months in the heat and humidity, to be processed in due course in Cairo or Rome. Many photographs were taken unofficially against regulations. Once taken some were sent home but most travelled around through any weather at the bottom of a kitbag: despite the wonders of digital processing there are limits as to just how much an image may be improved.

In respect of book extracts I have secured permission to quote wherever possible. This has sometimes been difficult where the original publisher has long disappeared and the author has died. Since I have not quoted at any length except where I have explicit permission, and since I have used extracts in a complimentary fashion, I see such use as helping to promote the work of others. For official documents I have quoted extensively since these are in the public domain and I have invariably noted the source.

Credits

In writing and research I tend to plough a lonely furrow, making numerous trips to museums and archives, coupled with questions to a handful of trusted colleagues. In preparing these volumes I have received invaluable help from Lt Col Robin Bolton RA, Lt Col Richard S. Clayton RAHS, Tom Culbert, Liz Deery at the Air Historical Branch, Mike Draper, Mick Elborn, Dennis Flynn, Chris Goss, 'Jeff' Jefford, Tinus le Roux, Gordon Leith and colleagues at the RAF Museum, Cathy Murray and family, Mark O'Boyle, Rupert Pengelly, Adrian Rigby, Chris Shores, Drs Marjolijn Verbrugge, Archivist at the Army Flying Museum, Alan Walton, Peter Warren, Andrew Whitton, Peter Young (my cousin) and numerous staff at The National Archive.

Several others have helped extensively and given many days or even weeks of their time for no reward other than helping to convert a framework into what I hope will be seen as a polished end product. I am indebted to Greg Baughen, who has read through my drafts and offered gentle suggestions for change or inclusion. My long-time writing pal Andrew Thomas has been generous to a fault with difficult photographs when my own collection suffered gaps. Chris Gibson has whiled away countless hours of his leisure time out on North Sea rigs by producing maps and diagrams from my clumsy drafts. Ray Hankin, one-time of *The Aeroplane* and other aviation titles, has undertaken the enormous task of editing with sensitivity and patience and of course, great competence. Charlotte Stear, editor at Crécy Books, has taken the material presented and converted it into a book.

Closer to home I have two huge thank yous to give. First to Poppy, my fox terrier, who routinely demands exercise, dragging me away from the computer every hour or so to play, thus ensuring that I keep relatively fit. And most importantly, to Christine, my super wife of fifty-seven years, who typed up all of my early articles in the days before word processing, who produced all 120 maps for my first book, and through each successive book has kept home and family together while I have selfishly plodded on. I appreciate your devotion more than you can know.

All credit to my supporters. If the book succeeds it will be in great part down to their assistance: if it fails, I take the blame!

Vic Flintham
Braughing, 2020

[1] Air Publication 3235

[2] Molony, *History of the Second World War; The Mediterranean and Middle East Vol V*, p433

Introduction

At the outset the point must be made that this is not a book about doctrine. The use of the term in a military context is essentially post-war and is defined by NATO[1] as the '…fundamental principles by which the military forces guide their actions in support of objectives. It is authoritative but requires judgement in application'.

Close air support in its various forms evolved during the Second World War in such a way that, with hindsight, it might be possible to suggest that there was doctrine. Obviously, there were approved ways of doing things, policies and procedures, and even directives. However, the approach at the time was a response to the immediate situation as appreciated locally; the quantity and type of resources available to meet that situation; the nature of the enemy; and the interpersonal relationships between key commanders. There then had to be a willingness to learn and apply the lessons learned. The questions to be asked at each stage in development were:

Was there a system? If yes

Did it work as expected? If yes

Did it achieve the intended outcome?

Regardless – what can we do better?

Much has been written about close air support and Army-Air relationships for a military or academic readership, but little in any detail about the control systems and, latterly, the part played by Air Observation Post (AOP) pilots. The evolution of close air support in the Second World War is most easily mapped by studying Allied forces in North Africa and Italy between August 1942 and May 1945. However, the evolving situation in North Africa is better appreciated by describing how the RAF did – or did not – support the Army in the earlier stages of the war.

The core of the Allied air forces was the (Western) Desert Air Force (DAF) whose pilots came predominantly from Great Britain, the Dominions and the USA, the latter flying under Canadian or British colours. The USAAF started its Mediterranean war embedded in the DAF and while separating and developing its own methods in detail, it remained operating in close collaboration with the DAF. By the end of the war 'Allied' air forces in theatre included American, Australian, Brazilian, British, Canadian, French, Greek, Italian, Jugoslav, New Zealand and South African units.

This is not a continuous history of the war in the theatre. Rather, a number of key battles or events has been taken to demonstrate how close air support and artillery direction developed so as to provide troops on the ground with immediate, accurate and potent support, whether by bomb or shell. As markers I have used:

El Alamein, October 1942

Operation *Torch,* November 1942

el Hamma, March 1943

Sicily, July 1943

Salerno, September 1943

Sangro River, November 1943

Cassino/Anzio, January 1944

Operation *Diadem,* May 1944

Operation *Dragoon,* August 1944

Gothic Line, August 1944

Battle of the Rivers, October 1944

Victory in Italy, May 1945

The development of close air support from the invasion of Sicily onwards will be covered in a second volume. While recognising that the first successful integration of Dominion air and land forces was demonstrated at El Alamein, there were earlier examples of failure and one notable success (East Africa) prior to October 1942. Those noted in this volume are:

Low Countries and France, 1940

Norway, 1940

Compass, 1940

East Africa, 1941

Crusader, 1941

In each chapter the intention has been to describe the battle in outline, note the land and air units involved and, where appropriate, the relevant system of close air support, plus the lessons learned and those applied. Five elements affect the impact of close air support:

Context – political, military, geography

Systems – breadth, ownership, review and upgrading, discipline, flexibility

Equipment – armament, munitions, aircraft, communications (radio, telephone)

People – personality of commanders, training, attitude, leadership, numbers, morale

Intelligence – accuracy, timeliness, confidence

To bring to life the people aspect, the following offers an invaluable insight. It is from a DAF pilot of 451 Sqn, a tactical reconnaissance unit, about a visit from the Commander XIII Corps in November 1941:[2]

> 'With our unpressed trousers, scruffy pullovers and dusty flying boots we looked like a collection of tramps. The General's appearance was in sharpest contrast. He had probably flown straight from GHQ Cairo. His belt, buttons and boots gleamed, his uniform seemed brand new and scarlet tabs burned brightly on his lapels. He told us that there was to be a battle shortly but he gave us no details.
>
> 'I'm sure you chaps are eager to move forward and get into the fray' he said. 'The Army relies greatly on the information you give us. You have a very important role to play. Good luck and good cheer in the days ahead.'
>
> His speech was designed for a fresh, untried, infantry unit just arrived in the desert from the rain-soaked training grounds of England and we didn't like it. We were dirty, smelly and had been in the fray for months. Whether the Army moved forwards, backwards or sideways our job was the same. Armies spend most of their days preparing to fight and living in comparative safety behind the lines. The soldier thinks in terms of the clash of arms, great victories like Blenheim or Waterloo. Air forces meet the enemy on a routine basis and our psychology is different. We abominate pep talks because every day is somewhat similar. Crisis is normal. Instead of stiffening the sinews for a decisive encounter, we sweat out a tour. Decorations are awarded not so much for individual acts of courage as for length of time on the job.'

The early chapters describe Army co-operation between the two world wars, the unhealthy situation applying in the first three years of the war and the chinks of light beginning to emerge through a door barely ajar. It is not surprising that innovation came through hard experience in the Western Desert, where the emphasis was on the immediate need to get on with the job as practically as possible and away from oversight by higher command.

In the end the effectiveness of support came down to the people who imagined, tested, applied and refined systems of delivering bombs and shells for the benefit of the 'poor bloody infantry' when and where it mattered.

Throughout the reader will find reference to air superiority and air supremacy. The terms need clarification since, except in the introductory chapter, they are used always in a local or regional context and not in any wider or conceptual way. Air superiority describes any situation where one party to battle has a distinct advantage in the air over the other in the setting of that particular action. Air supremacy, on the other hand, describes a scenario where, to all intents and purposes, one side is totally dominant in the air over a longer period of time and probably an enlarged geographic area.

Of course words like 'advantage' and 'dominant' are relative and subjective, but the setting will usually make clear the air state. For example, without air superiority Auster AOP pilots were confined to flying at extremely low level, popping up briefly at a couple of hundred feet to observe and call shot. And they would always be noting the gully or other topographical feature that could offer protection from marauding enemy fighters. With air superiority, AOP pilots could venture up to the desired 1,000ft, half a mile behind the bomb line, knowing that friendly fighters were probably keeping the enemy at bay. With air supremacy any pilot of any aircraft type was able to fly with impunity at any height and way beyond the bomb line because of the confirmed absence of opposition, subject only to the threat of anti-aircraft artillery (AAA). (In the case of the AOP pilots, they were usually secure from anti-aircraft fire because any enemy gun positions would have been noted and artillery fire called down upon therm.)

Air superiority is not simply measured in terms of aircraft operated by each side. The factors impacting on it are numerous, among which are:

Aircraft – numbers, performance, weapons

Maintenance – thoroughness, spares availability, facilities

Consumables – petrol, oil, lubricants, coolant

Munitions – bombs, rockets, bullets, shells

Aircrew – numbers, training, experience, morale

Intelligence – accuracy, timeliness

Landing grounds – size, state, location, facilities

Terrain and weather – inter-relationship, predictability

There are several reasons why this two-part study does not extend to covering the war in North-West Europe. Of necessity and practicality, there had to be a limit on its geographical scope (it could have also encompassed the Eastern Front, the Far East and the Pacific), otherwise the intended two volumes would have become several more. But more importantly, North Africa and Italy are deserving of concentrated focus because it was here that the whole concept of close air support was nurtured and developed and was where it proved most effective, particularly in the closing stages of the war in Italy.

That was not always so elsewhere. For instance, in the Normandy campaign, the potency and value of the Typhoon in combating tanks was considerably overrated[3] and exaggerated. Another marker is that on D-Day of Operation *Overlord,* 6 June 1944, of a total c15,000 sorties flown, just 100 were to provide close air support.[4]

A host of remarkable things happened in the Mediterranean theatre, one of which was the inter-relationship of armies and air forces and their flexibility, both in terms of systems and cross-cover. Some American Corps comprised more British than US troops, while both tactical air forces included wings or groups from British and American units working in close co-operation. General Ira Eaker, Commander in Chief Mediterranean Allied Air Forces, had this to say:[5]

> 'The Mediterranean theatre has been the primary crucible for the development of tactical air-power and the evolution of joint command between Allies. Ever since Alamein the Mediterranean has been the laboratory of Tactical Air Forces, just as England has been the primary testing ground of Strategic Air Forces.'

British Prime Minister Winston Churchill in North Africa 1943. Churchill had very clear views about close air support. Responding to a desperate bid by the French for more fighters during the Battle of France he stated "It is the business of the artillery to stop tanks. The business of the fighters is to cleanse the skies over the battle". In 1942, setting the tone for future co-operation, he instructed "Whenever our Army is established on land, and is conducting operations against the enemy, the system of organisation and employment of the Royal Air Force should conform to that which has proved so successful in the Western Desert". *Mark O'Boyle*

[1] NATO Glossary of Terms and Definitions

[2] Morley-Mower, *Messerschmitt Roulette,* p118

[3] See Gooderson, I, *Air Power at the Battlefront* for example

[4] Baughen G, RAeS conference May 2019

[5] Quoted in Slessor, *The Central Blue* p 566

1 Early History of British Air-Land Co-operation

Close air support by the Royal Air Force (RAF) for the Army reached its zenith in Italy in 1944. But the story of the evolution of that support began in the First World War where successful systems were devised. Between the wars the concentration was on bombing, which impacted on resources available for other applications of air power. Lessons from the Spanish Civil War were overlooked so that when Britain entered the Second World War in 1939 the RAF was ill-prepared for the coming battles.

The Great War

From the earliest stages of the Great War aircraft of the Royal Flying Corps (RFC) were involved in reconnaissance, which soon expanded to spotting for artillery. Throughout the course of the war procedures improved, depending initially on the pilot being able to identify the battery he was to work with and then observing the fall of shot. Corrections were notified by dropping messages on the battery. From 1915 airborne wireless came into use, together with the makings of a system.

Radios were heavy and took the place of the observer in two-seat aircraft like the B.E.2c or R.E.8. They were short-range wireless telegraphy (W/T) transmitters, relying on the pilot alone reading a squared map and transmitting by Morse code using a key strapped above his knee. Before transmission a 250-yard aerial had to be wound out and wound in before landing. The fact that aircraft like the B.E.2 and R.E.8 were inherently stable enabled the pilot almost to fly hands off, so long as airspeed was maintained.

The map and clock code system for noting and correcting shot has been described excellently by one expert:[1]

> 'These maps used 6000 x 6000 yard lettered squares to provide a common frame of reference. For artillery purposes the large square was divided into 3000 x 3000 yard quarters, called 'Zones', and labelled A–D (later alternate large squares used W–Z). Normally each Zone was the area for at least one battery. Wireless communications were air-to-ground only. Marker strips at the gun position were used (sparingly) to signal back to the aircraft if required. This process enabled air observers to report both target locations and their observations of the fall of shot. Before this reporting locations was difficult because there was no frame of reference apart from vague indications such as 'SW of village (name)', which provided neither brevity nor precision and in effect limited air observation to pre-arranged targets. The new procedure allowed opportunity targets to be attacked.
>
> For the Zone Call procedure all assigned batteries and artillery commanders had RFC receiving sets with RFC operators who listened for calls in their Zone. An example call (transmitted in Morse code) would be 'FB NF W21b34 N3' where F was squadron and B aircraft identities, NF ('now firing') meant HBs firing, then the map reference (main square W, 21 being in Zone C), b34 meant the North East quarter of square 21, 3/10ths (75 yards) to the right from the left side and 4/10ths (100 yards) up from the bottom. N3 being the third target during flight. The RFC wireless operator with the battery had to be able to pick target calls in his battery's Zone. With NF targets the goal was usually neutralisation, not destruction.[2]
>
> The battery could fire at once, but if already engaged only one gun or section was used for ranging. Once the ranging gun fired the air observer reported where the shell fell relative to the target by using the clock code. The problem was that this method was time consuming, and the aircraft had to be correctly positioned when the rounds fell so that they could be observed.'

RFC ground operators erected their aerials close to the artillery units to which they were attached and during the din of battle would have had to repair them under fire. The clock code was to be used into the Second World War.

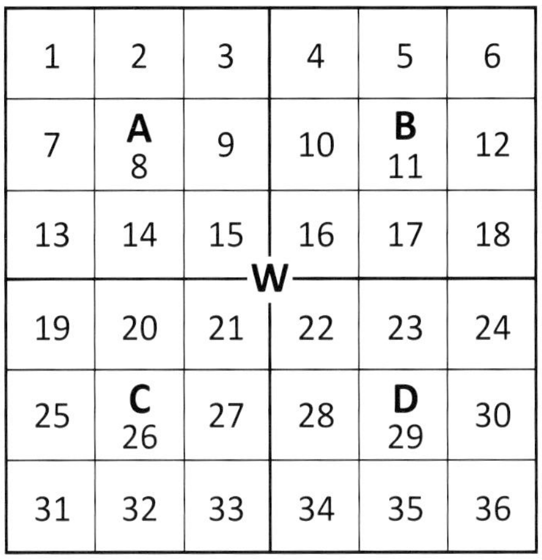

Map zones

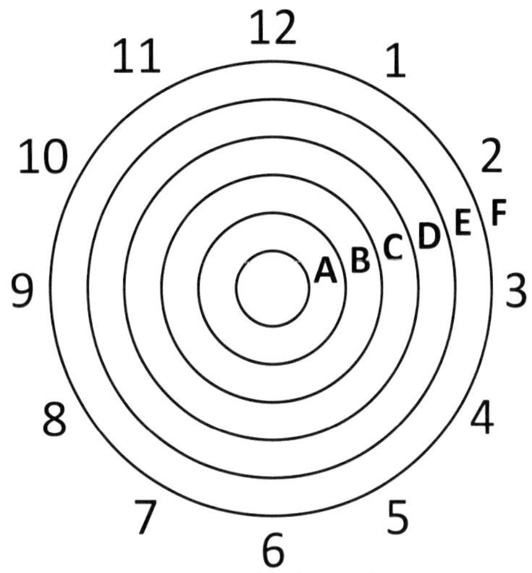

The clock code

From 1915 flying units were organised into brigades, each attached to an Army and comprising two wings (later three), plus a kite balloon wing. Each wing consisted of at least four squadrons, one equipped with aircraft for reconnaissance and artillery spotting (like the B.E.2c and R.E.8), the remainder with 'scouts' (fighters), like the Camel and S.E.5a, plus the occasional bomber squadron.

Later in the war aircraft like the B.E.2c, F.E.2b and Sopwith 1½ Strutter shot up enemy trenches. Many pilots had transferred from infantry regiments and thus were well versed in the demands of ground combat. While it was artillery that consistently wreaked havoc and caused great numbers of casualties on both sides, there were examples of aircraft working in concert with ground forces.

What was probably the first ever *planned* British close air support mission took place on 3 May 1917, conducted by 43 Sqn RFC during the Third Battle of the Scarpe in northern France. Two days earlier the squadron had been tasked to prepare to undertake counter-attack patrols against German forces facing the British at Fresnoy. (This was immediately after 'Bloody April', during which the RFC lost heavily against the German *Luftstreitkräfte* which, although inferior in numbers, enjoyed superior aircraft and better-trained and more experienced pilots.)

After reconnaissance on the 3rd identified the massing of enemy troops, five Sopwith 1½ Strutters took off from Treizennes to strafe trenches and artillery, flying down to 50ft with great success and no loss to their numbers. This was followed by a second mission in the afternoon. The 1½ Strutter had a fixed forward-firing Vickers gun with 300 rounds and a rear Lewis gun for which up to five 97-round drums were carried. On return from the sorties all ammunition had been expended. There was no counter-attack. In his autobiography the squadron CO commented:[3]

> 'Our success appeared to be due mainly to the enemy being so startled by the audacity of our attacks and bombardment that they could not bring themselves to throw at us any very heavy fire … the chief danger that we had to face was from our own artillery barrage.'

The Nascent Royal Air Force

From an early stage in the Great War both sides had engaged in bombing targets in their respective homelands and in February 1916, after a series of German Zeppelin raids, overland air defence of the UK was transferred from the Royal Naval Air Service (RNAS) to the RFC. By the summer of the following year, as London fell victim to the first Gotha bomber raids, Prime Minister David Lloyd George urged his war cabinet to review the use of aircraft for attack and defence and to make recommendations.

The response was to establish a committee of two under South African General Jan Christian Smuts, which met for the first time on 11 July 1917. The first report, published just eight days later, proposed a unified command for air defence, including the formation of dedicated fighter squadrons. Matters continued to move swiftly. The second report published on 17 August recommended the creation of an Air Ministry and amalgamation of the RFC and RNAS: this was approved by the Cabinet a week later.[4] The rationale behind the creation of a new force was primarily that aircraft now available were capable of waging war beyond the boundaries of the land or sea battle.

The Air Force (Constitution) Bill was introduced on 8 November and received the Royal assent three weeks later as the Air Force Act. Early in 1918 Lord Rothermere was appointed Secretary of State for Air and President of the Air Council. Sir David Henderson, who had commanded the RFC in France and who supported Smuts in his analysis, was appointed Vice-President, while Major-General Sir Hugh Trenchard became the first Chief of the Air Staff.

The new service came formally into being on 1 April 1918 as the Royal Air Force. In the days

Artillery Direction 1918

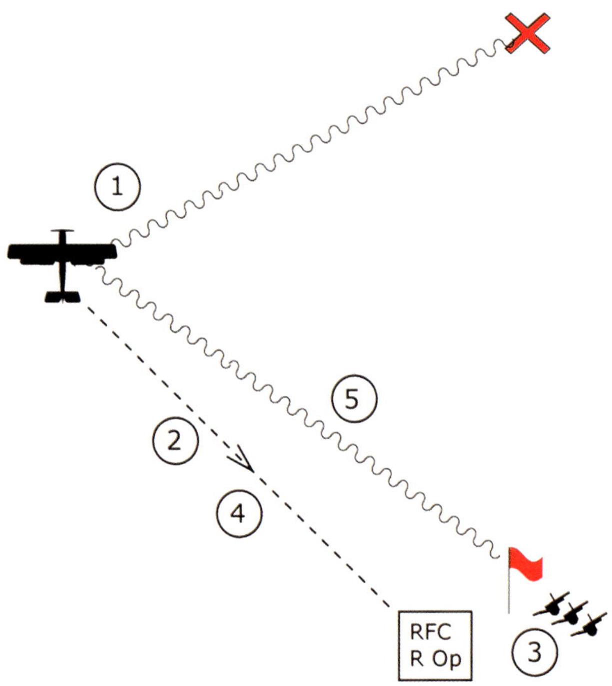

1) Spotter identifies target
2) Spotter one-way W/T to Control (RFC Radio Operator)
3) Radio Operator alerts artillery - shoots target
4) Spotter corrects shot if necessary
5) If required artillery alerts Spotter to its location with visual signal

immediately leading up to its formation the German Army, strengthened by divisions released from the Russian front, attacked the British line on the Somme front. From 21 March 1918 some fifty-eight divisions, supported by 6,500 artillery pieces, launched the assault against just fifteen British divisions. The RFC had 579 aircraft available on the Somme front, including 261 fighters, and all were immediately and heavily engaged. There was no time to celebrate the birth of the new service.

In the event the RFC performed superbly by flying murderous ground attack sorties that contributed to halting the German advance short of the objective of Amiens. With little mechanised transport, the Germans relied on horse-drawn carts so, sadly, horses became the target of many of the 250,000 rounds expended daily by British aircraft. On 9 April there was a second assault towards Hazebrouck and the channel ports, again repulsed. In five weeks the British Army lost 236,000 men, most of whom were taken prisoner. The RFC/RAF lost 1,032 aircraft of the 1,232 on charge.[5] Low-flying fighters on close support suffered a 30% attrition rate *daily*.

Table 1.1 – RAF aircraft and personnel at 1 April 1918

	RFC	RNAS	RAF total
Aircraft	17,350	2,950	20,300
Personnel	230,000	67,000	297,000

In respect of close support to the Army, the Chief of the Air Staff, by now Major-General Sir Frederick Sykes, had this to say in a report to the Cabinet in June 1918:[6]

> 'The Royal Air Force is called upon to co-operate with armies in an ever-increasing number of roles – reconnaissance, photography, observation of artillery fire, location of hostile batteries, contact patrols with infantry, counter-attack patrols, bomb attacks on communications, and (a role which has recently much increased in importance) machine-gun and bomb attacks on enemy troops and transport by large concentrations of machines flying at low heights, anti-tank defence, inter-communication – these duties are indispensable to an army in the field, and are regularly carried out.'

Support to the armies was described thus at Appendix A of the report:

> 'The work of aircraft attached to armies may be summarised as follows:
>
> (a) Reconnaissance and Aerial Photography.
>
> (b) Observation of Artillery Fire.
>
> (c) Contact Patrol Work.
>
> (d) Aerial Fighting.
>
> (e) Bomb Attacks.
>
> (f) Low Flying Attacks on Ground Objectives.'

In respect of the present book the notes on artillery spotting, interdiction and close air support are illuminating.

> '(b) Observation of Artillery Fire. This is carried out by two-seater machines, and the normal method of directing fire is by wireless. The work has grown increasingly complex and highly trained personnel is essential. Both the Pilot and Observer are trained to direct the fire of the batteries, but the work is usually carried out by the Pilot, while the Observer looks out for hostile aircraft.
>
> (e) Bomb Attacks. Systematic bombing both by day and by night has developed very extensively during the past year. By day the work is usually carried out by formations of both single-seater and two-seater machines, flying at from 10,000 to 20,000 feet. In the battle area it is necessary for the formations to be escorted by fast single-seater fighters. For more distant work, the formations are escorted over the 'Line' and met and escorted on the return journey. A very considerable amount of bombing is also carried out by night, this work

The first recorded planned close support mission by a British air arm was on 3 May 1917. From their base at Treizennes, Sopwith 1½ Strutters of 43 Sqn strafed trenches near Fresnoy in the Third Battle of the Scarpe, preventing a German counter-attack. Representative aircraft A1924 is at a UK aerodrome, possibly Larkhill, with F.E.2bs and an R.E.8 in the background. *Author's collection*

> is performed by special short-distance night-flying squadrons, and an escort is necessary. The objectives by day are troops, convoys, dumps, and other targets of tactical importance. By night the principal objectives are enemy aerodromes, railway stations, trains, billets, &c. These are frequently attacked from a low height.
>
> (f) Low Flying Attacks on Ground Objectives. These are carried out by single-seater machines such as 'Camels'. Light bombs are used in conjunction with machine gun fire, and the machines attack their objectives, which are generally troops or transport, from heights as low as twenty feet. Low flying attacks of this nature are also made on enemy aerodromes, with a view to dislocating his arrangements for aircraft co-operation.'

In the last few months of the war, the RAF and Army developed systems of close air support that were relatively effective and which, if analysed and developed both in terms of method and equipment, offered a sound platform for the future. 8 Sqn with the Armstrong Whitworth F.K.8, and subsequently 71 and 73 Sqns (Camel), were attached to the Tank Corps during the Allied attacks from Amiens in August 1918.[7] Their task was to identify and attack German anti-tank guns confronting the 500 British tanks leading the assault. At the same time several railway stations were attacked in interdiction missions by light bombers. Losses, though, were very high.

By September the decision had been taken to focus on specific targets rather than flying randomly over the front line (over which the Germans at this stage enjoyed air superiority) looking for targets of opportunity. The outcome was a system of quick response air support that worked effectively. On spotting a potential target, scouting aircraft with radio would contact a Central Information Bureau (CIB) which would either assign the target to artillery or to an RAF squadron. Being near the front, squadrons could scramble aircraft quickly. At the same time, if there were already fighter-bombers in the area, the scout could identify suitable targets for them by dropping indicator flares.

At this stage in the war improvements in radio technology and in aircraft design were such that there was space for both radio and observer. Thus, not only were ground targets referred back to the CIB, but enemy air formations for attack by fighters notified as well. Other innovations allowed the CIB to be alerted to a fluid front line in a ground battle, aircraft sounding a klaxon over where the front was assumed to be, in response to which ground troops fired an appropriately-coloured flare in confirmation.

These approaches offered great promise for the future. However, they highlighted a major deficiency, which was that without air superiority, artillery spotting, close air support or interdiction missions ran the risk of high losses, not only from ground fire, but also from enemy fighters. RAF aircraft at the time were un-armoured and suffered from inferior performance, so much so that the loss rate could not be sustained.

In August 1918 8 Sqn with its F.K.8 reconnaissance aircraft was attached to the Tank Corps in the Allied attacks from Amiens. On the 12th Capt Ferdinand 'Freddie' West in aircraft C8602 persisted in spotting German positions under attack from AAA and enemy aircraft despite serious injury. So serious were his injuries that his leg was amputated: for his bravery he was awarded the Victoria Cross. West is seen here at right with his observer Lt J G. G. Haslam at Auxi le Chateau with F.K.8 C8594 in July 1918. *AST collection*

At the war's end in November 1918 the huge challenge facing the infant RAF was nothing less than survival; both the Admiralty and War Office were desperate to reclaim their air arms. By then the Royal Air Force had 188 combat squadrons, fifteen flights, a vast training and support infrastructure, 22,647 aircraft, 103 airships, 23,260 vehicles and 291,170 personnel. The service used 401 landing sites in the UK – many of a very temporary nature – and 274 sites abroad.

In January 1919 Winston Churchill, now Secretary of State for Air, sought Trenchard's views on the shape of the post-war Air Force. Recognising that funds would be very limited, Trenchard kept suggestions on squadron strength to a bare minimum while ensuring that the foundations of an independent service – staff college, cadet college and apprentice school – were all provided for.

Post war, the situation was not helped by the dire economic climate and the much-reduced size of the nascent Air Force, now shrunk alarmingly to only twenty-eight squadrons – and most of these overseas. Also emerging was the Ten Year Rule, formally ratified in August 1919. This simply required that the armed forces should base their funding estimates on the assumption that the British Empire would not be engaged in any significant war during the following ten years. (In 1928 the rule became formally self-perpetuating at Churchill's demand!)

In 1919 Trenchard, now restored to the role of Chief of the Air Staff after an acrimonious dispute with Air Minister Lord Rothermere had caused him to resign, had proposed that the RAF could manage an insurgency in Somaliland. The idea of doing so was rejected initially by Field Marshal Sir Henry Wilson, Chief of the Imperial General Staff, who objected to the prospect of soldiers coming under RAF control. When it was put to him that the only ground forces required would be those already there, Wilson retracted and planning for military intervention from the air began in earnest, the government formally sanctioning the expedition in October. Significantly, in debate with the First Sea Lord, Admiral of the Fleet Earl Beatty, in December 1919, the latter had been prevailed upon to give Trenchard a year to prove the value of the RAF as an independent service. Meanwhile, in South Russia 47 Sqn Camels were flying close support sorties in support of White Russian forces.

Trenchard laid down the principles of the new force in a formal note in November 1919:[8]

> 'The principle to be kept in mind in forming the framework of the Air Service is that in the future the main portion of it will consist of an Independent Force, together with Service personnel required in carrying out Aeronautical Research. In addition there will be a small part of it specially trained for work with the Navy, and a small part specially trained for work with the Army, these two small portions probably becoming, in the future, an arm of the older services.'

The Sopwith Camel F.1 entered service with 4 Sqn RNAS in May 1917 and was soon engaged in trench-strafing and light bomb attacks. However, it was vulnerable and losses were high and so Sopwith developed the Salamander for such work. The company also converted one Camel, designated T.F.1 (trench fighter) serial B9278 with 110hp Le Rhône engine, armour plate and with two fixed Lewis guns firing down at 45°. *Author's collection*

The Sopwith T.F.2 Salamander was a dedicated trench fighter design based on the Snipe fighter but with an armoured 'box' around the pilot and protection for the fuel tank. Armament was two Vickers forward-firing machine guns and four 20lb or one 112lb bombs. Too late for the war the Salamander did not reach squadrons. *Author's collection*

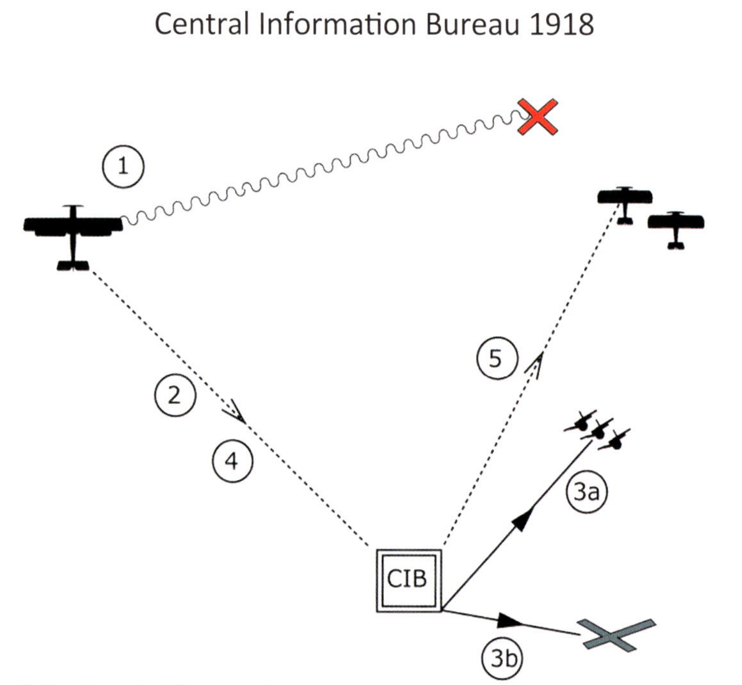

1) Spotter identifies target
2) Details passed to Central Information Bureau (CIB)
3) CIB alerts either artillery or airfield with target details
4) Spotter corrects shot if necessary
5) If Spotter observes enemy aircraft in air, refers to CIB who advise any airborne fighters

It is noteworthy that Trenchard anticipated Army co-operation shifting to the War Office. In respect of relations with the War Office the note continued:

> 'For co-operation with the Army it is proposed to provide eventually squadrons on the basis of a flight per division for work with the troops at all stages of their training, and in addition one or more squadrons for co-operation with the artillery both during their winter training and their annual gun practice. During the next financial year it is proposed to form two squadrons in all, one at Farnborough for co-operation with the troops at Aldershot and Salisbury, and the second at Stonehenge for work with the artillery. Small units will, if necessary, be provided in addition for co-operation with the Garrison Artillery School at Golden Hill, and the Anti-aircraft School when formed.'

It is perhaps not surprising that in designing the new service for slow growth in the context of a fight for survival, the RAF, with shallow traditions, struggled to retain an institutional memory. Thus, the experience of close air support in the Great War and the lessons that might have been drawn, were lost.

Post-War Structure

The first two Army co-operation units to be formed, in early 1920, were 2 Sqn, initially in Ireland then to Digby, and 4 Sqn at Farnborough, both with the Bristol F.2b. On 1 April 1924 two further squadrons were added – 13 Sqn at Kenley and 16 Sqn at Old Sarum, both also with the F.2b.

The RAF in the UK was organised in two commands – Inland Area and Coastal Area, the latter incorporating all units working with the Royal Navy. The Army co-operation squadrons worked with the Army on exercises throughout the inter-war years, with flights attached to Army divisions, but with no clear idea of what sort of future conflict the War Office envisioned. Some policies did emerge. For example, it was determined that it was dangerous to attack from the air troops reckoned to be fresh when advancing and more productive to do so when they were tired and withdrawing!

Initially the majority of RAF personnel were ex-Army (RFC) who would have continued to appreciate the challenges confronting the military. Over time, as the RAF recruited fresh intakes, the RFC veteran body was diluted and with it attitudes shifted. Another factor impacting on the lack of progress was that Army co-operation units were seen as backwaters, so postings to them were unpopular because they were seen as damaging to career prospects.

The Committee of Imperial Defence, chaired by the Marquess of Salisbury, met in 1923 to determine the future size and role of the RAF. It proposed raising the number of home defence units (which meant all UK squadrons apart from those allocated to Army co-operation and Coastal) from twenty-five to fifty-two by 1928. With its experience of the Independent Bomber Force, the RAF determined that future effective defence could be provided only through a bomber force, and this was reflected in government policy – '...the bomber will always get through'.[9] Thus, the expanded 'defence' force would comprise thirty-five bomber and seventeen fighter squadrons. It was also decided that Army officers would be attached to RAF units so as to promote better liaison between the two services.

In support of the military RAF policy was to concentrate on air superiority, thus protecting ground forces from attack by enemy aircraft.[10] At the time this meant essentially having a strong bomber force to suppress the enemy by bombing its airfields and munitions factories. Through exercises with the Army, the RAF also noted consistently the need for co-located tactical headquarters and good communications, together with advanced airfields. However, there remained a gap between appreciation of the need and doing anything about it, a state that continued well into the Second World War.

Air Defence of Great Britain (ADGB) Command was created in 1925 under Air Marshal Sir John Salmond to assume control of the main combat elements of Inland Area. In 1926 it comprised Fighting Area, Wessex Bombing Area and, later, No 1 Air Defence Group (ADG), which included the Special Reserve and Auxiliary Air Force squadrons. Inland and Coastal Areas continued in being.

In the early 1930s there was expansion of the RAF, but always with bombers at the forefront.

The Bristol F2b was widely used as a general purpose machine in the Middle East, India and at home where it served with Army co-operation squadrons from 1920 to 1931. In an aluminium dope finish J7686 of 2 Sqn was involved in Army Manoeuvres in 1925. *Author's collection*

The Ten Year Rule, although notionally applied, was overlooked from 1923 and effectively ended in 1931 after the League of Nations was seen to be powerless in halting the Japanese invasion of Manchuria. By 1934 there was recognition that Germany represented a potential future enemy, but it was not until 1938 that the British government countenanced the threat of a European land war with forces sent to mainland Europe.

There was a further reorganisation in 1933 when the bomber squadrons in Wessex Bombing Area and 1 ADG were redistributed to Western Area (HQ Andover), Central Area (HQ Abingdon) and 1 ADG (the Auxiliary bomber squadrons). Fighting, Inland and Coastal Areas remained.

By 1936, with civil war in Spain engaging German, Italian and Russian air force detachments, the government raised the target strength for the RAF in the UK to 1,736 combat aircraft in 124 squadrons by March 1939. In addition, large reserves of aircraft were to be funded and built. The final pre-war structural change in the United Kingdom involved the creation of four new commands to replace the previous arrangements. These were Bomber Command, Fighter Command (to include the Cinderella Army co-operation squadrons), Coastal Command and Training Command, all formed on 14 July 1936.

Though Army co-operation was under-resourced and lacking focus, the RAF had established a School of Army Co-operation in March 1920, responsible for training crews, initially on the F.2b. Early in 1921 it moved from Stonehenge to Old Sarum where it remained as such until September 1941, on becoming 41 Operational Training Unit (OTU). The flying component of the school was 16 Sqn, whose tasks included service trials of potential new aircraft. Courses were for up to twenty officers at a time and were of twelve weeks' duration. The syllabus included photography, air reconnaissance, artillery spotting, signals and military organisation. From creation, the school lived within 7 Group until April 1926, when it was disbanded and reformed within 22 Group. In the expansion of the RAF in 1936 this Group was tasked solely with the Army co-operation role, becoming part of the new Fighter Command, within which it remained until 24 June 1940. After that, it became independent as Army Co-operation Command under direct Air Ministry authority.

Seen flying over RAF Sutton Bridge is F2b F4503 of 13 Sqn. In the foreground are two Bessonneau hangars, while the tents at top right confirm a summer camp, in this case in late summer 1926. Sutton Bridge was established that year as an armament practice camp using nearby ranges on the Wash. *Author's collection*

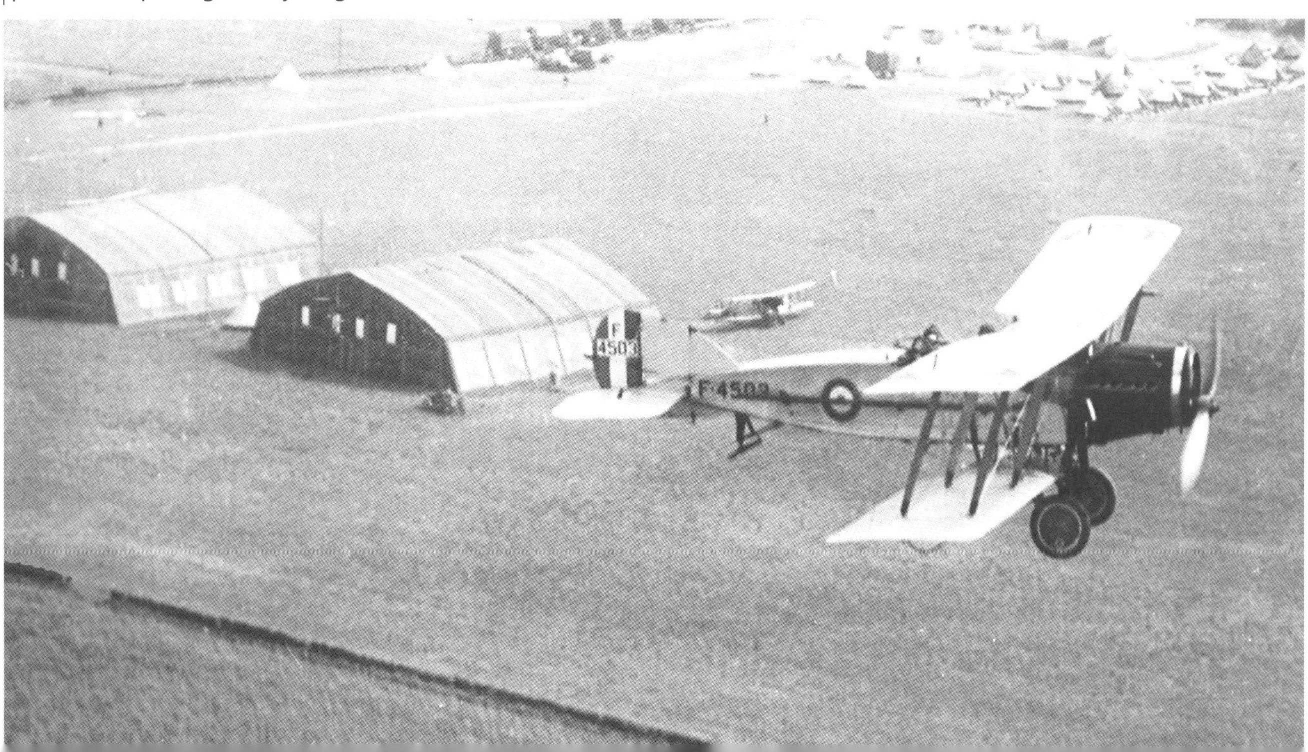

The two-seat Armstrong-Whitworth Atlas was designed at the outset as a replacement for the venerable F2b in the Army co-operation role. J9537 of 2 Sqn is being refuelled by a Morris-Commercial bowser probably at RAF Manston. *Author's collection*

The Atlas entered service with 26 Sqn in October 1927 and no fewer than 446 were built including a number of trainers, although the type only served with five home squadrons. In this photograph aircraft of 16 Sqn demonstrate their low-level formation flying skills at RAF Northolt in May 1932 with message hooks down. A system of using radio to communicate with ground units might have been more productive, if less spectacular. *Author's collection*

The Hawker Audax was a Hart variant build to Specification 7/31 as an Atlas replacement. K3693 of 16 Sqn, with its distinctive black bar fuselage marking, is here at North Coates in 1934. This is one of several Audaxes noted with the red centre of the roundel painted out, possibly for an air exercise. This aircraft saw its days out in India in 1944. *Author's collection*

The Army co-operation squadrons played an active part in air exercises in the 1930s but how realistic these were is debatable. This is 16 Sqn's operations room in the back of a Scammell lorry at Boscombe Down in September 1935; access appears to be via chair and box! The seated Army Air Liaison Officer is in discussion with a squadron leader umpire. *AST collection*

Audax aircraft of 26 Sqn in 1936 with K3095 in the foreground, again missing the centre spot on the fuselage roundel. 4 Sqn was first to fly the Audax in February 1932 but it was soon supplanted by the Hector. *Author's collection*

Aircraft and Expansion

The first type used extensively for strafing was the Sopwith Camel, its fixed twin Vickers machine guns (300 rounds per gun) firing at 450 rounds a minute. One Camel, B9278, was converted to a Trench Fighter (T.F.1) with three Lewis guns, two of which fired downwards, and armour. However, as the Salamander variant of the Snipe was in production, intended specifically for use against ground forces, it was not proceeded with. The T.F.2 Salamander of 1918 carried twin, fixed, forward-firing Vickers guns and armour, plus a light bomb load. Although nearly 300 were produced, the type equipped only 96 and 157 Sqns at the time of the Armistice before being scrapped.

The Bristol F.2b was supplied to the Army co-operation squadrons because it existed in great numbers and was robust. All told, 5,125 were built, many serving overseas in army support and policing roles. Armed with fixed Vickers and removable Lewis machine guns, they were safe but slow and, being large, were highly vulnerable in any strafing role. They were supplanted at home from 1927 by the Atlas, but remained in service in Palestine until 1932.

The first purpose-built Army co-operation type, to Specification 33/26, was the Armstrong Whitworth Atlas, which first flew in May 1925. It entered service with 13 Sqn from August 1927 and in due course equipped five squadrons at home, including newly formed 26 Sqn in October 1927. From then on, types designed for the Army co-operation role were given heroic names from classical mythology.

The Atlas was supplanted by the Hawker Audax, a type based on the Hart day bomber and constructed to meet Specification 7/31. It joined 4 Sqn in December 1931 and by September 1934 equipped the five home-based Army co-operation squadrons as well as a number overseas. High demand for the Kestrel engine led the Air Ministry to produce Specification 14/35 calling for an Audax replacement with an alternative engine. Hawker had tested a Napier Dagger engine in a Hart that led to a proposed straight-wing design with tailwheel (as opposed to skid) that became the Hector. The prototype flew in February 1936 and a contract was issued to Westland to build 178, the type replacing the Audax, first with 4 Sqn in May 1937. Speed increased slightly to 185mph but armament remained essentially the same. Not only did the Hector equip four of the original five Army co-operation squadrons, it went on to serve with 53 and 59 Sqns and five Auxiliary Air Force (AuxAF) units. With 613 Sqn, the type was involved in the defence of Calais on 26 and 27 May 1940.

The final pre-war Army co-operation type to enter service with the RAF was the Westland Lysander. Having built the Hector, Westland was invited to tender against Specification A.39/34 for a two-seat type. After discussion with RAF pilots, Westland came up with a monoplane design, with high-wing for visibility, short take-off and landing and good slow-speed characteristics.

The result was the Lysander that met Westland's criteria and, indeed, the specification, but in the event was too cumbersome to support effectively troops on the ground, even though armament was increased to two Browning fixed machine guns and a free Lewis or Vickers in the rear cockpit. The Lysander joined 16 Sqn in June 1938 and by the outbreak of war in September 1939 equipped the original five Army co-operation units. It then served in France where the squadrons suffered appalling losses, as described in the following chapter.

Table 1.2 – Characteristics of Army co-operation aircraft, 1918–1939

Type	Engine	HP	Speed/stall	Endurance	Bomb load
F.2b	Falcon III	280	110/45	3.00hrs	2x112lb
Atlas	Jaguar IVC	450	142/50	3.25hrs	4x112lb
Audax	Kestrel IB	530	170/55	3.00hrs	4x20lb
Hector	Dagger III	805	185/50	2.45hrs	2x112lb
Lysander	Mercury XII	890	230/40	3.30hrs	4x112lb

While defining the principles of close air support was muddling along in the UK, there were several important contributions emanating from India, where squadrons were working in close collaboration with the Army. A report in 1936[11] suggested that before take-off in support of an Army operation pilots should be briefed fully or, if not possible, by radio telephony (R/T) once in the air. If operations were planned for the following day, a full written briefing should be produced, whereas, at short notice, a situation report would suffice if aircraft were expected in the air within twenty minutes. Local bombing support was not to be conducted in formation.

A training exercise was conducted in late 1936 to evolve tactical methods for close air support. The analysis emphasised the need for good communications, both between column HQ and the advanced landing ground and between HQ and aircraft in the air. Advanced landing grounds should be as close as possible to the scene of operations and the preferred means of communications was to be land lines, both for reliability and clarity. Perhaps the most significant recommendation, also by now established in Britain, was that the Air Component commander should accompany the column commander at all times so as to ensure a speedy and accurate response to requests from ground forces.

The priority for close air support through the late 1930s was on air superiority and isolation of the battlefield,[12] and pre-war exercises concentrated generally on reconnaissance and artillery observation. In a report published in late September 1939, the Army stated its wish for Army co-operation aircraft to be under Army command and flown by Army-trained pilots.[13]

By the mid-1930s the potential of war was looming, resulting in the British government embarking on the first of a series of expansion schemes.[14] These included increasing the number of operational units, building many new airfields, increases in personnel and training and a demand for newer, more efficient aircraft. The schemes were lettered A to M, each comprising ambitious programmes for completion between 1937 (scheme C) and 1942 (scheme M).

The first two schemes, A and C of 1935, were intended to act as deterrents to Hitler at a time when emergence of the new *Luftwaffe* had been revealed publicly. Mainly, they proposed increases in bomber and fighter units and were intended to match German numbers, ignoring the question of relative aircraft performance. In respect of Army co-operation, the number of squadrons remained fixed at five until scheme F of 1936, which raised the number to eleven, including four reserve or auxiliary squadrons.

The School of Army Co-operation took on charge ten Cierva C.30A autogyros, built as the Avro Rota under licence. They were used for communications and observation of ground forces during exercises between 1935 and 1937, but were not considered to be sufficiently robust. The officers discussing K4235 of 16 Sqn include an Army officer with RAF brevet, one of a number of Army Officers flying with the Army co-operation squadrons. *AST collection*

Table 1.3 – RAF Army co-operation squadrons, 1920–1939

Sqn	Type	Base	From	To
2	F.2b	Oranmore, Digby, Manston	1.2.20	1.30
	Atlas	Manston	12.29	9.34
	Audax	Manston, Hawkinge	9.34	11.37
	Hector	Hawkinge	11.37	9.38
	Lysander	Hawkinge, Abbeville, Lympne	9.38	4.42
4	F.2b	Farnborough	30.4.20	10.29
	Atlas	Farnborough	10.29	1.32
	Audax	Farnborough	12.31	7.37
	Hector	Farnborough, Odiham	5.37	1.39
	Lysander	Odiham, France, Detling, Hawkinge	1.39	6.42
13	F.2b	Kenley, Andover	1.4.24	1.28
	Atlas	Andover, Netheravon	8.27	7.32
	Audax	Netheravon, Old Sarum	7.32	5.37
	Hector	Odiham	5.37	2.39
	Lysander	Odiham, France, Hooton Park, Odiham	1.39	9.41
16	F.2b	Old Sarum	1.4.24	1.31
	Atlas	Old Sarum	1.31	12.33
	Audax	Old Sarum	12.33	6.38
	Lysander	Old Sarum, France, Lympne	6.38	5.43
26	Atlas	Catterick	11.10.27	9.33
	Audax	Catterick	7.33	9.37
	Hector	Catterick	9.37	5.39
	Lysander	Catterick, France, Lympne, etc.	2.39	9.42
53	Hector	Farnborough, Odiham	28.6.37	1.39
	Blenheim IV	Odiham, France, Lympne	1.39	7.40[A]
59	Hector	Old Sarum, Andover	28.6.37	9.39
	Blenheim IV	Andover, France, Andover	5.39	7.40[A]
612[B]	Hector	Dyce	12.37	11.39
615	Hector	Kenley	11.37	2.39
614	Hector	Llandow	4.38	2.40
602[C]	Hector	Abbotsinch	1.11.38	14.1.39
18	Blenheim I	Upper Heyford	5.39	5.40
57	Blenheim I	Upper Heyford	5.39	5.40
613	Hind	Ringway, Odiham	4.39	4.40

A – to Coastal Command
B – to general reconnaissance
C – ex bomber then to fighter

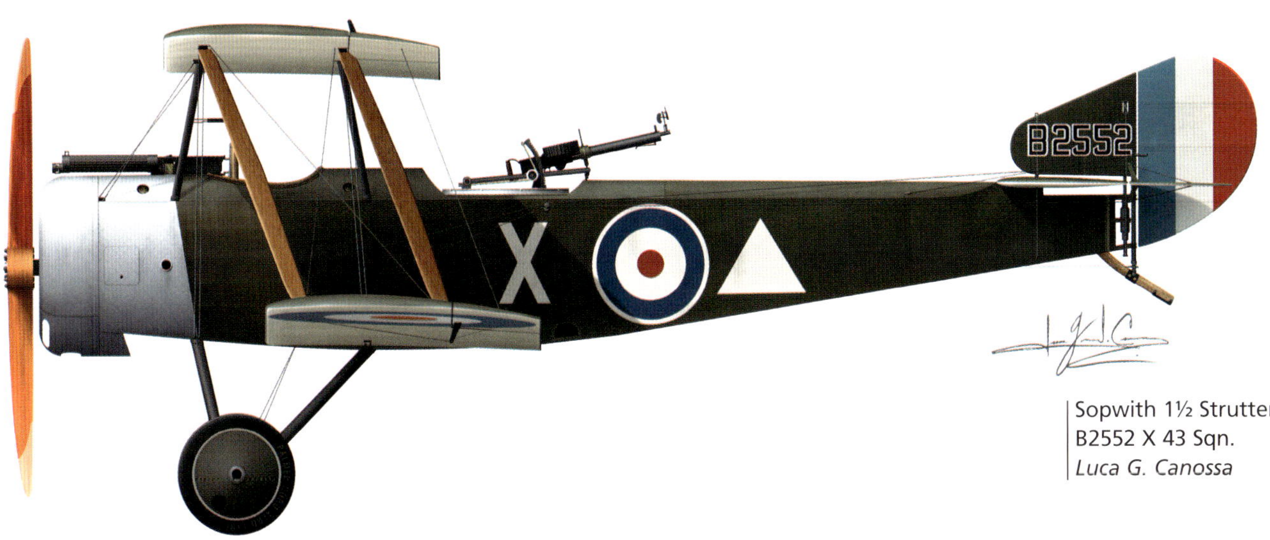

Sopwith 1½ Strutter B2552 X 43 Sqn.
Luca G. Canossa

The Hector was yet another Hart variant but with the H cross-section Dagger engine. To compensate for the change in the centre of gravity the wings were straightened. 13 Sqn aircraft demonstrate supply dropping in 1938. *Author's collection*

Prelude to War

In 1936 civil war broke out in Spain between complex alliances. In simple terms, on the one hand there were Republicans, embracing left-wing democrats and anarchists and supported externally by Russia and Mexico. In opposition were Nationalists, including right-wing Falangists and Monarchists, supported by Germany, Italy and Portugal. Germany, Russia and Italy all sent aircraft to take part in the conflict in large numbers, in the case of Germany masquerading as the Condor Legion.

In the United Kingdom there were mixed views about the wisdom of analysing and drawing conclusions from the application of modern aircraft, as there had been during the Abyssinian Crisis of 1935 involving the Italian Air Force. However, in 1937 a Joint Intelligence Committee sub-committee (JIC(S)) was formed to analyse aerial tactics, with special attention being paid to the use of the bomber. The sub-committee was to secure and dissect intelligence in relation to the composition, organisation, tactics, equipment, personnel and anti-aircraft defences of the forces involved. In addition, there would be review of attacks against naval objectives, close air support, air combat, and strategic and tactical bombing.

In respect of close air support, JIC(S) had this to say:[15]

> 'The combination of the noise of these weapons with the distracting or even terrifying roar of diving and zooming aircraft close overhead, produces demoralisation out of all proportion to the casualties inflicted. It is undoubtedly more effective in battle than bombing alone, especially high bombing. But these low attacks are hazardous and result in higher aircraft casualties than would be the case if bombing attacks were conducted at a safe height.'

While there was recognition in the sub-committee's Paper 4 of the role of close air support, it was highly qualified and suggested critically that it was only effective against poorly trained and motivated troops. The Air Ministry analysis was unsupportive and perhaps, not surprisingly, was able to describe air battles to suit its own priority of strategic bombing: protecting troops was seen as a gross misuse of resources. Wing Commander R. V. Goddard, in charge of Air Ministry intelligence in Spain, reported:[16]

With war clouds gathering, RAF aircraft were painted up in camouflage and post-Munich allocated codes rather than displaying the squadron number or unit badge. Hector K9690 PJ-B of newly reformed 59 Sqn is at Old Sarum on 21 November 1938. The Hector was short-lived in the Army co-operation squadrons, being replaced by the Lysander from 1938. *Author's collection*

The *Luftwaffe*, Italy's *Regia Aeronautica* and the Soviet Air Force all got first-hand experience of modern warfare during the Spanish Civil War. The *Luftwaffe* Condor Legion used large numbers of He 51s in the ground attack role, this He51b belonging to 1 Staffel, Jagdgruppe 88. *Author's collection*

Although it fully met a 1934 specification for an Army co-operation aircraft the Westland Lysander proved to be inadequate for its designed role: although robust and able to use very short fields it was slow and large, resulting in many losses in France. L4698 of 2 Sqn, seen here at Hawkinge in early 1939, is bereft of codes but clearly illustrates the wheel-spat bomb racks. *Author's collection*

> 'The salient feature of the war seems to be that, where armies are engaged, Air Forces become very much tied to Army tactical requirements, unless means are found to employ Air Forces in a definite and decisive strategic role.'

So, while the Germans were practising their war tactics and preparing for *blitzkrieg*, at least the British were trying to observe, learn and apply lessons, albeit getting it wrong. As one historian has noted:[17]

> '...prejudices shared by large parts of the British establishment were instrumental in influencing the conclusions drawn from the Spanish civil war. This, together with a tendency to interpret military operations in Spain in such a way that they supported an existing policy and/or strategy, made British military planners blind to what the Germans were learning in Spain. Vital information which could have been gained through observation and analysis of the Spanish civil war was instead learnt the hard way by Britain and its troops in May 1940.'

Late in the day the Cabinet prevailed over the Air Ministry and accelerated the demand for modern fighters and a defence system to include radar, recognising that the *Luftwaffe* bomber fleets conferred on Adolf Hitler, the German Chancellor, the ability to conduct pre-emptive strikes. It was only in 1938 that Britain recognised that it might need to send troops to mainland Europe in the event of war, at which time there was still no effective close air support system. Also in 1938, in a controversial move, Neville Chamberlain, the British Prime Minister, met Hitler and in effect conceded Czechoslovakia to Germany. Had Britain gone to war over the invasion of the Sudetenland she would have done it with biplane fighters and bombers. Appeasement bought time to modernise, but the priority remained.

While 53 and 59 Sqns were reformed in the Expansion period as Army co-operation squadrons, 18 Sqn was added to 22 Group in 1939. By 1938 all three squadrons were operating the Blenheim: seen here is Mk I L1171 of 18 Sqn. *Author's collection*

Lysander of 13 Sqn against a wintery backdrop in early 1939. The form of Army-Co-op squadron marking, the squadron badge within a six-pointed star, is clearly visible on the fin of the nearest machines. *Author's collection*

Atlas J9548 4 Sqn
Luca G. Canossa

53 Sqn based at Odiham replaced its Hectors with the Blenheim Mk IV from January 1939. In its reconnaissance role the type fared little better than the Lysander in Northern France without fighter protection. L4845/TE-C is still in the pre-war markings of the squadron in early 1940. *Author's collection*

[1] Evans, N F http://nigelef.tripod.com/p_artyint-cb.htm

[2] Destructive shooting, especially against guns, requires pinpoint accuracy, whereas neutralisation results in putting the guns out of action for the time being

[3] Douglas, W S, *Years of Combat* Collins, London, 1963

[4] Cab 23/3 minute 12

[5] Harvey, W F J *Germany Might Have Won in 1918* article in Air Pictorial March 1968

[6] Review of the Air Situation and Strategy for the Information of the Imperial War Cabinet by the Chief of the Air Staff. Air Ministry 27 June 1918. This and a number of key documents around the birth of the RAF are reproduced in the Royal Air Force Air Power Review Spring 2013 which is available on line

[7] Baughen, *Blueprint for Victory,* p179

[8] Cmd. 467 *Permanent Organisation of the Royal Air Force* 25 November 1919

[9] Stanley Baldwin, 1932

[10] TNA AIR10/1206 *Manual of Combined Naval, Military and Air Operations* 1925

[11] TNA AIR 75/31 *Combined Report on Air Cooperation Training* 1936

[12] TNA AIR 9/37 *Army Co-operation, Air Attacks in Direct Support of the Field Force* 1931

[13] TNA WO 193/678 *Air Requirements of the Army* 1939

[14] TNA AIR 41/8 *White Paper, Statement Relating to Defence*, March 1936

[15] TNA CAB 56/3 *JIC Paper 42 Report No 4 Low Flying Attack on Land Forces* 1937

[16] TNA AIR 2/3261 *Republican Spain: Visit of Air Staff Officers in February 1938*

[17] Cerdá, Néstor *The Road to Dunkirk: British Intelligence and the Spanish Civil War in War in History* Vol 13 No 1 2006

To War

At the outset of the Second World War in September 1939 the RAF was ill-prepared to support an expeditionary force. Light bombers were sent to France in significant numbers, together with the inadequate Lysander Army co-operation aircraft and Hurricane fighters purely in a defensive role. However, there was only a slow and cumbersome mechanism for calling up support where and when it might be needed. On the positive side, a trials flight of potential Air Observation Post (AOP) aircraft crossed the Channel: in due course the small, agile spotters would play a major part in the close air support system.

During the 'Phoney War' – the lull before the storm – the Allies launched a limited amphibious landing in Norway to counter the German invasion. That demonstrated the peculiar demands of such landings and in this case the vulnerability of aircraft carriers especially.

The RAF in France lacked the aircraft and systems to counter the German *blitzkrieg* in May 1940 and within a month the enemy was at the English Channel. The RAF devoted far more aircraft to protecting the troops evacuating Dunkirk than it has been given credit for, but retained sufficient to counter the German air onslaught in what was to become the Battle of Britain.

Defending France – the Phoney War

That Germany invaded Poland on 1 September 1939 is written large in history. By that time (actually on 23 August), the RAF had already been mobilised for war. Indeed, from this date war codes had been painted on aircraft. The first move was of nine squadrons of Fairey Battle light bombers of 1 Group to bases in eastern France on 2 September, the key element of an Advanced Air Striking Force (AASF) under AVM P. H. L. Playfair. A tenth squadron followed a week later.

These units were intended initially to offer tactical support to any French advance, but in due course were notionally tasked with the bombing of strategic targets in western Germany. (In December, two Battle squadrons returned to the UK to re-equip with Blenheims; they were replaced by two units already equipped with the latter type.)

Meanwhile, units of the British Expeditionary Force (BEF) began embarking at ports in the south of England from 9 September. By the end of the month 152,000 soldiers and 21,424 vehicles were in France[1] and soon there were ten divisions in three Corps on the Continent. Nine were allocated to the French First Army Group, near the coast to the north of Abbeville, and one within the Second Army Group to the east. When established, the BEF, under General Lord Gort, comprised the following in outline.

Table 2.1 – British Expeditionary Force, France, December 1939

British Expeditionary Force
GHQ inc three Inf Bns, HQ RA, RE, 1st Army Tank Bde, 5th Inf Div (six Inf Bns)
I Corps (inc two MG and two Pioneer Bns)
1st Div (1st Guards, 2nd, 3rd Inf Bdes)
2nd Div (4th, 5th, 6th Inf Bdes)
48th South Midlands Div (143rd, 144th, 145th Inf Bdes)
II Corps (inc two MG and two Pioneer Bns)
3rd Div (7th Guards, 8th, 9th Inf Bdes)
4th Div (10th, 11th, 12th Inf Bdes)
50th Northumbrian Motor Div (150th, 151st, 152nd Inf Bdes)
III Corps (inc one MG and one Pioneer Bns)
42nd East Lancashire Div (125th, 126th, 127th Inf Bdes)
44th Home Counties Div (131st, 132nd, 133rd Inf Bdes)
Saar front (att French Second Army)
51st Highland Div (152nd, 153rd, 154th Inf Bdes plus two MG and two Sapper Bns)
In training/reserve (from March 1940)
12th Eastern Div 35th, 36th, 37th Inf Bdes
23rd Northumbrian Div (69th. 70th Inf Bdes)
46th West Riding Div (137th, 138th, 139th Inf Bdes)

Each Corps had a HQ RA and RE plus various other HQ formations. Each Brigade comprised three infantry battalions, plus an anti-tank company. In total there were 114 infantry, eight machine gun, five pioneer, two sapper and one motorcycle battalions.

Table 2.2 – Advanced Air Striking Force (1 Group Bomber Command)

Sqn	Type	Base	From	To
Advanced Air Striking Force				
98	Battle	Chateau Bougon	16.4.40	15.6.40
71 Wing				
15	Battle	Bétheniville, Condé/Vraux	2.9.39	10.12.39
40	Battle	Bétheniville	2.9.39	3.12.39
114	Blenheim IV	Condé/Vraux, Moyencourt, Crécy	9.12.39	20.5.40
139	Blenheim IV	Bétheniville, Plivot, Poix	1.12.39	10.2.40
105	Battle	Villeneuve, Echemines, Nantes	10.2.40	16.5.40
150	Battle	Écury-sur-Coole, Pouan, Houssay	10.2.40	15.6.40
72 Wing *(Disb 6.2.40 105 Sqn to 71 Wing, 226 Sqn to 76 Wing)*				
105	Battle	Reims, Villeneuve	2.9.39	6.2.40
226	Battle	Reims	2.9.39	6.2.40
74 Wing *(Disb 10.2.40 103 Sqn to 75 Wing, 150 Sqn to 71 Wing)*				
103	Battle	Challerange, Plivot	2.9.39	10.2.40
150	Battle	Challerange, Écury-sur-Coole	2.9.39	10.2.40
75 Wing				
218	Battle	Auberive, St Lucien Ferme, Nantes	2.9.39	16.5.40
88	Battle	Auberive, Mourmelon-le-Grand, Les Grandes-Chapelles, Moisy	11.9.39	14.6.40
103	Battle	Béthenville, St Lucien Ferme, Ouzouer-le-Doyen, Sougé	15.2.40	15.6.40
76 Wing				
12	Battle	Berry-au-Bac, Amifontaine, Echemines, Sougé	2.9.39	15.6.40
142	Battle	Berry-au-Bac, Plivot, Berry-au-Bac, Faux-Villecerf, Villersfaux	2.9.39	15.6.40
226	Battle	Faux-Villecerf, Sougé	6.2.40	18.6.40
67 Fighter Wing				
1	Hurricane I	Vassincourt, Berry-au-Bac, Vassincourt, Berry-au-Bac, Condé/Vraux, Anglure, Châteaudun, Boos, Angers, Nantes	10.10.39	18.6.40
73	Hurricane I	Rouvres, Reims, Rouvres, Reims, Villeneuve, Gaye, Echemines, Ruaudin, Saumur, Nantes, Bagneux	10.10.39	18.6.40
501	Hurricane I	Bétheniville, Anglure, Le Mans, Dinard, St Helier	10.5.40	21.6.40
17	Hurricane I	Le Mans, Dinard, St Helier	8.6.40	19.6.40
242	Hurricane I	Chateaudun, Ancenis, Nantes	8.6.40	18.6.40

Protecting France against invasion along its eastern border with Germany was the massive Maginot defensive line of forts; its German counterpart was the Siegfried Line. To the north, Luxembourg, Belgium (with twenty-two Army divisions), the Netherlands (ten divisions), Denmark and Norway were all neutral and optimistically expected to retain their integrity. Along its eastern border, France deployed forty-three divisions plus one British and, facing Belgium, twenty-nine divisions plus nine British, with twenty-two in reserve. So ignoring the neutrals, the Allies fielded a total 104 divisions, of which only six were armoured, against which the Germans fielded three Army Groups.

German Army Group B in the north, aligned against the Netherlands, consisted of twenty-nine and a half divisions (three armoured). Group A, against Luxembourg and Belgium, comprised forty-five and a half divisions (seven armoured) and the strength of Group C, along the south-western German border, was nineteen divisions. In reserve were a further forty-two. Thus, by the Spring of 1940, some 136 German divisions confronted 104 Allied and thirty-two neutral divisions – notional parity.

The Germans had a number of advantages. First, they intended to knock out the neutrals whom they would overwhelm before any serious prospect of Allied intervention. Second, their tactics – *Blitzkrieg*, or lightning war – had been tried and tested in the invasion of Poland. Third, they could field 3,200 modern aircraft against 1,200 French and 500 British, most of which were inferior.

In addition to the AASF, which remained a part of Bomber Command until 15 January 1940, there was a BEF Air Component, elements of which had been created earlier. First on the scene were the four Hurricane fighter squadrons of 60 Wing formed in August, but two of these, 1 and 73, were quickly transferred to the AASF. 50 Army Co-operation Wing had been formed in January 1937 and its two Lysander squadrons and one Blenheim reconnaissance squadron moved to France late in September, followed by the similarly-configured 51 Wing early in October. The Air Component was completed by 52 Reconnaissance Wing's Blenheims and, in desperation, two squadrons of Gladiators in 61 Fighter Wing. These converted to the Hurricane in April 1940.

Since the BEF was under the overall command of the French there were problems with Army co-operation. The French system was unwieldy and there were lengthy response times to requests for air support. To intercept bomber raids, though, the Air Component brought with it mobile radar sets, installed at Boulogne, Calais, Lille, Arras, Cambrai, Aresne and Sedan, reporting to 1 Filter Centre at Arras. In due course further sets were erected at Verdun, Mont Haut, Bar-le-Duc and Troyes, reporting to a second centre at Reims.

The prescribed role of the fighters was solely to protect bases from attack by enemy aircraft, either through ground control direction or by standing patrols. As well as being proficient in gunnery the pilots were well trained in close formation flying, in vics of three, either as sections (three aircraft) or flights (six aircraft). Squadron leaders were expected to manage the squadron rather than lead it in battle – that was the role of flight commanders. There was no appreciation of the need to maintain loose formation and weave, nor was it expected that fighters would escort bombers or other types. Critically, there had been no training in any form of ground attack and, in any event, the machine guns of Hurricanes would hardly worry German armour.

Table 2.3 – British Expeditionary Force Air Component

Sqn	Type	Base	From	To
BEF Air Component				
212	Spitfire C, Blenheim IV, Hudson	Meaux, Lille/Seclin, Orléans/Bricy, Poitiers, La Rochelle	10.2.40	18.6.40
81	Tiger Moth	Laval, Amiens Mont Joie	17.9.39	5,5,40
50 Army Co-operation Wing				
4	Lysander II	Mons-en-Chaussée, Ronchin, Clairmarais, Dunkirk	24.9.39	25.5.40
13	Lysander II	Mons-en-Chaussée, Flamicourt, Douai, Abbeville, Châteaubriant	24.9.39	29.5.40
53	Blenheim IV	Plivot, Poix	20.9.39	7.3.40
16	Lysander II	Amiens, Bertangles	13.4.40	19.5.40
51 Army Co-operation Wing				
2	Lysander II	Abbeville, Labuissiére, Boulogne	29.9.39	20.5.40
26	Lysander II	Abbeville, Dieppe, Authie	3.10.39	22.5.40
59	Blenheim IV	Poix, Moyencourt, Poix, Crécy	5.10.39	7.3.40
52 Recce Wing (from 1.11.39)				
53	Blenheim IV	Poix, Crécy	7.3.40	20.5.40
59	Blenheim IV	Moyencourt, Poix, Crécy	7.3.40	20.5.40
60 Fighter Wing *(1 and 73 Sqns to AASF 10.10.39)*				
1	Hurricane I	Octeville, Norrent-Fontes	9.9.39	10.10.39
73	Hurricane I	Octeville, Norrent-Fontes	9.9.39	10.10.39
85	Hurricane I	Rouen/Boos, Merville, Lille/Seclin, Mons-en-Chaussée, Lille/Seclin, Merville, Boulogne	9.9.39	23.5.40
87	Hurricane 1	Rouen/Boos, Merville, Lille/Seclin, Le Touquet, Lille/Seclin, Amiens, Senon, Lille/Seclin, Merville	4.9.39	22.5.40
61 Fighter Wing				
607	Gladiator I	Merville, Vitry-en-Artois	15.11.39	3.40
	Hurricane I	Abbeville, Vitry-en-Artois, Norrent-Fontes	3.40	22.5.40
615	Gladiator II	Merville, Vitry-en-Artois, Poix, Abbeville	15.11.39	4.40
	Hurricane I	Abbeville	4.40	22.5.40
504	Hurricane I	Lille/Marcq, Norrent-Fontes, Vitry-en-Artois	12.5.40	20.5.40
63 Fighter Wing				
3	Hurricane I	Merville	10.5.40	20.5.40
79	Hurricane I	Merville, Norrent-Fontes, Merville	10.5.40	21.5.40
70 Bomber Wing				
18	Blenheim I, IV	Roye/Amy, Rosières-en-Santerre, Moyencourt, Crécy	24.9.39	9.5.40
57	Blenheim I, IV	Roye/Amy, Rosières-en-Santerre, Poix, Crécy	24.9.39	22.5.40

A number of Fairey Battle squadrons of the Advanced Air Striking Force was sent to France on 2 September, the day prior to Great Britain's formal declaration of war against Germany. Through the winter conditions were appalling, as evidenced in this shot of an aircraft of 142 Sqn at Berry-au-Bac in January 1940. *Author's collection*

Battle PH-X of 12 Sqn possibly at Amifontaine in the winter of 1940. Tented accommodation would have been miserable. *Author's collection*

The Air Component was under the overall command of Lord Gort until 15 January 1940 when Air Marshal A. S. Barratt assumed command of all British Air Forces in France (BAFF). The Air Component was commanded by AVM C. H. B. Blount.

One small, but for the future highly significant, deployment was that of three Taylorcraft and one Stinson Voyager of the independent D Flight from Old Sarum to France on 1 February 1940 for training in artillery direction. The flight, with three Army and one RAF pilots, went to the French artillery ranges at Mailly, eventually returning intact to the UK via Dieppe on 19 May.

During the early stages of the war in France the Lysanders of the Army Co-operation squadrons used the opportunity to test tactics with the Gladiators of 61 Wing and, being out of harm's way, none was lost in combat, although five were destroyed in accidents. The Battles, which might have needed to support the Army in close support in an emergency, fared less well, a number crashing in tight turns during exercises.

Early in the war the vulnerability of the Battle was illustrated when two aircraft of 88 Sqn were shot down on 20 September, followed by five of 150 Sqn ten days later while conducting a reconnaissance patrol just across the Franco-German border. RAF losses to the end of April 1940 were as shown.

Table 2.4 – RAF losses in combat, France, September 1939–April 1940

	Battle	Blenheim	Hurricane	Spitfire PR	Lysander	Total
September	8					**8**
October		6				**6**
November		2	1			**3**
December			2			**2**
January		3			1	**4**
February		1				**1**
March			4		4	**8**
April	1	1	6	1	5	**14**
Total	**9**	**13**	**13**	**1**	**10**	**46**

Hurricane P3886/UF-K 601 Sqn. *Luca G. Canossa*

The Low Countries 1940
Emden
North Sea
Amsterdam
NETHERLANDS
The Hague
Rotterdam
Waalhaven
River Maas
GERMANY
Zeebrugge
Ostend
Bruges
Antwerp
Dusseldorf
Munchen Gladbach
Dunkirk
Nieuport Canal
River Scheldt
Albert Canal
Veldvezelt
Hasselt
Maastricht
Ledegem
Wevelghem
Brussels
River Dyle
Vroenhoven
Cologne
Aachen
BELGIUM
Liege
Lille
Gembloux
Bonn
Namur
River Maas
Arras
Amiens
Prüm
FRANCE
Wiltz
Ardennes
LUXEMBOURG
Sedan
Luxembourg
0 Miles 100
0 Km 100
River Meuse
Reims

The Brief Norwegian Campaign

Having occupied Poland and while preparing her army for the forthcoming invasion of France via the Low Countries, Germany began seizure of Norway on 9 April 1940. Britain's response was to despatch a strong naval force, to land troops at three locations – at Harstad, off Narvik in the far north and at Namsos, to the north of, and Andalsnes to the south of, Trondheim. The carriers HMS *Ark Royal* and HMS *Glorious* were recalled from the Mediterranean, to join HMS *Furious* in due course.

The reasons for the invasion were simple, as were the reasons for Allied concern. Norway was neutral, but her fjords and ports were coveted because they would provide bases for German naval vessels venturing into the Atlantic. Further, Germany relied on huge imports of iron ore from Sweden, which were shipped through the northern port of Narvik. Two distinct and very brief campaigns resulted, one hopeless, the second achieving limited objectives.

The German invasion, Operation *Weserübung*, was made via also neutral Denmark (which fell in a day), providing springboard airfields for operations against Norway. By the end of day one the Germans, who had fielded seven divisions (including two of mountain troops), occupied most of the key cities and airfields, having met little resistance initially. The troops were supported by *Fliegerkorps X*, which included 102 fighters (Bf 110 of ZG 76), 233 bombers (He 111 of KG 4 and KG 26 plus Ju 88 of KG 30), thirty-nine dive-bombers (Ju 87 of StG 1) and 165 reconnaissance types. Some 580 Ju 52/3m transports were also used to move troops and supplies.

Britain had contemplated a pre-emptive strike and while the Norwegian government had blocked this, there was a plan of sorts. The first engagements were naval, the Home Fleet, sailing off the southern coast of Norway without carrier support, being bombed by ninety He 111s and Ju 88s on the 9th with the loss of a destroyer. HMS *Furious* joined the fleet on the 10th, but with no fighters embarked. The following day her Swordfish attacked vessels in Trondheim without success.

British-led landings took place between 14 and 18 April with two objectives – to capture Trondheim in the centre, with its important airfield at Vaernes, and Narvik in the far north. The first to land, at Harstad and with limited cover from aircraft of the Fleet Air Arm (FAA), was *Rupertforce* on 15 April, followed by the two Trondheim forces between 15 and 18 April. The three forces involved were as set out below.

The Allied force of some 38,000 men was given scant air support throughout. What was provided was more a victory of hope over planning. 263 Squadron with Gladiators was embarked on HMS *Glorious*, flown on by FAA pilots. Selection of the type was because it had good short-field performance and was also in use by the Norwegian Air Force. On 23 April *Glorious* was off Norway and the day following, from 150 miles offshore, Gladiators were flown off in two flights of nine, each flight led by a Skua to aid navigation. Their destination was frozen Lake Lesjaskog, albeit by now beginning to melt with the onset of the thaw.

With little fuel, few servicing personnel and limited supplies, the squadron was doomed from the outset. There was no liaison with the Army units

Gladiators of 263 were despatched to Norway in HMS *Glorious*: the aircraft was considered suitable due to its good short-field performance and also because the type was flown by the RNoAF. N5641/HE-G 263 Sqn at Bardufoss. *Author's collection*

Great care was taken to hide the small British force in Norway from the *Luftwaffe*, which enjoyed air superiority. This Gladiator at Andalsnes, with wheel discs removed to prevent ice and mud binding the brakes, is covered with scrub, as is the FAA Skua in the background. *Author's collection*

On 11 April 1940 Swordfish from HMS *Furious* bombed ships in Trondheim harbour without success. K8399/593 of 818 NAS is ashore in 1940, possibly at Hatston. *Author's collection*

the squadron was presumably intended to protect and no early warning system, so the only possible tactic was to mount standing patrols. The makeshift aerodrome was spotted by *Luftwaffe* reconnaissance aircraft and bombed several times during the day with the destruction on the ground of ten Gladiators and fracturing of the ice. Six German aircraft were brought down with eight more probables, but with total German air supremacy, neither the Allied armies nor the *Luftwaffe* would notice the difference. The following day four remaining aircraft were flown out to a plateau at Setermoen where, with little remaining fuel, the aircraft were destroyed and the pilots evacuated. The troops at Namsos and Andalsnes, with no artillery or air support, were overwhelmed and withdrew between 30 April and 3 May, the carriers having been forced to return to home waters.

The Allies now concentrated on Narvik. The hapless personnel of 263 Sqn were re-grouped and a further eighteen replacement Gladiators flown on to HMS *Glorious*, which set sail for Narvik on 14 May. This time the aircraft were destined for Bardufoss airfield, which had been extended and improved considerably in advance. Keen to withdraw from the coast, *Glorious* launched two sections of Gladiators, each led by a Swordfish, but in the face of a strong gale. One flight flew into a mountainside but the other managed to return and land safely back on. Eight Gladiators reached Bardufoss eventually on 22 May and immediately flew defensive sorties, the remaining eight aircraft following the next day.

Several aircraft flew south to Bodø on the 26th from where they were successful in bringing down a number of transports and escorting bombers. Through ensuing days the biplane fighters protected the troops from attack as the Germans advanced on Narvik, their numbers boosted by Hurricanes of 46 Sqn. These had embarked on HMS *Glorious* with the Gladiators, but had not flown off since their intended base at Skaanland was not ready. They returned to Bodø on 26 May and quickly transferred to Bardufoss.

By now the German Army had invaded France and the Low Countries. At Narvik demolition and evacuation was the order of the day. The two RAF squadrons continued to mount defensive patrols, there being no radar or other early warning. On 2 June the *Luftwaffe* attacked in force and 46 Sqn flew around forty sorties, 263 Sqn flying fifty-five. Cover of the Army continued to the last and in this brief period the RAF destroyed some twenty-eight enemy aircraft. Demolitions complete, on 7 June ten Hurricanes were flown on to HMS *Glorious*, a remarkable feat by pilots who had no experience of carrier landings in aircraft without arrester hooks. Ten Gladiators also landed on, but sadly *Glorious* was sunk on the 8th by the German battleships *Scharnhorst* and *Gneisenau* with the loss not only of the aircraft but, tragically, all but two of 46 Sqn's pilots.

Table 2.5 – Allied Expeditionary Force, Norway, April 1940

Allied Expeditionary Force – Norway
Mauriceforce (landed Namsos N of Trondheim from 14 April)
146th Brigade
5eme demi-Brigade French Chasseurs Alpins
Sickleforce (landed Andalsnes S of Trondheim from 18 April)
15th Brigade
148th Brigade
Light and heavy AA, RE
Rupertforce (landed Harstad W of Narvik from 15 April)
24th Guards Brigade
27eme demi-Brigade French Chasseurs Alpins
13eme demi-Brigade French Foreign Legion
Polish Highland Brigade (four battalions)
RA, light and heavy AA, several tanks, RE
Royal Navy
3 Aircraft carriers
4 Battleships
2 Battle cruisers
21 Cruisers
21 Destroyers
17 Submarines
Sloops and minesweepers
French and Polish navies
6 Cruisers
12 Destroyers
2 Submarines

Table 2.6 – Fleet Air Arm units, Norway, 1940

FAA units Norway
HMS *Furious (10.4.40–28.4.40: 9.5.40–28.5.40)*
816 NAS Swordfish I (9.4.40–28.4.40)
818 NAS Swordfish I (14.4.40–27.4.40)
804 NAS Sea Gladiator (9.5.40–28.5.40)
818 NAS Swordfish I (12.5.40–26.5.40)
801 NAS Skua (25.5.40–25.5.40)
HMS *Glorious (9.4.40–18.4.40: 22.4.40–12.5.40: 18.5.50–8.6.40 sunk)*
802 NAS Sea Gladiator (9.4.40–8.6.40)
803 NAS Skua (22.4.40–26.4.40)
804 NAS Sea Gladiator (22.4.40–4.5.40)
823 NAS Swordfish I (30.4.40–12.5.40)
701 NAS Walrus (9.5.40–18.5.40, then based Harstad)
HMS *Ark Royal (10.4.40–21.4.40: 22.4.40–28.4.40: 3.5.40–14.6.40)*
810 NAS Swordfish I (10.4.40–8.10.40)
820 NAS Swordfish I (10.4.40–30.4.40)
821 NAS Swordfish I (10.4.40–23.4.40)
801 NAS Skua (22.4.40–15.5.40)
803 NAS Skua (26.4.40–28.4.40)
803 NAS Skua/Roc (3.5.40–25.5.40)
820 NAS Swordfish I (4.5.40–8.10.40)
803 NAS Skua/Roc (31.5.40–14.6.40)
701 NAS Walrus (7.6.40–14.6.40, ex Harstad)

The battleships, and all cruisers with the exception of four AA cruisers, carried one or two Swordfish floatplanes of 700 Naval Air Squadrons (NAS) for local spotting.

Northern France May 1940

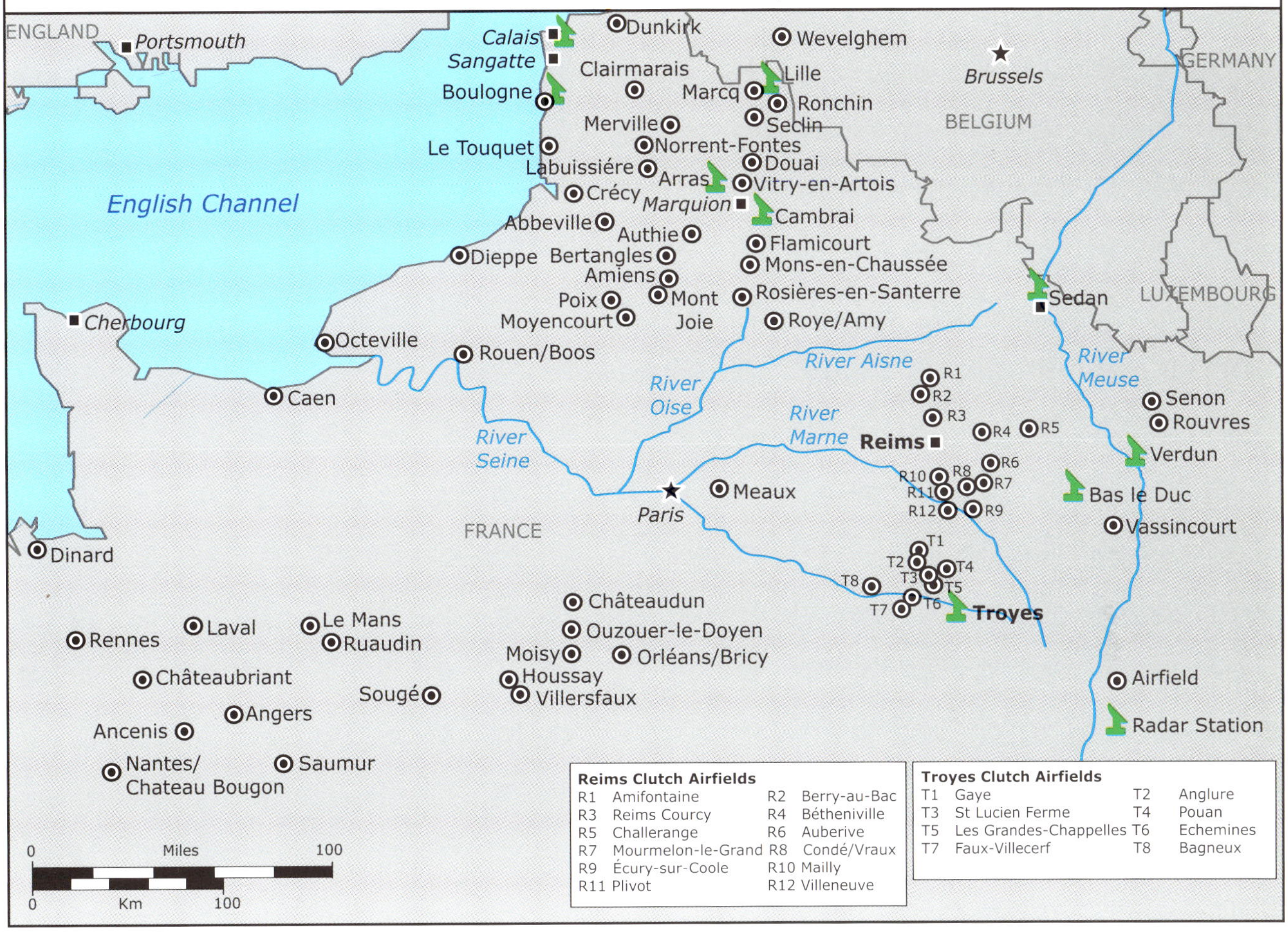

Thus ended this brief campaign, which served only to highlight the vulnerability of the fleet to an opponent who enjoyed air supremacy and also the need for support aircraft and a system within which they could work effectively. One objective that was achieved was that the port of Narvik was out of action until April 1941.

Assault on France and the Low Countries

Cooperating with the Army had become such an alien concept that the Air Staff tended to see the RAF role as stepping in when the Army had failed rather than helping the Army to succeed.[2]

On 10 May the long anticipated German assault began; the 'Phoney War' was over. In a month France would be overwhelmed and British troops evicted from continental Europe. The advance was bold, fast and efficient, with armour outstripping infantry and backed up throughout by close-support aircraft well protected by fighters. As predicted, the Germans ignored Dutch and Belgian neutrality, charging swiftly through both countries, while at the same time invading France through Luxembourg.

Attacking through the Netherlands, Army Group B had the task of drawing British and French divisions north into Belgium in order to remove them from northern France. This would make easier the assault by *Panzer* units of Army Group A through the allegedly impenetrable Ardennes Forest towards Sedan. There was an Allied plan to hold the Germans on the River Dyle stretching across the centre of Belgium and, accordingly, British and French units moved up to reinforce the Belgians. Rotterdam was bombed on 14 May, after which the Netherlands surrendered. While the French First Army Group with the BEF was being outflanked from the Netherlands and under direct pressure across the Dyle, Army Group A had swept through northern France from the Ardennes and forced a wedge between the French Seventh and Second Army Groups. By 21 May the coast had been reached at St Valery.

When the assault began the RAF had a total of twenty-nine operational squadrons in northern France. For Army co-operation there were five Lysander squadrons plus nine Battle and five Blenheim light bomber squadrons. For bomber escort and defence there were ten Hurricane squadrons. The Lysanders were now intended to act as local tactical reconnaissance, the Blenheims to provide longer range recce and the Hurricane squadrons airfield protection. The Battles and Blenheims of the AASF were relieved of bombing targets in Germany, supporting instead the Army along the eastern battle area by bombing bridges and bottlenecks. Their three Hurricane squadrons were to protect the AASF bases.

Road and rail targets to the north would be attacked by Blenheims of 2 Group from the UK, but there were misgivings about using bombers in support of the Army in this way. To quote from the operational instructions of the day:[3]

> 'Bomber aircraft have proved extremely useful in support of an advancing army, especially against weak anti-aircraft resistance, but it is not clear that a bomber force used against an advancing army, well supported by all forms of anti-aircraft defence and a large force of fighter aircraft, will be economically effective.'

Arraigned against the Allies and in support of German Army Groups A and B, were two *Luftwaffe* air fleets, comprising in total 3,500 modern aircraft.

Table 2.7 – Luftflotte 2, May 1940

Luftflotte 2 (Army Group B fronting Netherlands and Belgium)	
Bombers (485 serviceable)	
KG 4	He 111, Ju 88
KG 27	He 111
KG 30	Ju 88, He 111
KG 54	He 111
KG 77	Do 17
LG 1	He 111, Ju 88
Ground attack (246 serviceable)	
StG 2	Ju 87
StG 77	Ju 87
IV/LG 1	Ju 87
LG 2	Hs 123
Reconnaissance (55 serviceable)	
Various	He 111, Ju 88, Do 17
Fighter (539 serviceable)	
JG 1	Bf 109E
JG 2	Bf 109D, Ar 68
JG 3	Bf 109E
JG 20	Bf 109E
JG 21	Bf 109E
JG 26	Bf 109E
JG 27	Bf 109E
JG 51	Bf 109E
I/LG 2	Bf 109E
TrGr 186	Bf 109E
ZG 1	Bf 110C/D
ZG 26	Bf 110C/D

Table 2.8 – Luftflotte 3, May 1940

Luftflotte 3 (Army Group A fronting Luxembourg and France)	
Bombers (579 serviceable)	
KG 1	He 111
KG 2	Do 17
KG 3	Do 17
KG 28	He 111
KG 51	He 111
KG 53	He 111
KG 55	Do 17
KG76	Do 17
Ground attack (110 serviceable)	
StG1	Ju 87
StG 2	Ju 87
TrGr 186	Ju 87
StG 51	Ju 87
Reconnaissance (44 serviceable)	
Various	He 111, Ju 88, Do 17
Fighter (554 serviceable)	
JG 2	Bf 109E
JG 3	Bf 109E
JG 51	Bf 109E
JG 52	Bf 109E
JG53	Bf 109E
JG 54	Bf 109E
JG 76	Bf 109E
JG 77	Bf 109E
I/LG 2	Bf 109E
ZG 2	Bf 110C/D
ZG 26	Bf 110C/D
ZG 52	Bf 110C/D
ZG 76	Bf 110C/D
LG 1	Bf 110C/D

(As described in Appendix 1, *Geschwader* were subdivided to *Gruppen*, typically comprising around forty aircraft and these were deployed to air fleets in much the same way as British battalions were to brigades. It thus follows that not all elements of any given *Geschwader* were allocated to a single air fleet. Where two types are shown, the dominant one appears first.)

The AASF Hurricane squadrons moved back from Vassincourt to Berry-au-Bac (1 Sqn) and to Reims from Rouvres (73 Sqn), to be reinforced immediately by 501 Sqn at Bétheniville. Within 63 Wing, 3 and 79 Sqns brought their Hurricanes from the UK to Merville. Two days later 504 Sqn became the tenth fighter squadron in France.

As the German Army pressed ahead relentlessly, the *Luftwaffe* attacked Allied airfields, destroying a number of aircraft on the ground. Counter-attacks saw 600 Sqn send six Blenheim fighters to attack Ju 52s landing at Waalhaven in the Netherlands, shooting down five. Much of the Dutch and Belgian air forces were lost, either in bombing raids or combat. The Germans planned to use Waalhaven as a springboard for further adventures and it was thus the subject of further Allied attack to prevent them from doing so.

For the next two weeks the RAF flew hundreds of sorties daily to slow the onslaught, but the cost

Eleven Battle squadrons were deployed to France as part of the AASF including 88 Sqn, some of whose aircraft are seen here at Mourmelon-le-Grand in 1940. Nearest are K9244/RH-L and K9282/RH-P: noteworthy is the different presentation of fuselage roundel on the nearest three aircraft. *Author's collection*

was high. The Hurricane, used mainly as a point defence fighter, was outclassed by the Bf 109E but still managed to bring down some bombers. This main tasking of the Hurricanes in turn meant that the vulnerable and now unescorted Battles and Blenheims represented easy pickings for the German fighters. When Hurricanes did escort bombers they were often drawn off by 109s flying high cover over targets, leaving the light bombers at the mercy of lower cover fighters. The Lysanders were proving next to useless, many being lost to fighters and groundfire.

By night, medium bombers of Bomber Command flying from the UK hit lines of communication and airfields. For example, on 10/11 May, Whitleys of 77 and 102 Sqns attacked roads and railways leading into the Netherlands while Wellingtons bombed Waalhaven airfield. By day, fighters of 11 Group, Fighter Command, patrolled the Dutch and Belgian coasts and from the 12th Coastal Command Beauforts and FAA Swordfish also attacked Waalhaven.

The Germans had captured two bridges over the Albert Canal, at Vroenhoven and Veldwezelt, and on 12 May these were a key target for AASF bombers. Five Battles of 12 Sqn, with volunteer crews (because the bridges were so well defended), took off in the morning from Amifontaine. Their Hurricane escort from 1 Sqn was soon engaged by covering Bf 109s, leaving the light bombers unprotected. All were shot down, the pilot and observer of the lead aircraft

Allied Central Air Bureau France 1940

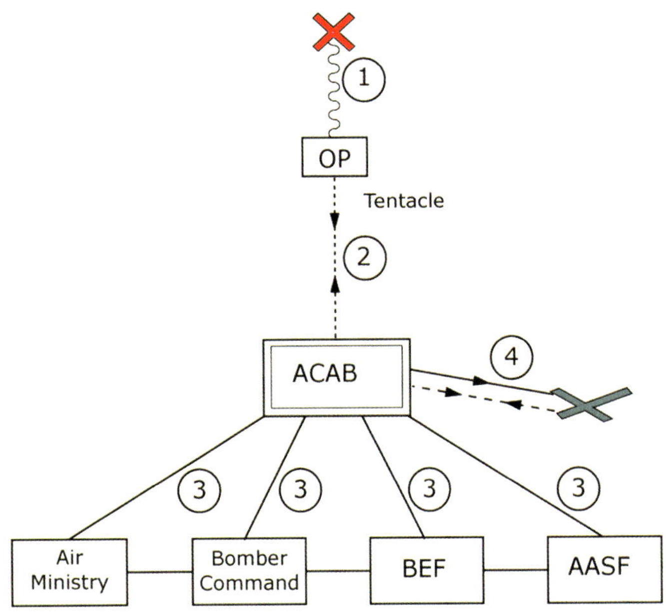

1) Ground reconnaissance OP (tentacle) identifies target or threat
2) OP alerts Allied Central Air Bureau (ACAB) by R/T
3) ACAB seeks confirmation from Air Ministry, Bomber Command, British Expeditionary Force and Advanced Air Striking Force before committing aircraft
4) ACAB instructs light bomber airfield by landline or W/T once parties agree

Hurricanes of 73 Sqn on patrol over France in October 1939 during the Phoney War. The Hurricanes achieved some success but were no match for the Bf 109s of the *Luftwaffe*, many of whose pilots had experience with the Condor Legion in Spain. Losses, particularly of inexperienced pilots, were high.

Sergeant Thomas Pyne of 73 Sqn awaits while his Hurricane 'A' is re-armed. In the prelude to the evacuation from Dunkirk, Pyne was to be shot down and killed near Sedan on 14 May 1940 flying Hurricane P2812. *Author's collection*

Blenheim IV reconnaissance aircraft of 53 Sqn at Poix in the Spring of 1940. The nearest aircraft displays the wartime code PZ and shows the under-fuselage bomb rack. On the original photograph at left is a Tiger Moth, probably of 81 Sqn. *Author's collection*

The Gladiator was hopelessly outdated by 1940 but 607 and 615 Sqns were sent to France in November 1939. Few returned to the UK and from 13 May those still remaining were spread around the fighter squadrons. Pictured is an aircraft of 607 Sqn at Vitry-en-Artois. *Author's collection*

The censor has managed to obscure the identity of this OO coded Lysander of 13 Sqn at Mons en Chaussée in 1940. The aircraft seems to have blown a tyre: the spat side covers were removed to avoid snow or mud building and binding the wheels. *Author's collection*

attacking the Veldwezelt bridge, Fg Off Donald Garland and Flt Sgt Thomas Gray, both being awarded the Victoria Cross. Two dozen Blenheims of 15 and 107 Sqns from 2 Group bombed Maastricht at about the same time, losing ten to flak and fighters. Again, the escorting Hurricanes, of 85 and 87 Sqns, were preoccupied in combat with the fighter cover. The ground forces were just holding their own, but Sedan was threatened by General Guderian's XIX Corps, its divisions having reached the Meuse (Maas).

Breakthrough at Sedan

The British and French were struggling with limited reconnaissance capability, poor communications and lengthy lines of command. The speed of the German offensive caused uncertainty and anxiety as to exactly where the enemy had reached. In the UK Winston Churchill had just replaced Chamberlain as Prime Minister, but was to some extent preoccupied with the pointless campaign in Norway. The French High Command, under General Maurice Gamelin, was rigid and slow to respond to a rapidly changing picture.

Indeed, French generalship was poor, lacked imagination and thrust and was considered overall to have had a Great War mindset of static warfare in which artillery played the key role. For that reason, and despite evidence from Spain and Poland that ought to have been taken into account, the High Command viewed an attack through the Ardennes as impossible because German horse-drawn artillery could never negotiate the difficult terrain.

The thousands of tanks massing, in theory protected against prying aerial reconnaissance by fighter patrols, were spotted. What was not known was their intended direction of advance. Once the breakthrough came, Ju 87 Stukas worked in concert with the Army as airborne artillery, to devastating effect.

By 13 May the Dutch Air Force had been almost destroyed, rendering the country's position hopeless. On the morning of 14 May Rotterdam was bombed by fifty-seven He 111s of KG 54, resulting in the deaths of 913 civilians. Early the next day the Dutch government understandably capitulated. In France replacement Hurricanes and volunteer ferry pilots struggled to locate their intended destinations due to a severe shortage of maps. Given that the main task for the fighters was the protection of their own airfields, it is clear that any chance of them helping to support the Army through reconnaissance, escort or strafing, was negligible. Thus, apart from destroying the odd bomber that might otherwise go on to inflict damage on ground forces, their very presence seemed almost pointless. So desperate was the situation that some of the recently retired Gladiators of 615 Sqn were distributed to squadrons for local defence and staff officers pulled from HQ to fly them.

Throughout the campaign the *Luftwaffe* fielded a large number of Henschel 126 light, two-seat observation aircraft, always flying ahead of ground units while seeking out Allied defences and protected by a covering screen of fighters. That the

In February 1940 the first Spitfires went to France with 212 Sqn, later to become 1 Photographic Reconnaissance Unit (PRU). Spitfire PR C P9385/LY operated with 1 PRU, which also operated Blenheims, and a Hudson. *Author's collection*

Hs 126 bore a strong resemblance to the Lysander was unfortunate in that a number of them would have been left alone, whereas some Lysanders fell victim to friendly fire. Another Henschel type, the Hs 123, was a single-seat biplane ground attack aircraft which served in immediate support of the Army, often based on makeshift strips close behind the advancing front line.

On the 15th on the Sedan front AVM Playfair was ordered to fly the maximum possible sorties against bridges across the Meuse to hold up the advance. From 0630 to 1820 there were at least nine missions, including two French, with the RAF Battle and Blenheim sorties alone numbering 123. The early raids suffered few losses, but by the afternoon the bridges were protected by Bf 109s and alert anti-aircraft (AA) units. Hurricanes escorting the bombers were soon distracted and engaged Ju 87s attacking French positions: at least six were shot down at this stage lacking protection from covering Messerschmitts. The Battles and Blenheims suffered appalling losses, with the fighter squadrons also badly hit, to the extent that the final raid by 2 Group Blenheims lacked escorts.

The day proved disastrous for the RAF: thirty Battles, ten Blenheims and four Lysanders were shot down, mainly by fighters, while twenty-seven Hurricanes were lost, along with fifteen pilots killed, among them a number of campaign veterans. The cost to the *Luftwaffe* was forty-six aircraft, of which only eight were Bf 109s.

Overnight, the AASF squadrons were ordered to retire south, HQ moving to Troyes. Throughout the 15th *Luftwaffe* bombers returned to the attack on airfields, including Berry-au-Bac, Bétheniville and Rosières. They were often escorted by Bf 110s, which shot down half of the Hurricanes lost.

Seven *Panzer* divisions had advanced 60 miles, outstripping their own infantry and artillery but doing so under the protective umbrella of air superiority. As well as the fighter shield, medium bombers struck at lines of communication, long-range reconnaissance and short-range probing was done by Hs 126s while Hs 123s and Ju 87 Stukas acted as airborne artillery. The lighter aircraft, easy prey for Allied fighters had it not been for German dominance of the air, were all based close to the front, their personnel skilled at rapid turn-around on the ground.

At home, Air Marshal Sir Hugh Dowding, AOC Fighter Command, was struggling to retain his fighter squadrons in the UK under pressure from Churchill and the French government when the position in France was clearly hopeless. By drawing the 7th Army north and then attacking in strength through the Ardennes, the Germans had wrong-footed completely the Allied

The Battles began their war in earnest with the German invasion of France on 10 May. Often flying without cover against heavily defended targets they suffered serious losses. K9264/PM-L is from 103 Sqn. *Author's collection*

high command. Against increasing pressure, French General Gaston Billotte ordered a withdrawal from the Dyle Line to the Scheldt, forgetting to advise either the Belgians or the British commander. There was an inevitability of defeat as withdrawal turned into a rout over the next week.

Concerned to do its best to protect troops from the constant and overwhelming *Luftwaffe* bomber and ground attack sorties, the RAF now committed many more Hurricanes to the fray – but with care. Initially eight half-squadrons were sent to France, to be attached to existing units in order to bolster aircraft numbers and to operate under a pre-existing command structure. In reality, the half squadrons were flights, comprising a range of pilot experience and skill, which meant that neither an elite unit was potentially lost, nor just novices sent like lambs to slaughter. If these flights were lost, then the core of each squadron remained in the UK to face the inevitable forthcoming aerial onslaught. Further units were sent to France over the next few days, as shown in Table 2.9. Late on the 16th it was agreed to commit further fighter units to France, the equivalent of six more squadrons, but due to lack of space they would operate from UK airfields, being based temporarily in France for either a morning or afternoon.

The unstoppable German advance, coupled with poor intelligence and French indecision, now resulted in a chaotic retreat to the coast and ultimately eviction of the BEF. The details of the ground actions, often heroic, are well recorded. However, both the British Army and Royal Air Force were to pay a high price for having failed to develop effective systems for support and the right aircraft, policies and training to make them effective. The RAF could now do no more than mount standing patrols and sacrifice yet more of the light bombers and their crews in suicidal attempts to bomb key communications and advancing columns.

What was left of the Belgian Air Force – a handful of biplane fighters and light bombers – withdrew to France on Thursday 16 May. In the afternoon RAF Hurricane reinforcements began arriving for aerodromes in the Lille and Abbeville areas. Ground crew and spare pilots were flown in by de Havilland Flamingo and Bristol Bombay transports. So desperate was the situation, and so ambiguous were Hurricane ferry pilot orders, that according to one source a number stayed and flew Hurricanes operationally with 87 and 504 Sqns.[4] The AASF Hurricane squadrons, not being reinforced, withdrew to the south while the last four Battles of 105 and 218 Sqns were distributed among the remaining six squadrons.

The light transport and communications aircraft of 24 Sqn were ordered back to Le Bourget and 615 Sqn transferred to the small aerodrome at Moorsele, outside Courtrai and now near the front line. The control centre at Merville reported into the main centre at Arras, directing fighters towards the incoming bomber streams. Just nine German aircraft, including the newly deployed twin-boom Focke-Wulf Fw 189, were destroyed for the loss of thirteen Hurricanes in the air and five pilots killed.

Table 2.9 – Half-squadron fighter reinforcements, 16/17.5.40–18/20.5.40

Sqn/Flt	Type	Base	Reinforcing
Fighter reinforcements			
60 Wing			
242/A	Hurricane I	Lille/Seclin	85
111/A	Hurricane I	Merville	87
61 Wing			
56/B	Hurricane I	Vitry-en-Artois, Norrent-Fontes	607
229/B	Hurricane I	Norrent-Fontes	607
245/A	Hurricane I	Moorsele, Norrent-Fontes	615
253/B	Hurricane I	Norrent-Fontes	504
63 Wing			
601/A	Hurricane I	Merville, St Valery	3
213/B	Hurricane I	Merville	79
67 Wing			
17	Hurricane I	Merville, Lille/Marcq, Norrent-Fontes	
32	Hurricane I	Abbeville, Moorsele, Merville	
151	Hurricane I	Abbeville, Vitry-en-Artois	
14 Fighter Group			
56/A	Hurricane I	Abbeville, Lille/Marcq, Lille/Seclin	
213/A	Hurricane I	Abbeville, Lille/Marcq, Lille/Seclin	
111/B	Hurricane I	Abbeville, Vitry-en-Artois, Valenciennes	
253/A	Hurricane I	Abbeville, Vitry-en-Artois, Valenciennes	
145/A	Hurricane I	Vitry-en-Artois, Abbeville, Merville	
601/A	Hurricane I	Vitry-en-Artois, Abbeville, Merville	
253/A	Hurricane I	Hawkinge (UK)	
229/A	Hurricane I	Hawkinge (UK)	

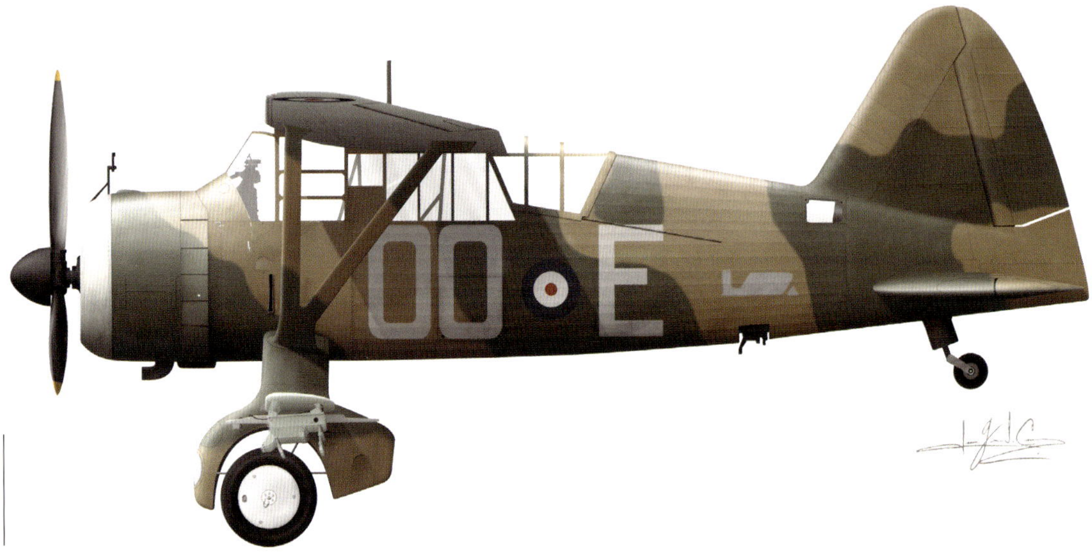

Lysander
L????/OO-E 13 Sqn
France 1940.
Luca G. Canossa

85 and 87 Sqns with the Hurricane were part of the BEF Air Component and remained in France until late May. P3408/K is an aircraft of 85 Sqn.
Author's collection

The scene at Poix in early May 1940. In the foreground is a French H-75A Hawk with 52 Recce Wing Blenheims behind. TR-Y and TR-Z belong to 59 Sqn while PZ-W and others to the rear are from 53 Sqn.
Author's collection

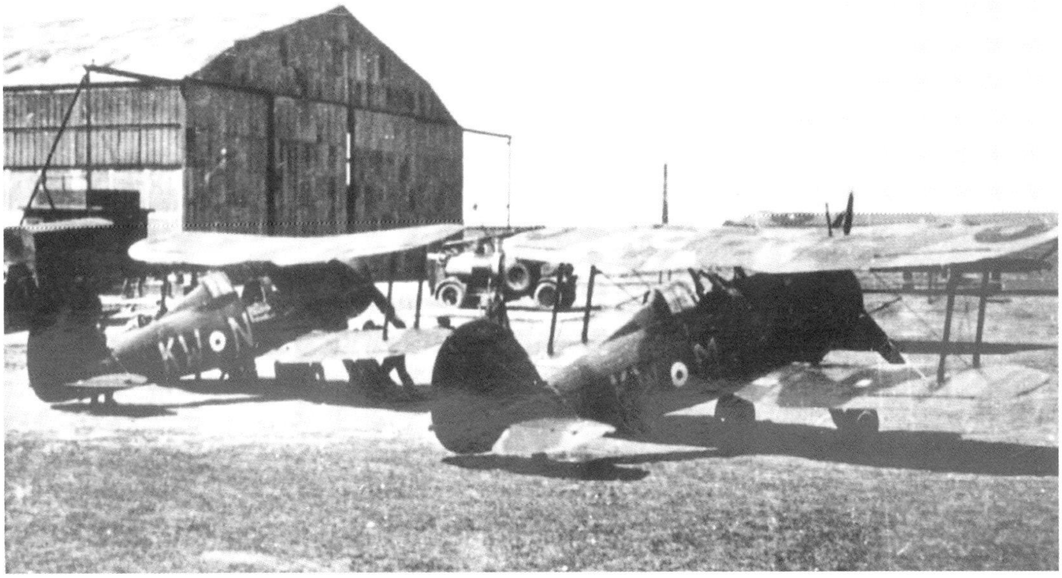

Gladiators of 615 Sqn at St Inglevert in April 1940 before the squadron converted to the Hurricane. *Author's collection*

By now the French had accepted defeat. Winston Churchill flew to Paris to discuss the situation with his counterpart and the French military commander Gamelin. From Churchill:[5]

> 'In the course of his appeal Général Gamelin said that fighters were needed...to stop the German tanks. At this I said "No. It is the business of the artillery to stop tanks. The business of the fighters is to cleanse the skies over the battle".'

During the 17th the pattern continued: patrols up against bombers and the wretched Stukas operating in support of their army and bombing retreating columns, slowed by an increasing number of refugees. In the morning twelve Blenheims of 82 Sqn had taken off from Watton to bomb a concentration of vehicles near Gembloux. They were to meet Hurricanes of 87 Sqn over the target, but by then they had been intercepted by Bf 109s of I/JG 3; only one aircraft returned. The shambles was compounded when Blenheims, given poor intelligence, bombed French troops on the Cambrai road. Overnight, Bomber Command moved to tactical bombing when fifty-three bombers were briefed to attack the Meuse crossings, but they struggled to find their targets, 25% returning with their bomb loads.

The following days were equally chaotic. On the 18th, thirty-three Hurricanes were shot down with seven pilots killed against forty-six Germans destroyed: two-thirds of the RAF losses were from the reinforcement units. There were several reports of enemy fighters shooting at RAF pilots who had taken to their parachutes, with at least one killed in this manner. As the raids on airfields continued unabated, Vitry was evacuated.

Twenty German divisions had poured through the Allied lines and were now advancing rapidly towards the coast. On 19 May the Lysander squadrons were ordered to return to the UK from where the Air Component was now controlled. Arras was evacuated and effective communications were near impossible. From now on it was a matter of squadrons patrolling in the hope of encountering bombers and their escorts with reconnaissance Blenheims trying to make sense of where the front line might be. For some time the Hurricanes had sought out the enemy ahead of the front to try to reduce the level of attack against retreating Allied units. The newly appointed Churchill now made his first broadcast as Prime Minister. He said:

> 'In the air, often at serious odds, even at odds hitherto thought overwhelming, we have been clawing down three or four to one of our enemies, and the relative balance of the British and German air forces is now considerably more favourable to us than at the beginning of the battle. In cutting down the German bombers we are fighting our own battle, as well as that of France.'

RAF claims were around double *total Luftwaffe* losses, a number of which was lost to fighters of the French Air Force. At this stage in the withdrawal troops on the ground should have witnessed the desperate fighting above them and on the 20th, in a change of role, Hurricanes turned to ground attack, on columns approaching Arras, for which their pilots were not trained. Limited success against soft-skinned targets was counter-balanced by their ineffectiveness against German armour, given that armament was limited to machine guns.

A bottleneck at Marquion over the Canal du Nord was bombed by Blenheims of 21 and 107 Sqns escorted by aircraft from 17, 56 and 151 Sqns. Although several bombers were hit by AA, none were lost. The escorting Hurricanes were now instructed to strafe convoys, which reportedly slowed the advance, some German troops taking to the fields. During the day, the Air Component began a withdrawal to England with a new Back Component HQ at Hawkinge.

607 Sqn swapped its Gladiators for Hurricanes from March 1940. Seen is a squadron aircraft refuelling at Vitry-en-Artois. *Author's collection*

The question might well be asked what a Whitley is doing in a book about close support to the Army. During the battle in northern France and the low countries aircraft of Bomber Command made raids on railway and road junctions to slow the movement of German forces. Whitley DY-P of 102 Sqn is seen taking off from Driffield. *Author's collection*

Coastal Command played its part in slowing down the Germans with Beauforts from 22 Sqn detached to Manston attacking the airfield at Waalhaven. Beaufort I OA-F is pictured low over the Channel. The squadron also undertook anti-shipping sorties during the Dunkirk evacuation. *Author's collection*

On 12 May five Battles of 12 Sqn with volunteer crews made a suicidal low-level attack on bridge over the Albert Canal at Veldwezelt. Four were brought down and the lead pilot, Fg Off Donald Garland, and his navigator Sgt Thomas Gray were both awarded the Victoria Cross. Downed PH-P is here being examined by German troops. *Author's collection*

A wide range of impressed civil and military transports operated by pilots of 24 and 271 Sqns and the civilian Air Transport Auxiliary (ATA) was to fly spare and wounded pilots to the UK, but many groundcrew had to find their own way via Cherbourg. Tuesday 21 May saw the lull before the storm. The German Army reached the coast and most of the BEF was cut off to the north, in west Flanders. As the Air Component raced to complete its evacuation, every effort was made to recover unserviceable aircraft and equipment. But by the time the last aircraft departed, of 261 Hurricanes allocated seventy-five had been destroyed totally, sixty-six returned to England and 120 were left in France, a loss that Fighter Command could ill afford.[6]

The loss of France was probably inevitable and no amount of refined systems of air-land co-operation by the Allies would have made any real difference. The Germans had a unified command, clear plans, confidence, training, competence through experience in Spain and Poland and certainly air superiority, both in tactics and numbers. By way of contrast, the Allies were not fighting cohesively, failed totally to appreciate German intentions, had limited intelligence of German dispositions and suffered poor communications. In terms of RAF aircraft, the Hurricane alone could be considered up to the task for which it was deployed, but these were always flown in penny numbers, in tactically naive formation and were invariably outnumbered. *Luftwaffe* losses were assessed at 364 lost or seriously damaged.

The AASF soldiered on pointlessly for another few weeks, reinforced by 17 and 242 Sqns from 8 June, but all units left France eventually through Normandy by 21 June. After the Air Component withdrawal, Fighter Command mounted patrols along the French and Belgian coasts, critically between Boulogne and Dunkirk, and these now included the use of Spitfires. At extreme range from home station, with no intelligence and no training in ground attack (nor the weapons for it!), there was little they could do to support the retreating British Army. The best that could be hoped for was to cover the impending evacuation by protecting troops from constant air bombardment.

Operation *Dynamo* – Dunkirk

On Saturday, 25 May Churchill decided that evacuation of the BEF from France was essential and to be concluded as a matter of urgency. At the same time Hermann Göring persuaded Hitler that if the *Panzers* now stayed put to remain clear of danger, his *Luftwaffe* would obliterate the British and French troops concentrated behind the beaches around Dunkirk. While these key decisions were being taken, a so-called 'Reserve Bombing Force', comprising Lysanders and Hawker Hectors of 613 Sqn, bombed an enemy battery at Sangatte outside Calais to no effect, while eleven Swordfish of 815 NAS, operating within Coastal Command, bombed enemy vehicles. Fighter Command flew 151 sorties, either escorting bombers and reconnaissance aircraft or disrupting bombing.

On 21 May aircraft of 21 and 107 Sqns attacked a German bottleneck across the Canal du Nord at Marquion. Blenheim IV L8740/YH-(?) of 21 Sqn is pictured at RAF Watton in Spring 1940. *Author's collection*

In desperation, on 16 May a number of Hurricane squadrons was added to those already in France, but with most basing in the UK overnight due to airfield congestion. 32 Sqn Hurricane I L3147/LZ-B is seen at Hawkinge on 31 July 1940 during the Battle of Britain. *Author's collection*

Operation *Dynamo* – the evacuation of the BEF – was announced at 1857hrs on 26 May, the original intention being to use the three ports of Boulogne, Calais and Dunkirk. In the event, only the ruined port of Dunkirk and its beaches were available, although significant numbers, including the remnants of the AASF, escaped through ports in Normandy.

Over the next nine days, 338,226 men were evacuated, but at a huge cost in ships. Of the reported 765 vessels involved, many small and of shallow draft, 228 were destroyed by bombing, including six destroyers. By 1 June there were still 39,000 men, now including a number of French troops, in a pocket of just 60 square miles. With great courage, the BEF and French units fought a rearguard action during the day, withdrawing as night fell, until the perimeter was around 12 miles from the sea. Meanwhile, the squadrons of 11 Group now rotated over Dunkirk and beyond, attempting to prevent *Luftwaffe* bombers – and especially the deadly Ju 87s – from attacking the assembling troops.

The operation was directed by Vice-Admiral Bertram Ramsay from HQ in Dover. He asked AVM Keith Park for continuous cover for the eighteen hours of daylight until the evacuation was complete, but with just sixteen squadrons to draw on at any one time this was an impossible task. Typically, an 11 Group airfield was more than 50 miles from Dunkirk, reducing patrol time over the evacuation area to forty minutes. There was no radar to warn of incoming raids and with the vast numbers of aircraft committed by the *Luftwaffe* there was no point in merely fielding sections of three aircraft. Park took the decision to send fighters out in squadron strength, but with inevitable gaps between patrols.

The fighters flew at 18,000ft–23,000ft, splitting into sections, one to attack the covering Bf 109s and 110s, the other dropping for the bombers. The fighter squadrons fought bravely over a wide skyscape, often out of sight of the troops awaiting evacuation. The sheer weight of *Luftwaffe* forces meant that inevitably, despite losses, some got through resulting in the destruction or serious damage to many ships. With the pressure of action – for Hurricane pilots it had been continuous for some months – a number of squadrons was withdrawn for rest and rebuilding, replacements from 12 Group being brought in to relieve them.

There was also night action by the *Luftwaffe*. On 30/31 May He 115s sowed mines off Dunkirk, Ostend and Zeebrugge while Ju 88s bombed Zeebrugge harbour. Unfortunately, the only night fighters available to counter them were single Blenheims of 604 Sqn, too few to prevent these operations.

'*Where was the RAF?*' was a question raised by soldiers and sailors after Dunkirk. The answer was that its aircraft were often above cloud, too far away to be seen, out to sea, or not recognised for what they were. There were no dedicated ground support aircraft or close air support systems to help those holding the perimeter: the best that could be done was to take out enemy bombers before they reached their targets.

In total, thirty squadrons were engaged, comprising fourteen Hurricane, fifteen Spitfire and one Defiant. In nine days they flew 2,739 sorties in 100 patrols totalling 4,822 hours, an average of 1¾ hours per sortie. Sixty-one pilots were killed, fifteen wounded and six taken prisoner. The RAF lost 142 fighter aircraft, but against this the pilots of 11 Group had claims of 270 aircraft destroyed accepted and many more probables. These claims were not considered excessive, apart from those made by 264 Sqn Defiants. They appeared to have had a field day on 29 May, but claims of thirty-five aircraft destroyed were more than double the number of *Luftwaffe* aircraft lost that day.

Table 2.10 – 11 Group Fighter Command, Dunkirk, 26 May–3 June 1940

Sqn	Type	Base	Claims	Losses aircraft/aircrew
11 Group fighter squadrons				
17	Hurricane I	Kenley	4	6/3k, 2w
64	Spitfire I	Kenley	8	7/4k
79 #	Hurricane I	Biggin Hill	2	0/0
229	Hurricane I	Biggin Hill	8	8/4k, 1w
242	Hurricane I	Biggin Hill	22	6/2k, 2w
213	Hurricane I	Biggin Hill	18	10/4k, 1w
43 $	Hurricane I	Tangmere [a]	8	2/1k, 1w
145	Hurricane I	Tangmere [a]	14	9/4k
601 #	Hurricane I	Tangmere [a]	6	2/1k
72 $	Spitfire I	Gravesend	3	1/1w
610	Spitfire I	Gravesend	8	8/7k
245	Hurricane I	Hawkinge	5	7/2k, 1pow
605 #	Hurricane I	Hawkinge	1	4/2k, 1pow
611 $	Spitfire I	Digby [b]	3	7/2k
32	Hurricane I	Wittering	2	1/1pow
266 $	Spitfire I	Wittering [b]	1	2/2k
66 $	Spitfire I	Duxford [b]	1	4/1k
264	Defiant I	Duxford [a]	53	10/11k
92	Spitfire I	Northolt [b]	8	0/0
609 $	Spitfire I	Northolt [b]	8	9/5k, 1w
56 #	Hurricane I	North Weald [a]	7	5/1k, 1w
111 $	Hurricane I	North Weald [a]	5	3/1w
151	Hurricane I	North Weald [a]	2	3/1w
19	Spitfire I	Hornchurch	23	7/1k, 1w, 2pow
41	Spitfire I	Hornchurch	4	2/1k, 1w
54 #	Spitfire I	Hornchurch	9	3/1k
65 #	Spitfire I	Hornchurch	19	3/1w
222 $	Spitfire I	Hornchurch	5	6/2k, 1pow
74 #	Spitfire I	Rochford	8	2/0
616	Spitfire I	Rochford	5	5/1w
604	Blenheim I	Manston		
Total			**270**	**142/61k, 16w, 6pow**

Notes:
Operating up to c30 May
$ Operating from c30 May
a Operated from forward bases – Hawkinge or Manston
b Operated from forward base – Martlesham

Blenheims of 2 Group Bomber Command flew numerous interdiction missions during May and early June in France and the Low Countries. Ten squadrons were involved mainly based in East Anglia: this is Blenheim IV R3612/BL-V of 40 Sqn at Wyton. *Author's collection*

But it was not just fighter squadrons that were engaged in supporting the evacuation at Dunkirk. Bomber Command flew 651 sorties against essentially tactical targets while aircraft of 16 Group Coastal Command, supplemented by units of the FAA, flew 327 sorties in direct support and many more further afield, keeping a watchful eye on enemy shipping, especially E-boats.

No 2 Group Blenheims flew numerous daylight sorties against German positions close to the receding front. They appear to have been well briefed with target information from 53, 57 and 59 Sqn Blenheims which flew daily reconnaissance sorties out of Eastchurch and Gatwick. Bombing missions were usually accompanied by fighters and losses were relatively light.

Medium bombers also flew at night against known German dispositions: these comprised 3 Group Wellingtons (East Anglia), 4 Group Whitleys (Yorkshire) and 5 Group Hampdens (Lincolnshire). Seven Wellingtons and a Whitley were lost and nineteen crew killed.

On 26 May eleven Swordfish of 812 NAS attacked German positions at Gravelines with 250lb bombs. Throughout the Dunkirk operation Hudsons of 206 and 220 Sqns patrolled the adjacent coast, keeping a watchful eye for surface vessels. At the same time Ansons of 48 and 500 Sqns and FAA Swordfish were searching for E-boats off the Dutch and Belgian coasts and the Blenheim fighters of 235 Sqn were providing cover over the evacuation beaches.

Some close support was attempted, also on 26 May, when Swordfish of 825 NAS were spotting for the guns of HMS *Arethusa* and HMS *Galatea* firing on German positions around Calais. Trying to evade attacking Bf 109s during violent manoeuvres, one aircraft lost its observer overboard. The squadron lost eight aircraft on 28 and 29 May with four crew killed.

During 31 May one of the few recorded examples of genuine close support, albeit fortuitous rather than planned, was when Skuas and Rocs of 801 NAS and Swordfish of 826 NAS bombed positions opposite the Nieuport Canal confronting elements of

Table 2.11 – 2 Group Bomber Command squadrons, Dunkirk, 26 May–3 June

Sqn	Type	Base	Losses aircraft/aircrew
2 Group bomber squadrons			
107	Blenheim IV	Wattisham	5/4k,1pow
110	Blenheim IV	Wattisham	
21	Blenheim IV	West Raynham	3/1k
101	Blenheim IV	West Raynham	
82	Blenheim IV	Watton	
15	Blenheim IV	Wyton	1/1w
40	Blenheim IV	Wyton	
53	Blenheim IV	Eastchurch	4/6k, 2w
59	Blenheim IV	Eastchurch	3/3k,1pow
57	Blenheim IV	Gatwick	
Total			**16/14k, 3w, 2pow**

Note: In addition to the squadrons shown, 114 and 139 Sqns were rebuilding following their actions in France while 105 and 218 Sqns were converting from the Battle to the Blenheim

Table 2.12 – 16 Group Coastal Command squadrons, Dunkirk, 26 May–3 June

Sqn	Type	Base	Claims	Losses aircraft/aircrew
16 Group coastal squadrons				
220	Hudson I	Thornaby	2	
22	Beaufort I	North Coates		
812 NAS	Swordfish I	North Coates		
206	Hudson I	Bircham Newton	1	
233	Hudson I	Bircham Newton		
815 NAS	Swordfish I	Bircham Newton		
235	Blenheim IVF	Detling		7/9k
254	Blenheim IVF	Detling		2/5k
500	Anson I	Detling	3	4/5k, 5w
801 NAS	Roc, Skua	Detling	1	3/4k, 2w
826 NAS	Albacore	Detling		
48	Anson I	Thorney Island	1	2
818 NAS	Swordfish I	Thorney Island		
806 NAS	Roc, Skua	Worthy Down		2/1k
825 NAS	Swordfish I	Worthy Down		8/5k, 1w, 9pow
Total			**8**	**28/29k, 8w, 9pow**

Note: The Worthy Down and Thorney Island units were forward based at Detling

With the evacuation from northern France in Operation *Dynamo* precious Spitfires were committed to the fray, despite reservations about imminent attacks on the British Isles and thus the need to conserve the best fighters. Spitfire I X4330/QJ-G of 616 Sqn in May 1940. *Author's collection*

the 12th Infantry Brigade. A strong German attack had just been launched and the bombing caused retreat. Two Skuas were lost in the raid.

The RAF, including the seconded FAA squadrons, thus sought to protect the soldiers on the beaches and in the port area. Dowding had worked hard to persuade the British Cabinet that some of his squadrons should be held back for the feared onslaught against the British Isles, so the maximum possible cover was never committed. After the fiasco in France, where fighters were held for defence and outdated and inappropriate types used for Army co-operation, the Air Marshals now had to rethink how the RAF might work better with the Army. Throughout, the prevailing logic had been that only a strong bomber force could defeat Germany by depriving her of the means of production. In the event, not until Wellingtons, Whitleys and Hampdens had given way to Lancasters and Halifaxes with improved navigation systems, would Bomber Command make much difference to the progress of the war.

Table 2.12 – 16 Group Coastal Command squadrons, Dunkirk, 26 May–3 June

Sqn	Type	Base	Claims	Losses aircraft/aircrew
16 Group coastal squadrons				
220	Hudson I	Thornaby	2	
22	Beaufort I	North Coates		
812 NAS	Swordfish I	North Coates		
206	Hudson I	Bircham Newton	1	
233	Hudson I	Bircham Newton		
815 NAS	Swordfish I	Bircham Newton		
235	Blenheim IVF	Detling		7/9k
254	Blenheim IVF	Detling		2/5k
500	Anson I	Detling	3	4/5k, 5w
801 NAS	Roc, Skua	Detling	1	3/4k, 2w
826 NAS	Albacore	Detling		
48	Anson I	Thorney Island	1	2
818 NAS	Swordfish I	Thorney Island		
806 NAS	Roc, Skua	Worthy Down		2/1k
825 NAS	Swordfish I	Worthy Down		8/5k, 1w, 9pow
Total			**8**	**28/29k, 8w, 9pow**

Note: The Worthy Down and Thorney Island units were forward based at Detling

Over the Dunkirk beaches Defiants of 264 Sqn were brought into play. They suffered at the hands of German fighters, despite which, on 29 May, they rather optimistically claimed thirty-five enemy aircraft shot down. L7026/PS-V and others are seen in day fighter camouflage. In August the squadron reverted to the night-fighter role. *Author's collection*

Operation *Dynamo* required all hands on deck, including aircraft of the FAA. Skuas and Rocs of 801 and 806 NASs maintained patrols from Detling and bombed German positions beyond the perimeter, losing five aircraft. These aircraft, two Skuas and a Roc, are from 806 NAS and sport the L6 code on the fin. *Author's collection*

Coastal Command Ansons of 48 Sqn patrolled over the evacuation beaches from Thorney Island. Squadron aircraft are seen lined up at Evanton in 1939. *Author's collection*

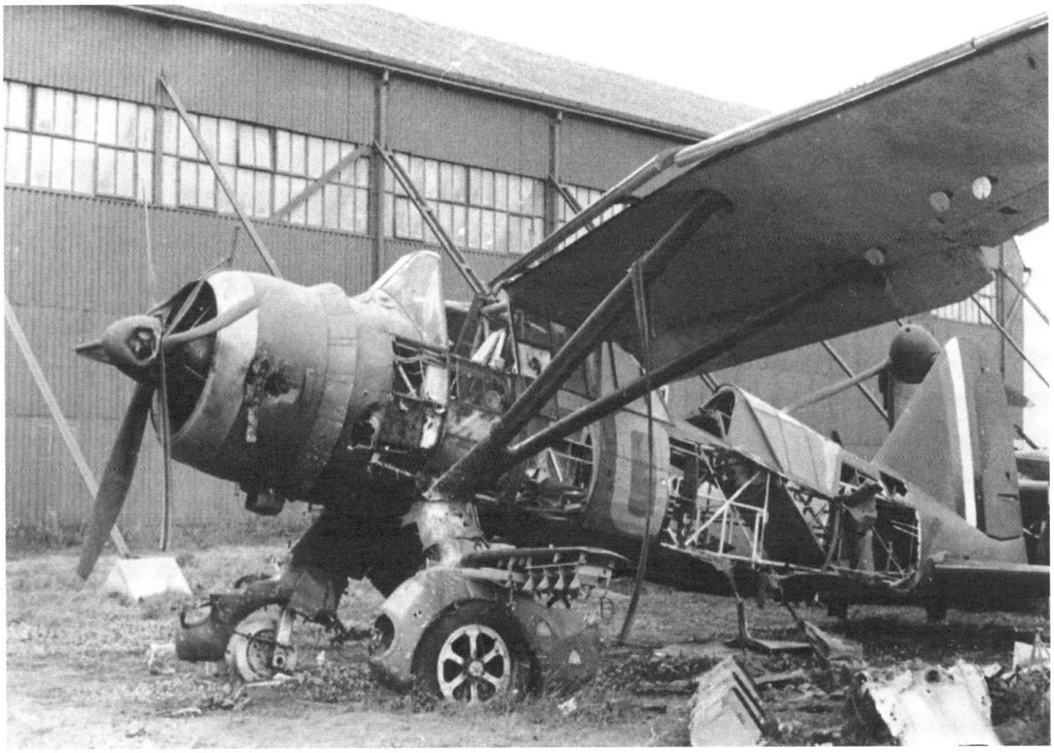

The end in France. A Lysander of 13 Sqn lies derelict and abandoned on a French airfield in June 1940. *Author's collection*

Of Operation *Dynamo,* Prime Minister Churchill tellingly said to the House of Commons on 4 June:[7]

> 'Wars are not won by evacuations. But there was a victory inside this deliverance, which should be noted. It was gained by the Royal Air Force.'

And echoing the Churchill sentiment, General Albert Kesselring, Commander-in-Chief of Luftflotte 2, had this to say about Goring's bluster:[8]

> '...Göring for some incomprehensible reason had pledged himself to the Führer to wipe out the English with his Luftwaffe. ...I pointed out to Göring that the modern Spitfires had recently appeared, making our air operations difficult and costly – and in the end it was the Spitfires which enabled the British and French to evacuate across the water.'

Transport aircraft from 24 and 271 Sqns plus Flamingo airliners of BOAC were used to fly replacement aircrew, other personnel and stores into French airfields. On the return trips they took wounded home to the UK. These Harrows are from 271 Sqn, then based at Doncaster but also operating from Hendon. *Author's collection*

[1] From Ellis, L *History of the Second World War: The War in France and Flanders 1939-1940* HMSO, London, 2004
[2] Baughen, *The RAF in the Battle of France,* p127
[3] Richards, *Royal Air Force 1939-1945 Vol I*, p110
[4] Cull, *Twelve Days in May,* p160
[5] As quoted in Cull, *Twelve Days in May*, p170
[6] Richards, *Royal Air Force 1939-1945 Vol I*, p126
[7] Churchill, *Their Finest Hour,* p103
[8] As quoted in *The Battle of France Then and Now,* p366

Army Co-operation Command

In the aftermath of the Battle of France and while the Battle of Britain was being fought in the air over southern England, plans were cobbled together to provide what would have been desperate measures to counter an invasion of the United Kingdom. At the same time the RAF, and indeed the Army, began to take stock. Trials were conducted, a system of control tested and developed, and despite indifference – if not objection – from Bomber Command, Army Co-operation Command was formed. New ideas were then applied and further refined in a number of large-scale exercises. Army flying got off the ground with the formation of specialised AOP squadrons and the Glider Pilot Regiment, whose aircraft would be flown by Army pilots (although some RAF pilots flew gliders in Operation *Varsity*).

A further development was the introduction of new aircraft for the close support role, albeit that the role was still not clearly defined. Thus, the Curtiss P-40 Tomahawk and then the North American P-51 Mustang supplanted the Lysander, while Fighter Command Hurricanes began to fly ground attack sorties. In the course of reviews, procedures in use in the Western Desert were also examined and no doubt influenced thinking.

Short-Term Measures

In the immediate aftermath of defeat in, and retreat from, France and the Low Countries, the British government not only made plans to counter the threatened invasion, it also began a process of review of the military lessons to be learned. The situation was desperate: the Army was disorganised and seriously short of equipment, much of which had been lost in France. The RAF was also consolidating after the loss of so many Battle and Blenheim light bombers and Hurricane fighters, not to mention the unwieldy Lysander, which had proved of little value in its Army co-operation role.

For the RAF there was nothing new in stop-gap problem solving. For instance, in December 1939 a shortage of maritime surveillance aircraft led to the formation of six coastal patrol flights equipped with de Havilland Tiger Moth and impressed Hornet Moth aircraft. Their task – to warn of off-shore U-boat and surface vessel activity by flying what became known as *Scarecrow* patrols. At least one Tiger Moth is known to have been fitted with underwing bomb racks for 25lb bombs. The flights were disbanded on 27 May 1940, the same day that Operation *Banquet* was inaugurated. Knowing that an intended German invasion was imminent, a set of desperation measures was established to support the now depleted RAF in the event of an invasion by land, sea or air. (Originally *Plan ZZ*, then *Plan Julius Caesar*.)

The plan called for the transfer of a wide range of non-combat aircraft types to operational commands and stations and their preparation for warlike roles. A number of these intended transfers would have an impact on air–land co-operation since all were intended to provide immediate and close support. Most of the aircraft were to be made capable of carrying light bombs or guns for an offensive role; there was no question of any protective or defensive measures. Pilots would come from the pool of instructors and students at an advanced stage in their training. The various *Banquet* plans included the following, which give some indication of the seriousness of the situation.

Banquet 6 Group – operational use of Bomber Command Group Pools (later Operational Training Units (OTUs)).

Banquet 22 Group – transfer of Army co-operation assets to 2 Group, Bomber Command.

Banquet Alert – transfer of second-line FAA aircraft to Coastal Command.

Banquet Comm – for further impressments of light aircraft for communications.

Banquet Light[1] – transfer of Training Command Tiger Moths, Cadets and Magisters to 22 Group and based at Lysander stations. Aircraft to be fitted with bomb racks for light bombs, flown by a single pilot at 800ft and dived on to ground forces. At the

After the withdrawal of troops from France and with the threat of imminent invasion, a series of emergency *Banquet* plans was drawn up to use a variety of aircraft to counter any landings. In *Banquet Light* it was proposed to use Tiger Moths and other trainers from the elementary flying schools, flown by instructors, as (very) light ground attack machines. Tiger Moth R4922 of 7 EFTS. *Author's collection*

time there were 663 Tiger Moths and an assumed 410 civil light aircraft available.

Banquet Master – conversion of Master trainer to makeshift fighter with six machine guns (twenty-five produced and later used for gunnery training).

Banquet Technical – bringing into service retired airframes like the Wallace, used for technical training.

Banquet Training – transfer of second-line or stored aircraft to Bomber Command, including Hind, Harvard, Battle and Audax.

Banquet Transport – conversion of Harrows to bombers.

In the event *Banquet* was not implemented, but training for it continued, just in case. Thus, pilots nearing completion of elementary training on Tiger Moths spent additional time on the principles and practice of bombing. What is significant is that 22 (Army Co-operation) Group within Fighter Command would have transferred to Bomber Command to provide the Army with support. Before *Banquet* was cancelled on 30 September 1943, some of its principles were applied to the first 1,000 bomber raid on Cologne that required aircraft, instructors and pupils from OTUs to make up the numbers. One other short-term measure that had its origins in *Banquet* was the allocation of a number of Gladiator biplane fighters to stations to form defence flights.

Taking Stock

On 12 June a committee of five was set up under General Sir William Bartholomew[2] to review the recent events in France and the lessons to be learned from them. Just one senior RAF officer – AVM C. H. B. Blount, who had commanded the BEF Air Component – was among the thirty-seven witnesses. In its introduction the committee had this to say:

> '(iii) Air Superiority. Whilst being fully conscious of the magnificent effort of the R.A.F. in the face of great German numerical superiority, the Committee feels that urgent action is required to place co-operation between the two services on a better basis.'

The review made a number of specific military recommendations, including the proposition that the brigade, rather than the division, should be the basic fighting formation with its own organic anti-aircraft

Tiger Moth 3 EFTS T-7021/31. *Luca G. Canossa*

Plan *Banquet Master* envisaged the conversion of Master trainers to light fighters by the installation of six machine guns. Some Masters were fitted with a single fixed Vickers gun and provision for practice bombs as noted on this Master III, W8647/PA-M 'Lydia' of 55 OTU. *Author's collection*

artillery (AAA), anti-tank (AT) and field artillery. HQs were too large and needed to be divided into command post and rear organisation. In respect of air power, it noted in some detail the way in which the *Luftwaffe* operated in support of the Army, but drew some wrong conclusions, committee members demonstrating a lamentable lack of appreciation of the application of air power.

The analysis was thus skewed and presented a warped case for the way in which the RAF might operate in future in support of the Army. The sections relating to the use of air power are noted fully since they serve to illustrate the military mindset, which was to hinder speedy change.

> '6(b) The outstanding features of the German air action and the lessons learnt were: (i) The concentration of the maximum air effort to assist in achieving the immediate object in view. There were abundant examples of this … (including) the concentration on our roads at the time of the withdrawal to the coast and finally the concentration on the points of embarkation. At such times attacks at other points were slight … Apparently at no time during the period when the defeat of the Allied armies in the north was the aim of the German High Command were there any serious diversions of the aircraft against strategical objectives.'

The conclusion drawn was that the *Luftwaffe* was at the beck and call of the Army and only concerned with immediate support, both when and where instructed. No effort was wasted on, for example, interdiction. This ignored the considerable number of raids against lines of communication, aerodromes and so on.

> '(ii) The close co-operation between the enemy's army and air forces. There is little doubt that the policy of equipment, organization and training of the enemy had been directed to this end. Air action, both in time and place was always intimately connected with the tactical situation on the ground … This indicated not only good organization and communications for the purpose, but the siting of many of their landing grounds close up behind their advanced troops. Efforts should at once be made to simplify and improve our own intercommunication between ground and air for similar purposes. Another example of the close co-operation which existed was the many instances in which troops were ferried across the demolished zones by troop carriers to land in fields close to our forward localities almost immediately after contact on the ground was made.'

There seems to have been no recognition of the fact that the *Luftwaffe* had secured air superiority in numbers, aircraft performance and pilot experience. There was, though, legitimacy in noting that better communications were essential.

> '(iii) The outstanding value of air attack as "supporting fire" to cover the assault of armoured and, at times, infantry formations. According to the reports from formations concerned, it was this feature which contributed to the successful "breakthrough" against the French on our right more than any other factor. Although this "close tactical bombing", which is carried out by dive bombers with both M.Gs[A] and bombs, is a form of artillery "preparation". It can be carried out under circumstances of time and place when effective artillery fire would not be possible. It is accurate and has the great advantage of placing the fire to conform with the observed movements of the assaulting troops – an extremely difficult, if not impossible problem for the artillery observer in a ground O.P.[B]'

Again, there seemed to be no recognition that the short-range dive-bomber could only be effective with its own air cover and against troops lacking AA protection.

> 'c) It is imperative to ensure forthwith that a system comparable to that of the Germans should be introduced into our Army and Air Force. Even the brigade group must be able to call up immediate support by wireless, a process which ought to be easier in the defence than in the attack.'

The idea that a brigade group (functioning within a division, within a corps, within an Army), might have been able to call directly on close air support with no sense of the wider battle, or indeed the resources available, was at best naïve.

> 'd) Use of aircraft for intercommunication
>
> The enemy used aircraft for the control of his armoured divisions to the fullest

[A] Machine guns

[B] Observation post

In the aftermath of Dunkirk Gladiators were allocated to RAF stations to form defence flights. However, Gladiator N2306, ex 605 and 615 Sqns, is a bit of a mystery as the original caption describes it as belonging to 239 Sqn in 1943, which at the time was flying the Mustang! The rudder displays an Army Co-operation Command symbol. *Author's collection*

extent, and even carried unit commanders. It is recommended that we should study this development in the control of our own formations. In the meantime the aircraft employed by the Germans for this purpose are easily [*sic*] recognisable and when seen should be attacked with the greatest vigour.'

Again, ignorance of what actually occurred is demonstrated. The biplane Hs 123 light ground attack fighter produced a terrifying noise from its BMW engine, but soon demonstrated vulnerability. In France in May 1940 'Although effective against ground forces, the elderly biplane was very vulnerable to enemy fighters, so much so that I.JG21 (Bf 109E) was assigned for II(S).LG 2's protection.'[3] Further, the Hs 126, was easily confused with the Lysander, which the report heavily criticised as being extremely vulnerable! Many of both types were destroyed by BEF fighters.

'e) General effect on morale

The magnificent work done by the R.A.F. in the face of German numerical superiority, is appreciated by all. The Committee, would, however, like to point out that by the nature of things, neither the actual bombing carried out by the R.A.F. in support of the B.E.F. nor its effect was seen by the man in the field. All day he saw swarms of enemy bombers escorted by fighters and suffered from their attack. Occasionally he saw, or heard above the clouds an attack by our fighters. Unlike the German soldier, he had never seen aircraft closely co-operating with him to defeat his own particular enemy opposite to him. All this had a very definite effect on morale and gave the impression that the enemy superiority was complete and that our own air force hardly existed. Radio news reports that the Ruhr and Hamburg had been bombed were cold comfort. There are three steps which can be taken to put matters right.

First, as matter of training, all ranks must be taught how the R.A.F. work, where fighters patrol, and get their greatest successes, the localities and nature of the targets bombed and the effect on the battle in which the soldier is taking part etc.

Secondly, early provision should be made of suitable close support aircraft together with the developments of organization and training to use them.

The Curtiss Tomahawk entered RAF service with 26 Sqn in February 1941 and eventually equipped sixteen Army co-operation squadrons in the UK and four in the Middle East. Some 885 Tomahawks were taken on charge of which most served in the UK. Mk I AH864/RM-G seen at Gatwick is a 26 Sqn mount. *Author's collection*

Thirdly, until such aircraft are available, the R.A.F. must 'show the flag' to the troops in the forward areas – even at the expense of other tasks – by carrying out some bombing with existing machines in sight of our lines.'

It was self-evident that the RAF needed a quite different type of aircraft from the Lysander and in the event two complementary types were required: the *small*, slow, ideally high-wing, aircraft for observation and an effective fighter-bomber. The suggestion that, regardless of air superiority or true need, the RAF should send aircraft to bomb just across the front line, regardless of relative demand but in sight of own troops in the forward area, was misguided; such close support would normally be the function of artillery. How many squadrons would be required to cover a 100-mile front?!

In paragraph (f) on reconnaissance, the report notes that after the fifth day of the German assault the Lysanders, which were attached by squadron to corps, could not operate in the tactical reconnaissance role, whereas the German counterpart, the Hs 126, could. Thus, again there is a recognition of the need for air superiority if close support is to be effective. (Some eighty-eight Lysanders were shot down and at least thirty lost on the ground.)

There were further recommendations in respect of communications and the structure of the field artillery, both areas that would impact on air-land co-operation. It was thought that in future there should be three batteries of two troops, each with four guns. Finally, it was noted that infantry had to be deployed to aerodromes to defend them against the prospect of paratroop landings, resulting in the formation of the RAF Regiment in 1942.

While the Bartholomew Committee was sitting there were simultaneous reviews, including one at the War Office, on the air aspect. MO7 had been set up in January 1940 under Lt Col F. W. Festing to look at close land-air co-operation and was now reviewing that aspect of the recent fighting, while there were others on areas like the operation of artillery.

In post-Dunkirk 1940 two types of air support were envisaged. Direct Support was the use of air forces to isolate the battlefield; Close Support was the use of air forces in a 'close', presumably impromptu, air support role.[4] These descriptions were not especially helpful.

Trials

There had been in France a system for securing air support and in theory it would have been effective had the subsequent battle been relatively static, communications reliable, and air superiority achieved. But, in the light of a rapidly advancing enemy, extended lines of command and overwhelming German air superiority, the system was found wanting.

An Allied Central Air Bureau (ACAB) was established at Chauny, near Reims, in November 1939, a signals organisation using telephone landline with W/T backup. Its task was to analyse and prioritise the need for bombing or further reconnaissance based on reconnaissance reports from the air and also from joint air/ground recce units. The unit needed continuous communication with the Air Ministry, Bomber Command, the BEF and the Advanced Air Striking Force as well as the ability to accept information from air and ground assets. However, communication was one-way and there was not the opportunity to alert forward formations as to what, if anything, they might expect by way of support. The official narrative on close air support had this to say.[5]

The Tomahawks of Army Co-operation Command routinely flew *Rhubarb* sweeps over France from 1941. SP-T of 400 Sqn appears to have ground-looped on return. Noteworthy is the Crossley FE1 crash tender which carried a 300gal water tank, 7.4gal foam tank and four 60lb CO_2 cylinders. *Author's collection*

'It became clear from signals exercise that special provision was required for getting back directly to ACAB at Chauny up-to-the-minute information about the ground situation and requirements for air action. For this purpose a special ground reconnaissance unit comprising a joint air/army mission but best known by its code name of 'Phantom', was set up under command of a RAF officer with an army officer borrowed from GHQ as his second in command and head of the army element.

The task of 'Phantom' was to get rapid information back to BAFF[c] at all costs and for the purpose it was provided with mobile wireless stations or 'tentacles' to be sent out to forward positions from which the course of the battle could be observed and reported.

This unit – a measure of whose value can be gained by the fact that when the battle began BAFF usually had information thirty hours sooner than the French Army Group – was in fact the origin on the one hand of the Air Support Signals Unit (AASU), and on the other hand of the GHQ Reconnaissance Regiment.'

Thus a foundation had been laid, but one that needed significant refinement in the light of experience. An effective system for close air support required a number of characteristics that proved difficult either to achieve or sometimes to reconcile. Those characteristics were:

- A local commander might need air support urgently: however, he could not have a whole picture of the battle.
- The higher command would have an overall picture of the battle, but not necessarily an immediate one.
- Reconnaissance aircraft could identify targets for immediate attack.
- There needed to be a centre to absorb information and decisions.
- Separate comms channels were essential to avoid delay.
- Squadrons would need to be close to the front and briefed in general about the ebb and flow of the battle and thus where and when they might be needed.
- It follows that the air and land HQs needed to be joint.
- The front line – the 'bomb line' – would need to be clear at all times.
- Pilots would need a simple map system in order to be certain about the location of intended targets.

The War Office now commissioned exercises to experiment with close support techniques and appointed Lt Col J. D. Woodall to manage them. Woodall had been the BEF's nominee at the ACAB in France and was to be assisted by Gp Capt A. Wann, who had commanded the Fairey Battle units in the AASF. They oversaw a series of experiments in Northern Ireland using Battles of 88 and 226 Sqns and Lysanders of 231 Sqn, which had just been formed from 416 Flt. The first experiments were between 5 September and 22 October 1940 and the resultant report built upon the limited experience in France to pave the way for formal structures for close support, especially in North West Europe.

The objectives of the trials were to determine:[6]

- The most suitable form of organisation for close support bombers.
- Appropriate tactical methods for close support bombers.
- Signals installations required for control.

In support of Army Co-operation Command were the Blenheims of 2 Group – if Bomber Command was prepared to release them. This line-up of Mk IV aircraft of 82 Sqn at Watton includes in the foreground P6915/UX-A. *Author's collection*

[c] British Air Forces in France

This detailed shot shows the external bomb-carriers on a Blenheim IV of 235 Sqn at Bircham Newton. The eight 40lb bombs appear to be a mix of armour-piercing and general purpose.
Author's collection

The Lysander soldiered on in Army co-operation squadrons until well into 1942. Mk III T1532/KO-D belongs to 2 Sqn, in 1940 based at Sawbridgeworth, Hertfordshire.
Author's collection

In 1942 2 Sqn switched types and codes, as seen when Mustang I AG623/XV-W was demonstrated to the press at Sawbridgeworth in July 1942. The Mk I was powered by the 1,150hp Allison V-1710 engine which gave limited performance at height. However, the type was ideal for Army co-operation Tac/R, being fast with long range or loiter time and steady in the dive.
Author's collection

Over the winter of 1942/43 various aircraft were involved in trials with Army Co-operation Command, none more unusual than the Fairey Fulmars of 809 NAS attached to 33 Wing and operating from Clifton. This example, coded 6G, is seen taking the wire on HMS *Victorious* with canopies open for speedy exit of crew in the event of a prang. *Author's collection*

- The establishment of Royal Air Force and Army personnel required for a close support bomber organisation.
- Methods to be employed by Army formations in obtaining close bomber support.
- Times in which support under various circumstances can be given.
- Methods of controlling close support bombers and directing them on to targets.
- The need for close relations between Air and Army at command level, at field HQ and on the front line.
- An independent signals network with no competition for time or frequencies and no hierarchical delays.

The outcome of initial trials was a system of communications, separate from other signals organisation, to take requests from tentacles, assess them speedily against a wider picture of the situation through having a combined air and land HQ, and then communicate the requirement to squadrons. The critical need was for speedy 'impromptu' support and key to this was a new Close Support Bomber Control (CSBC) with RAF and Army staff.

Wann and Woodall had tried to apply fresh thinking rather than being drawn to (possibly wrong) conclusions about operations in France. For example, they were satisfied that the *Luftwaffe* did not have systems for impromptu support, so there was little to learn in that particular area. What was important was up-to-the-minute intelligence and first-class staff work between Army and Air Force.

Major Charles Carrington, an academic, was attached to Bomber Command as a liaison officer and was in turn involved in the air-land trials. He added a proposal that tactical reconnaissance aircraft should ideally also be in the signals net so that if they detected a target or threat they could alert the CSBC direct. Three important principles were determined as being essential in whatever system was to be applied, and these emerged independently through evolution in fighting in the Western Desert.

Wann-Woodall Proposals 1940

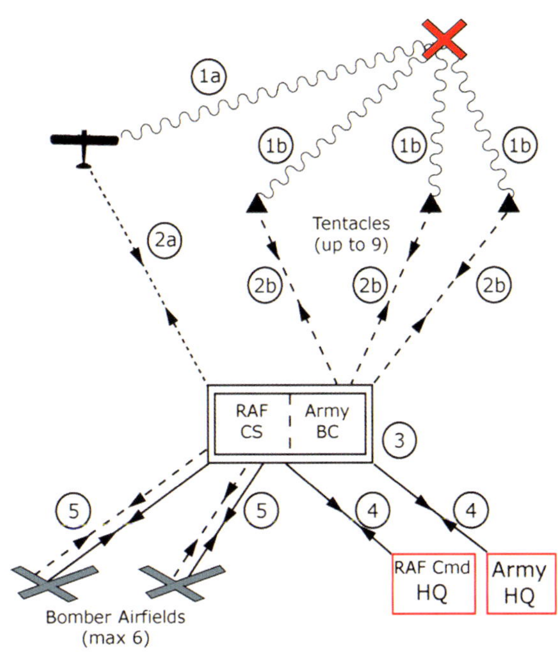

1) Spotter or OP at Tentacle identifies target or threat
2) Either then alert Close Support Bomber Control
3) Decision taken on support to be given
4) If uncertainty referral to RAF Command HQ and/or Army GHQ
5) Requirement conveyed to light bomber airfield(s)

- Scope for the involvement of aircraft outside the specialist types immediately available.

While the trials were being conducted, structural change was under way with the intended establishment of an Army Co-operation Command. On 23 September Anthony Eden, then Secretary of State for War, sent a memo to Sir Archibald Sinclair, Secretary of State for Air, proposing the new Command. The Air Ministry had little choice but to agree with the idea – albeit reluctantly – and the new Command came into being on 1 December 1940 with Air Marshal Sir Arthur Barratt as AOC. Barratt had headed the RAF in France so was ideally placed to develop improved ways of working, but his Command was hardly operational. He had two groups, one training and development, and one notionally operational but, in reality, outside his direct control.

The new Command was formed from 22 Group and at the outset now comprised two new groups:

70 (Army Co-operation) (Training and Development) Group, Farnborough

1 School of Army Co-operation, Old Sarum – Lysander, Tomahawk, Blenheim

2 School of Army Co-operation, Andover – Lysander, Blenheim

71 (Army Co-operation) (Operational) Group, Farnborough

Squadrons as shown in Table 3.1

In addition, Barratt could call on the two light bomber squadrons (88 and 226) in 75 Wing (Northern Ireland; later 31 Wing) and the Blenheim squadrons of 2 Group, always assuming that Bomber Command was prepared to release them.

Table 3.1 – RAF Army co-operation squadrons UK, 1939–August 1941

Sqn	Type	Base
Army co-operation squadrons		
2	Lysander	Bekesbourne, Hatfield, Sawbridgeworth
4	Lysander	Ringway, Linton-on-Ouse, Clifton
13	Lysander	Speke, Hooton Park, Odiham
16	Lysander	Lympne, Cambridge, Weston Zoyland
26	Lysander	Lympne, West Malling, Gatwick
168	Tomahawk	Snailwell
171	Tomahawk	Gatwick
225	Lysander	Old Sarum, Tilshead, Thruxton
231	Lysander	Aldergrove, Newtownards
239	Lysander	Hatfield, Gatwick
241	Lysander	Longman, Bury St Edmunds
268	Lysander	Bury St Edmunds, Snailwell
613	Lysander	Netherthorpe, Firbeck
614	Lysander	Grangemouth, Macmerry
Royal Canadian Air Force		
110	Lysander	Old Sarum, Odiham
400	Lysander, Tomahawk	Odiham, Gatwick
112	Lysander	Old Sarum, High Post

The 71 Group (operational) squadrons were at the call of local Army commanders, so the AOC had limited authority and was accountable primarily for the development of procedures by conducting trials.

Table 3.2 – 2 Group Blenheim squadrons, 1 December 1940

Sqn	Base
2 Group Blenheim squadrons	
107, 110	Wattisham
21, 82	Watton
114	Oulton
139	Horsham St Faith
18	Great Massingham
101	West Raynham
105	Swanton Morley

The remit of the new Command extended initially to three key tasks in support of the Army:

- Tac/R – tactical reconnaissance, or noting things of relevance on or near the front line.
- Arty/R – artillery spotting, noting and correcting the fall of shot.
- Photo/R – tactical photo-reconnaissance.

Exercises and trials continued into 1941, including anti-invasion exercises that inevitably had an Air Component. These included Exercise *Dragon* (5–8 January) and Exercise *Victor* (22–25 January), the latter without troops and concerned with signals effectiveness. The threat of invasion demanded some hard decisions about the nature of the role of bombers in covering troops defending beaches against invasion. In essence, the Army wanted squadrons on call by divisional commanders to respond to immediate tactical needs, whereas the RAF insisted on responding to the slightly wider operational need by hitting invasion forces at sea or while landing. On all potential invasion beaches the fixed defences were noted and bomb lines agreed. The 2 Group bombers would have been spread thin, having a notional establishment of eighty-four aircraft across nine squadrons, but allowing for serviceability and crew shortage the number would have been sixty at best.

There was structural change within 70 Group in May when 2 School of Army Co-operation dissolved into 6 and 42 OTUs, but a major change took place in August 1941 with the disbanding of 71 Group into wings.

Reorganisation

The euphemistically-named Government Code & Cipher School (GCCS) had been established in 1919 to protect government codes and break those of enemies or potential enemies. It moved to Bletchley Park in August 1939 and work concentrated on breaking coded German radio traffic sent through Enigma and later Lorenz machines. The product was distributed only at the highest level as *Ultra* decrypts.

It had been determined through *Ultra* intercepts that Hitler had parked any thought of invasion of the United Kingdom through the winter of 1940/41. However, it was assumed that there might be a change of thinking, so the Army was reorganised into six regional commands in the Spring. Then, between 15 and 22 August, new RAF wings were formed to work directly with the regional commands. This was the new structure:

SCOTCO. Scottish Command, Edinburgh. 15th and 52nd Divisions. 32 Wing RAF

NORCO. Northern Command, York. I, IX and X Corps. 33 Wing RAF

EASTCO. Eastern Command, Luton. II, IV and XI Corps. 34 Wing RAF

SECO. South-East Command, Reigate. VII and XII Corps. 35 Wing RAF

SOUTCO. Southern Command, Salisbury. V and VIII Corps. 36 Wing RAF

WESTCO. Western Command, Chester. III Corps. 37 Wing RAF (no aircraft)

The initial allocation of squadrons was in relation to the regions most likely to come under attack in the event of a German invasion. All were equipped initially with Lysanders, which had the dual roles of Tac/R and Arty/R until better equipment and more specific systems came along. Allocations are shown at Table 3.3 below. In this table main bases only are shown; in reality squadrons moved in their entirety or sent detachments to a number of Army commands, sometimes for short duration or exercises.

This frequent movement of units between commands gave plenty of opportunity to exercise in a range of environments. However, it also denied one of the key requirements of effective land-air co-operation, which was a close relationship between local Army and RAF personnel. Close support remained the responsibility of 2 Group Bomber Command and its Blenheims, but still subject to the Command's other priorities. One small but significant change was made in July when the CSBC was renamed Army Air Support Control (AASC), which embraced an Air Support Signals Unit (ASSU).

Through 1941 the threat of invasion diminished, especially with the German assault on Russia in Operation *Barbarossa* in June. Wann, Woodall and Carrington continued to improve and refine the systems and techniques of air support, despite serious Air Ministry opposition to any prospect of the Army having control of aircraft. The view was that since the Army in the UK was stuck in respect of a role in the short term, all RAF assets should be concentrated on key strategic tasks and these included bombing German industry and cities. The attitude at Bomber Command was well described by Carrington[7] in his diary note on a discussion with the Senior Air Staff Officer (SASO), AVM Robert Saundby in May.

> 'SASO said with no little heat that the Army must stand on the defensive for a year or more. With a conscript army and five years' start for the Germans, no Continental expedition was practicable yet. All the Army can do is 'stretch out its neck'. Fifteen or twenty squadrons were quite inadequate even for a small field force… The Army must wait until the whole Air Force can be thrown in. The unity of the Air Force must be maintained.'

The new organisation, and more importantly the evolved system of air control, was almost immediately put to the test in Exercise *Bumper*, held in East Anglia and the East Midlands from 28 September to 3 October.[8] The exercise involved 250,000 troops and SOUTCO provided the Allied Army (under Lt Gen H. R. L. G. Alexander), while EASTCO generated the notional German Fourth Army (under Lt Gen L. Carr). Each had the equivalent of two corps (infantry) plus an armoured division. They also each fielded an Air Support Signals Unit (ASSU) with the enemy force having access to 2 Group HQ. The exercise highlighted a number of weaknesses, but also proved in principle the value of the new AASC system. Eight hundred sorties were flown and in his summing up the umpire, Lt Gen B. L. Montgomery, had this to say about air support:

Mustang I AM148/RM-G 26 Sqn. *Luca G. Canossa*

Hawker Typhoons from several squadrons were also involved in trials, as indicated by the temporary white nose on this aircraft of 182 Sqn. R8893/XM-M is seen in a dispersal pen at RAF Martlesham Heath in November 1942. *Author's collection*

'13. Air Support. On the air aspect, the C.-in-C. mentioned the following points. (A) Don't use your air support 'in penny packets'. (B) The fighter appears to present a serious menace to troops and transport on the move. (C) The Air Support Control should be at Army HQ if this is as far forward as it ought to be. It does not follow, however, that it should not be sent to some lower formation's HQ if the main weight of air support is being directed to this formation's area.'

During its existence Army Co-operation Command enjoyed the benefit of additional units attached for trials or exercises. These are shown at Table 3.4.

Table 3.3 – RAF Army Co-operation Command, August 1941–June 1943

Sqn	Type	Wing/base[c]	From	To
Army Co-operation Command				
2	Lysander	34/Sawbridgeworth	8.41	7.42
2	Tomahawk	34/Martlesham Heath	8.41	4.42
2	Mustang	34/Sawbridgeworth	4.42	6.43
4	Lysander	33/Clifton	8.41	6.42
4	Tomahawk, Mustang	33/Clifton	8.41	6.42
4	Tomahawk, Mustang	34/Bottisham	3.43	6.43
13	Blenheim	36/Odiham	8.41	11.42
16	Lysander	36/Weston Zoyland	8.41	7.42
16	Mustang, Tomahawk	36/Weston Zoyland	4.42	6.43
26	Lysander, Tomahawk	35/Gatwick	8.41	6.43
26	Mustang	35/Gatwick	1.42	6.43
225	Lysander, Hurricane	36/Thruxton	8.41	8.42
225	Mustang	32/Macmerry	8.42	12.42
231	Lysander, Tomahawk	RAFNI/Long Kesh	8.41	3.43
231	Tomahawk, Mustang	33/Clifton	3.43	6.43
239	Lysander, Tomahawk	35/Gatwick	8.41	8.42
239	Mustang	34/Twinwood Farm	8.42	11.42
239	Mustang	36/Odiham	11.42	11.42
239	Mustang	38/Stoney Cross	12.42	2.43
239	Mustang	35/Gatwick	3.43	5.43
241	Lysander, Tomahawk	34/Bottisham	8.41	5.42
241	Lysander, Tomahawk	32/Ayr	4.42	11.42
268	Lysander, Tomahawk, Mustang	34/Snailwell	8.41	5.43
309	Lysander, Mustang	32/Dunino, Kirknewton	8.41	6.43
400	Lysander, Tomahawk	35/Dunsfold	8.41	6.43
414	Lysander, Tomahawk	35/Croydon, Dunsfold	8.41	6.43
613	Lysander, Tomahawk	33/Doncaster	8.41	4.42
613	Mustang	34/Twinwood Farm	4.42	7.42
613	Mustang	33/Ouston	7.42	6.43
614	Lysander, Blenheim	32/Macmerry	8.41	8.42
614	Blenheim	35/Odiham	8.42	11.42
63	Mustang	33/Catterick	6.42	11.42
63	Mustang	32/Macmerry	11.42	6.43
168	Tomahawk	34/Snailwell	6.42	11.42
168	Mustang	35/Odiham	11.42	6.43
169	Mustang	33/Doncaster	6.42	11.42
169	Mustang	34/Duxford	7.42	3.43
169	Mustang	36/Andover	3.43	6.43
170	Mustang	36/Hurn	6.42	6.43
171	Tomahawk, Mustang	35/Gatwick	6.42	1.43

[c] Includes detachments

Table 3.4 – RAF Army Co-operation Command temporary detachments and support units, August 1941–June 1943

Sqn	Type	Wing/base	From	To
809 NAS	Fulmar	33/Clifton	12.42	1.43
174	Hurricane IIB	35/Odiham	12.42	3.43
175	Hurricane IIB	35/Odiham	12.42	2.43
182	Typhoon	34/Sawbridgeworth	12.42	1.43
183	Typhoon	33/Church Fenton	1.43	3.43
318	Hurricane I	35/Detling	3.43	6.43
1494 Flt	Lysander	RAFNI/Long Kesh	12.41	6.43
1472 Flt	Tomahawk, Battle	33/Dishforth, Catterick	6.42	6.43
1498 Flt	Lysander	38/Hurn	3.43	6.43

New Aircraft

It now remained for Barratt to support the Army within the limitations of equipment and backing from the Air Ministry. Through the course of his tenure he oversaw developments in artillery spotting, tactical reconnaissance and the introduction of airborne forces. There is little evidence that his ideas were influenced by the practical experience of the Western Desert Air Force (WDAF), at least in the early stages of his command, although he did visit WDAF between 27 August and 9 September 1942 during the Battle of Alam Halfa. Most of the changes in ACC were incremental, refined in the light of revisions in equipment and organisation. The Command was to be disbanded on 31 March 1943, its constituent units going into Fighter Command and 2nd Tactical Air Force, ready for the invasion of France the following year.

Even as the services were handling the further withdrawal of troops from Normandy ports in June 1940 and preparing for the inevitable air assault, weapons began to arrive from the USA to make good those lost on the Continent. One weapon relevant to the development of air-land co-operation was the Curtiss P-40 fighter. Both Britain and France had placed orders and those destined for France were diverted to RAF stocks; the first crated airframes arrived in April 1940.

The P-40A, named Tomahawk in RAF service, was inferior to fighters then in service, especially at altitude, so it was relegated to the Army co-operation role, soon displacing the Lysander. The first model, of which 140 were delivered from direct orders, came with limited armament and no armour and as the Mk I it was issued to training or second-line units. The Mk IIA had four British machine guns in the wings and was generally similar to the US P-40B (110 delivered). The largest delivery, by now lend-lease rather than direct purchase, was the Mk IIB (P-40C), of which 930 were due, but some were diverted to the US military in China, the USSR and elsewhere. Around 635 were in British service, either in the UK or North Africa. The Mk IIB Tomahawk was powered by an Allison V-1710-33 engine producing 1,040hp and served in sixteen front-line squadrons in the UK. It was not fitted with a camera, so recce was by eye, note and radio.

This Tiger Moth, far from being a trainer, is the182 Sqn hack, seen here during an exercise. *Author's collection*

The Tomahawk remained in service for a relatively short time, to be supplanted by the North American P-51 Mustang. This type had been designed and built to a British requirement and, like the P-40, was initially powered by the Allison V-1710 in its early versions. This also restricted performance at altitude, so until the Packard Merlin engine became available for later marks the type was used by Army Co-operation Command from May 1942. The Mk I (600 supplied) featured four 0.50in and two 0.30in machine guns while the Mk IA packed four 20mm cannon. Most importantly, the Mustang was fitted with a single, oblique F24 camera, thus becoming Army Co-operation Command's first true Tac/R aircraft. Later marks served with the RAF in NW Europe and Italy.

A visitor to 182 Sqn during the trials was this Vultee Vigilant HL430 of 651 Sqn. One of the host squadron's Typhoons is just visible to the right. *Author's collection*

Table 3.5 – Key characteristics of Army close support aircraft, 1940–1943

Type	Max speed	Cruising speed	Ceiling ft	Range mls	Armament	Gross weight lbs
Lysander	215	180	26,000	600	3x.303 mg	5,920
Hurricane	315	275	35,600	460	8x.303 mg	6,600
Tomahawk	350	300	30,000	600	6x.303 mg	7,610
Mustang	390	340	32,000	1,050	6x.5/.3 mg	8,600
Typhoon	410	350	35,200	510	4x20mm can	13,250

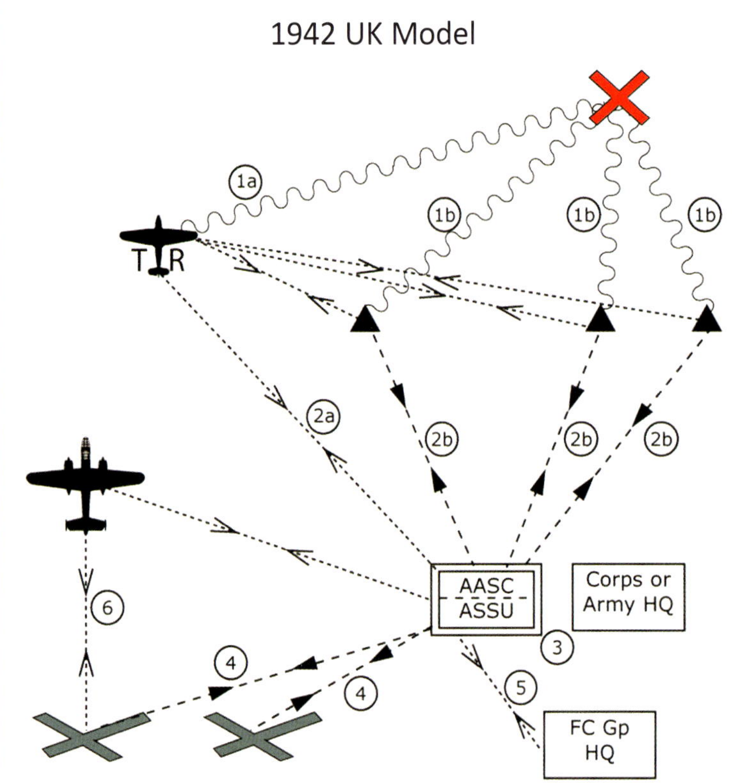

1) Tac/R aircraft or OP tentacle identifies target or threat
2) Either alert Army Air Support Unit (AASU) and via associated Air Support Signals Unit (ASSU)
3) Decision taken on support to be given
4) Light bomber airfield(s) advised
5) Fighter cover requested from Fighter Command Group if required
6) Close support bombers launched

The Hawker Hurricane was used extensively in North Africa in the close support role and a few were operated briefly by ACC squadrons in the UK. The Hawker Typhoon was used only by Fighter Command prior to the disbanding of ACC. Data for both are shown in table 3.5 above by way of comparison.

The experience of using ground attack fighters in the Western Desert, coupled with that of 11 Group Fighter Command when searching for a wider role by late 1941, resulted in the allocation of 257 Sqn to Western Command for training with the Army. The squadron was based at Honiley, Warwickshire, and fielded a mix of Hurricane I, IIb, IIc and Spitfire VB fighters. The intention was that the benefits of experience would be passed on to other fighter squadrons. Fighter Command could see a role in supporting the Army, but in its own time and on its own terms.

Tactical Reconnaissance

Just prior to the war MI6, the Secret Intelligence Service, commissioned several flights by a civilian Lockheed 12A twin, flown by businessman and inventor Sidney Cotton, for surreptitious photography over Germany. On the outbreak of war there was a need for faster, higher-flying aircraft for both strategic and tactical photo-reconnaissance (PR) and several Spitfires were assigned to this role, operating from Heston, Middlesex, under the guise of No 2 Camouflage Unit (CU). On 5 November 1939 the first Spitfire went to France as the Special Survey Flight (SSF). The parent 2 CU became the Photographic Development Unit (PDU), while on 10 February 1940 SSF morphed into 212 Sqn at Lille-Seclin with several Spitfires.

The primary task of 212 Sqn was to search for and record German preparations for the invasion of France and for that purpose was split into three small flights. Once the assault began there were immediate demands for photographic images of the enemy lines of communication, for which Bomber Command and the AASF became insistent customers. Following German occupation of France 212 Sqn was disbanded and its aircraft returned to Heston, on charge to the PDU which, from 8 July, became 1 Photographic Reconnaissance Unit (PRU).

Demand for the PRU's product came from a number of quarters, Bomber Command and the Admiralty among them, and to ensure objective access to its resources it had been placed under Coastal Command (administered by 16 Group) from 10 June. With a need for low-level photography, a Spitfire (N3117) was adapted to accommodate an 8in F24 camera mounted at 15° to the horizontal. Given the aircraft's vulnerability, the PR IG retained its eight-gun armament and had extra fuel tankage to increase range. For the next six months the unit kept a careful eye on the German invasion barges in the Channel ports.

Army Co-operation Command was slow to get to grips with Photo/R, but it assumed some limited responsibility. On 10 March 1941, 1416 Flight was resurrected in 71 Group with six PR IG Spitfires at Hendon, transferring to 34 Wing (Eastern Command) in August before moving to Benson on 5 September. Its function was to secure photographs of the French and Belgian coasts showing any signs of an impending invasion for the Joint Intelligence Committee and GOC Home Forces and by doing so free 1 PRU and its successors to concentrate on strategic reconnaissance.

Table 3.6 – ACC specialised tactical reconnaissance, 34 Wing

1416 Flt	Spitfire PR, Blenheim	Hendon, Benson	10.3.41	5.9.41
140	Spitfire PR, Blenheim	Benson	17.9.41	20.5.42
140	Spitfire PR, Blenheim	Mount Farm	20.5.42	16.3.43

At this time it also acquired a few Blenheims, upgrading to squadron status as 140 Sqn. In May 1942 140 Sqn moved to Mount Farm, in effect an outstation of Benson, prior to absorption into Fighter Command and then 2nd TAF in March 1943.

Air Observation Posts

> 'Today the speed of fighters and the development of flak has made the 1914–1918 method of spotting hazardous and obsolete. It is still essential however for a gunner to know how and when his shells are falling, and his problem is very like that of the army commander, to whom accurate information of an enemy's movements and dispositions is essential. The supply of accurate information ... has placed upon pilots and observers of Army Cooperation aircraft a great responsibility.
>
> Since Army Cooperation pilots are required to supply military information, on which the course of an engagement may depend, it is essential that they should possess a sound basis of military knowledge. The Army Cooperation pilot ... must be a military encyclopaedia as well as an airman. Considerable training in all this work is very necessary... like so many activities of Army Cooperation since Dunkirk they must remain military secrets.'

So wrote Air Marshal Barratt in 1942.[9] While he could not refer to the development of Army flying at this time, he did so obliquely by underscoring the need for gunners who could fly rather than airmen who could direct shoots.

The emergence of effective artillery observation from the air, as practised in the Second World War, was due largely to the perseverance of one man – Major H. C. Bazeley. Trained as a private pilot in 1934 and later secretary of the Royal Artillery Flying Club (RAFC), he was posted to 16 Sqn before becoming an instructor at the School of Army Co-operation (SAC) from 1937 until early 1940. It was at the RAFC that discussions began about the idea of *gunners* observing and directing artillery from the air. Given that the system in use at the time for correcting the fall of shot was by W/T and therefore slow and outdated, the RAF remained opposed to allowing Army pilots to fly its aircraft.

During summer 1939 trials were conducted using light aircraft including, among others, de Havilland Moth, Piper Cub and Taylorcraft, the latter being found to be most suitable. The tests were to determine how quickly and accurately shot could be observed and reported, the level of visibility from air to ground, and the capability of each aircraft type to operate from strips close to the guns. On 1 February 1940 D Flight was formed under Bazeley, who described the joint War Office/Air Ministry objectives[10] as being to determine:

> a) The possibilities and limitations of the use of light aircraft as Air Observation Posts (AOP).
>
> b) The most suitable type of aircraft for this purpose.
>
> c) The organisation most suited for the operation and maintenance of aircraft used for this purpose.

D Flight went to France on 19 April with three Taylorcraft Plus Ds (W5740, W5741 and G-AFZJ) and a sole Stinson Voyager, on loan from the manufacturer (X1050), to continue trials. As noted in the previous chapter, the trials were far from complete when the Flight had to make a hurried return to the UK. In December 1939 G-AFZJ had undertaken trials on Salisbury Plain with a Spitfire to assess the light aircraft's ability to avoid and evade a fighter. In France the Taylorcrafts were subject to further evasion tests against Hurricanes of 85 Sqn. Both exercises confirmed that small and manoeuvrable types could do so effectively.

To test the potential of fighters in support of the Army, 257 Sqn was detached to 37 Wing in Western Command late in 1941. The squadron had a mix of Hurricanes and Spitfires, the former exemplified by Mk I V6864/DT-A, photographed at Martlesham Heath in January 1941. *AST collection*

Typhoon Ib DN334/HF-D 183 Sqn. *Luca G. Canossa*

Tactical photo reconnaissance fell within the ambit of 71 Group in 1941 with the reformed 1416 Flight. Initially operating six PR Spitfires the unit operated within Eastern Command's 34 Wing from RAF Hendon. The flight expanded to become 140 Sqn, applying the ZW code as seen on this Spitfire PR IG. *Author's collection*

From July 1940 the first Army pilots started training within the School of Artillery and the first dedicated AOP course was between October and December, seven RA officers learning to fly. Through 1941 Bazeley managed to continue with trials, but was denied aircraft or support from the RAF, which still resisted the idea of conceding flying to Army pilots. However, D Flight survived within 70 Group Army Co-operation Command and from it 1424 AOP Flight formed on 20 September 1941 at Larkhill, equipped with Tiger Moth, Piper Cub, Taylorcraft Plus D and a Vigilant. The Flight in turn expanded to become 43 Operational Training Unit (OTU), formed on 1 October 1942 and still at Larkhill, but soon moving to Old Sarum.

There were challenges faced by pilots when spotting and correcting the fall of shells and some of the problems and solutions determined by trials were described in conference papers in July 1941.[11] The RAF had used the simple clock code with W/T and abbreviated Morse message that in practice proved to be less accurate than using the formal artillery system of correction, but which could be taught to non-gunner pilots. It was further determined that fighters were too fast to be able to handle artillery shooting. In general, it was expected that success would be achieved by a small, light, aircraft using R/T in direct contact with a battery and flying just behind the bomb line, not above 1,000ft and ideally with the protection conferred by air superiority.

Eventually, with great reluctance, the RAF agreed to a formula that satisfied all parties. Squadrons would be formed, each to be commanded by a Major, Royal Artillery, and gunner pilots would fly light aircraft. The squadron adjutant would be RAF, as would aircraft fitters and riggers, but drivers and signallers would be Army. Levels of equipment were agreed and the first squadron, 651, formed at Old Sarum in August with Taylorcraft Plus C and Plus D aircraft. The unit worked up during Exercise *Bumper* and through the early months wider discussions were held about the AOP's role in battlefield scenarios that differed from what was deemed to be the norm, an example being working with the Navy when shooting ship's guns in support of landings. In July 1942, 651 Sqn was sent to Scotland to work up with V Corps that would be part of the force landing in North Africa in Operation *Torch*.

As the number of units grew, so did the need for an appropriate aircraft. The Taylorcraft was deemed to be the best of those trialled, although the D Flight experts would have preferred the Miles M.38 Messenger, which the Air Ministry was not prepared to order. In desperation, Stinson Vigilants were ordered through lend-lease, but few were delivered and those that were proved to be too complex for front-line service. The Army eventually settled on the American Taylorcraft design and after initially using civilian-impressed examples, acquired the D.I from Taylorcraft Aeroplanes (England) Ltd, British licence holder for production. The Mark I was under-powered and without armour or flaps, but over time the aircraft was developed by the progressive introduction of design improvements and more powerful engines.

Table 3.7 – Air Observation Post squadrons to June 1943

Sqn	Type	Wing/base	From	To	Onwards to
Air Observation Post squadrons					
651	Taylorcraft	Old Sarum	8.41	7.42	
651	Auster I	32.Dumfries	7.42	10.42	North Africa. Italy
652	Tiger Moth	34.Bottisham	6.42	12.42	
652	Auster I	32.Dumfries	1.43	2.43	
652	Auster I	32.Methven	4.43	6.43	UK. N W Europe
653	Auster I, III	35.Penshurst	9.42	6.43	UK. N W Europe
654	Auster I	33.Firbeck	9.42	11.42	
654	Auster I	34.Bottisham	12.42	2.43	North Africa. Italy
655	Auster I, III	36.Old Sarum	12.42	3.43	
655	Auster I, III	35.Detling	3.43	6.43	North Africa. Italy
656	Auster I	34.Westley	1.43	1.43	
656	Auster I, III	34.Stapleford	3.43	6.43	Far East
657	Auster I	33.Ouston	1.43	3.43	
657	Auster I, III	34.Westley	5.43	6.43	North Africa. Italy
658	Auster III	36.Old Sarum	5.43	6.43	UK. N W Europe
659	Auster III	33.Firbeck	4.43	6.43	UK. N W Europe

In common with the Army co-operation squadrons AOP units were allocated to commands, as shown in the table below. From the disbanding of ACC, the AOP squadrons went to Fighter Command if they were destined to take part in the invasion of Europe, or to overseas commands.

By 1944 AOP squadrons were typically assigned to a Corps, a squadron having three flights plus a HQ flight, each of four aircraft, and a complement of twenty-one pilots of captain rank. The support establishment was set at 105 Army (drivers, cooks, clerks, batmen) and sixty-three RAF (adjutant, fitters, riggers). For rapid mobility each squadron had twelve 3-ton lorries, twelve jeeps, motorcycles and bowsers.

Above: D Flt of the School of Army Co-operation went to France in April 1940 for operational trials, taking with it three Taylorcraft Plus D and this Stinson Voyager X1050 which was on loan from the manufacturer. In the event the Taylorcraft design proved more suitable for artillery spotting.

Right: Spitfire PR IV X4784/ZW of 140 Sqn shows off its overall pink finish over the Oxfordshire countryside in 1941. The colour worked well against the sky, albeit compromised by the code letters. *AST collection*

Airborne Forces

Any description of Army Co-operation Command would be incomplete without brief reference to airborne forces. The 1st Parachute Brigade was formed under Lt Col Richard Gale on 1 September 1941, shortly after which the 1st Airlanding Brigade was established. On 29 October, Maj Gen F. A. M. Browning was appointed OC Parachute and Airborne Forces and in December the Glider Pilot Regiment came into being, followed in January 1942 by 38 Wing, Army Co-operation Command.

Parachute troops had undertaken two raids by Spring 1942. The first was Operation *Colossus*, to destroy an important aqueduct in southern Italy; the second, on 27 February 1942, to recover a German radar from Bruneval on the French coast in Operation *Biter*. Paratroopers were transported in converted Armstrong Whitworth Whitley bombers from 78 Sqn and 51 Sqn respectively.

Table 3.8 – Airborne Forces units

Unit	Type	Wing/base	From	To	Comment
PTC		Ringway	21.6.40	31.8.40	
CLS/E	Whitley	Ringway	31.8.40	1.9.41	ex PTC
AFE	Whitley	Ringway	1.9.41	12.41	ex CLE
Glider units					
GEU.S	Hector, Hotspur	Ringway	18.7.41	25.1.42	Within CLE
296 Sqn	Hector, Whitley, Albemarle	Netheravon	25.1.42	6.43	ex GEU
295 Sqn	Whitley, Halifax	Netheravon	3.8.42	6.43	Note 1
Parachute units					
PES	Whitley	Netheravon	15.12.41	22.1.42	Within CLE
297 Sqn	Whitley, Albemarle	Netheravon, Hurn	22.1.42	6.43	ex PES
298 Sqn	Whitley	Thruxton	24.8.42	10.42	Note 2

Notes:
PTC – Parachute Training Centre (in 22 Group)
CLS/E – Central Landing School/Establishment (in 22, then 70 Group); incorporated Parachute Training Sqn, Glider Training Sqn and Development Unit
AFE – Airborne Forces Establishment (in 70 Group)
PES – Parachute Exercise Squadron
Note 1 – nucleus from 296 Sqn
Note 2 – nucleus from 297 Sqn

With the formation of 38 Wing, new squadrons were formed from training units which, themselves, went through a number of stages of development. The training establishments, while spawning operational units, also expanded. By the time ACC disbanded, 38 Wing, which became 38 Group, fielded two glider and two parachute squadrons.

AASG to TAF and a System

> 'Army/Air Co-operation? Nothing in it! All you need is willingness to cooperate and good signals!'

This sentiment is attributed widely to Air Marshal Sir William Sholto Douglas when AOC-in-C Fighter Command, November 1940 to November 1942. Under his leadership, though, Fighter Command was slow to appreciate the demands of Army co-operation.

Late in 1941 the War Office managed a war game-cum-simulation called *Striker*. It was to test ideas about the demands of the invasion of France and was followed by further trials and exercises. Fighter Command was in 1942 taking the offensive to the enemy with fighter sweeps over the French and Belgian coasts, for which fighters like the Hurricane and Typhoon were adapted to be fighter-bombers. While the RAF was concentrating on its bomber campaign and Coastal Command was fighting the Battle of the Atlantic, there was scarce interest in supporting an Army which, in northern Europe, was passive. Fighter Command did participate in Exercise *Repulse* in March 1942, but with a lack of enthusiasm.[12]

After the trials a number of Taylorcraft Plus C aircraft were impressed for military use with D Flt and then 651 Sqn. C2 G-AFVB was impressed into military service as HH985.

In May 1942 Air Cdre Henry Thorold and Col Claude Oxborrow, senior staff officers at Home Forces GHQ, put forward a modest plan[13] for a composite Army Air Support Group (AASG) within ACC comprising twelve mobile squadrons. These would build experience and systems under Army command and help train other squadrons of fighters and light bombers under RAF command. Predictably, despite its modesty, the proposal was rejected. But it was followed by a comprehensive RAF plan,[14] devised by Air Vice-Marshal John Slessor, now Assistant Chief of the Air Staff (Planning), aimed specifically at supporting the opening of a second front in France.

Field Marshal Sir Alan Brooke, Chief of the Imperial General Staff and Chairman of the Chiefs of Staff Committee, argued for retaining ACC, desperate to have a tactical air force under Army command. In the event, the differences between Army and RAF were referred to Churchill who, on 5 October 1942, chaired a meeting of the Chiefs of Staff. He subsequently determined that the Slessor Plan would prevail, having this to say:[15]

> 'Whenever our Army is established on land, and is conducting operations against the enemy, the system of organisation and employment of the Royal Air Force should conform to that which has proved so successful in the Western Desert. The characteristics of this system are that the whole Air Force will be under command of the Air Officer Commanding-in-Chief, whose relationship to the Army Commander-in-Chief will be that laid down in my [Middle East] Directive of 7th October 1941. This fact must be the starting point in our investigation of the part to be played by the Royal Air Force in Continental operations based on the United Kingdom.'

The Army was now planning for the liberation of Europe by conducting exercises like *Dryshod* and relatively small-scale operations, like *Jubilee* (the raid on Dieppe) in August 1942. Come November and a major force was sent to North Africa for the *Torch* landings (Chapter 7). The RAF had been reluctant to provide bomber support for the Dieppe raid; the large number of fighters committed were heavily involved, but in air combat rather than in supporting troops on the ground. Indeed, no ASSU had been embarked. In the *Torch* landings air support would be provided by the Fleet Air Arm initially and then Eastern Air Command, embracing elements of the Desert Air Force.

As preparations began for opening a second front in France there was one major exercise to come involving Army Co-operation Command before it was disbanded. Exercise *Spartan* took place between 1 and 12 March 1943 and was designed to test assumptions and systems relating to 'seaborne' invasion and breakout from the bridgehead.

Taylorcraft Plus D G-AGDB was a trials aircraft fitted with a raised Perspex canopy and importantly a Blackburn Cirrus Minor engine of 90hp compared with the original Lycoming of just 55hp. The sprightly performance with the new engine is obvious. The aircraft became the basis of the Auster Mk I and was given the serial LB267. *Author's collection*

The Taylorcraft D1 morphed into the Auster I, as exemplified by LB278. *Author's collection*

The Armstrong Whitworth Albemarle was built to a bomber requirement and was unusual in being of composite steel and wood construction. In its designated role it was a failure but was converted as a special transport and glider tug. This Mk I, P1442, was a tug with 296 Sqn. *Author's collection*

Although designed as an assault glider the General Aircraft Hotspur was never used operationally, being used in the training role. Hotspur Mk II HH464 displays the underwing 'Oxydol' trainer markings, so-called from the design of a contemporary washing powder packaging. *Author's collection*

Below: Both parachute and glider airborne forces were formed within Army Co-operation Command. An early operation in February 1941, *Colossus* was against an aqueduct at Calitri in southern Italy with paratroopers flown in by Whitley aircraft of 78 Sqn. These are Whitley Mk V Z6743/EY-V and Z6625/EY-L. *AST collection*

The exercise was smaller in numbers than *Bumper*, but was offensive and more refined in respect of air support. The 'British' force was 1st Canadian Army, comprising three Corps (six divisions and a tank brigade, plus Army and Corps assets) and was operating from Southland, south of a line between Swindon and Slough. The 'German' occupying force was provided by Eastern Command's Sixth Army, with four divisions in two Corps, plus a Brigade Group.

Each army had an air force comprising composite groups. Eastland's air force, X Composite Group, used fixed bases, while Z Composite Group had both fixed and mobile bases, including advanced landing grounds. There were, in addition, several numbered 'airfields' – in effect wings – that could service, fuel and arm aircraft. Z Group also had the benefit of 1 Mobile Operations Room Unit (MORU) to handle requests for air support. Both forces had an Air HQ, air stores

Table 3.9 – Exercise *Spartan* – Eastland ('German') X Group units

X Group – 'Eastland' (enemy)			
Sqn	**Type**	**Base(s)**	**Cmd**
303, 350	Spitfire VB, VC	Heston, Debden	FC
167, 411	Spitfire VB, VC	Kidlington, Fowlmere	FC
453	Spitfire VB	Westcott, Newmarket	FC
421	Spitfire VB	Croughton, Gransden Lodge, Fowlmere	FC
124	Spitfire IX	Croughton, Duxford	FC
181, 183	Typhoon IB	Cranfield, Snailwell	FC
151	Mosquito II	Wittering	FC
4	Mustang I	Barford St John, Cranfield, Duxford	ACC
169	Mustang I	Barford St John, Gransden Lodge, Bottisham	ACC
2	Mustang I	Westcott, Newmarket, Cranfield, Duxford	ACC
613	Mustang I	Bottisham	ACC
268	Mustang I	Bottisham, Snailwell	ACC
98	Mitchell II	Foulsham	BC
21	Ventura I, II	Methwold	BC
464, 487	Ventura I, II	Feltwell	BC
652	Auster I	Sawbridgeworth	ACC
655	Auster I, III	Fowlmere	ACC
656	Auster I, III	Westley	ACC

parks, signals and other support. The aircraft of X Group were specially marked with black spinners and black underside to the port wing, with a white panel along the forward fuselage.

From the table above it will be noted that the fighter and support squadrons of X Group, part of the occupation force of Eastland, started on airfields in Oxfordshire and Buckinghamshire, close to the assumed front line, and gradually retreated to East Anglian airfields. X Group also had the benefit of three AOP squadrons.

The exercise demonstrated conclusively that composite wings were effective and workable. As a consequence, in the summer the support squadrons of Fighter Command, with the light bombers of 2 Group Bomber Command and the assets of Army Co-operation Command, were transferred to the new 2nd Tactical Air Force (TAF). The MORU worked well,

Table 3.10 – Exercise *Spartan* – Southland ('British') Z Group units

Z Group – 'Southland' (British)			
Sqn	**Type**	**Base(s)**	**Cmd**
Fixed base force			
129	Spitfire VB	Tangmere	FC
504	Spitfire VB, VC	Ibsley	FC
616	Spitfire VI	Ibsley	FC
96	Beaufighter VIF	Ford	FC
16, 170	Mustang I	Ford	ACC
400, 414	Mustang I	Dunsfold	ACC
Mobile force			
19	Spitfire VB	121 Airfield	FC
132	Spitfire VB	122 Airfield	FC
412	Spitfire VB	Hurn, Odiham, 124 Airfield	FC
182, 247	Typhoon IB	121 Airfield	FC
174, 184	Hurricane IIB, IID	122 Airfield	FC
175	Hurricane IIB	123 and 124 Airfields	FC
26	Mustang I	123 Airfield	ACC
239	Mustang I	123 and 124 Airfields	ACC
88, 226	Boston III	Charmy Down	BC
653	Auster I	Penshurst	ACC

Note:
121 Airfield (Wing) was Middle Wallop, then Membury
122 Airfield – Chilbolton, then Grove
123 Airfield – Stoney Cross, and for the Mustangs two ALGs at Eastmantown Down and Red Barn
124 Airfield – Lasham
Hurricanes and Typhoons were newly operating in the army support role.

Exercise *Spartan* was a major test of potential invasion forces for the forthcoming assault on France, planned for 1944. Friendly Southland forces included Spitfire VBs of 132 Sqn then based at Chilbolton but here seen at Newchurch in October 1943. The second aircraft is BM648/FF-B. *Author's collection*

616 Sqn operating within Southland was unusual in operating the Spitfire VI. Ground crew training at King's Cliffe seems a jolly affair, but a defensive position next to a fuel bowser may not be the most intelligent arrangement. *Author's collection*

In *Spartan* a number of Mustang squadrons operated on both sides. These XC coded Mustang Mk Is are from 26 Sqn operating out of Stoney Cross as part of Southland's mobile force. *Author's collection*

but there were to be further refinements to enable it to control four airfields. The Canadian report[16] on the exercise had this to say of the Southland air activity, which rather reflects the RAF preference for interdiction as opposed to very close air support:

> '...there was bombing activity against lines of communication, and some intervention by aircraft on the battlefield. The writer gathered that Air Vice-Marshal Whitworth-Jones was disposed to use his resources mainly against the enemy's rear areas, and from remarks which he heard dropped on the morning of 6 Mar when Sir Archibald Sinclair the Secretary of State for Air and his party visited HQ Second Army, he gathered further that some R.A.F. opinion held that the commander 'Z' Group had gone too far in this direction.'

Typhoons also operated for both sides with 182 and 247 Sqns flying from Middle Wallop and then Membury. R8981/XM-X, with individual code repeated on the cannon fairing, is a 182 Sqn machine. *Author's collection*

In *Spartan* both sides were allocated one squadron of night fighters, in the case of Southland Beaufighters of 96 Sqn. In this obviously posed photograph Beaufighter VIF V8748/ZJ-R was caught at Drem in September 1943 with six WAAFs forming a human chain taking ammunition boxes to the tail of the aircraft! *Author's collection*

Also a part of the 'friendly' mobile force were two squadrons of light bombers, 88 and 226. One of the former's aircraft is Boston IIIA BZ377 RH-F. *AST collection*

Above: The aircraft of the enemy Eastland force, apart from the light bombers, were required to wear a white horizontal band along the forward fuselage. In the case of 421 Sqn the requirement was artistically interpreted on its AU-coded Spitfire VBs, seen here at RAF Croughton. In the background are ON-coded aircraft of 124 Sqn. *AST collection*

Below: 303 (Polish) Sqn was flying for Eastland from Heston which may not have amused the squadron OC, Polish ace Sqn Ldr Jan Zumbach, an aggressive pilot with eleven kills at the time. Spitfire V EN951/RF-D was one of three similarly coded aircraft flown by Zumbach. *Author's collection*

In Britain inter-service rivalry, poor analysis of operations (especially the retreat from France), overriding RAF commitment to strategic bombing, lack of appropriate equipment and endless trials and exercises, meant that it took time for a system of close air support to evolve. In contrast, in the Western Desert, far from the politics of Whitehall and oversight from the chiefs of staff, effective systems were developed step by step, battle after battle.

Some writers have asserted that the Western Desert Air Force (WDAF) benefitted from 'doctrine' developed in Britain. However, the Wann-Woodall report was confined to home commands and not sent to the Middle East, while Barratt's visit was to take ideas away, not to convey them. The new system that was in place after the *Spartan* exercise was finely described in summary by now Lt Col Carrington:

> '... the system called for the joint staff at the control centre (ASSU) to evaluate air-support requests as they came in, checking the proposed target locations in relation to the

Mustang Is NM-H and NM-M of 268 Sqn seen here in late 1942. In Exercise *Spartan* the squadron was one of five Mustang units flying with Eastland forces, operating from Bottisham. *AST collection*

In the exercise four Typhoon squadrons were equally split between opposing sides. JR128/HF-L hails from 183 Sqn operating from Cranfield. *Author's collection*

This Auster I of 655 Sqn shows well not only the white bar on the forward fuselage but also the port wing black underside, the other distinguishing mark of the Eastland units. The aircraft is here dropping a message at its base at Fowlmere, shortly to become a USAAF P-51 station. *Crown copyright*

'bombline'. A deconfliction measure to reduce fratricide, the bombline was based on a physical feature easily identifiable to both airmen and soldiers, projected forward of friendly troops, beyond which aircraft were permitted to engage targets. If the target was accepted by the ASSU, the squadron designated for the task was contacted via direct communications, and the Air Liaison Officers (ALOs) attached to the squadron were alerted to brief the pilots, who had then to identify their targets by means of photographic maps with grid references.'

In contrast to the Boston squadrons with Southland, the enemy force was equipped with a sole Mitchell unit and two of Venturas. Mitchell II FV985/VO-S of 98 Sqn. *Crown copyright*

Four squadrons in RAF Bomber Command were equipped with the Ventura light bomber, but it was not a success in the bomber role and most were operated by Coastal Command. Ventura AE854/SB-J was operated by 464 Sqn, one of two Ventura units under Eastland command. *Author's collection*

[1] TNA WO 199/2471 *Banquet Light*

[2] TNA CAB 106/AL118 *Report on Operations in Flanders 1940*

[3] Smith and Kay, *German Aircraft of the Second World War*, p319

[4] TNA WO 106/5162 *Army Air Requirements, Summary of Decisions made at a Meeting Held at the Air Ministry, 2 August 1940*

[5] TNA WO 277/34 *Historical Monograph Army Air Support and Photographic Interpretation, 1939-1945, Chapter II Air Support and the Battle of France, 1939-1940: The BEF and its Air Support*

[6] TNA AIR 39/140 *Close Support by Bomber and Fighter Aircraft.* (Wann-Woodall Report)

[7] Carrington, *Soldier at Bomber Command,* p65

[8] TNA WO199/797

[9] Article in *Flying and Popular Aviation* September 1942

[10] Bazeley, *The Air Observation Post,* p14

[11] TNA AIR 39/47 *Artillery Reconnaissance Co-operation*

[12] Carrington, *Soldier at Bomber Command,* p80

[13] TNA AIR 20/2812 *Army Co-operation: the Thorold paper*

[14] TNA CAB 80/37 COS(42)351 *Continental Operations 1943 – Operational Organisation and System of Command of the RAF* 21 July 1942

[15] Quoted in Hall, *Strategy for Victory*, p126

[16] Report No 94 Historical Officer Canadian Military HQ 12 May 1943

Evolution in Africa

As England became the focus of the German air assault, the British and Dominion Allied forces were fighting land battles in North and East Africa and their air forces developing systems of increasing sophistication with which to support the Army. Italian forces invaded Egypt from Libya in September 1940, but were held despite the Allies having inferior equipment. Then, in December the Allies hit back, getting as far as Benghazi, but with extended supply lines.

The British and Dominions were also fighting the Italians in East Africa, using biplanes like the Hartbees and Gladiator to some effect. The most significant marker from that theatre was the embryonic first use of 'cab-ranks' of fighters to provide immediate close-support to advancing troops. No sooner was progress being made than troops and squadrons were withdrawn to Egypt. This was to cover Axis attacks in Greece, Syria and Lebanon and to provide support for the defence of Malta.

At the outbreak of war there were six Blenheim light bomber squadrons in the Middle East including 84 Squadron based at Shaibah. The squadron soon moved to Egypt and here seven of the VA coded aircraft are seen over the Western Desert in November 1940. *Author's collection*

By early 1941 the Germans were in North Africa and in March Rommel struck east, soon reaching the Egyptian border. With squadrons spread so thinly the British held on and slowly began to re-equip with more Hurricane units and the first Tomahawks. A counter-attack – *Battleaxe* – failed, but there was another milestone in the journey to cohesive close air support when a conference of military leaders in Cairo agreed independently on procedures which were similar to those worked out in the UK in trials and exercise. Thus, the scene was set for the next Allied assault against Axis forces.

Background

At the outbreak of war the RAF was spread thinly across the Middle East with aged aircraft protecting Egypt and the vital Suez Canal. Units were organised geographically and were part of a 1939 Combined Plan[1] that required both air and land to co-operate in defence of Egypt. The deployment of units is shown at Table 4.1.

During the next nine months there were few changes. 113 Sqn acquired the Blenheim IV and 80 Sqn was in the process of changing its Gladiators for Hurricanes. 30 Sqn was equipped partially with the Blenheim IF fighter and 230 Sqn with Sunderlands joined 228 Sqn at Alexandria. There was also structural change in that 202 Group formed on 21 September 1939 under Air Cdre Raymond Collishaw as a composite group controlling all the squadrons in Egypt. Thus, defence of Egypt and ultimately support of the Army in the Western Desert fell to a geographical command as opposed to the functional command structure that existed in the UK. Writing of Army co-operation as it was some three years into the war and referring to the Middle East, one respected historian[2] noted that the essential principles of co-operation were threefold, being: intimate relations; an independent signals network; the function of the whole available air power.

Table 4.1 – RAF in the Middle East at the outbreak of war, September 1939

Sqn	Type	Base	Role
Mediterranean Command Gibraltar 200 Group			
202	London II	Gibraltar	AS
Middle East Command			
202 (Egypt) Group			
250 (Bomber) Wing Ismailia			
30	Blenheim I	Ismailia	LB
55	Blenheim I	Ismailia	LB
14	Wellesley	Ismailia	LB
251 (Bomber) Wing Heliopolis			
113	Blenheim I	Heliopolis	LB
70	Valentia	Helwan	Trspt
216	Valentia, Bombay	Heliopolis	B/Trspt
252 (Fighter) Wing Fort Shefa Khana			
80	Gladiator I	Amriya	F
112	Gladiator I, II	Helwan	F
253 (Advanced Bomber) Wing Maaten Bagush			
33	Gauntlet, Gladiator	Mersa Matruh	F
45	Blenheim I	Fuka	LB
208	Lysander I, II	Qasaba	AC
211	Blenheim I	el Daba	Recce
228	Sunderland	Alexandria, Kalafrana	AS
254 (Bomber) Sudan Wing Khartoum in 203 Group			
47	Wellesley	Khartoum	LB
223	Wellesley	Summit	LB
British Forces in Iraq			
84	Blenheim I	Shaibah	LB
RAF in Palestine and Trans-Jordan			
6	Lysander	Ramleh	AC
British Forces Aden			
94	Gladiator I, II	Khormaksar	F
8	Blenheim	Khormaksar	LB
203	Singapore	Isthmus	AS

> 'The most important difference between England and Egypt at this stage [1942] was that the third principle, though perceived in England, was not acted upon; in Egypt, under the stress of war, it was acted upon. [The AOC] did not have to struggle against the rigidities and dogmas of the functional Command system; he could use the RAF in the Middle East as a single unit.'

Throughout the war in North Africa and Italy effective systems evolved through necessity and economy. They probably also flourished because the Western Desert Air Force (WDAF) included a large proportion of personnel from the Dominions who, with non-regular British airmen, brought a practicality and impatience at protocol and what would now be called doctrine. Conditions and the ebb and flow of battle kept formal discipline to a minimum.

This and the next chapter of the preparatory stages in reaching any sort of effective system describe the foundations of Army co-operation in East and North Africa prior to the first *major* battle where air and land were coordinated on a large scale – El Alamein.

Egypt, Italy and the Western Desert

On 10 June 1940, with the collapse of France imminent, Benito Mussolini, Italian Prime Minister, alias fascist dictator, committed his country to war on the side of the Germans. This now presented major problems for the British since strong Italian forces occupied Libya and, to the south, Abyssinia, Eritrea and Italian Somaliland. The Italian *Regia Aeronautica* had a 3:1 numerical superiority over the RAF, so Air Chief Marshal Sir Arthur Longmore, AOC-in-C Middle East, was now faced with deploying his handful of squadrons to best effect. He decided to go on the offensive immediately by attempting to reduce the imbalance by sending twenty-six Blenheims to attack El Adem airfield on 11 June. Eighteen Italian aircraft were destroyed or damaged for the loss of two Blenheims. In July, another decision was to send 45 Sqn with its Blenheims to Sudan to support the two Wellesley squadrons based there.

With Italy now in the war the Mediterranean was, for the time being, effectively closed as a supply route and Malta isolated. This meant that supplies and reinforcements by sea had to travel around the

Cape of Good Hope to use Egyptian Red Sea ports. For aircraft, though, there was an alternative. From September aircraft were shipped to Takoradi in the Gold Coast, assembled and ferried to Egypt via Khartoum, a route pioneered by the RAF between the wars. While the route involved overflying French Equatorial Africa, fortunately this was one colony that had gone from Vichy France to Free France.

From 1 September Italian troops were seen to be massing on the Egyptian border and on the 13th, in *Operazione E*, they invaded with four divisions, soon reaching Sidi Barrani and capturing its airfields before halting at Maktila. The British withdrew to Mersa Matruh, the RAF being left to reflect on the loss of the forward airfields and the need to keep closely supporting the Army without compromising its primary role of destroying the Italian Air Force. From now on the forward HQs of Army and Air were co-located. Over the next few months the Army, under General Archibald Wavell, consolidated and built up reserves of men and equipment ready for an attack on Libya. Meanwhile, the RAF was receiving and assimilating new equipment like the Hurricane fighter and trying to conserve stock through maintenance.

Of significance to the development of Army/Air co-operation were the instructions[3] issued by Collishaw to the units under his command in relation to support for a large-scale raid on Sidi Barrani on 22 October by a battalion of the Cameron Highlanders. They included:

> 'Intention:
>
> 3. To provide fighter protection for our forces during daylight, prior to, and after the attack.
>
> 4. To occupy and Harass enemy forces in the Sidi Barrani area during the attack by our ground forces.
>
> 5. To neutralize enemy air forces which might be employed in attacking our ground forces during the withdrawal on the morning after the attack.'

Within a heading 'Method of Execution', the order listed the units to be involved and their bomb loads and so forth. This included the following:

> '11. The roles of fighters will be as follows. Gladiators on patrol to watch for and intervene against enemy air attacks on our ground forces. Enemy fighters which leave the vicinity of our ground forces are not to be pursued. Hurricanes on patrol to protect the Gladiators from air attack to which they are particularly vulnerable when engaged on the protection of ground forces.'

Assault into Libya – Operation *Compass*

Initially planned as a five-day raid into Libya, Operation *Compass*, planned for December 1940, ended as a 500-mile advance as far as El Agheila. The attack was made by Western Desert Force (from January 1941 XIII Corps) under Lt Gen Richard O'Connor, comprising some 31,000 soldiers, 275 tanks and 120 guns of the 7th Armoured and 4th Indian Infantry divisions. RAF support began with a heavy bombing raid on 7 December by Wellingtons of 148 Sqn from Malta against Tripoli and Castel Benito airfield and by Egyptian-based Wellingtons against Benina and El Adem. One result was twenty-nine Italian aircraft claimed as destroyed on the ground.

As it moved from rear bases 60 miles up towards Maktila, the Indian Division was given fighter cover. From here on 6 and 208 Sqns from Qasaba were at the immediate call of the two divisions. The Blenheim

Unescorted the Blenheim was vulnerable to air attack. Blenheim I L8482/OB-W of 45 Sqn has come to grief at Fuka on 20 February 1940. *Author's collection*

light bomber squadrons each had a small army liaison section, Air Intelligence Liaison (AIL), attached to brief and de-brief pilots. At the outset the squadrons were connected by landline to Corps or divisional HQ.

The attack started against military encampments around Maktila on 9 December and by the following day Sidi Barrani had been recaptured. The battle was a truly combined services affair, naval vessels contributing a bombardment from offshore. The weary Gauntlet fighters of 33 Sqn were withdrawn from use on the 12th and from then fighters began using Sidi Barrani as a forward base.

On the 13th 3 Sqn RAAF lost five Gladiators in combat. Busy covering ground forces and moving in to attack Italian bombers, they failed to notice Fiat CR.42 fighters above them. As Collishaw had warned in his order that is noted above, fighters supporting a ground battle needed top cover.

Hurricane and Gladiator fighters patrolled ahead of the advancing Army to engage approaching enemy aircraft and in this way aircraft of 274 Sqn intercepted a number of Savoia-Marchetti SM.79 bombers, shooting down five. Throughout the month airfields were also bombed and strafed with a view to reducing the numerical superiority of the *Regia Aeronautica*. The initial objective, the port at Sollum, was captured on the 16th, by which time the Italian inventory had been reduced by 237 guns, seventy-three tanks and countless vehicles, all captured. To all intents and purposes the Italian air effort stalled after the first week. From now on the main problem for the RAF was keeping pace with the advancing Army and finding forward airfields from which to operate with minimal infrastructure. Thus, 73 Sqn was at Gazala on 30 January and two days later at El Adem.

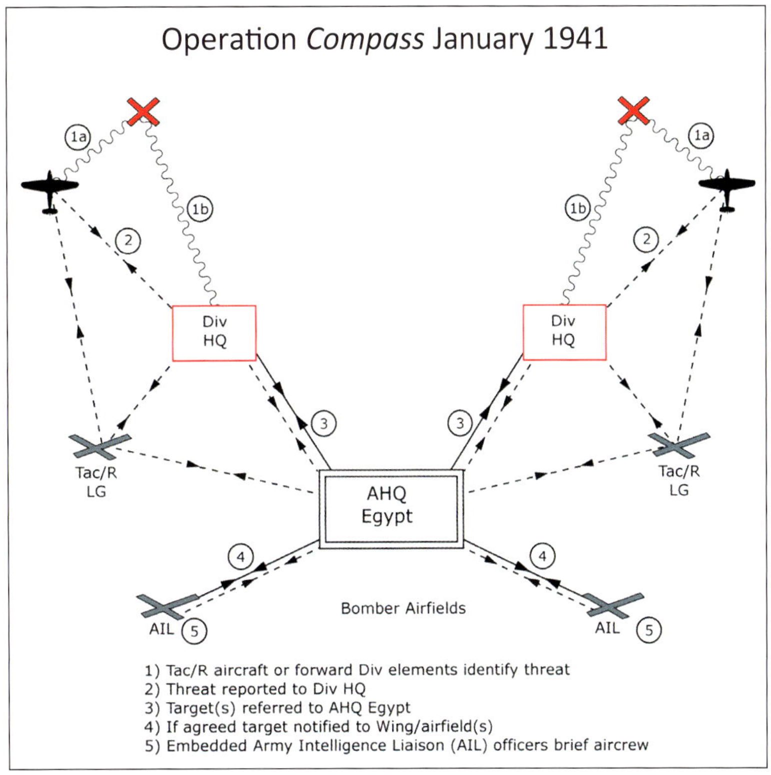

With Army support, the RAF became adept at mobility, moving up 31 Air Stores Park (ASP) and 51 Repair and Salvage Unit (RSU), together with explosives and fuel support, to convert Italian material for RAF use. In the attack on Bardia, the RAF provided photographic reconnaissance, bombing of enemy strongpoints holding up the advance and laid a bomb 'curtain' in front of advancing troops, according to one source.[4]

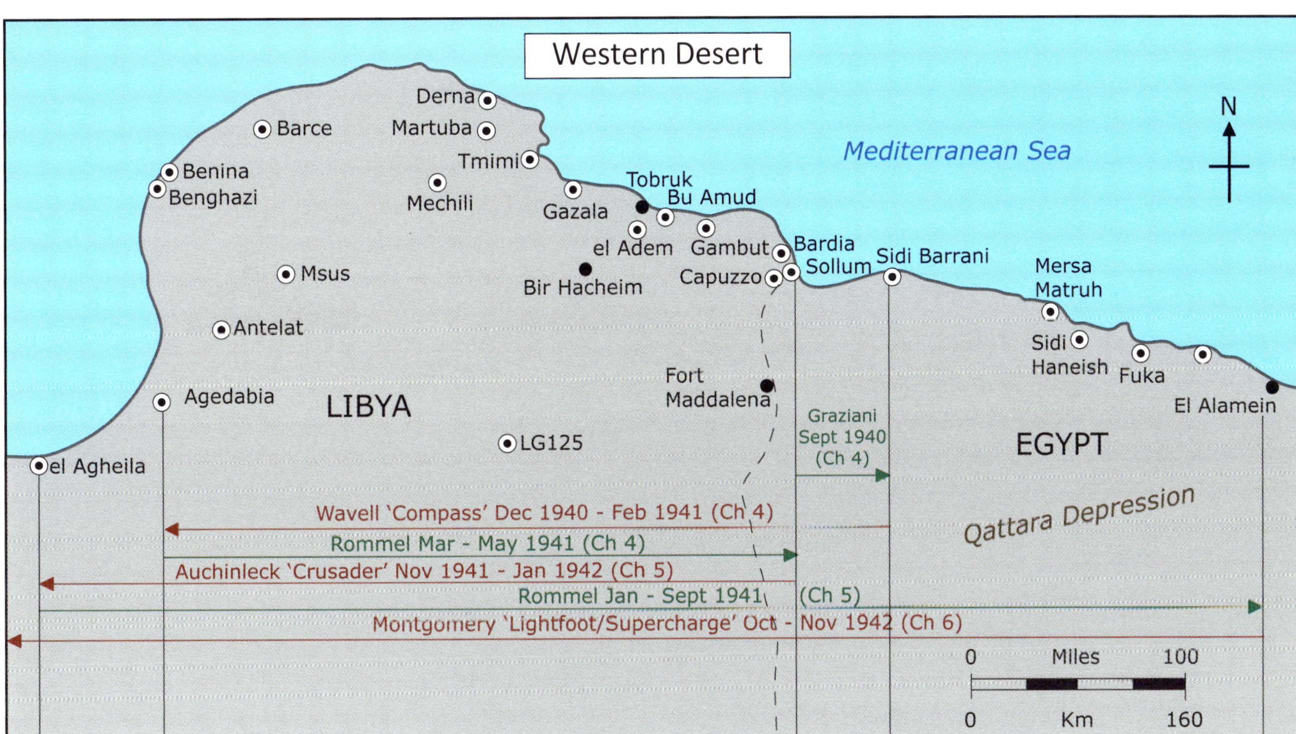

Initially the sole fighter squadrons in the Middle East – all four of them – were equipped with the Gladiator. This anonymous aircraft belongs to 112 Sqn which, together with 33 and 80 Sqns, was responsible for the defence of the Egypt base. *Author's collection*

In September 1940 3 Sqn RAAF began to assemble at Helouan to support defence of the Suez Canal. Equipped with Gladiators the squadron pilots were in action from 19 November. Walking from his aircraft, N5752/NW-C, is Fg Off A. H. Boyd (right) with Fg Off A. C. Rawlinson and Flt Lt B. R. Pelly. *Author's collection*

The battle went well for O'Connor. On 22 January Tobruk fell, followed by Derna on the 26th. Accordingly, 73 and 274 Sqns moved up to Gazala and 3 RAAF (now re-equipping with Hurricanes) and 208 Army co-operation squadrons to Tmimi. The RAF now faced the prospect of no airfields for several hundred miles between Derna and Benghazi, so the latter now became an objective.

In the event Benghazi was captured on 6 February and with it the local airfields, essential if the RAF was to keep up with the Army. By now the Australian 6th Division had replaced the Indian 4th (which had gone south to Sudan), fighting the final battle of this campaign by taking Beda Fomm on 7 February. Tired and with hugely extended lines of supply, the Army now stopped short of El Agheila, having destroyed the Italian 10th Army and advanced 350 miles. The fighting cost the Italians dearly in manpower (130,000 taken prisoner) and hardware – 1,300 guns, 400 tanks and at least 1,650 aircraft, of which 1,100 were captured on the ground, mainly in need of repair. The Allied cost was 500 killed, 1,373 wounded and fifty-five missing.

Although there were some aspects of co-operation that worked, there was nonetheless considerable scope for improvement. Frequently the RAF was unaware of where ground forces were, so there was the risk of fratricidal bombing, the Army generally having failed to appreciate the value of Tac/R. Telephone land lines were partial and often congested. For the future, AILs would be allocated to all support squadrons and an RAF liaison officer to the armoured division to both advise on the front line and to request air support.

In January, despite the first German units reaching Sicily initially, then Libya, Army units were withdrawn for Greece. The reason was a fear that the Germans were about to invade, which they did on 6 April. But by that time further RAF squadrons had been sent to Greece. The depletion of the Army and Air Force in the Western Desert was shortly to prove disastrous.

There had been changes to the structure of the RAF and Dominion air forces since March 1940, as illustrated in Table 4.2. Number 251 Wing had disbanded while 250 Wing was limited to just one General Reconnaissance Unit (GRU) with several Wellington mine de-gaussing aircraft. The units of 253 Wing had transferred into 202 Group in June and several squadrons had been transferred to Greece following the Italian invasion on 28 October, including 30, 84 and 211 (Blenheim) and 80 (Gladiator) sqns, plus a flight of Wellingtons from 70 Sqn. Significantly, 257 Wing was created on 20 December at Shallufa, comprising three Wellington squadrons (two recently arrived from the UK), plus 216 Sqn with Bombay bomber/transports. The final (for the time being) adjustment came with the formation on 1 January 1941 of 258 (semi-mobile advanced fighter) Wing at Aboukir, comprising three Hurricane squadrons, now intended to move forward with the Army.

A flight of 3 Sqn RAAF Gladiators over Gerawla. *Author's collection*

Table 4.2 – British and Dominion air force units, Egypt, December 1940

Sqn	Type	Base	Role
AHQ Egypt Maaten Bagush (ex 202 Group)			
258 (Mobile Fighter) Wing			
33	Hurricane I	Fuka	F
73	Hurricane	Dekheila	F
274	Hurricane I	Sidi Haneish	F
252 (Fighter) Wing			
112	Gladiator	Sidi Haneish	F
3 RAAF	Gladiator, Gauntlet	Maryut	F
253 (Bomber) Wing			
55	Blenheim IV	Fuka	LB
45	Blenheim I	Qotaifiya	LB
113	Blenheim IV	LG68	LB
257 (Bomber) Wing			
37	Wellington	Fayid	B
38	Wellington	Fayid	B
70	Wellington	Kabrit	B
216	Bombay	Heliopolis	B/Trspt
Army Co-operation			
6	Lysander	Qasaba	AC
208	Lysander, Hurricane	Qasaba	AC
203 Group			
228	Sunderland I	Alexandria	AS
230	Sunderland I	Alexandria	AS
HQ ME Command			
11	Blenheim I	Helwan, Fuka	LB
39	Blenheim I	Helwan, Qotaifiya	LB
267	Various comms types	Heliopolis	Comms

East Africa

When Italy declared war, British forces in East Africa and Aden were spread thinly and equipped mostly with outdated equipment. The Italians occupied Abyssinia, Eritrea and Italian Somaliland with some 330,000 troops and 200 aircraft. To the west of Abyssinia and Eritrea, Sudan had two squadrons (47 and 223) of Wellesley light bombers, 14 Sqn with Gladiators and Blenheims and a flight of 112 Sqn Gladiators. The Sudan units were formed into 203 Group from August 1940 under Air Cdre L. H. Slatter.

The Gladiators were first complemented, and then replaced, by Hurricanes. Mk I P2544/YK-C of 274 Sqn is here at Amriya in October 1940 about to have the trolley-acc connected. *Author's collection*

Lysanders featured in the early stages of the desert war in the Army co-operation role with both 6 and 208 Sqns. Mk II L6876/JV-U 6 Sqn in 1940. *AST collection*

Table 4.3 – RAF and Dominion units in Sudan, June 1940–November 1941

Sqn	Type	Base	From	To
Dominion air units Sudan				
47	Vincent, Wellesley	Carthago, Malakal, Sennar	6.40	21.12.40
	Wellesley	Gordon's Tree, Asmara	21.12.40	
223	Wellesley	Summit, Gazouza	6.40	10.4.41
14	Gladiator, Blenheim IV	Port Sudan	6.40	9.4.41
112 Flt	Gladiator I, II (to K Flt)	Summit, Carthago, Gedaref	3.6.40	20.8.40
K Flt	Gladiator (ex 112 Sqn)	Port Sudan	20.8.40	9.12.40
K Flt	Gladiator	Mersa Tachai	13.2.41	10.4.41
45	Blenheim I	Carthago	29.7.40	28.11.40
430 Flt/ 1430 Flt	Gauntlet, Vincent	Khartoum, Gedaref, Gazouza, Blackdown	3.8.40	10.4.41
1 SAAF	Gladiator det	Khartoum	7.8.40	31.10.40
	Fury, Hurricane	Khartoum, Gazouza	9.40	31.10.40
	Gladiator, Hurricane	Gazouza, Port Sudan, Tessebei	31.10.40	6.4.41
237	Hardy, Lysander	Gordon's Tree, Blackdown, Barentu, Asmara	18.9.40	26.5.41
94	Gladiator	Berbera	20.3.41	28.3.41
GRB 1[A]	Blenheim IV	Gordon's Tree, Asmara	11.3.41	13.8.41
CSG[B]	Battle, Hartbees, Gladiator		21.5.41	
51 Flt SAAF	Ju 52/3m	Khartoum	4.41	
16 SAAF	Ju 86 (ex 12 Sqn), Maryland (to 35 Flt)	Addis Ababa	1.5.41	18.8.41
41 SAAF	Hartbees	Addis Ababa	1.5.41	
3 SAAF	Hurricane	Addis Ababa	18.7.41	27.8.41
35 Flt SAAF	Maryland (ex 16 Sqn)	Addis Ababa, Aiscia	18.8.41	
3 SAAF	Mohawk	Aiscia, Alomata	15.9.41	

Note:
A – Free French Bomber Flight
B – Close Support Group

To the south of Abyssinia, Kenya had four Dominion squadrons. 1, 11 and 12 Sqns, South African Air Force (SAAF), were equipped respectively with a Fury/Hurricane mix, Hartbees (a tropicalised version of the RAF's Hawker Audax) and Ju 86 (airliner converted to bomber). 1 Sqn, Southern Rhodesian Air Force (SRAF), flying the Audax, Hardy and Hart, was re-numbered 237 Sqn RAF to avoid confusion with 1 Sqn SAAF. OC RAF East Africa was Gp Capt (shortly to be Air Cdre) W. Sowrey.

At various times Hurricanes served with 1, 2 and 3 Sqns in East Africa. This somewhat worn aircraft displays the markings of 3 Sqn and is probably seen at Gordon's Tree. *Tinus le Roux*

Table 4.4 – Dominion units in Kenya, June 1940 – November 1941

Sqn	Type	Base	From	To
Dominion air units Kenya				
237	Audax, Hardy, Hart	Nairobi dets Buna, Malindini, Garissa, Wajir, Umritsar	6.40	18.9.40
1 SAAF	Fury, Hurricane	Mombasa	6.40	30.9.40
	Gladiator (to 2 Sqn)	Mombasa	24.7.40	30.9.40
11 SAAF	Hartbees (to 40 Sqn)	Archers Post	6.40	18.6.40
	Battle	Archers Post, Husseini, Vitooria d'Africa, Jijiga	12.8.40	5.6.41
12 SAAF	Ju 86 (to 16 Sqn)	Nairobi, Garissa W, Gobwen, Mogadishu	6.40	30.4.41
40 SAAF	Hartbees (ex 11 Sqn)	Archers Post, Marsabit, Neghelli	18.6.40	21.5.41
PR Flt	Envoy, Double Eagle	Nairobi	22.6.40	28.11.40
60 SAAF	Anson (ex PR Flt)	Nairobi	28.11.40	24.4.41
2 SAAF	Fury (ex 1 Sqn),	Mombasa, Nanyuki, Garissa E	1.10.40	17.4.41
	Gladiator, Hurricane			
3 SAAF	Hurricane	Mombasa, Nairobi, Aligabe, Garissa W, Jijiga	24.10.40	18.7.41
41 SAAF	Hartbees	Garissa, Buna, Mogadishu, Jijiga, Combolcia, Alomata	11.40	30.4.41
14 SAAF	Maryland	Nanyuki, Nairobi	5.12.40	24.4.41
34 Flt SAAF	Anson	Mombasa	20.12.40	
50 SAAF	Valentia, Rapide	Nairobi	12.40	
CSF[A]	Hartbees, Gladiator	Buna, Miesso, Combolcia	4.41	
15 SAAF	Battle (ex 11 Sqn)	Jijiga	5.6.41	19.8.41

Note:
A – Close Support Flight

Across the Red Sea from British Somaliland were four RAF squadrons at Aden. Long-term resident 8 Sqn was still flying the Vincent as part of a hotchpotch that included Blenheim, Swordfish and Martin Maryland; 39, just arrived from India, and 203 Sqns flew the Blenheim while the air defence unit, 94 Sqn, managed with the Gladiator.

The Italians occupied a great deal of territory, but its forces were isolated and supply hazardous from the homeland via Libya. In contrast, Dominion forces in effect surrounded the Italians and had easier supply lines from Egypt to the north and South Africa/Kenya to the south.

Battle was joined on 11 June 1940 when 47 Sqn Wellesleys raided Asmara (Eritrea) and 12 Sqn SAAF Ju 86s struck Moyale. During the next few months there was ongoing air combat as each side made bombing raids and defended against them. From the outset the Italian land and air forces fought strongly and, indeed, chivalrously, but gradually attrition hit the *Regia Aeronautica* more severely than it did the Dominion air forces.

Italian troops made an incursion into northern Kenya on the 18th, taking El Wak and on 4 July attacked Kassala in Sudan, across the border from Eritrea. In August much of British Somaliland was occupied, the few troops stationed there being evacuated across the Red Sea to Aden. Gradually, while the Allied air forces fought for air superiority, their slender resources were reinforced whereas those of the Italians weakened. Nonetheless, the Allied air forces needed every serviceable aircraft. As an indication of the pressure on availability, there were two instances of transports being pressed into service as bombers. On 4 August a Bombay of 216 Sqn bombed Zula near Diredawa and on the 14th a SAAF Valentia dropped a home-made oil drum weapon on an Italian fort on the Kenyan border.

Table 4.5 – RAF units, Aden, June 1940–November 1941

Sqn	Type	Base	From	To
British Forces Aden				
94	Gladiator I, II	Khormaksar, det Berbera, Sheikh Othman	6.40	19.4.41
8	Vincent, Blenheim I, Swordfish, Maryland I	Khormaksar, det Berbera	6.40	10.41
39	Blenheim I	Sheikh Othman	6.40	22.11.40
203	Blenheim I, IVF	Khormaksar	6.40	10.4.41
11	Blenheim I	Sheikh Othman	15.6.40	22.11.40
223	Wellesley det	Perim Island	13.8.40	11.40
GP Flt	Vincent (ex 8 Sqn)	Khormaksar	22.11.40	26.5.41

Blenheim I
L8376/UQ-D 211 Sqn.
Luca G. Canossa

In the south, 11 Sqn SAAF had donated its Hartbees army support aircraft to 40 Sqn, having itself re-equipped with Battles, while a PR flight had formed at Nairobi, later to grow into 60 Sqn. In October two fighter squadrons, numbers 2 and 3, came up from South Africa to Mombasa with Furies, Gladiators and a few Hurricanes and 41 Sqn, with more Hartbees, formed at Garissa in November. Elsewhere, 14 Sqn formed in December with Marylands at Nanyuki, north of Nairobi and a new coastal reconnaissance flight, number 34, was created with Ansons at Mombasa. On the debit side, 237 Sqn was reassigned to Sudan.

By the end of the year 1st South African Division and three independent brigades were ready for the assault on southern Abyssinia and Italian Somaliland respectively.

The situation in Sudan was broadly similar. 112 Squadron had sent a flight of Gladiators from Egypt, followed by 45 Sqn's Blenheims in July. In August, a utility army support unit, 430 (later 1430) Flt formed with Gauntlet and Vincent and flights of 1 Sqn SAAF joined them periodically from Kenya, together with 237 Sqn in September. Aden had also been reinforced with another Blenheim squadron, No 11, arriving from India mid-June.

The Dominion air forces kept up steady bombardment of military objectives, especially airfields and motor parks, but also against Italian forces occupying new bases in Kenya and Sudan. On 31 October Lt Gen Alan Cunningham was appointed OC East Africa forces in preparation for the invasion of Italian Somaliland. In the north, the first British offensive of the Second World War kicked off on 6 November to recover Gallabat, taken by the end of the day, albeit with the loss of five Gladiators.

The next attack was in Kenya, from 15 December, to oust the Italians from El Wak before invading Somaliland. On the right, 22 East African Brigade would fight from Buna to the port of Kismayu, 24 Gold Coast Brigade from Garissa and 1 South African Brigade from Wajir. They were to enjoy integrated air support from 40 Sqn Hartbees, 12 Sqn Ju 86s and four Hurricanes of 2 Sqn, all located near to the front. At this time 4th Indian Division arrived at Port Sudan from the Western Desert, as did more Hurricanes for 1 Sqn SAAF. In Aden, 8 Sqn divided its Vincents to form a provisional General Purpose Flight (GPF) to combat local incursion.

In mid-January Kismayu fell while to the west 25th East African Bde, supported by 40 Sqn SAAF, advanced into Abyssinia along Lake Rudolph. In the north, British forces occupied Kassala and the East Africa war became a true tri-service affair when naval forces bombed Mogadishu and mined its harbour. The force comprised 826 and 829 NAS with Albacores and 803 NAS with Fulmars, flying off HMS *Formidable* on 2 February. 1 Bomber Brigade, comprising the Kenya-based SAAF bombers, was renamed 2 Wing and the OTUs in Nairobi were closed temporarily in anticipation of their aircraft and instructors being required for the forthcoming offensive.

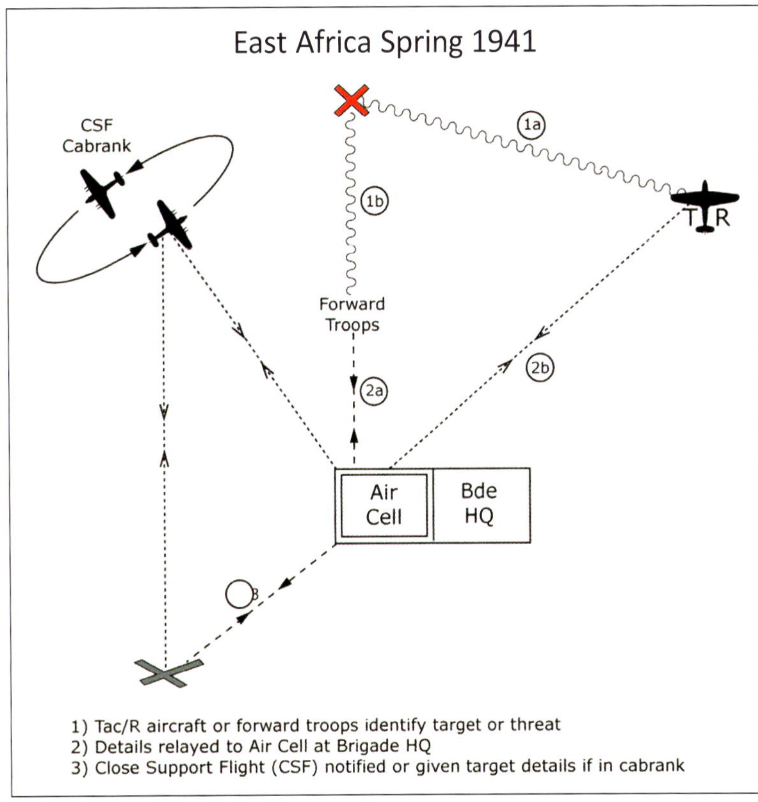

Several squadrons in the Middle East got away with employing flamboyant markings, sometimes in place of unit codes. Here a rigger is applying the finishing touches to a 274 Sqn lightning flash on Hurricane I V7830. *Author's collection*

The African divisions in the south made steady progress and, as they moved forward, their close-support Hartbees from 40 and 41 Sqns moved with them. Afmadu fell on 11 February, Kismayu on the 14th and Mogadishu on the 20th. Swordfish of 814 NAS, embarked on HMS *Hermes*, had flown several bombing missions against Kismayu. The heavy cruiser HMS *Shropshire* was also off the coast and shelled the port of Modum, directed by a Maryland of 14 Sqn SAAF. HMS *Formidable* was now in the Red Sea and fourteen of her Albacores bombed Massawa in Eritrea.

Already in Sudan when Italy declared war were two squadrons of obsolescent Wellesley bombers. Included in the inventory of 223 Sqn based at Summit was L2673/X of 223 Sqn. *Author's collection*

By the beginning of March, 1 Sqn had at last re-equipped fully with Hurricanes, passing its Gladiators to 237 Sqn. A number of squadrons, their aircraft the worse for wear from intense flying, were now based at Mogadishu, ready for the push north towards Jijiga in Abyssinia. A small but symbolic and welcome reinforcement came in the form of Blenheim IVs of the Free French GRB 1, which operated under the auspices of 47 Sqn.

As an indication of the close co-operation between the SAAF and the Army, on 8 March 1941 a Maryland of 12 Sqn SAAF flew 700 miles from Mogadishu to Awash where a bridge was photographed.[5] From the films, accurate measurements were made and a replacement Bailey bridge constructed on the assumption that the Italians would blow the bridge in the face of the Allied advance – which they did.

Berbera in British Somaliland was taken by a small force from Aden on 20 March, covered by Blenheims of 203 Sqn and Gladiators of 94 Sqn, the latter remaining there to help consolidate gains. Asmara was occupied on 1 April and the following day Swordfish of 813 and 824 NAS from HMS *Eagle*, together with Blenheims of 14 and 223 Sqns, attacked ships attempting to leave Massawa.

With most of Eritrea and the Somalilands now in Allied hands, on 3 April the AOC Middle East, AM Sir Arthur Longmore, called a conference of the AOCs for Sudan, East Africa and Aden, to discuss the final arrangements for clearing Italian strongholds in northern Abyssinia, the capital of which, Addis Ababa, was taken on the 5th.

In a most important development, the previously close ties between land and air forces fostered by Sowrey were strengthened by the creation of a close support flight. This comprised four Gladiators and four Hartbees under the control of 22 East Africa Brigade, within which there was a close support controller with a small air cell. Even with the few aircraft available, sorties were mounted to cover advancing troops, signalling the first fully-integrated and operational Allied close support organisation of the war. While there is no evidence of formal analysis and reporting back to the Air Ministry in London, Longmore would have been aware of this highly significant development and, once they had shifted to the Western Desert, many of the South African pilots would have become accustomed to close co-operation with land forces.

The Allies having achieved almost complete air superiority, 203 Group was now stripped of a number of its units for transfer to the Western Desert where the situation had become perilous. Accordingly, 14, 223, 237 Sqns, 1 Sqn SAAF and K and 1430 Flts, departed for Egypt. With them went 94 and 203 Sqns from Aden and 14 Sqn SAAF from Kenya. Despite heavy losses the Italians were instructed to hold out in order to pin down as many Dominion forces as possible in order to provide relief for the German advance in Libya.

A flight of Gloster Gladiators of 112 Sqn was also in Sudan in early 1940. Gladiator II N5839/RT-Z, seen here in Egypt, was one of its charges. *Author's collection*

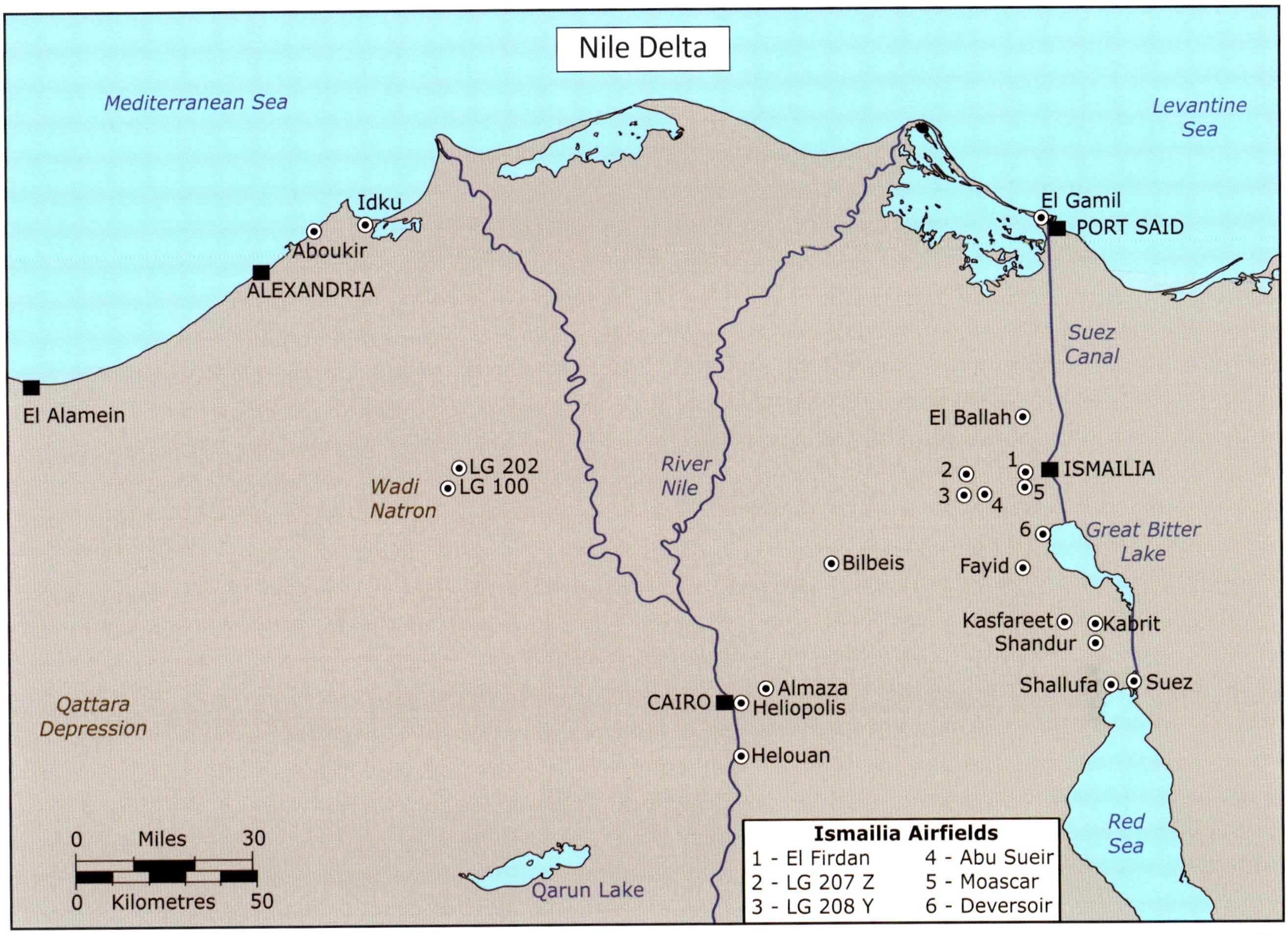
Nile Delta
Mediterranean Sea
Levantine Sea
Idku
Aboukir
ALEXANDRIA
El Alamein
El Gamil
PORT SAID
Suez Canal
El Ballah
1
ISMAILIA
2
3
4
5
6
LG 202
LG 100
Wadi Natron
River Nile
Great Bitter Lake
Bilbeis
Fayid
Kasfareet
Kabrit
Shandur
Shallufa
Suez
Almaza
CAIRO
Heliopolis
Helouan
Qattara Depression
Red Sea
Qarun Lake
0 Miles 30
0 Kilometres 50
Ismailia Airfields
1 - El Firdan
2 - LG 207 Z
3 - LG 208 Y
4 - Abu Sueir
5 - Moascar
6 - Deversoir

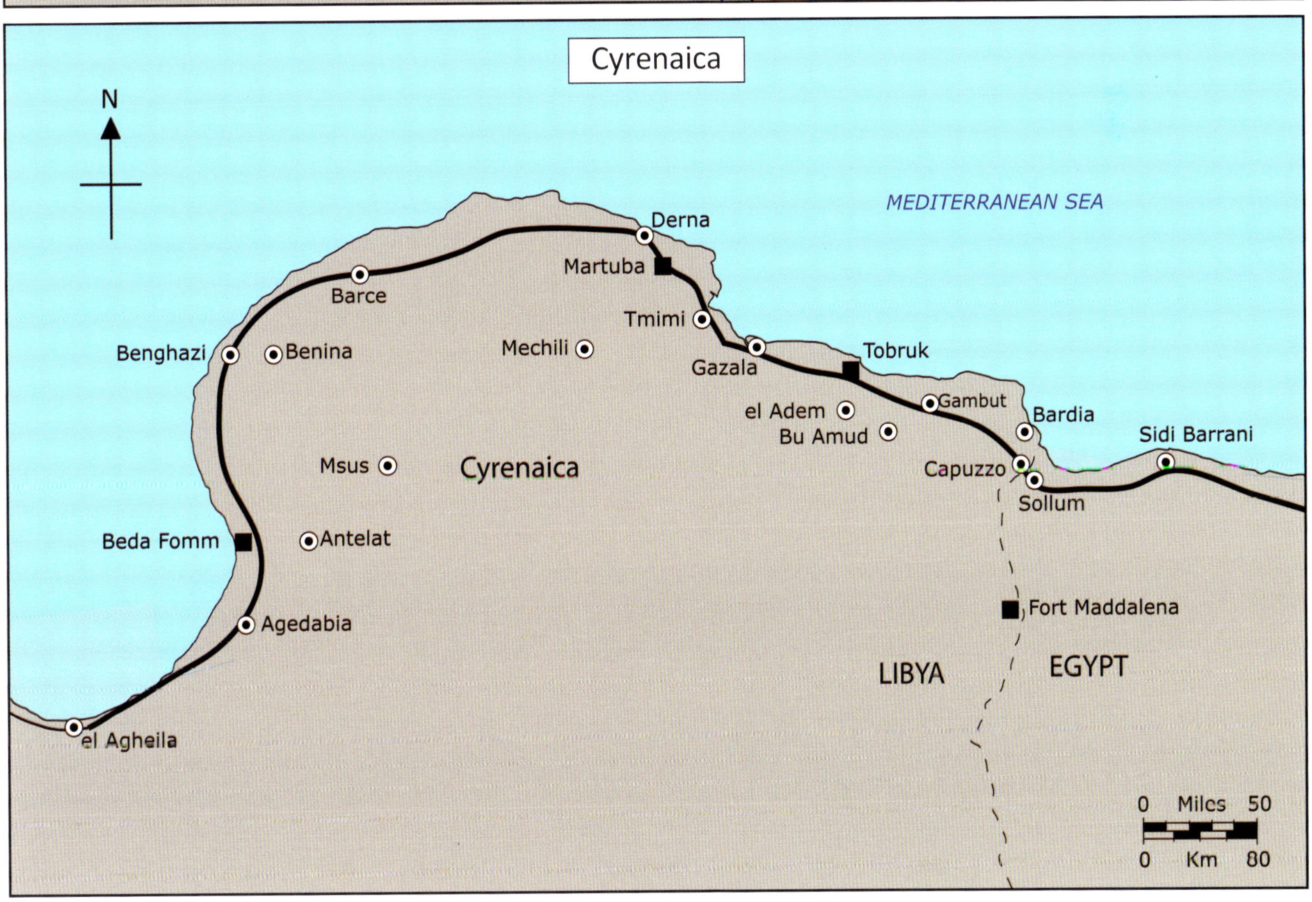
Cyrenaica
N
MEDITERRANEAN SEA
Derna
Martuba
Barce
Tmimi
Benghazi
Benina
Mechili
Gazala
Tobruk
Gambut
el Adem
Bu Amud
Bardia
Sidi Barrani
Msus
Cyrenaica
Capuzzo
Sollum
Beda Fomm
Antelat
Fort Maddalena
Agedabia
LIBYA
EGYPT
el Agheila
0 Miles 50
0 Km 80

The Gladiator's open-cockpit predecessor, the Gauntlet, was also involved in the East Africa campaign in small numbers. This South African Gauntlet II of 2 Sqn appears to have light stores racks fitted under the wings. *Author's collection*

This photo of Vincent K4883 is a bit of a mystery. *South African Air Force at War* gives it as being with 24 Sqn in East Africa in 1941, possible since the squadron formed at Nakuru in March of that year. The official record card gives the aircraft as having been operated by 8 Sqn in Aden and struck off charge in October 1940. In any event, Vincents were operated by 8 Sqn across the Red Sea. *SAAF*

The Gladiator served extensively in the early years of the war in East Africa and the Middle East. N2287 coded G-EO originally served with 94 Sqn but is seen here in South African service at Jijiga in May 1941. *Author's collection*

A Close Support Flight (later Group) was attached to 22 East African Brigade and provided immediate coordinated cover for advancing forces. The Flight included Gladiators and Hartbees as typified by aircraft 429 of 40 SAAF. *Author's collection*

Notwithstanding the start of the rainy season, fighting in northern Abyssinia continued. Dessie was taken on 26 April and Amba Alagi on 18 May, leaving the Italians cooped up at Gondar. 41 Sqn SAAF and what was now the Close Support Group at Combolcia, near Dessie, remained to support the final assault on Gondar. By July the *Regia Aeronautica* presence in Abyssinia comprised just two CR.42 fighters and a sole Caproni Ca.133 bomber. Late in August, 3 Sqn SAAF relinquished its Hurricanes, the pilots collecting from Nairobi newly prepared Curtiss Mohawks with which they returned to Aiscia mid-September. On 15 September a Command restructuring saw Lt Gen Sir William Platt heading East Africa Command and Sowrey given overall charge of the air forces (apart from Aden), that now comprised 2 Wing SAAF and 47 Sqn.

In a final attempt to reinforce its presence at Gondar with troops and supplies, the Italians sent SM.75 transports down the Red Sea and into Jibuti (now Djibouti) in (Vichy) French Somaliland: the Mohawks of 3 Sqn SAAF were charged with intercepting them. The final assault on Gondar was not until November, the outpost surrendering finally on the 27th.

The Hardy was a Hawker Hart development for use in the Middle East. 47 were built and after service with 30 then 6 Sqn the balance were transferred to 237 Sqn one of whose DV coded aircraft is seen in East Africa. The large low-pressure tyres are just visible.
Tinus le Roux

A wide variety of resources was applied to supporting the Army including a Bombay of 216 Sqn, which bombed Zula near Diredawa on 4 August 1940. In this photo, showing the unusual refuelling pump, L5522 is seen at Heliopolis in 1941. *Author's collection*

The latest fighter to be added to the SAAF inventory and used in Ethiopia was the Curtis Mohawk IV. Although slower than the Hurricane it had longer range and could carry a 400lb bomb load. 2506 of 3 Sqn in Ethiopia during operations against Gondar.
AST collection

The simple close air support arrangement organised by the newly promoted Air Cdre Sowrey had worked admirably. After victory in the region General Cunningham had this to say of the (primarily) South African Air Force contribution:[6]

> '...its air force commander with his own communication advanced with the commander of the leading troops. The value of this arrangement from the army point of view cannot be over stressed [*sic*]. Air support for the forward troops of the nature called for by the situation was 'on tap', and engendered the greatest confidence amongst both commanders and men.'

'On tap' refers to the limited, but in terms of morale critical, precursor to the cab-ranks of fighters, not to be seen in the air war until two years later.

The Hawker Hartbees was a development of the Audax built under licence in South Africa. It had a slightly more powerful engine (608bhp compared to 530bhp) and additional armoured crew protection. Aircraft 813 of 41 Sqn SAAF is at Addis Ababa in 1941, where a transport Ju 52/3m is undergoing maintenance. *Author's collection*

The SAAF converted fifteen Ju-86Z transports to the maritime reconnaissance and bomber role to serve with a single K model. The bomber was used extensively in East Africa, first with 12 Sqn, then with 16 Sqn. The externally carried bomb-load is clearly visible. *Tinus le Roux*

Distractions and Diversions

Though Dominion forces had occupied Libya westwards as far as El Agheila, there was anxiety because it was clear that Germany was about to play a significant part in the Mediterranean. All resources – land, sea and air – were now stretched thinly across the region, not in East Africa alone.

The Italian invasion of Greece in October 1940 had resulted in the transfer of a number of RAF squadrons there, depleting those available to defend the Army against any assault in Libya. On the 30th Air Cdre J. H. D'Albiac, AOC RAF Palestine and Transjordan, was sent to Greece to organise an Air Component. The initial RAF deployment in November comprised 30, 84 and 211 Sqns with Blenheims and the trusty Gladiators of 80 Sqn. In January 1941 they were joined by the Gladiators of 112 Sqn and 11 Sqn with Blenheims, followed a month later by 33 Sqn's Hurricanes. The final addition before the Germans invaded in April was yet another Blenheim squadron, 113, taking the total to five. Post-invasion, 208 Sqn Lysanders and Hurricanes were brought in, supplemented for a week by Beaufighters of 252 Sqn, which were en route from the UK to Egypt.

The action on Greece, and later Syria, also diverted the support available from other Egypt-based units. This included three Wellington bomber squadrons (37, 38 and 70), 216 Sqn's transports, 230 Sqn's Sunderland maritime patrol and specialist units like de-gaussing Wellingtons and 2 PRU. But air support was not solely down to the RAF. The Royal Navy had on hand three carriers between January and April and their aircraft, some temporarily shore-based, took an active part in Greek operations. They were, with their embarked squadrons:

HMS *Eagle* – 805 det Fulmar; 813, 824 Swordfish

HMS *Formidable* – 803, 805 det, 806 det Fulmar; 826 Albacore; 829 Swordfish, Albacore

HMS *Illustrious* – 806 Fulmar; 815, 819 Swordfish

The Gladiators were supplemented by Hurricanes of 33 Sqn also from Amriya. Hurricane I V7419/NW-? with pilots at a cold Larissa in April 1941. In the centre, recumbent in leather flying jacket, is Sqn Ldr M. T. St John Pattle, the highest-scoring RAF pilot with forty-plus victories. *Crown copyright*

Beaufighters of 252 Sqn were employed for a short time to cover the evacuation of British forces from Greece. Tired-looking Beaufighter Mk If T4831/BT-D. *Author's collection*

On Crete in mid-May the remnants of 33, 80 and 112 Sqns – around a dozen Hurricanes – plus a few Fulmars of 805 NAS, tried to protect 28,500 troops against 650 aircraft of the *Luftwaffe*. Needless to say, ground forces were once more subject to concerted attack by an enemy that had total air superiority. Yet, despite that, 50% of troops were evacuated. But it cost the Navy dearly, with the loss of three cruisers and six destroyers plus many more warships damaged. The Army claimed that the RAF had deserted it, and in the aftermath the Royal Navy pressed for a functional Coastal Command in Egypt to cover ships of the Mediterranean Fleet. In Greece, D'Albiac had applied his limited resources not in support of the Army but in strategic bombing (by a handful of Wellingtons and Blenheim Is) and in air defence.

Following the collapse in Greece and evacuation of Allied forces from Crete at the end of May there would then be insurrection in Iraq (April/May), followed immediately by involvement in Syria and Lebanon (June/July). In each case a commitment was required from the RAF.

And there was one other vital obligation to be fulfilled in the Mediterranean, essential to the British ability to wage war – the defence of Malta. Both fortress and harbour, the small island, only twenty minutes flying time from Sicily, had limited air cover initially. At the beginning of 1941 its safeguard was in the hands of just a Maryland reconnaissance squadron (No 69), Sunderlands of 228 Sqn, whose operational patch extended to Alexandria and of 830 NAS with Albacores for anti-shipping strikes. Protecting these was 261 Sqn with a handful of Sea Gladiators and Hurricanes. The perilous position of Malta was such that some reserves and reinforcements needed for operations in the Western Desert had to be diverted to the island.

The widespread distribution of RAF squadrons to address one crisis after another did nothing for the cause of better Army co-operation. Indeed, dissipation of forces almost certainly held back any chance of structural improvement

Rommel and the Western Desert

On 12 February 1941 *Generalleutnant* Erwin Rommel arrived in Tripoli as head of the *Afrika Korps*, comprising at that time the 5th Motorised and 15th *Panzer* Divisions. It was supported by *Luftwaffe* units in Sicily and elements of StG 1 Ju 87s and ZG 26 Bf 110s in Libya. A week later RAF Cyrenaica was formed, controlling 258 Wing HQ at Benghazi and with the handful of aircraft available to it spread along the coastal airfields. With the Wing HQ was a mobile radar (216 AMES), which supported, from west to east, a flight of 208 Sqn at Agedabia, 3 Sqn RAAF at Benina and two flights each from 6 and 208 Sqn at Barce. The advanced element of 31 Air Stores Park (ASP) was also located at Barce. Farther back, protecting the vital port of Tobruk with its own 235 AMES radar, were 73 Sqn Hurricanes at Gazala, a flight of 70 Sqn Wellingtons at El Adem (which also housed the core of 31 ASP and 51 RSU) and finally 55 Sqn Blenheims at Bu Amud.

In March, Rommel began probing the British defences, now depleted by the loss of three divisions and two brigades to Greece, and on the 11th 258 Wing began to withdraw to Tobruk. The full-scale attack started on 31 March, Stukas bombing retreating troops and Allied fighter squadrons moving back. The Germans reached Derna on 6 April, by which time 73 Sqn was at Bu Amud with a radar unit.

First aircraft deployed to Greece were Blenheims of 30, 84 and 211 Sqn. Blenheim I L6670/UO-? Is here landing, possibly at Tatoi, after a raid on troop concentrations in Albania late in 1940. *Author's collection*

Charged with escorting the light bombers and also protecting friendly troops from attach by enemy aircraft, the Hawker Hurricane bore the brunt of air combat in the Western Desert from 1940 to 1942. Hurricane IIB BE334 of 274 Sqn in late 1941 carrying underwing fuel tanks. *Author's collection*

The main vehicle for delivering bombs close to the front line was the Bristol Blenheim. This Mk I of 45 Sqn is seen here at Fuka. *Author's collection*

Connected and ready to go. This anonymous Hurricane I is seen in a typical Western Desert setting. *Author's collection*

The Allied withdrawal was at best uncoordinated, so much so that on 3 April 6 Sqn, under the control of 2nd Armoured Division at Antelat, found that the Division had moved back without a word. The Army claimed subsequently that it had been misinformed by a tactical reconnaissance report of a large enemy force (actually a Long Range Desert Group patrol) converging on Msus, which was a main supply and fuel dump. The RAF rejoinder was to the effect that the pilot reported what he saw – it was up to the attached Army intelligence officer to interpret the report. This was yet another pointer to the need for systematic improvements in Army co-operation. On 8 April, as a result of poor communications, a significant part of Wavell's forces was captured at Mechili while waiting for 3rd Armoured Brigade, which had been overwhelmed at Derna.

Tobruk was surrounded by 10 April and two days later 3 Sqn RAAF was back at Mersa Matruh. Petrol and stores at Sollum were destroyed to avoid them falling into enemy hands. Tobruk was held by 20,000 troops, mainly Australian, who were subjected to Stuka attacks. On 14 May seventy aircraft bombed the harbour to try to prevent resupply by sea of the beleaguered garrison. Holding Tobruk was essential in order to deny Rommel a forward supply base.

The Allied air forces continued to do their best to cover the retreat and on 16 April Hurricanes of 3 Sqn RAAF covered a Walrus of 700 NAS, catapulted from the cruiser HMS *Gloucester*, spotting for her guns in a bombardment of Bardia. The fighters were also protecting Blenheim bombers attacking German-held airfields. On the 17th 3 Sqn was withdrawn to begin conversion to the Curtiss Tomahawk. By mid-April Allied forces had withdrawn to the border, maintaining a defensive line south from Bardia, but also holding Tobruk. On the night of 30 April Rommel attacked the town, but had to withdraw after a fierce counter-offensive by the Australians destroyed more than half his tanks. Ominously, Bf 109 fighters of JG 27 now started appearing, despite which the Hurricanes of 274 Sqn tried to protect the Tobruk garrison from strafing attacks.

Gladiator II SAAF N5852 1 Sqn. *Luca G. Canossa*

After short-term failure to take Tobruk, Rommel was ordered to withdraw and build resources ready for a further attack. The order was picked up by *Ultra* intercept and Wavell was instructed to take the offensive immediately, mounting an attack in Operation *Brevity*.

Even as Crete was being invaded by the Germans, a key convoy of five merchant ships with escorts, part of Operation *Tiger*, was hurrying to Alexandria. One, the SS *Empire Song*, hit several mines and exploded, but the remaining vessels were able to land 238 tanks and sixty-four Hurricanes, beginning 12 May.

Operation *Brevity*, launched towards Sollum on 15 May at little more than brigade strength, was unfortunately named. After reaching Capuzzo the force, including more than eighty tanks, was repulsed and the operation called off after just twenty-four hours. Fighter cover had been provided by 73, 274 and 1 SAAF Sqns, all with Hurricanes, while the Blenheims of 14, 45 and 55 Sqns were available to attack enemy ground forces. Later, on 27 May, German forces recaptured the important Halfaya Pass in Operation *Skorpion*.

The RAF now maintained pressure on Axis troops with strafing attacks and bombing raids on airfields, costing a number of Blenheims brought down by Bf 109s of JG 27. Then, from 23 May, 204 Group light bombers were heavily involved in the Cretan operations with the further loss of aircraft and aircrew.

Table 4.6 – RAF Units Egypt, 1 June 1941

Unit	Type	Base
202 Group RAF Cairo		
228	Sunderland I	Alexandria
230	Sunderland I	Alexandria
2 JAF	Do 22K	Alexandria
272	Beaufighter Ic	Abu Sueir
13 RHAF	Anson 1	Dekheila
1 GRU	Wellington DWI	Ismailia
2 PRU	Maryland, Hurricane	Heliopolis
252 (Fighter) Wing		
30	Hurricane I	Amriya
94	Hurricane I	Ismailia
451	Hurricane I	Aboukir
112	Tomahawk	Fayid
805 NAS	Buffalo	Dekheila
257 (Heavy Bomber) Wing Shallufa		
37	Wellington IC	Shallufa
38	Wellington IC	Shallufa
70	Wellington IC	Kabrit
216	Valentia, Bombay	Heliopolis
148	Wellington IC	Kabrit
204 Group RAF Maaten Bagush		
253 (Army Co-operation) Wing Maaten Bagush		
1 SAAF	Hurricane IIB	Sidi Haneish
2 SAAF	Hurricane IIB	Sidi Haneish
274	Hurricane I	Gerawala
45	Blenheim IVF	Wadi Natrun
113	Blenheim IV, IVF	Maaten Bagush
39	Maryland I	Wadi Natrun
258 (Fighter) Wing Maaten Bagush		
6	Hurricane I	Qasaba
33	Hurricane I	Amriya
73	Hurricane I	Sidi Haneish
250	Tomahawk IIB	Sidi Haneish
259 (Medium Bomber) Wing		
14	Blenheim IV	LG 21
55	Blenheim IV	LG 95
203	Blenheim IV	Kabrit
12 SAAF	Maryland II	Shandur
24 SAAF	Maryland II	Shandur

Reorganisation and Another Failed Attack

There was now to be a number of significant changes. The AOC-in-C Middle East, Air Chief Marshal Sir Arthur Longmore, had been recalled to London on 3 May for consultations and during his stay had been relieved of his command. His uncompromising and direct approach annoyed Churchill, who had challenged consistently (and ignorantly) the demands for aircraft and personnel for RAF Middle East. Longmore's deputy, Air Marshal Arthur Tedder, was appointed in his stead.

A restructuring saw 202 Group retaining control of the heavy bombers and defence of the Egyptian Delta under AVM Thomas Elmhirst while 204 Group, now for the time being under Raymond Collishaw, controlled the tactical squadrons. Later in the year the two groups would evolve into AHQ Egypt and AHQ Western Desert respectively – one fixed, one mobile.

In June 1941 there was one further attempt at relieving Tobruk, Operation *Battleaxe*, involving XIII Corps and its 7th Armoured and 4th Indian infantry divisions. This operation, the first in which Tedder managed the Allied air effort, was important for the future of Army co-operation in several ways, primarily for the lessons learned and their subsequent application. The air and land commanders' HQs were 80 miles apart, the communications systems failed and there was rarely any effective indication of the bomb line. However, 204 Group applied its limited resources in such a cohesive way that all relevant and available airpower was applied as appropriate. Indeed, FAA pilots and a motley selection of fighters were incorporated into composite squadrons that also included pilots of newly arrived RAF squadrons still awaiting their ground crews.

RAF fighters provided high cover to protect advancing troops from Axis bombers and their fighter protection, but not the low-level airborne artillery that the Army felt it deserved. One notable addition to the armoury was a sole cannon-armed Hurricane, soon lost, but an indication of the shape of things to come in close-support. The official history of the RAF at war[7] had this to say:

Hurricanes of 73 Sqn escorting Blenheims over Derna. *Author's collection*

> 'The preliminary air action kept down activity by the enemy air force; and the approach-march of the troops on 14th June, and their operations on the following two days, were duly conducted under the fighter 'umbrella'. This served its purpose well.'

However, the umbrella was held high. From 9 June the RAF struck at the Axis airfields at Derna, Gazala and Martuba in an attempt to reduce the effectiveness of the *Luftwaffe* and *Regia Aeronautica*, although they appear to have made little impact. On 14 June, while the RAF undertook further strafing raids on airfields by Hurricanes led by Maryland 'navigators', the Allied force approached the front line in three elements. The armoured units had hurriedly brought into play some of the newly arrived tanks. However, in the short time he had had since *Brevity,* Rommel had improved his defences. While from the 15th the central force made headway, the flanking elements came unstuck and after three days withdrew with the loss of half of its tanks. By the 18th both sides were back where they had started.

Battleaxe was another expensive failure. The RAF alone lost thirty-one Hurricanes, four Tomahawks on their initial strafing outing with 250 Sqn, and three Marylands. Twenty-five aircrew were killed, mainly Hurricane pilots, and a number more were taken prisoner – and this all for the loss by the *Luftwaffe* of six Bf 109s, two Ju 87s and a Bf 110. The commanders now jointly took stock and gradually improvements were made in respect of integration.

Even as the battle was raging changes were being introduced. Recovery, repair and return of damaged aircraft was a shambles in Egypt, being just a part of the administration role. So on 17 June 206 (Maintenance) Group formed at Heliopolis under Air Cdre C. B. Cooke, who quickly improved the situation. In the immediate aftermath of the failure Wavell was replaced by Lt Gen Sir Claude Auchinleck and from now on he and Tedder co-operated closely in planning and operations. Formal relationships between Tedder and Admiral Cunningham were rather less cordial, the latter demanding his own 'Coastal Command' to provide long-range reconnaissance. At this stage, though, his warships were routinely departing Alexandria without advising the RAF, foolhardy to say the least.

A joint commanders conference in Cairo on 4 September discussed and agreed further details of air support. There was distinction drawn between direct and indirect support and recognition that in the former case – support on the battlefield – it was more productive to attack lines of communication than tanks or troops dispersed near the front line. As units of 253 Wing worked up with the Army a refined system of operating was determined. In the future each corps and armoured division would have an Air

Although the Gladiator had largely been superseded by the Hurricane or Tomahawk by 1941, a few were still around. Gladiator II N5851 of 6 Sqn is seen being recovered on a Fordson six-wheel lorry in 1941. *Author's collection*

In the early stages of the war in the Western Desert recovery and repair was slow and inefficient, not improving until 1942. Hurricane IIB BD930/R, being lowered by Coles crane onto a Queen Mary aircraft transporter, shows to good effect the distinctive markings of 73 Sqn. *Author's collection*

Support Control (ASC) linked by W/T to forward tentacles functioning with brigades. Brigades, in turn, would have an RAF Forward Air Support Link (FASL) with R/T to take advice from Tac/R aircraft. Bids for impromptu support, or immediate changes to planned support, would go via the ASC, which would evaluate and then pass back by landline to the Rear Air Support Link (RASL) for action.

Coincidental to the Cairo Conference, there was a similar debate in London presided over by Churchill. A key part of his instructional memorandum, dated 5 September 1941, is quoted in full by Hall.[8]

> 'Upon the military Commander-in-Chief in the Middle East announcing that a battle is in prospect, the Air Officer Commanding-in-Chief will give him all possible aid irrespective of other targets, however attractive. Victory in the battle makes amends for all, and creates new favourable situations of a decisive character. The Army Commander-in-Chief will specify to the Air Officer Commanding-in-Chief the targets and tasks which he requires to be performed, both in the preparatory attack on the rearward installations of the enemy and for air action during the progress of the battle.
>
> It will be for the AOC-in-C to use his maximum force on these objects in the manner most effective. This applies not only to any squadrons assigned to army co-operation permanently, but also to the whole air force available in the theatre. Bombers may, if required, be used as transport or supply machines to far ranging or outlying columns of troops, the sole object being the success of the military operation. As the interests of the two Cs-in-C are identical it is not thought that any difficulty should arise. The AOC-in-C would naturally lay aside all routine programmes and concentrate on bombing the rearward services of the enemy in the preparatory period. This he would do not only by night, but by day attacks with fighter protection. In this process he will bring about a trial of strength with the enemy fighters, and has the best chance of obtaining local command of the air. What is true of the preparatory period applies with even greater force during the battle. All assembly or refuelling points for marching columns of the enemy should be attacked by bombing during daylight with strong fighter protection, thus bringing about air conflicts not only of the highest importance in themselves but directly contributing to the general result.'

Wellingtons usually operated at night against concentrations near the front line. These LF-coded Wellington IC bombers of 37 Sqn are out from their base at Shallufa. *Author's collection*

Large numbers of Ju 87 dive-bombers were employed by both German and Italian forces. Ju 87D-3 S7+EP of StG 3 was a captured example. *Author's collection*

With great clarity, in exactly 300 words, the Prime Minister, in his secondary role of Minister of Defence, spelled out both policy and procedure for air support. The principles of what the Army could expect were further described by Churchill,[9] in the context of the delivery of 250 Bofors AA guns to the Middle East for troop protection.

> 'Nevermore must the ground troops expect, as a matter of course, to be protected against the air by aircraft ... Above all, the idea of keeping standing patrols of aircraft over moving columns should be abandoned. It is unsound to distribute aircraft in this way, and no air superiority will stand any large application of such mischievous practice.'

During the summer there were further changes of personnel and structure. One of considerable future importance was the appointment of New Zealander AVM Arthur 'Maori' (corrupted to Mary) Coningham to command 204 Group on 30 July, replacing Collishaw. Then, on 3 October, 201 (Naval Co-operation) Group formed at Alexandria with Sunderland, Beaufighter and Beaufort squadrons. Later in the month 257 Wing was elevated to become 205 (Heavy Bomber) Group. There were also numerous – and frequent – changes to the designation and composition of wings that finally settled down in December after the start of the major offensive, Operation *Crusader*.

Through the summer and autumn of 1941 squadrons were preparing for the battle ahead, but for the sole, hard-pressed Army co-operation squadron it was the constant grind of business as usual. No 6 Sqn had gone to Palestine, then Sudan, while 208 was in Greece, then Palestine, leaving newly arrived 451 Sqn RAAF to hold the fort. (Although essentially a fighter unit, for a time in the summer 73 Sqn also acted in this role.) Under the command of XIII Corps and based at Qasaba, this notionally Australian squadron was little short of being dysfunctional with resentment against flying in a dangerous, non-glamorous and tedious role, being commanded by English officers and flying a mix of tired Lysanders and Hurricanes. The tasks of this unit – for which few of the pilots had been trained – were threefold.

- Tactical reconnaissance, or Tac/R, that meant flying as low as possible, noting dispositions of men and vehicles on map or kneepad and either dropping notes to army units or landing back and de-briefing the ALO.
- Artillery spotting, or Arty/R, that involved stooging around over the front line at 1,000ft and talking directly to a battery by R/T and correcting shot (now by distance fore and aft, or left and right, rather than by the dated clock method).
- Photo reconnaissance, Photo/R, that involved flying straight and level over a defined area at a prescribed height with no opportunity to deviate in order to avoid AA fire. The results were handled by squadron camera crews and then whisked to Corps HQ for interpretation.

The Valentia transport soldiered on for a few years into the war, as a transport bringing stores up to the advanced airfields. K3614/T of 70 Sqn had been adapted to have a dorsal gun mounting on the upper fuselage. *Author's collection*

Hartbees 851 41 Sqn.
Luca G. Canossa

Because of lack of experience, as fresh aircraft and pilots arrived from the UK they were attached to existing squadrons while their units were awaiting their groundcrew. This proved costly despite the 6 Sqn record saying, 'They are fighter pilots but can carry out simple tactical reconnaissance.'[10] Thus, six pilots from each of 213, 229 and 40 (SAAF) Sqns were attached to 73, 6 and 451 (RAAF) Sqns respectively. Lacking experienced support, four of the 229 Sqn trainees were shot down within a few days, two while flying their first mission.

It might be thought that equipment would be bespoke and flying procedures well organised, but clearly they were not. Flying Officer Geoffrey Morley-Mower, one of 451's English pilots, described the camera fit on the Hurricane:[11]

> 'Some of our Hurricanes were equipped with cameras, three of them, mounted to the rear of the pilot. The massive old-fashioned air cameras, designed for a larger platform than the frail Hurricane, weighed the tail down so badly that the nose would rise in flight even with the elevator trim fully forward. On these aircraft thick elastic cords fastened the stick to the dashboard, relieving the pilot of the physical effort of holding the nose level by main force. To climb the pilot didn't have to move the stick from its position of maximum dive. Half a notch on the elevator trim and the aircraft would lurch upward … This effectively turned a racehorse into a carthorse. The very thought of encountering fighters while flying one of these overburdened, unbalanced aircraft made one nervous.'

Speed on these sorties was restricted to around 180mph in order to get the right amount of overlap on photographs. Sorties were rarely short and could take two plus hours; they were flown with another squadron aircraft acting as cover and weaving to check for the presence of enemy fighters. Army co-operation Hurricanes were fitted with eight guns, but these were generally used for opportunistic strafing. Against the Bf 109 the Hurricane could fly only in tight circles, until the enemy ran out of fuel or ammunition or gave up. If there was time and distance, the alternative was to run for cover.

In terms of protection, it has often been stated that the Tac/R aircraft flew with fighter top cover. It might have been assumed that this was *formal policy* from above, but it appears not to have been so. Morley-Mower, by now a flight commander, described securing cover for a difficult sortie.[12] Having been assigned one on 15 November, to an area west of Gambut (35 miles beyond the front line) that involved flying over a clutch of well-defended airfields packed with fighters, it occurred to him to seek help:

> 'A wing of Hurricanes and Tomahawks [258 Wing] had begun to operate from LG110…and I had seen the sweeps going out. A fighter wing is an impressive sight. It had not occurred to me that they had much connection with us. They were the glamorous fighter types, an object of envy. They occupied a different sphere.
>
> We belonged to the same nation, the same service even. We flew over the same ground, but they could have been Russians for all that we knew of their operations. Being such amateurs at war, we had to learn everything from scratch, but we didn't have the luxury of being able to try, try, try again. The first time might easily be the last time. The Luftwaffe was out, but why was it out? My guess was that it was responding to the fighter wing, not to our puny little reconnaissance penetrations.'

The reference to the *Luftwaffe* 'being out' related to the loss of two 451 Sqn pilots on 12 November, shot down by Bf 109s while there was an Allied fighter sweep in progress thousands of feet above. As a consequence, Morley-Mower flew over to LG 110 with his cover pilot to ask Wg Cdr Kenneth Cross, OC 258 Wing, for protection for his own upcoming sortie. Cross apparently agreed and the two Tac/R pilots waited until a wing sweep was underway at 1400hrs, before following them off. The outcome was a successful sortie that was critical in terms of gathering information on Axis dispositions immediately before the *Crusader* offensive. (It later transpired that one of the senior Australian pilots had also informally scrounged fighter cover, but had failed to discuss it within the squadron!) Later, Morley-Mower observed:

> 'The connection I had discovered between the fighter operations and our recce sorties was valid for only two weeks. As the air war progressed our fighters gradually achieved air superiority and once again everything changed. But air superiority never fully applies to reconnaissance. The necessity to infiltrate enemy lines and to outfly fighters remained, and being low down we were always at some risk. A badly planned sortie, no matter how the air battle was going, could kill you.'

In June 1941 the Curtiss Tomahawk began replacing the Gladiators of 112 Sqn, as seen here with Tomahawk IIB AK461/A etc. at Sidi Haneish in July 1941. At this stage the squadron's GA unit code was not applied. *AST collection*

[1] TNA AIR 41/44 *The Middle East Campaign: Operations in Libya and the Western Desert, September 1939-June 1941*
[2] Terraine, *A Time for Courage,* p352
[3] 202 Group Operational Order No 39
[4] Ehlers, *The Mediterranean Air War,* p56
[5] Noted in Shores, *Dust Clouds in the Middle East,* p121
[6] Quoted in Pitchfork, *The Sowreys,* p 141
[7] Richards, *The Royal Air Force 1939-1945* volume 1, p336
[8] Hall, *Strategy for Victory,* p108
[9] Playfair, *History of the Second World War: The Mediterranean and Middle East* vol III, p287
[10] Noted in Shores vol 1 p226
[11] Morley-Mower, *Messerschmitt Roulette,* p40
[12] Morley-Mower, *Messerschmitt Roulette,* p120

Crusader and Gazala

The game of Western Desert ping-pong was now to take another turn. On 18 November 1941 the British Eighth Army struck westwards again, in the process relieving the garrison at Tobruk. By intercepting the Axis Mediterranean supply routes the Royal Navy and RAF made a major contribution to the forthcoming battles. More immediate support included the jamming of enemy tank communications. Air support was relatively unstructured, forward Army units not bothering to mark the front line and therefore heightening the risk of the RAF bombing friendly troops. Poor weather and difficulty in finding and preparing new landing grounds added to the lack of cohesive movement and close air support.

In a couple of months the Army had reached beyond Benghazi, but now suffered from extended supply lines and the withdrawal of some units for India, given that Britain was now also at war with Japan. In addition, the dire situation in Malta meant that some squadrons destined for Egypt and the Western Desert were detained on the island temporarily. On a more positive note, the Kittyhawk and the improvements in performance and ordnance carrying that came with it, was beginning to replace the Tomahawk and the first Hurricane tank-busters were ready for service.

In January 1942 German General Erwin Rommel struck east against the depleted British Army. Despite 2 Army Air Support Control arriving from the UK in March, the intended system for close air support was found wanting in retreat. By June Axis forces had crossed into Egypt and were halted at El Alamein, just 80 miles short of Alexandria.

Operation *Crusader*

From June 1941 the RAF and Dominion air forces had received more aircraft, the army more tanks and guns. Tobruk had been held bravely and despite the best attempts of the Axis air forces and navies, resupplied regularly by sea. In the autumn, though, the Australian government regrettably, but understandably, insisted on withdrawal of its forces from the port, a process that added significantly to the problems confronting the planners. Fighter aircraft were now required to move from the offensive to the defensive, flying patrols over convoys. In due course airfields in the vicinity of Tobruk had become untenable, but from time to time Tac/R Hurricanes of 451 Sqn had been based on a small strip on the clifftop.

Before summarising Operation *Crusader* it is worth a reminder of the context. On 22 June Germany had turned on the Soviet Union in Operation *Barbarossa*, abrogating its non-aggression pact and quickly making considerable headway. Hitler had given up thoughts of an invasion of Britain and although the *Luftwaffe* retained a considerable number of aircraft in France and the Low Countries, others were released from there and the eastern front for the Mediterranean theatre. In the desert Rommel was concentrating on defeating the garrison at Tobruk with air attacks on Allied shipping bringing in supplies. In November 1941 the entry of the United States into the war was not foreseen, although in reality a gap of only three weeks separated it from the beginning of *Crusader*.

The main problem for Axis forces remained that of supplies reaching North Africa and an extended supply line from the ports at Tripoli and Benghazi. The supply shortage was due in large part to the combined efforts of the Royal Navy and the RAF. Malta-based bombers hit Italian ports and Tripoli and Egypt-based Wellingtons struck at Benghazi and Greek ports. According to the Official History,[1] between 1 June and 31 October 1941 at least 220,000 tons of Axis shipping was sunk on Africa convoy routes – 94,000 tons was by the RN and 115,000 by the RAF and Fleet Air Arm. Of that claimed sunk from the air, 75% was by Malta-based units. 90% of the sinkings were of laden, southbound, vessels.

The Official History was compiled well before the existence was widely known of the *Ultra* intercepts and has this to say about the aircraft attacks on enemy shipping in the Mediterranean: 'So complete was our intelligence that no important convoy escaped their attention.' While that was true, the cost of applying

Generalleutnant Erwin Rommel commanded the *Deutsches Afrika Korps* (DAK) and as such was the bane of Allied forces. Popular with his troops he commanded them with panache, but too often outran his meagre supply lines. *Alan Walton*

In November 1941 there were fifteen Hurricane squadrons controlled by AHQ Western Desert, some of which were charged with defence of the Delta. Uncoded Mk I Z4641 belongs to 274 Sqn. *Crown copyright*

Ultra intelligence was high. For one thing, maritime patrol aircraft had to make numerous unnecessary sorties, implying that convoys were found by aerial reconnaissance so that the source of intelligence was not compromised. This strategy, although far removed from close air support, was nonetheless to have a huge impact on the course of subsequent ground battles in favour of the Dominion forces.

Churchill had been pressing for early attack on Rommel, but the local commanders resisted until they had sufficient tanks, guns and aircraft, and properly trained personnel. In the event the operation was planned for mid-November, the primary objective being to drive the enemy from Cyrenaica. This would have the effect of removing the threat of Axis attack on Egypt, easing shipping passage through securing ports, the relief of Tobruk and the acquisition of forward air bases. Equally important, a major assault would ease German pressure on the Soviet Union and hopefully raise the siege on Malta.

Following the failed *Battleaxe* operation to relieve the siege of Tobruk, the Army was reorganised, Western Desert Force becoming the Eighth Army, now under the leadership (for a short time) of Lt Gen Alan Cunningham. The air forces were also restructured, 204 (Operations) Group, including the tactical wings west of Burgh-el-Arab, being redesignated AHQ Western Desert on 21 October.

Although the RAF and Dominion squadrons were strong in numbers and with a more efficient maintenance organisation returning damaged aircraft to service quickly, numbers could not obscure the inferiority of equipment. The Messerschmitt Bf 109F was far superior to the Hurricane in nearly all respects and the defence of Egypt rested on several squadrons of the elderly

Hurricane I P2544/YK-? of Wg Cdr J. H. Lapsley OC 274 Sqn. He was shot down over Tobruk on 19 April 1941 by Bf 109Es of I/JG 27 and injured in the ensuing crash landing. *Author's collection*

fighter. However, on the plus side, there was now an effective network of fixed radar stations, while the tactical air force would be supported by mobile Chain Overseas Low (COL) radars of AMES 216 and 235.

There was also an imbalance in the training and experience of pilots. In general German pilots, and in many cases Italian too, had more experience and arguably had been better trained. In the summer of 1941, the RAF put in place improvements with the introduction into the Middle East of a number of operational training units, but it would be some time before the benefits of them would show.

As well as refined pilot training, air force infrastructure had been revised with dramatically improved maintenance and repair processes and with new, but as yet untried, systems of co-operation with the Army that included co-location of headquarters. Plans were also in place, and understood by the Army, for the rapid acquisition of forward airfields and movement of tactical squadrons and their equipment, priority being given to ground personnel, radars, fuel and munitions.

The air support system had also been upgraded. Air Support Controls (ASC) now had a two-way W/T radio link from tentacles to Brigade HQ where the Forward Air Support Links (FASLs) had a two-way R/T link to Corps Tac/R aircraft. The Rear ASLs likewise had two-way R/T radio link connecting airfields and advanced landing grounds to the ASCHQ. And RAF staff here also had two-way R/T with support aircraft and receive-only R/T from Tac/R aircraft. A further change was the description of bomb lines by reference to ground features rather than map references.

In respect of numbers, at the outset of *Crusader* aircraft available to the air arms were as follows:[2]

Table 5.1 – comparative strengths of air arms

Air Arm	Total	Serviceable	%
WDAF	657	554	84
Luftwaffe	244	121	50
Regia Aeronautica	296	192	65

Air units available to support *Crusader* are shown at Table 5.2. As well as the offensive element, on the eve of the operation AHQ Western Desert also controlled directly a number of transport, reconnaissance, casualty evacuation and other specialised units. Additionally, the five Wellington squadrons (37, 38, 70, 108 and 148) of newly formed 205 Group were on call to attack tactical targets, as were Beaufighters of 201 Group (252 and 272 Sqns) for fast strike. To supplement Hurricane units, 73 Sqn in Egypt formed a 'Battle Flight' comprising its most experienced pilots, basing it near the front line. Hurricanes were by now being adapted locally to carry eight 40lb bombs on wing racks and the first use of the fighter-bombers was on 20 November against German M/T north of Bir-el-Baheira.

One further support unit was a detachment of six Wellington ICs of 109 Sqn whose function was radio jamming, specifically that of German tank communications in the 28–34 MCS waveband. The first three aircraft were deployed to LG 75 on 14 November.[3]

Table 5.2 – AHQ Western Desert units, 18 November 1941

AHQ Western Desert		
30	Hurricane I	LG 05
RNFS	Hurricane I	LG 05
33	Hurricane I	Giarabub (Oasis force)
80	Hurricane I bomber	LG 111
450	Hurricane I	Burgh el Arab
113	Blenheim IVF	Giarabub (Oasis force)
203 det	Beaufort	
253 (Army Co-operation) Wing (Sidi Barrani)		
208	Lysander, Hurricane I	LG 112 (XXX Corps)
237	Hurricane I	LG 75 dets 112, 132 (reserve)
451	Hurricane I	LG 75 dets 131, 132 (XIII Corps)
258 (Fighter) Wing (Bir Khamsa)		
112	Tomahawk IIB	LG 110
250	Tomahawk IIB	LG 109
2 SAAF	Tomahawk IIB	LG 110
4 SAAF	Tomahawk IIB	LG 110
3 RAAF	Tomahawk	LG 110
RNFS	Hurricane I, Martlet	Sidi Haneish
262 (Fighter) Wing (Sidi Haneish)		
94	Hurricane I	LG 124
229	Hurricane IIC	LG 12 dets 111, 123
238	Hurricane IIC	LG 123
260	Hurricane I	LG 115 dets 101, 109, 124
274	Hurricane IIB	LG 103
1 SAAF	Hurricane IIB	LG 130
3 SAAF (Medium Bomber) Wing (Maaten Bagush)		
11	Blenheim IV	LG 116
12 SAAF	Maryland II	LG 24
21 SAAF	Maryland II	LG 76
24 SAAF	Maryland II, Boston III	LG 112
270 (Medium Bomber) Wing (Fuka)		
8 det	Blenheim IV	Fuka
14	Blenheim IV	LG 75
45	Blenheim IVF	LG 75
55	Blenheim IV	LG 17
84	Blenheim IV	Amiriya
GRB.1 FF	Blenheim IV	Abu Sueir

The Eighth Army comprised two corps, the Tobruk Garrison and a small 'Oasis' force, plus a South African division in reserve. In outline their composition was:

Table 5.3 – Eighth Army, November 1941

XXX Corps (500 tanks)		
	7th Armoured Division	
		Three armoured brigades, one with field artillery
	1st South African Division	
		Two infantry brigades, both with field artillery
	22nd Guards Brigade	
		Two infantry battalions
	Support Group with three regiments and a battery of 25pdr guns plus two infantry battalions	
	Divisional troops, including armoured cars, LAA and two tank regiments	
XIII Corps (130 tanks)		
	2nd New Zealand Division	
		Three infantry brigades
	4th Indian Infantry Division	
		Three infantry brigades
	Divisional troops, including three regiments of field artillery	
Tobruk Garrison (130 tanks)		
	70th Infantry Division	
		Three infantry brigades
	Polish Carpathian Rifle Brigade	
		Five infantry battalions plus artillery
	32nd Army Tank Brigade	
	4th Anti-Aircraft Brigade	
Oasis Force		
	29th Infantry Brigade, including an armoured car regiment	

Tac/R squadrons were attached to both Corps, and Hurricane (33) and Blenheim IVF (113) squadrons provided support to the Oasis force. The survey flight of 60 Sqn SAAF was working directly to the survey company at Eighth Army HQ.

Confronting the Dominion forces were some 244 German and 296 Italian aircraft, of which roughly half were serviceable immediately. On the ground was the Italian XX Corps, with one armoured and one motorised division, plus a reconnaissance group and *Panzer* Group Afrika, consisting of two German *Panzer* and one special purpose divisions and four Italian infantry divisions. Against the 760 deployed Allied tanks (with another 280 in reserve), Axis forces could muster around 440.

Despite the disparity in numbers, Rommel was intending to attack Tobruk, planned for 23 November, suggesting that reconnaissance capability by the *Luftwaffe* and the intelligence it was able to provide was not as effective as it should have been. Given the composition and weaponry available to the garrison, it also reflects great credit on the effectiveness of the Allied anti-aircraft artillery defending the port.

Tedder's plan in support of Eighth Army was to secure air superiority, to mount night bombing attacks on supply routes and by doing so, in due course, help the Army move forward. The overall air plan involved four stages:

D-35 to D-6 – softening up of enemy airfields and supply routes

D-5 to D-day – protect Army moving forward

D+1 to D+5 – close support during armoured battle

D+6 onwards – harass enemy in retreat

Just after the first phase began Air Cdre Basil Embry arrived in Cairo, to be attached temporarily to the Tactical Air Force, having been requested by Tedder to bring to the theatre the latest ideas from the UK. He was appointed Senior Air Staff Officer to Coningham, whose style was very different. Embry suggested the appointment of *true* wing leaders (not merely administrators holding the rank) from among the most experienced officers available. He also worked hard to change the defensive mentality that had evolved through escort duties. That led to agreement that Hurricanes would operate below 15,000ft, where they were at less of a disadvantage to the Bf 109F. There was also accord that squadrons would weave as a whole, not just as

Beaufighters were used for strafing M/T as well as hunting ships. This trio is possibly from 16 Sqn SAAF. *Author's collection*

At this stage in the war close support was provided by the Blenheim squadrons. Blenheim IV Z9546/AD-D of 113 Sqn in 1941. *Author's collection*

flights and that they should work in paired units within their wings. Perhaps surprisingly, Embry did not suggest the adoption of the finger four formation, borrowed from the *Luftwaffe* and now applied in the UK.

Composition of the two wings, with paired squadrons, was:

258 Wing – 2 SAAF & 4 SAAF; 250 & Royal Navy Fighter Squadron (RNFS); 112 & 3 RAAF

262 Wing – 94 & 260; 229 & 238; 274 & 1 SAAF

During the softening up period innovative tactics were developed. Attacks on airfields were difficult because they were hard to spot from low level and heavily defended besides. The approach was to allocate a squadron of Blenheims and three of fighters to the attack, during which the Blenheims flew at around 10,000ft, coming from an unexpected direction. When they spotted the airfield and if enemy aircraft were visible, they bombed. A squadron of ground attack fighters were a few minutes behind, at low level, noting the bomb bursts and continuing the attack. A squadron of fighters would be in close support to the bombers, while the third of the fighter squadrons acted as top cover for the entire circus.[4] For Beaufighters, which would fly at low level out to sea and then turn inland to shoot up motor transport (M/T) along the coast road, there were special protocols. Several aircraft would operate in concert, turning in at 50-mile intervals. Not only would this type of interdiction destroy supplies and M/T, it would also have a serious impact on morale among rear echelon troops.

From 14 October to the advance the RAF conducted some 3,000 sorties. Most often, Marylands of the SAAF Wing attacked Benghazi and airfields while Blenheims specialised in beating up M/T, 113 Sqn concentrating on the Agedabia–El Agheila road as well as airfields. Among weapons used were barbed caltrops, anti-personnel/tyre puncturing devices whose origins date back to Roman times. Airfields, including Benina, Berka, Derna, Gambut, Gazala, Martuba, Msus and Tmimi, were bombed round the clock. Wellingtons attacked at night, sometimes with the support of flare-dropping Albacores, and from 7 November 4,000lb 'Cookie' bombs were used against Benghazi. By way of contrast, marauding Hurri-bombers of 80 Sqn were armed with eight 40lb bombs, useful against soft-skinned M/T and personnel.

By the middle of November Axis reconnaissance aircraft had spotted the build-up of forces at Giarabub, some 20 miles into Libya; the airfield there was bombed on the 15th with losses to both sides. Allied PR and survey aircraft had been operating throughout the preparatory phases of the battle so that the Army had a clear view of both the lie of the land and enemy dispositions. Allied aircraft losses in the four weeks amounted to around fifty, including twelve Wellingtons, twelve Hurricanes, nine Blenheims, eight Marylands and five Tomahawks.

In preparation for the advance, tactical squadrons – which, exceptionally, had aircrew messes, as opposed to separate officers' and sergeants' messes – organised themselves in three elements. One was to stay on the original base, one was a rear party and one was an advanced party. The latter components were able to service aircraft for up to seven days away from base and were highly mobile. The decision was taken to use inland landing grounds that were firmer underfoot wherever possible. The downside was the difficulty in locating them from the air since they had no immediate coastal reference points, although it could be made easier by the use of rockets and smoke candles. Forward landing grounds were prepared and stocked at night.

During the lead-up to the battle the three Tac/R squadrons flew sorties to pinpoint enemy formations. They were always escorted by Hurricane top cover. The Allied air forces made every effort to prevent enemy reconnaissance aircraft from functioning effectively and by the opening rounds the Axis airfields and their based aircraft had taken a pounding, as had stores dumps and motor transport.

The British were fortunate that on 17 November, D-1, there were dust storms, followed by thunder and heavy rain, which affected especially enemy coastal airfields at Gambut and Gazala that were soon mudbaths. The Allied airfields, on firmer ground, fared slightly better.

Before describing the battle, about which practically every historian on the subject has used the 'fog of war' cliché, a brief note on the geography may help. The border between Egypt and Libya, marked by a wire fence, ran due south from Sollum (then in Axis hands) through the Halfaya Pass, continuing south and to the east of Giarabub oasis (150 miles south of Tobruk). To the north of Sollum the coastline ran for around 25 miles, to include the port of Bardia and then due west for around 40 miles, to the besieged garrison at Tobruk. A road ran west from Bardia and there were tracks from Fort Capuzzo, through Sidi Rezegh, on a ridge to the south-east of Tobruk, and from Halfaya Pass to Bir el Gubi, some 30 miles south of Tobruk.

Starting from Fort Maddalena, the intention was that XXX Corps, with most of the tanks, would strike north-west towards Tobruk. To the north, XIII Corps would advance through the wire to work up the coast, striking westwards towards Tobruk, having cleared the enemy garrisons at Sollum and Bardia. There was to be a diversion in the south where the Oasis Force would set out from Giarabub to Jalo to create the impression that this was the main thrust, inland towards El Agheila.

The Battle

The battle started at 0600 on 18 November, the 7th Armoured Brigade driving forward to Gabr Saleh with 450 tanks. To its left, the 22nd Armoured Brigade made for Bir el Gubi and on the right 4th Armoured Brigade moved due north, flanking XIII Corps' New Zealand Division. Between the Kiwis and the coast, the 4th Indian Division also advanced. Enemy forces were to the north and west and in due course to the east, as XIII Corps worked north, bypassing the coastal garrisons. Several sorties were flown by 109 Sqn Wellingtons, their objective being the jamming of Axis tank radio communications, successfully so according to accounts by prisoners.

On the first day considerable progress was made, but that was to be short-lived. On the 19th the Italians halted 22nd Armoured Brigade at Bir el Gubi and the *Afrika Korps* XXI *Panzer* Division counter-attacked the 4th Armoured Brigade from the north-east. Such was the lack of communications, that evening General Sir Claude Auchinleck, C-in-C Middle East, telegraphed Churchill: 'Until we know the area reached by our troops today it is not possible to read the battle further…'.

On the first two days the RAF mounted numerous escorted bomber raids and fighter sweeps on airfields, meeting with little air opposition, although some aircraft were lost to AA fire. In the south, 33 Sqn moved to its forward base at LG 125, well into Libya. But overall, close air support was a mess. Gp Capt Kenneth Cross, OC 258 Wing, while highly complementary about the support from the Royal Army Service Corps (RASC), had this to say:[5]

> 'W/T communication from forward formations to Army HQ and vice-versa simply did not work. The result was that even the location of

The Free French Air Force Groupe *Lorraine* GRB 1 formed in September 1941 in Syria and shortly after moved to Egypt. Its aircraft were used to the end of January 1942, at which time it returned to the Levant. Blenheim IV Z7633 plus light load of 250lb GP bombs. *Author's collection*

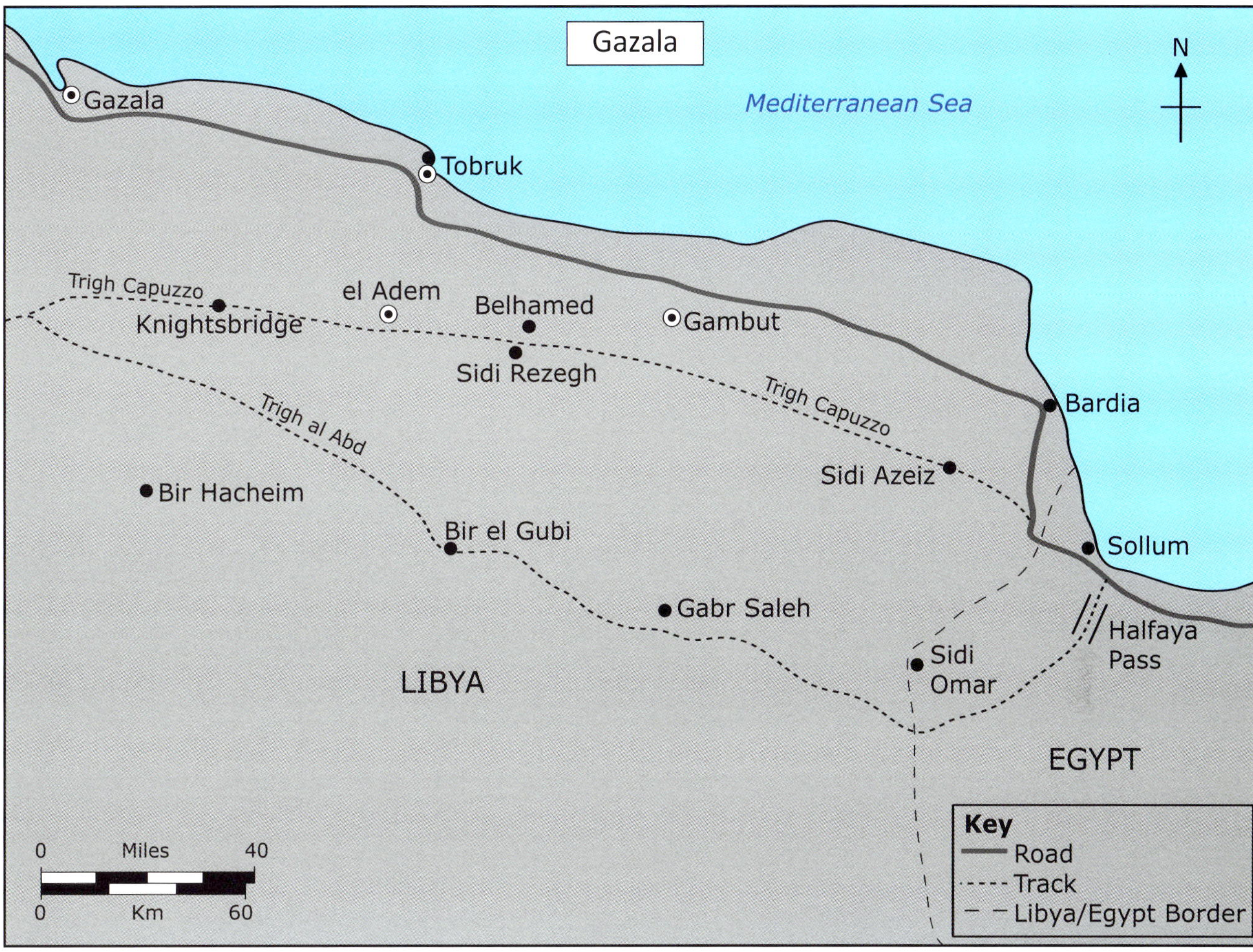
Gazala
Mediterranean Sea
N
Gazala
Tobruk
Trigh Capuzzo
el Adem
Belhamed
Gambut
Knightsbridge
Sidi Rezegh
Trigh Capuzzo
Trigh al Abd
Bardia
Sidi Azeiz
Bir Hacheim
Bir el Gubi
Sollum
Gabr Saleh
Halfaya Pass
Sidi Omar
LIBYA
EGYPT
0 Miles 40
0 Km 60
Key
Road
Track
Libya/Egypt Border

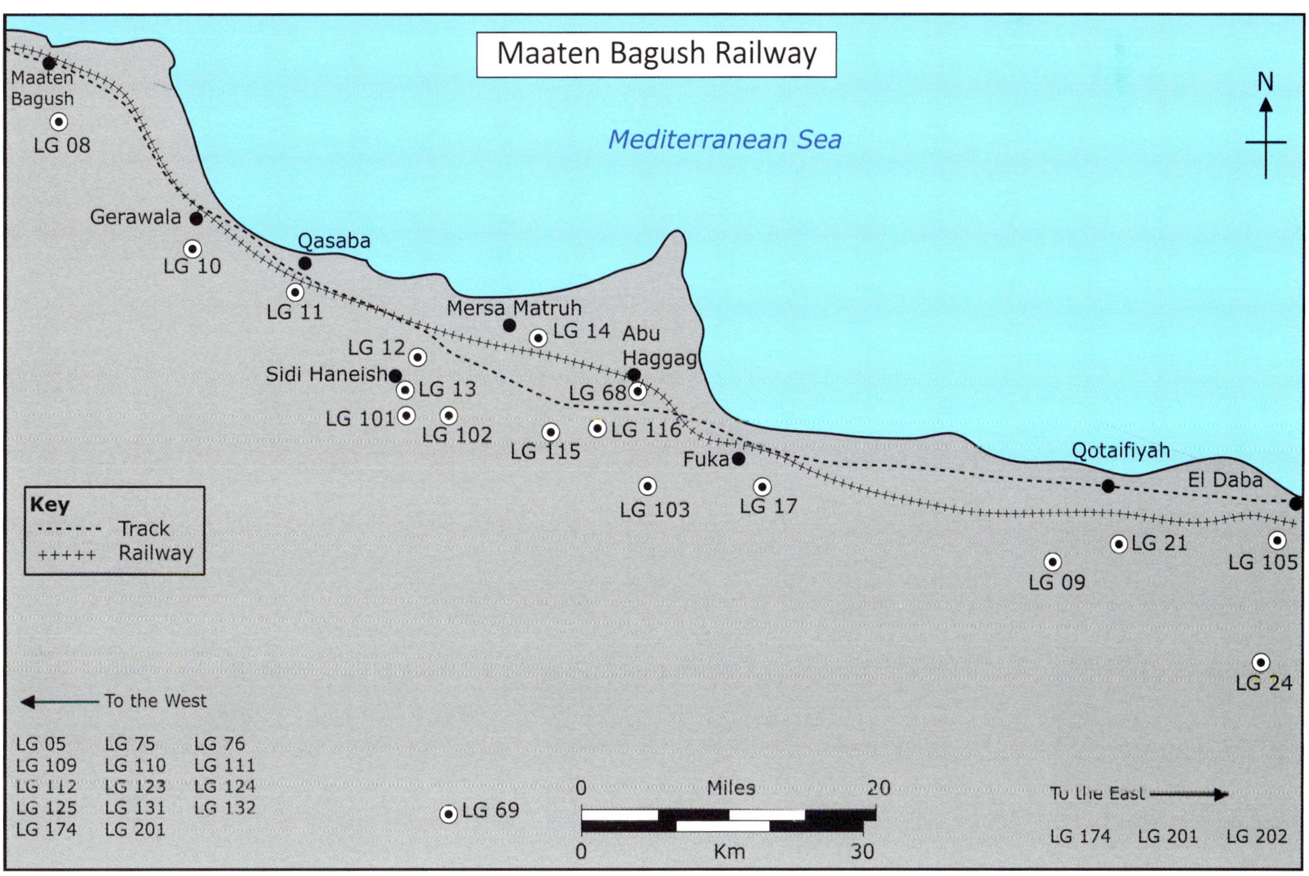
Maaten Bagush Railway
Maaten Bagush
LG 08
Mediterranean Sea
N
Gerawala
LG 10
Qasaba
LG 11
Mersa Matruh
LG 14
Abu Haggag
LG 12
Sidi Haneish
LG 13
LG 68
LG 101
LG 102
LG 115
LG 116
Fuka
LG 103
LG 17
Qotaifiyah
El Daba
Key
Track
Railway
LG 21
LG 105
LG 09
LG 24
To the West
LG 05 LG 75 LG 76
LG 109 LG 110 LG 111
LG 112 LG 123 LG 124
LG 125 LG 131 LG 132
LG 174 LG 201
LG 69
0 Miles 20
0 Km 30
To the East
LG 174 LG 201 LG 202

The Wellington squadrons played a major part in interdiction, securing air superiority through bombing airfields. Wellington IC 'S' of 37 Sqn is here taking off from Shallufa: note the different presentations of the single individual code letter. *Author's collection*

friendly formations was often unknown and this made planning bomber operations difficult and sometimes impossible … The most serious result was the under-utilisation of the light bomber force which waited hour after hour bombed up and ready to go, but no information about targets came from the Army. Army intelligence did not pass on to us accurate locations of enemy formations even with the air reconnaissance squadron working directly under Corps HQ.'

He goes on to note that, in the event, RAF fighters had a better idea of what was going on than did the Army.

There was increased air activity from the 20th because improved weather meant that Axis airfields became usable again. The RAF mounted sweeps against them and now the enemy was coming up prepared to fight. Despite the Corps' Tac/R sorties, little if any information was being passed up the line, so there was little that could be done in the way of close air support, given uncertainty as to the location of troop formations. Instead, light bombers attacked obvious targets, safely away from any front line and escorting fighters did their best to protect them. At night, Wellingtons attacked airfields and depots with assistance from Albacores of 826 NAS. The increased enemy response led to the loss of five Marylands, two Blenheims, six Tomahawks and six Hurricanes. This pattern of activity, with heavy losses, critically of pilots, was to continue for the next ten days.

The XV *Panzer* Division attacked the NZ Division from the west on the 20th, while XXI *Panzer* Division made a 90° turn to the north-west so as to attack 7th Armoured Brigade from behind. By 22 November the brigade had lost 113 of its 141 tanks, while XV *Panzer*

Hurricane D of 73 Sqn ran into a Wellington during a crash landing at a very muddy Mersa Matruh late in 1941. *Alan Walton*

The Royal Naval Fighter Squadron consisted of Naval pilots shore-based at Dekheila for defence but also used to supplement Air Force squadrons in escort duties. It flew Hurricanes and Martlets: Hurricane I Z4932/OL-B force-landed but lived to fight another day. *Author's collection*

Division destroyed 4th Armoured Brigade, again attacking from behind. 70th Division had begun the breakout from Tobruk, but this had to be suspended. On the 23rd the 5th South African Brigade was eliminated and the chaotic nature of the widespread distribution of Allied forces encouraged Rommel to make an eastwards dash for the wire.

The radio jammers of 109 Sqn, making considerable impact in support of the Army, were having a hard time of it. Flying very low and slow and often unescorted, two had by now been shot down with the loss of their crews, while a further four were damaged, two in an attack on their base at LG 75.

The turmoil was exemplified on 24 November when RAF fighters spotted an Axis column heading east for Sidi Omar and due to pass just to the north of advanced landing grounds 123 and 124. While Cross instructed his squadrons to strafe the soft elements, according to Embry he personally instructed the aircraft of both tactical fighter wings to retreat to LG 128. However, this could not easily be located, so aircraft ended up at LG 122 at Sidi Haneish where, by dusk, some 175 fighters were distributed wingtip to wingtip. Earlier in the day German tanks were seen approaching XXX Corps' advanced HQ at Gabr Saleh where Gen Cunningham was briefing; hurriedly, he departed aboard a 108 Sqn Blenheim. The following day, with Rommel now reversing his thrust, the squadrons were back where they had started. It was around this time that Arthur Coningham, AOC WDAF, complained to Tedder that the Army was not able to defend the airfields due to confusion and lack of information.

Such was the caution exercised by Cunningham, who now wanted to retreat back to the frontier, that he was relieved of his command on the 26th and replaced by acting Lt Gen Neil Ritchie. The retreat was halted and two days later the NZ Division captured Sidi Rezegh, then linked up with 70th Division. In the air, mixed formations of German and Italian fighters escorted Ju 87 missions against Allied forces. These were usually broken up, but with greater loss to the Allied squadrons than to the enemy. Fed up with getting little advanced warning of incoming raids from the west, Wg Cdr Fred Rosier, OC 263 Wing, attempted to fly into Tobruk to check why the radars there were giving no warning. His escorting squadrons were intercepted and after landing in the desert to pick up a downed pilot, his own aircraft was damaged and he had to walk back to base. A surprising number of downed pilots were either collected in single-seat fighters or walked back to Allied lines.

Cairo Conference September 1941
Post Operation *Brevity*

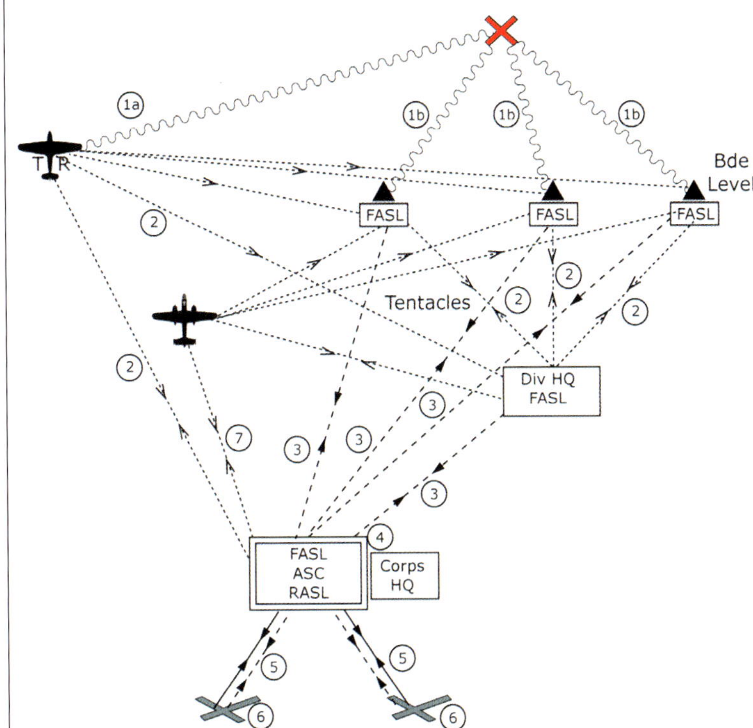

1) Tac/R or Brigade tentacle identifies threat
2) Call noted by Div HQ and Air Support Control (ASC)
3) Forward Air Support Link (FASL) requests support from ASC
4) ASC confers with Corps HQ
5) If request agreed squadrons at landing ground(s) notified
6) Pilots briefed by Air Liaison Officers (ALOs)
7) Bomber support aircraft despatched; calls monitored

Note – for simplicity only one division is shown on diagram

The RNFS was parented by 775 NAS at Dekheila which also had on charge a number of Fulmar including N4002. *Alan Walton*

Shipping aircraft via the Mediterranean was high risk, and via the Cape time-consuming. The solution was to ship crated aircraft to West Africa, assemble them at Takoradi, in what was then the Gold Coast. The aircraft flew across Africa east to Sudan then north to Egypt, wearing special markings to facilitate rescue in the event of an accident en route. These are seen on Hurricane I Z4769/3 which completed the route between 28 and 31 August 1941. *Author's collection*

The Takoradi-Cairo delivery route was supported from the outset by PAA-Africa. Blenheim IV Z79** Is here seen with the distinctive white search and rescue marking on the rear fuselage. The Company mascot, Leo the lion, looks intent on remonstrating with the photographer! *PAA-Africa Alumni Association*

Tobruk Relieved

On 28 November, the weather worsening, Rommel decided to retreat and address the blocking of his supply line by the NZ Division: in the process units of XXI *Panzer* Division drove into 21st NZ Regt HQ. For several days there was violent fighting south of Tobruk before, on 3 December, German forces set out east again to relieve the garrisons of Bardia, Halfaya and Sollum, but these were spotted and attacked from the air. Four days later, with his forces desperately short of fuel, Rommel decided to give up the siege of Tobruk and retreated to Gazala. At this time the Battle Flight of 73 Sqn replaced 33 Sqn at Giarabub.

69 Sqn based on Malta employed a mix of types in the reconnaissance role. Some of the sorties were artificial in that they provided cover for 'locating' surface vessels whose courses were already known through *Ultra* intercepts. Baltimore IV FA465/B over Malta. *Author's collection*

On 22 November Rommel had received additional aircraft to take his inventory up to 300, after which, on 2 December, Hitler ordered *Fliegerkorps II* from the Eastern Front to the Mediterranean theatre with a view to neutralising Malta and regaining naval and air superiority encompassing Italy and the North African ports. By the 8th Rommel had some 120 Bf 109s, of which half were F models.

Ritchie now reorganised and gave 70th Division responsibility for leading the drive west to take Cyrenaica. XXX Corps retired to mop up the pockets of resistance and regroup following its heavy losses. The air war became even more intense with many sorties flown and continuous dogfighting on 4 and 5 December. On these two days the Dominion air forces claimed thirty-three Ju 87s, fourteen Bf 109s, two Bf 110s and twenty-nine Italian fighters destroyed or damaged.

The RAF now had serious problems in moving forward to maintain contact with the Army. Among the difficulties were a lack of advanced landing grounds (and no support from the Army in defending them), unfavourable weather and poor information on Allied positions. Light bombers stood by to give support, but to whom and where? From 7 December the RAF repaired the Gazala airfields and brought in 10,000 gallons of aviation fuel and shortly after Mechili, then Msus, were stocked with 15,000 and 10,000 gallons respectively. From late December Kittyhawks began replacing Tomahawks, starting with 112 Sqn and 3 Sqn RAAF.

With Axis forces now concentrated at Gazala and almost surrounded, a rout looked possible. However, 7th Armoured Division was unable to close the gap fast enough because of soft sand to the south. The air forces were standing by for three days (14–16 December), but not called upon due to problems of identification of any bomb line and the close proximity of opposing forces. Thus, a great opportunity was wasted, the Army demonstrating a total lack of appreciation of the potential of close air support.

By Christmas Eve the front was stabilised, but given the inadequacies of his equipment Tedder asked for more modern aircraft and in the short term got six Spitfire Vs, two Mosquitoes and ASV Wellingtons. After a month of fighting Rommel now withdrew his forces to El Agheila, completed by mid-January. To quote from one notable historian:[6] 'At last, on December 17, for the first time since the British and Axis armies had become entangled in Operation *Crusader*, the plots on the battle maps began to assume a coherent pattern.'

On 2 January 1942 Bardia was taken in a highly controversial operation because medium bombers were used in close support of the Army, during which 385 sorties were flown, starting 27 December. On the 17th Sollum and Halfaya were taken, along with some 30,000 prisoners and supplies. By mid-January, though, the British attack had petered out. At 1,000 miles, the supply line from Egypt had become too long, added to which for several weeks Benghazi harbour was unusable. Allied aircraft were hampered by lack of fuel and general wear and tear. Further, the entry of Japan into the war resulted in the immediate despatch of a number of squadrons to India and the Far East, together with two Australian and one British infantry divisions.

Between 18 November 1941 and 20 January 1942 the RAF had flown an average of 190 sorties daily for the loss of c300 aircraft. The Axis deficit was 259 German and 204 Italian aircraft destroyed, mostly on the ground. Many of the RAF losses were from light AA, which the Germans operated most efficiently by firing barrage rather than attempting to hit individual aircraft.

Army co-operation had failed, not through willingness or capability on the part of the RAF, but through inexperience, hesitation and lack of communication on the part of the Army. Systems were in place, but not used properly, so that the average response time to a FASL call for support was in excess of two and a half hours.[7] In a joint service exercise in July, target and bomb line marking systems had been agreed, but in the heat of combat had not been applied.

One relative success was the introduction of the fighter-bomber in the form of converted Hurricane Mk 1s serving with 80 Sqn, which moved forward just behind the front line. In early January squadron pilots went to Egypt to collect newly delivered Hurricane Mk IICs, armed with four 20mm Hispano cannon and with wing hardpoints for bombs or added fuel tanks. However, overall, shortcomings resulted in Rommel being able to withdraw and regroup. Worse was to come before any lessons were learned and applied.

The Martin Maryland was a light reconnaissance-bomber operated mainly by the squadrons of 3 Wing SAAF. This aircraft is probably AH336 which served with 223 Sqn, the light bomber OUT in the Middle East. *Tinus le Roux*

Attack aircraft were critical in preventing supplies reaching North Africa from Italy and Greece. These included the torpedo-bomber Beauforts of 39 Sqn based in Egypt until August 1942, when they moved to Malta. Mk II DD906/C at low level over the Mediterranean. *Author's collection*

The Assault on Malta

Aircraft and naval vessels based on Malta played a key role in supporting military action in North Africa by attacking and destroying supply convoys from Italy to Tripoli. Some 90% of Axis shipping sunk was when outbound with full loads. At the highest level within the Axis high command, it was decided that Malta must be eliminated. From 22 December 1941 the island was subject to constant bombing by the *Regia Aeronautica*, *Fliegerkorps II* in Sicily, *Fiiegerkorps X* in Greece and Crete, and *Fliegerführer Afrika*. In addition, Axis air forces and navies did their best to prevent convoys of weapons, fuel, armaments and food reaching the island. What little managed to evade the blockade came by submarine, by small, fast vessels or by air.

Bases on Malta were critical for interdiction of Axis convoys. While the island was under siege it was supplied by surface vessel but also by submarine, at least one of which was converted solely for supplies. The craft here are seen in Valetta harbour early in 1943. *Mark O'Boyle*

Early Hurricane deliveries to the Middle East included aircraft still retaining their black port undersides, as evidenced by this Mk I without tropical filter being prepared for 213 Sqn. *Alan Walton*

RAF defences comprised three Hurricane day fighter squadrons and, in effect, two night-fighter flights with Hurricanes and Beaufighters. For attacks on shipping or ports there were the equivalent of three Blenheim light bomber and two Wellington squadrons, but these were soon destroyed in bombing raids or flown to Egypt, leaving two FAA anti-submarine squadrons. Photo-reconnaissance was handled by 69 Sqn.

If Malta was to survive there was a desperate need for aircraft to replace the rapidly diminishing Hurricane force. Thus, the first fifteen Spitfire Mk Vs arrived, flown in from HMS *Eagle* on 7 March – and not a day too soon. They were the forerunners of thirteen batches of deliveries between March and October, totalling 367 aircraft from the 385 that had been launched, a loss rate of 5%. With proper reception arrangements the aircraft were operational almost immediately after arrival.

As a result of the enormous Axis pressure on Malta, through relentless bombing especially, several key convoys had made it from Italy to Tripoli. That meant that by the latter part of January Rommel had shorter supply lines and was receiving regular reinforcements of men and machines. On the other hand, the British had extended supply lines, were short of fuel and had lost significant units, both land and air, to the Far East. Tedder, for instance, was deprived of 450 aircraft transferred to India, including four Blenheim light bomber squadrons. A further problem was that US aircraft deliveries, originally destined for the RAF, were now being diverted to Russia.

The attempts to re-provision Malta, primarily to enable forces there to deny passage to Axis supply convoys, was a truly tri-service affair. One example, on 21 March, was when convoy MW10 from Alexandria had reached the critical area between

Table 5.4 – HQ RAF Malta, mid-1941–June 1942

Sqn	Type	Base	From	To
185	Hurricane I, II, Spitfire VC	Hal Far, Ta Kali, Luqa	12.5.41	29.7.44
249	Hurricane II, Spitfire VB, VC	Ta Kali	21.5.41	23.10.43
126	Hurricane II, Spitfire VB, VC	Ta Kali, Luqa	28.6.41	23.9.43
229	Hurricane IIC	Hal Far	28.3.42	29.4.42
601	Spitfire VC	Luqa	20.4.42	23.6.42
603	Spitfire VC	Ta Kali	20.4.42	3.8.42
89 det	Beaufighter IF	Luqa, Ta Kali	10.12.41	8.42
1435 Flt	Beaufighter II, Hurricane NF	Ta Kali	4.12.41	22.6.42
110 dets	Blenheim IV	Luqa	41	17.3.42
107 dets	Blenheim IV	Luqa	11.5.41	1.42
18	Blenheim IV	Luqa	13.10.41	1.42
21	Blenheim IV	Luqa	25.12.41	14.3.42
104	Wellington II	Luqa	14.10.41	14.1.42
40	Wellington IC	Luqa	31.10.41	14.2.42
830 NAS	Swordfish I	Hal Far	1.7.40	31.3.43
828 NAS	Albacore	Hal Far	18.10.41	28.6.43
69	Maryland, Hurricane IIC, Mosquito I, Beaufighter I, Spitfire IV	Luqa, Ta Kali	10.1.41	9.2.44

The South African Air Force operated two squadrons of Bostons in the Western Desert between December 1941 and December 1943 when the type was replaced by the Marauder. The Boston was used mainly against enemy formations close to the front line. Seen here after a landing mishap is an aircraft of 12 Sqn SAAF. *Mark O'Boyle*

Crete and Cyrenaica. The Army, supported by WDAF bombers, made diversionary raids against Martuba and Tmimi to draw off Axis bombers. Egypt-based aircraft of 201 and 205 groups also joined those aircraft able to operate from Malta.

The pressure on Malta continued until May 1942, at which stage Hitler removed the imperative to neutralise Malta, the *Luftwaffe* needing to divert aircraft to France, the Eastern Front and Cyrenaica. Aircraft and ships on the fortress island were therefore once again able to exert pressure on Axis convoys, making an enormous contribution to Rommel's eventual defeat.

Rommel Strikes East

In poor weather and sensing Allied weaknesses, Rommel struck east without warning on 21 January, in three columns with 100 tanks. They were faced only by XIII Corps. The Kittyhawks of 239 Wing and Hurricanes of 33 and 274 Sqns were bogged down at Antelat airfield, close to the advancing columns. Eventually a strip was cleared sufficiently of water to allow one aircraft away at a time and most were able to depart for Msus, 40 miles back, where they were joined by 229 Sqn. But with no British troops between the Axis advance and Msus, the squadrons were obliged to fall back further, to Mechili. The Army was confused and in poor shape and it too retreated quickly, Benghazi being lost on the 28th.

Blenheims remained the mainstay of the close support/light bomber force into 1943. Blenheim IV Z5893/W of 14 Sqn shows the distinctive white bar unit marking and the rearward-firing machine gun under the nose. *Author's collection*

Hurricanes Mk IIc of 94 Sqn over the Western Desert. The aircraft display both Middle East 'sand and stone' and temperate camouflage schemes. *Author's collection*

Rommel's advance now put the Army to flight. It was incapable of defending airfields or even appreciating any ground-based threat, with the consequence that in order to preserve their aircraft, squadrons too had to move back. By the end of January they were widely dispersed – 33, 73, 112 and 250 Sqns at Gazala, 80 at LG 109, 94 and 3 RAAF at LG 110 (to collect Kittyhawks), 450 at Sidi Haneish and 237 Sqn off operations. The situation became so serious that on 8 February, 234 Mobile Defence Fighter Wing was assigned temporarily from AHQ Egypt to WDAF. By 10 February the enemy had overrun Tmimi and reached Gazala. Here they were halted by Allied forces holding prepared positions and a new front line established, running south for 45 miles to Bir Hacheim, held by Free French. However, despite the rapid withdrawal of an Army in disarray, there were occasions when WDAF fighter-bombers were directed to new targets by Tac/R fighters. From now until May both sides consolidated their positions and found some breathing space within which to train and to bring equipment levels up to reasonable strength.

During the period 7 February to 25 May WDAF flew in excess of 14,000 sorties, losing 300 aircraft in the process. At no time were targets refused, air superiority being maintained even in retreat and extensive damage inflicted on Rommel's supply lines. Key targets were reconnaissance aircraft, invariably heavily escorted by Bf 109F fighters. Axis airfields were also subject to constant attack, Martuba especially. Airfield shoot-ups were not all one-way, though: on 26 February seven Kittyhawks of 112 Sqn were damaged or destroyed on the ground at Gambut by a strafing attack by Bf 109s of 5/JG 27. Operations designed to relieve the pressure on the Army also extended out to sea, that on 12 May being a good example. Based on local intelligence, Beaufighters of 252 Sqn, escorted by Kittyhawks of 250 Sqn, intercepted fourteen Ju 52 transports, each flying twenty fully-equipped infantrymen from Crete to Derna. Nine were brought down, together with one Bf 110 escort, for the loss of one Beaufighter.[8]

Air superiority remained a priority, typified by the response to a large Axis raid on Tobruk on 25 April that Kittyhawks and Tomahawks were scrambled to intercept. The *Luftwaffe* lost four Bf 109s and a single Ju 87, but at heavy cost to the defenders – three Tomahawks and three Kittyhawks shot down, all by 109s, and five aircraft damaged. One pilot was killed, one posted missing and one wounded.

There were several changes and improvements to procedures and equipment within WDAF during this difficult period. VHF radios were being introduced with much better quality reception, although limited to line of sight. Ideally, their receivers were Forward Air Support Links (FASLs) located with forward tentacles (or, in retreat, rearward tentacles). In March, 2 Army Air Support Control (AASC) arrived from the UK, to be based at the Army/Air HQ to offer theoretically-improved communications between forward tentacles and combat aircraft, new W/T links supporting faster signals. In the background, 'Y' service – radio signals interception – coupled with prisoner-of-war interrogation, was providing more accurate intelligence on the scale and location of supply dumps, enabling precision air strikes to make maximum impact.

Also in March – and in the light of experience – a change was made so that the forward links at tentacles now reported directly to Air Support Control HQ. Further, an Army Liaison Officer (ALO) was appointed to each wing in an attempt to reduce reaction times and determine clearer bomb lines. The Tac/R squadrons attached to Corps were now extremely fast at passing their output up the line. Pilots were debriefed by ALOs and squadron IOs, initial reporting being done up the line by R/T and a full report following by W/T to Corps, to Army and to AHQWD. By April, Tac/R Hurricanes were fitted with VHF and reporting in flight direct to the AASC.

2 AASC did not find everything to its liking, though. Extracts from its war diary[9] are illuminating:

> '22 March – Bombers are flying 140 miles to tgt[A] bombing from 6000ft after a delay of 2 to 3 hours. It is difficult to imagine what type of direct support tgt can be taken on by these methods. Too many people have to be consulted before a/c can be launched.
>
> 25 March – All tentacles will in future listen in to Tac/R sorties in case of a tgt materializing.
>
> 7 April – Dawn tgt laid on at 0200 hrs. with A.A.H.Q. operations, confirmed by 0730 but not engaged until 0920 hrs. CONC[B] by that time dispersed, one fire started. A request from 50 Div. in afternoon was accepted, a/c in the air in 52 mins. from time of request. 1 tank recovery vehicle hit and many near misses at SIDI BREGHISC. 6 a/c were flown on each tgt. This is the first damage done to the enemy as a result of this unit's activities over a period of one year and 51 days!
>
> 8 April – An S.O.S. from 50 Div. for ground strafing had to be refused. Even 2 sqns of cannon fighters earmarked for the job would be greatest help to fwd tps[C] in this type of warfare. A later request from 50 Div. in S. BREGHISC area had to be refused as a fighter escort was standing by to cover a convoy into TOBRUK. On such things must Army Air Support be dependent at present.'

PR aircraft were also active, some Spitfire Mk IVs having arrived in theatre for 2 PRU that operated a flight from Gambut. A drawback was that cameras in use at the time limited their effectiveness in identifying detail, critical when the enemy was using large numbers of captured vehicles. Overall, there was a degree of conflict and confusion with the Army using its Tac/R aircraft and the WDAF its Spitfires to reconnoitre the same areas, and with a variable speed and quality of reporting.

Procedures for attacking M/T were refined, ideally this being done line abreast at right angles to a convoy, each pilot selecting a different target. Against M/T concentrations Hurri-bombers used 40lb bombs with contact fuses, dropped from 1,000ft; 500lb bombs were preferred against troops in the open. From March, Kittyhawks were also fitted for bombs, usually a 250lb device carried underbelly.

Gazala to El Alamein

From early May Auchinleck was planning to recover the lost ground, but was thwarted. On 26 May Rommel struck again, having intelligence on Allied strength and dispositions through a communications leak in the US embassy in Cairo. The Axis forces were combined in two groups, each identified by the name of their commander – *Gruppe Crüwell* (three Italian divisions, one German brigade) would strike against XIII Corps infantry brigades holding the northern half of the line; the *Panzer* divisions of *Gruppe Rommel* would bypass the southern flank at Bir Hacheim and turn to hit Allied armour of XXX Corps from the south. Having been spotted advancing by 40 Sqn SAAF, the northern *Gruppe* made limited progress against the intended objective of breaching the minefields and forcing a way through for supplies to reach Rommel's *Gruppe*. At the same time enemy aircraft struck at WDAF forward airfields.

[A] Tgt – target
[B] concentration
[C] Forward troops

Hurricane I V7670 was abandoned by 208 Sqn at Gambut, where it was recaptured in February 1942. Simply marked with crosses on wing and fuselage it was probably simply used as a decoy, and on recovery was put back into service. *Author's collection*

By now the situation regarding the strength of the opposing air forces had reversed. WDAF could field 290 serviceable aircraft out of a total of 320. Axis forces had 497 serviceable out of a local total of 704, but with large numbers additionally available on Greece, Crete, Sicily and mainland Italy.[10] An increasing number of WDAF fighter units was now operating in the fighter-bomber role, the latest being 3 Sqn RAAF.

There were still concerns about close air support procedures, even while a major battle was threatened. These further extracts from the 2 AASC war diary suggest more than a hint of incompetence on the part of the Army:

> 'May 9 – Preliminary conference with S.A.S.O. Western Desert on training of fighter-bomber squadrons in direct air support. Exercises are to be arranged and the existing procedure will be applied to demands from these squadrons. The target pro forma will be reinstated and a ground sign, assisted by smoke, will whenever possible be put out to assist in location of target. An interchange of RAF and army officers is also being arranged. With fighter bombers available direct air support may become a reality at last and not a political gesture.
>
> May 11 – Target request from 13 Corps Tac/R had to be refused as TOBRUK convoy was preoccupying fighter escort.
>
> 22 May – … to 13 Corps to confirm procedure laid down in pamphlet 3A and encourage use of ground strips and smoke signals.
>
> 24 May – The policy has been adopted for the immediate future of putting out artificial landmarks to be uncovered as an aid to air navigation in the event of a breakthrough. The landmark will be a letter A, apex west with a number of bars placed north, east or west depending on the formation. This should confuse the enemy as much as ourselves.'

Table 5.5 – AHQ Western Desert units, 26 May 1942

AHQ Western Desert		
Unit	**Type**	**Base**
208	Hurricane II, Tomahawk IIB	Sidi Azeiz
40 SAAF	Hurricane I, Tomahawk IIB	Sidi Azeiz
6	Hurricane IID (from 4/6/42)	Gambut
15 SAAF	Blenheim IV	Amriya, Kufra
60 SAAF	Maryland	Sidi Barrani
1437 Flt	Maryland, Baltimore	Maktila
3 SAAF (Medium Bomber) Wing (Baheira)		
223	Baltimore	LG 116
12 SAAF	Boston III	LG 21
24 SAAF	Boston III	LG 21
211 Group		
243 (Fighter) Wing (Gambut)		
33	Hurricane IIB	Gambut
274	Hurricane IIC	Gambut
80	Hurricane IIC	Gambut
73	Hurricane IIC (NF)	El Adem
335	Hurricane I	LG 10
145	Spitfire VB (from 3/6/42)	Gambut
233 (Fighter) Wing (El Adem)		
4 SAAF	Tomahawk IIB	Gambut
5 SAAF	Tomahawk IIB	Gambut
2 SAAF	Kittyhawk I	Gambut
260	Kittyhawk I	Gambut
239 (Fighter-bomber) Wing (Gambut)		
112	Kittyhawk I	Gambut
250	Kittyhawk I	Gambut
450	Kittyhawk I	Gambut
3 RAAF	Kittyhawk I	Gambut
AHQ Egypt		
94	Kittyhawk I	Maryut
213	Hurricane IIC	LG 12
238	Hurricane IIB	LG 121
14	Blenheim IV	El Firdan
805 NAS	Martlet	Maaten Bagush
GRB.1 FF	Blenheim IV	?
55	Baltimore II	LG 99

Note: Available when required were the six Wellington squadrons of 205 Group, plus the two Albacore and two Beaufighter squadrons in 201 Group.

Allied fighters were scrambled to intercept repeated bombing sorties by escorted Ju 87s making for Bir Hacheim and Italian CR.42 fighters routinely making strafing attacks on Allied M/T. By 28 May 15 *Panzer* Division was out of fuel and ammunition and resupply convoys were not making it eastwards around the southern flank of the defensive box at Bir Hacheim. Eighth Army now asked Coningham to ignore air superiority and concentrate his squadrons on attacking the enemy's supply columns. In a typically cavalier fashion, Rommel headed back and personally took the lead to bring much-needed supplies to his armoured units. In the north, the Axis suffered a setback as Gen Crüwell was captured when his Storch, searching for 50th Division positions, was shot down.

Two days later *Gruppe Rommel* was well established in what became known as the 'Cauldron', an area about 10 miles by 10 between two tracks, Trigh Capuzzo and Trigh el Abd. Between them and the minefields to the west was 150th Infantry Brigade's defensive box and 1st Army Tank Brigade, both of which were now cut off. The *Panzer* divisions put in a very heavy attack on the box, but were held off. Despite air support from the RAF (notwithstanding serious sandstorms), but with no support from the Eighth Army to the east, 150th Brigade refused the offer of surrender and on 1 June was wiped out after being assaulted by four Axis divisions with Stuka support.

In six days to the end of May WDAF aircraft had flown more than 1,500 sorties, mainly against supply convoys, plus Tac/R missions, losing around fifty aircraft, but claiming 200 vehicles destroyed and many more damaged. Not only had the fighters attacked ground targets, they were also committed heavily to keeping Stukas at bay.

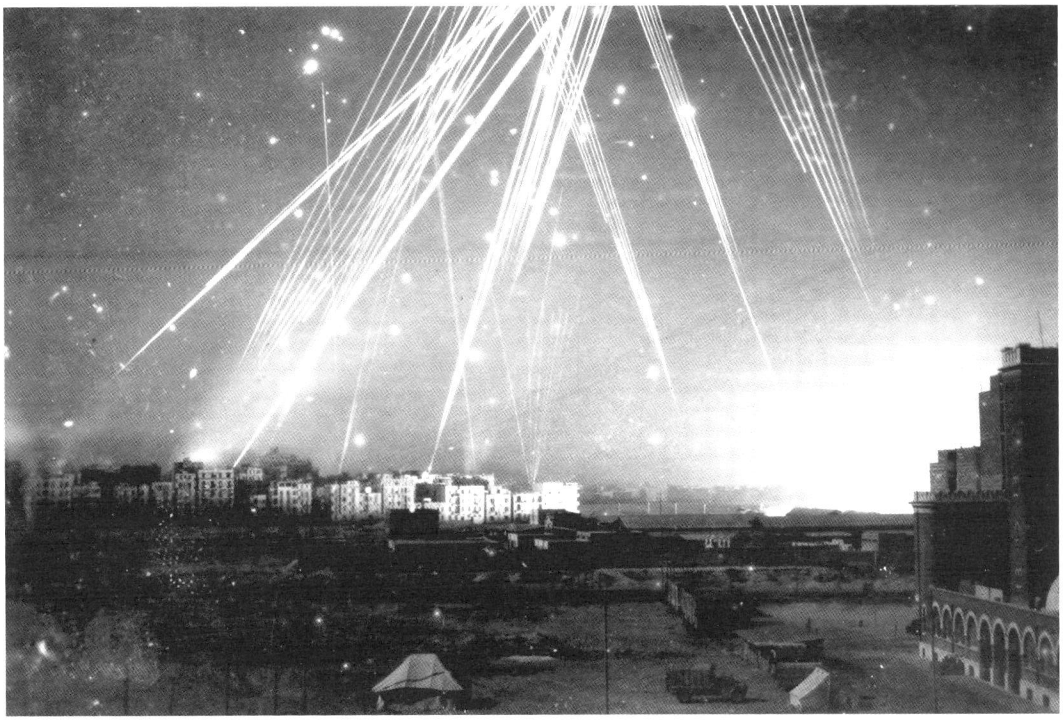

Attack was not all one-way. Alexandria was subjected to occasional bombing raids, but was heavily defended by AAA. *Alan Walton*

The Eighth Army now shortened its line running south-east from Gazala, concentrating its armour some way back at El Adem. Meanwhile, Rommel turned his attention to the remaining box, held by the Free French at Bir Hacheim. The outpost was attacked from 3 June and eventually taken on the 10th after fierce fighting and despite constant air cover. In a week the box was covered by some 1,500 sorties, 950 of them by fighters, of which twenty were lost. Pilots were flying three to four sorties daily.

Not to be outdone by Rommel, *Feldmarschall* Kesselring, Commander-in-Chief South, also took to the front. In this instance he flew as an observer in a Ju 87 on a bombing sortie over Bir Hacheim. His aircraft was damaged and force-landed 20 miles south of Tmimi, an escorted Storch being sent out to recover him. On 7 June the WDAF was diverted from Bir Hacheim to try to influence a fierce tank battle south of Knightsbridge, but shortly after resumed support for the French until the end. On 9 June Hurricanes dropped supply canisters on the box and at night Bombays of 216 Sqn also dropped supplies. Fighting here saw the introduction of the Hurricane IIDs of 6 Sqn.

On 10 June Bir Hacheim was evacuated. The valiant French defenders who, by their own admission, could not have held out without direct air support, had bought a precious eight days. As a *Luftwaffe* historian noted:[11] '...for our Army and Air Force, nine days [*sic*] of losses in material, personnel, armour and petrol. Those nine days were irrecoverable.' Yet again the 2 AASC war diary brings to life the pressures and chaos of the battles. Indeed, the handwritten original, from which extracts have been taken, conveys a clear sense of urgency and desperation:

'27 May – Two specific calls for support by Free French were answered with good effect by fighter bombers in 40 and 53 mins from set to attack.

28 May – Air policy for day fighter cover over arena of armd battle ACROMA, EL ADEM, KNIGHTSBRIDGE. Then later 2 sqns fighter bombers available harass southern supply route round BIR HACHEIM. Bostons available later when fighter force returns from base. Large enemy force building up all day south of ACROMA, bombed on third request at 1300 hrs with good effect. Fighter bombers bombed and strafed without ceasing, first on supply routes by BIR HACHEIM – EL GUBI, in afternoon to assist 13 Corps hq against a thrust from south and finally against a large enemy coln mvg[D] into arena from south-east. A great deal of traffic through control all day ... Over 150 messages passed through control with 10 target requests and 29 fighter or bomber reports. GII[E] acted almost entirely on a directif which was changed at intervals during the day.

29 May – All effort during day was concentrated in supply echelons moving north inside minefield trying to join up with armour around Knightsbridge. These attacks by Kittybombers were particularly successful, were well sustained, and probably materially delayed or even prevented the refuelling of some enemy round KNIGHTSBRIDGE. Tac/R reports were of little value here either because of delay in getting them or because of the area covered. All arrangements were complete for putting out night tgt indicators against close

[D] Column moving

[E] General staff officer grade 2, typically a major

By May 1942 the Tomahawk had largely been replaced by the Kittyhawk. 4 Sqn SAAF was one of the remaining units flying the type: squadron pilots illustrate a wide variety of flying kit. *Tinus le Roux*

leaguers[F] and Wellingtons were available but the confused situation on the battlefield at the end of the day and the appreciation of enemy movement during night precluded use being made of them. Tentacle with 8 R.T.R.[G] not heard of after 1430.

30 May – From 1154 onwards tgts were received from 69, 150 Bdes, 50 Div, 13 Corps and 30 Corps, all directed at a gap appearing about the TRIGH CAPUZZO. BGS[H] Army finally consolidated information and appreciated that TRIGH CAPUZZO, nicknamed PAUL and ROTUNDA UALEB 'PETER' were main gaps. All available fighter bombers and fighter effort was concentrated on these two and from 1345 hrs a continuous strafe was carried out on a text book tgt of tanks and MT concentrated in a minefield gap. Flak was very heavy and strong fighter cover was put up but in spite of this casualties to a/c were light.

31 May – Intention was to have a day of recuperation as far as sqns were concerned. [Enemy assumed to be west of minefields and regrouping, but assumption was wrong.] Some confusion was caused in afternoon by BGS 13 Corps asking for support direct from air ops which had just been vetoed by BGS 30 Corps. BGS Army arbitrated and the tgt was engaged. The system of laying on tgts direct from BGS etc at Corps to S.A.S.O.[I] without reference or information to control is extremely dangerous. Control may often have had a late request from a div or bde on the front which conflicts with the information then in possession of corps. A.S.C. alone must be responsible for bombline and the safety of our Troops.'

As the situation at Bir Hacheim deteriorated support to the French became a priority as did trying to speed up the decision-making process given the prevailing uncertainty as to the ebb and flow of battle.

'2 June – 1100 50 TNK[J] mvg S on Hacheim. This constituted a direct threat to Hacheim and fighter bombers were first on it in the hope of delaying attack until 7 Bde could interrupt. Towards evening enemy were attacking HACHEIM from both sides and a call for support at 2000 hrs had to be refused owing to weather conditions and time.

3 June – Policy for day was priority to HACHEIM and any good bombing tgts in CAULDRON. During night deciphered enemy messages warned us of Stuka attack at dawn, later postponed to 0800. Stukas arrived punctually but we failed to intercept. 1030 As an anti-Stuka measure all bombs were removed from fighter bombers and every effort was made to intercept. This was successful and 7 Stukas were shot down in one raid on HACHEIM.

It has been decided, at request of S.A.S.O. that GII ASC should be allowed to be fully in the military picture and speak with authy. of Army Cmd. Hitherto he has been, unofficially, in touch with Cmd's appreciation but RAF have not felt that he represented the considered Army view. He will now be allowed discretion in implementing the policy of the Army Cmd. as given to him from time to time by B.G.S. or GI Ops[K] and will refer to them only when he feels unable to make a decision in the light of this directive.

[F] Siege
[G] Royal Tank Regiment
[H] Brigadier General, Staff
[I] Senior Air Staff Officer
[J] Tanks moving
[K] General staff officer grade 1 operations, chief of staff and usually a lieutenant-colonel

4 June – Arrangements were made to bomb 369400, objective of 7 Armd Div at 0530 hrs tomorrow as a prelude to attack. Bombline is only 3 kms from tgt and I feel that this is much too close for Bostons to attempt first time. A landmark is being put out.

5 June – 6 Bostons bombed strong position successfully from 1510 to 1529. 7 Armd Div went in successfully immediately afterwards. Air reported landmark, V with sides 100 yds long as being very clear. Policy for the day, which was adhered to in spite of 15 requests for support, was to husband resources, particularly of fighter-bombers, until a definite threat developed, which it was expected to do.

6 June – Enemy thrust started last night had been directed as expected on KNIGHTSBRIDGE which during the day was attacked from E and SE. Information was scarce in the morning and it was not till 1100 that a policy for the day was formed. This was to concentrate on any tgts in the Cauldron, particularly against MT movement.'

General Ritchie had intended to destroy the Axis forces in the Cauldron in Operation *Aberdeen*, but the attack was coordinated poorly and repulsed. In early June, WDAF had embraced two notable equipment changes which, although too late to influence the present battle, would soon make a significant difference in the balance of power. The first fighter Spitfires in North Africa were allocated to 145 Sqn at Gambut, where the first nine Hurricane Mk IID 'tank-busters' equipped 6 Sqn. Fitted with two 40mm cannon, they were to prove devastating against tanks, albeit vulnerable to AA fire. Their first, abortive, sorties were on 7 June, but the following day they attacked tanks near Knightsbridge to some effect, albeit with the loss of two aircraft to AA. For the future, pilots noted that dispersed tanks mixed with M/T did not present a favourable target. More Hurricanes (213 Sqn) were added to the WDAF, having been replaced in Egypt by 127 Sqn.

With hardly a pause for breath and relying heavily on recently-acquired booty, Rommel's divisions moved eastwards on 11 June, where the columns were picked up by RAF reconnaissance. Problems of identification were exacerbated by duplication of effort with one system, but two methods, for calling for air support. As noted earlier, Corps had their own Tac/R squadrons, now 208 and 40 SAAF, calling in possible targets for air strike. The RAF operated reconnaissance through a forward-based flight of 2 PRU (Hurricane and Spitfire IV) at Gambut, whose product took longer to process.

Axis armour maintained the relentless drive on Egypt, the British losing 138 tanks in a major battle south of Knightsbridge on 12 June. There was also an extensive air battle around El Adem involving all Hurricane units and the sole Spitfire squadron that were scrambled to intercept a large force of Ju 87s and Ju 88s. The day was the worst of the battle so far for WDAF, with sixteen Kittyhawks, five Hurricanes and three Tomahawks becoming casualties. Much more serious was the loss of eleven pilots, of whom six were killed.

By *Crusader* there were five squadrons of Tomahawks operating in the ground attack role, including two South African and one Australian. If there was any doubt about ownership of Mk IIA AN325/W seen here being re-armed, the bush hat confirms it as belonging to 3 Sqn RAAF. *AST collection*

By the 14th the Eighth Army was on the verge of collapse and huge forward stores at Belhamed were destroyed, including 5.7 million litres of fuel. Three days later Tobruk was surrounded, to be taken on the 21st with the loss of a further 6.8 million litres of fuel, 7,000 tons of water, 2,000 vehicles and 300,000 rounds of artillery ammunition. By now the RAF fighter wings had moved back, first from Gambut to Sidi Azeiz and then to Sidi Barrani. Communications were breaking down. On 12 June the 2 AASC diary recorded: 'No information, even of bombline, was available early, but fighter recces were made at dawn.' Then, on the 14th: 'At 0900 we heard that a withdrawal was planned and that Army HQ was to go right back to MAKTILA. Everyone astonished as it seemed that enemy morale was at lowest ebb and that one more drive could settle him.' Thus, while supporting totally the Army, WDAF was now having to act independently of it, identifying Axis units and attacking them.

On 16 June, 21 *Panzer* Division suffered continual air attacks, which its own air force was incapable of countering. By this time Tedder had a plan for withdrawing squadrons to 20 miles behind the bomb line, but with the loss of Gambut WDAF was outside effective range of the front. Yet again there was confusion as Allied units were out of touch, both laterally and hierarchically, and decision making difficult. Units were cut off and for the RAF any bomb line was impossible to determine. Coningham was now told that the Army could not protect the airfields, leaving them vulnerable to Axis columns, the whereabouts of which could only be determined by the Air Force.

Many Allied formations were now back at the Egyptian border and, with disaster looming, Auchinleck relieved Ritchie of his command, taking personal control and deciding to withdraw in a running battle to a line south from El Alamein. The closely-packed retreating columns would have made easy targets for Axis air forces had they been nearer and not pinned down by Allied fighters. There was limited action on 27 June, given that *Luftwaffe* Messerschmitt units were desperately short of fuel. On this day a second Spitfire unit, 601 Sqn, arrived in Egypt.

The withdrawal was completed by 30 June and the Army settled in to hold the line just 80 miles west of Alexandria. While there was no doubting the bravery of the fighting soldier, the Army as a whole demonstrated a degree of incompetence bordering on the criminal. The French and New Zealanders had fought with distinction, but the Army – and Egypt – had been saved by the Air Force. In the retreat from Gazala to El Alamein, WDAF had received just twelve requests for air support from the Army: every other mission conducted was based on the RAF's own assessment of need.[12]

The cost to WDAF of the cover for the retreating Army in just five weeks was more than 200 aircraft and 123 pilots, fifty-nine of whom were killed, many of them experienced leaders. In addition, seventeen pilots were lost in trying to protect Malta-bound convoys. In the way that some British commentators have of making a victory out of disaster – Dunkirk and Arnhem for instance – one senior commander[13] was able to write subsequently that Rommel's drive '… allowed the Eighth Army and Desert Air Force [*sic*] to fall back on their supplies to end up like a coiled spring to be released at Alamein.'

Defending the El Alamein Line

With the withdrawal to El Alamein, Auchinleck organised his forces extremely quickly into sound defensive positions. His front was about 40 miles long, from the sea to the Qattara Depression, and rather than try to cover the whole extent of the line he created five defensive boxes. Three corps were under his command, but of these X Corps, with its armoured divisions, was reorganising in the Nile Delta. XXX Corps held the north of the line, with five infantry divisions and an armoured brigade group. XIII Corps held the southern sector; it had two infantry divisions, one armoured, plus a French brigade group. Boxes each comprised a brigade plus battery of field artillery, anti-tank and anti-aircraft guns. The bulk of the units were held back, though, to intercept or to come to the aid of any box under attack should the enemy break through between them. The north was more heavily defended, the intention being to force Axis units to attack in the south.

From 1 July Rommel assaulted the El Alamein Line, but with limited resources and little organised air cover. Axis air forces had flown 580 German and 177 Italian bomber sorties against Tobruk in a single day and were exhausted.[14] Their fuel was rationed too. With no air cover and WDAF response time for direct support now down to thirty-five minutes, the Axis divisions could make little headway. The 90th Light Division attacked the El Alamein box, but was repulsed. Elsewhere though, 15 and 21 *Panzer* Divisions overwhelmed 18 Brigade holding the Deir el Shein box, 10 miles to the south and at the western end of the Ruweisat Ridge.

The Tomahawks also flew as cover to other fighter squadrons engaged in low-level tasks. However, they were no match for the Bf 109 as evidenced by Tomahawk IIA AN422/TA-U of 2 Sqn SAAF, which was shot down south-west of Martuba on 12 December 1941 by aircraft of JG 53. The pilot, Capt P. J. Robbertse, became a prisoner of war. *AST collection*

For a brief period in Spring 1942 260 Sqn operated the Tomahawk, a flight of which is seen here at Port Said in March. *Author's collection*

On 7 August 1942 Churchill decided to appoint Lt Gen William Gott to succeed Auchinleck as commander Eighth Army. Unaware, Gott boarded Bombay L5814 of 216 Sqn at Burgh el Arab for Cairo. Shortly after take-off the aircraft was attacked by Bf 109s of II/JG 27, resulting in a crash landing which all aboard survived. However, the fighters returned to strafe the aircraft resulting in the deaths of those remaining on board, including Gott. His replacement was Bernard Montgomery. *Author's collection*

Between 1 and 7 July the WDAF pounded Axis airfields, including those at Gazala, Tmimi and Sidi Barrani, flying 5,458 sorties.[15] Axis forces were then to take the western end of the Ruweisat Ridge, after which Rommel stopped attacks to draw breath. On the 9th, 21 *Panzer* Division attacked the box at Bab el Qattara; the defenders, 6 NZ Brigade, held out. Auchinleck had been aware through intelligence of Axis intentions and he thus launched an attack in the north by South African and Australian divisions against two positions held by similar Italian formations. The attack was backed with heavy air support, but at huge cost: twenty-six fighters were lost or badly damaged, together with twelve pilots, of whom five were killed.

Rommel also moved key units north, but on the 14th had to rethink as Allied forces attempted to retake the Ruweisat Ridge. An Axis counter-attack achieved some success, due in part to a lack of accord at this time between Allied infantry and armoured units. On 16 July Rommel's *Afrika Korps* suffered a serious loss when a bomber raid on Mersa Matruh destroyed 50,000 gallons of fuel and 2,200 tons of ammunition.

Throughout July and August, despite heavy losses, WDAF kept the upper hand. The Air Force was consolidated, new wings created, more cannon-armed Hurricanes delivered and, as noted, a second squadron of Spitfires (601 Sqn) deployed; Table 5.6 demonstrates clearly the concentration of units. Each day there were up to seven Boston or Baltimore missions of eighteen or so aircraft, all escorted by fighters, with the newly arrived Spitfires providing top cover. Very few of the light bombers were lost, despite their escorts sometimes peeling off to attack Ju 87s or CR.42s coming in the opposite direction.

An increasing number of Hurricanes and Kittyhawks were fitted for carrying ordnance and one flight of Hurricanes of 7 Sqn SAAF was equipped to drop the unusual Jefferis 'sticky bomb'. Formally the 'Grenade, Hand, Anti-tank No 74' it comprised a glass sphere containing nitroglycerine with a powerful adhesive on the exterior to enable it to stick to a non-dusty/clean tank. The Hurricanes were fitted with three tandem light series bomb racks, one under each wing and one under the mid-fuselage enabling twenty-four bombs to be carried.[16] The first operational use was in September 1942 but the weapon proved to have little value since it was impossible to aim and the fighter-bombers were particularly susceptible to AA fire.

Within the limitations of fuel, Bf 109s were either roaming on unplanned (*Freie Jagd*) sorties or stuck with escorting vulnerable bombers. WDAF, which had expanded slightly since the retreat from Gazala, now concentrated its various wings in a complex of landing grounds south of Amriya, for which there was an effective air defence radar network to give early warning of incoming raids, allowing squadrons to be scrambled. Even so, it was surprising that there was no Axis aerial assault on these airfields. In general, WDAF was operating defensively when necessary, but more usually beyond the line by attacking obvious enemy formations and airfields.

On most days there were fighter patrols over the boxes, not providing close support but there to head-off any threat from the air, which was done most successfully. At night there was no let-up for Axis troops as the Wellingtons of 205 Group pounded away against targets illuminated by Naval Albacores.

With consolidation on the front, there were now changes in preparation for the inevitable battle ahead. In early July, reflecting the importance of his command, Tedder was promoted to Air Chief Marshal. Lt Gen Bernard Montgomery was in Egypt on 12 August ready to assume command of Eighth Army and just three days later Auchinleck was relieved as Commander-in-Chief, to be replaced by Gen Sir Harold Alexander. The Eighth Army was also receiving new equipment. Lend-lease M3 Grant medium tanks from the US and 6-pounder anti-tank guns were proving themselves and the Grant's successor, the improved M4 Sherman, was in the pipeline. Also, in mid-August, 5 AASC arrived, to be located with the joint forward HQs.

Subject to the changes at the head of the Army, the RAF now had systems, equipment and men in place to support any campaign to retake Cyrenaica. And now, at least, it was Rommel who had the overextended supply lines and lacked immediate air cover. Axis attacks on Malta had slowed so that naval and air units on the island were able once more to interdict supply shipping from Italy and Greece to Libya. The US had entered the theatre with heavy and medium bombers, initially based in Palestine. From here on, battles were destined to go the way of the Allies.

Table 5.6 – AHQ Western Desert units, 5 July 1942

AHQ Western Desert		
240 Wing (Heliopolis)		
208	Hurricane II, Tomahawk IIB	Heliopolis
40 SAAF	Hurricane I, Tomahawk IIB	LG 39
6	Hurricane IID	LG 91
15 SAAF	Blenheim IV	El Ballah
1437 Flt	Maryland, Baltimore	Heliopolis
2 PRU	Maryland, Hurricane II, Spitfire IV	Heliopolis det LG 100
3 SAAF (Medium Bomber) Wing (Baheira)		
223	Baltimore II	LG 207
12 SAAF	Boston III	Bilbeis
24 SAAF	Boston III	LG 97
211 Group		
7 SAAF (Fighter) Wing (LG 89)		
33	Hurricane IIC	LG 154
73	Hurricane IIC (NF)	LG 89
7 SAAF	Hurricane I	LG 89
335	Hurricane I	Idku
233 (Fighter-bomber) Wing (Amriya)		
5 SAAF	Tomahawk IIB	LG 85
2 SAAF	Kittyhawk I	LG 85
4 SAAF	Kittyhawk I	LG 85
260	Kittyhawk I	LG 85
239 (Fighter-bomber) Wing (Amriya)		
112	Kittyhawk IA	LG 91
250	Kittyhawk I	LG 91
450	Kittyhawk I	LG 91
3 RAAF	Kittyhawk I	LG 91 Amriya
243 (Fighter) Wing (Amriya)		
213	Hurricane IIC	LG 154
238	Hurricane IIB	LG 92
274	Hurricane IIC	LG 92
145	Spitfire VB	LG 154
244 (Fighter) Wing (Amriya)		
601	Spitfire VC	LG 154
80	Hurricane IIC	LG 92
127	Hurricane IIB	LG 92
1 SAAF	Hurricane IIB	LG 92
AHQ Egypt		
417 RCAF	Spitfire VB	Kasfareet
94	Hurricane IIC	El Gamil
805 NAS	Martlet	Maaten Bagush
14	Blenheim IV	LG 207
GRB.1 FF	Blenheim IV	LG 207
55	Baltimore II	LG 207

[1] Richards, *Royal Air Force 1939-1945 Vol II*, p169
[2] TNA WO 277/34 Army Air Support
[3] Granfield, *Bombers Over Sand and Snow*, p176
[4] Townshend Bickers, *The Desert Air War*, p71
[5] Cross, *Straight and Level*, p159
[6] Macksey in Purnell's *History of the Second World War Volume 2*, p755
[7] Terraine, *A Time of Courage*, p359
[8] Shores et al, *Mediterranean Air War Vol Two*, p209
[9] TNA WO169/6638 *War Diary of 2 AASC*
[10] Terraine, *A Time of Courage*, p371
[11] Quoted in Richards, *Royal Air Force 1939-1945 Vol II*, p202
[12] Richards, *Royal Air Force 1939-1945 Vol II*, p225
[13] De Guingand, F, *Generals at War* ,p182
[14] Terraine, *A Time of Courage*, p375
[15] Richards, *Royal Air Force 1939-1945 Vol II*, p212
[16] TNA AIR 20/4315 *The attack of Ground Targets by Fighters*

6 Alam Halfa and El Alamein, August–November 1942

Preparation for the Offensive

British forces had suffered from coordinated German land and air assault in the Battle of France and subsequently in the Western Desert. While that had prompted thought and some research into how the RAF might best support the Army on the battlefield, the desire for co-operation at the highest levels was at best lukewarm. It was not until the desert war in Egypt and Libya that the first serious attempts were made to utilise the Air Force in immediate support of an Army assault.

In Egypt the war had ebbed and flowed, the Italians attacking from Libya in September 1940, to be firmly repulsed early in 1941. German troops were now deployed in Libya and under Field Marshal Erwin Rommel began an attack on the British in February 1941, crossing eventually into Egypt in June. With around only thirty serviceable aircraft, the RAF was in no position to offer much support to the retreating Army.

But by November the British Eighth Army outnumbered Axis forces, launching Operation *Crusader* which was designed to recover ground lost in Libya and relieve the garrison at Tobruk that had been surrounded by the Germans in their Spring advance. The attack drove forward 300 miles but was held, Rommel counter-attacking in two stages, eventually ending in late June 1942 with his forces poised on a line to the west of El Alamein, only 80 miles from Alexandria. Due to Gen Claude Auchinleck's poor handling of forces against a numerically inferior enemy, he was replaced as GOC-in-C Middle East and GOC Eighth Army by generals Sir Harold Alexander and Bernard Montgomery respectively.

The Army commanders now expected a further attack, plans for the containment of which were put in place. However, the main consideration was an all-out attack on Axis forces once Eighth Army troops had been equipped and trained properly. Prime Minister Winston Churchill was keen for this new attack to commence in September, but the Army chiefs were adamant that success would depend on prepared formations attacking in ideal moon conditions late in October.

The key to successful collaboration in Egypt was to be the personal relationships between Army and Air Force commanders. At the highest level, General Alexander, the GOC-in-C, worked well with Air Chief Marshal Sir Arthur Tedder, AOC-in-C RAF Middle East Command. For the forthcoming battles, Lt Gen Sir Bernard Montgomery, newly appointed commander of the Eighth Army, formed a close relationship with Air Vice-Marshal Sir Arthur Coningham, under whose guidance the Western Desert Air Force had matured from the disparate units within 204 Group.

Coningham was only too well aware that his job was to give the Army full and unstinting support. His HQ was at Burgh al Arab, about 28 miles south-west of Alexandria and only 50 miles to the east of El Alamein. Montgomery shared his HQ, but because of Army and RAF staff numbers combined, there was also the need for a shared, rear, HQ at Wadi Natrun. Thus, from Autumn 1942, at staff level the Army and RAF were able to integrate fully and share their intentions, which in turn enabled the RAF to plan properly its support for the Army.

The Battle of Alam Halfa

The expected Axis attack on the line started on 31 August. It presented no surprise to Montgomery since he was well apprised of the intentions and limitations of Rommel and his forces. Aerial reconnaissance and decrypts of German communications through *Ultra* signal intercepts allowed unprecedented insight into German planning. The German commander was determined to exploit his position and catch the British before they had re-equipped fully, but the risks were huge since the Axis forces were starved of supplies. Indeed, according to General Bayerlein, Chief-of-Staff of the *Afrika Korps*, by August supplies crossing the Mediterranean were only 20% of the minimum required for conduct of an offensive.[1]

Table 6.1 – Luftwaffe, Mediterranean, Autumn 1942

Fliegerführer Afrika[2]		
Stab, II/JG 27	Bf 109F-4, G	Qotaifiya
I/JG 27	Bf 109F-4	Turbiya
III, 10./JG 27	Bf 109F-4	Qasaba, Fuka
III and 10./JG 53	Bf 109F-4	Qasaba
I/NJG 2	Ju 88A, C	
III/ZG 1*	Bf 109E-7, Bf 110	Bir el Abd
III/ZG 26	Bf 110 C, D, E and F	Crete
10./ZG 26	Do 17Z-2	Barce
Stab StG 3	He111H-5, Bf 110E-3	Qasaba
I, II, III/StG 3	Ju 87R-2, 4	Qasaba, El Daba
I, II/LG 1	Ju 88A-4	Crete
II/KG 77	Ju 88A-4	Crete
II/KG 100	He 111H-6	Crete
2.(F)/123	Ju 86R-1	Crete
4.(H)/12	Bf 110F-3	Crete
2.(H)/14	Bf 109E,F Bf 110E	

* renamed II./SchG 2 1 November
X Fliegerkorps included bomber and reconnaissance units operating from Crete and Greece. *Transportverbande Ob.Süd* provided Ju 52/3m and Me 323 transports.

The front along which Axis troops would have to attack was only some 30 miles in length, sea at the northern end and the impassable (by armour) Qattara Depression to the south. While there may be popular notions of the desert as featureless flat scrub or heaving dunes à la Lawrence of Arabia, the Egyptian Western Desert was far from featureless, containing high, rocky ridges interconnected by tracks. So while there were stretches where cover could be non-existent, and there were heaving sand dunes, there were also plenty of areas where formations could organise or regroup or where ambushes could be set. (To get some appreciation of the terrain the reader is recommended to download Google Earth and to zoom in on the area to the south of El Alamein. From a mass of ochre, features begin to emerge, including high, rocky outcrops and the odd oasis.)

Montgomery deployed his two Corps with care, knowing that there would be a feint to the north and the main attack in the south, where the Germans believed defences to be weakest. Three infantry divisions of XXX Corps held a 12-mile front to the north while XIII Corps deployed two infantry and two armoured divisions some way behind the notional front line. On the night of 30 August RAF Wellingtons bombed Axis troop concentrations, targets being lit by flares dropped from Fleet Air Arm Albacores.

The British Army now had excellent support from a well-equipped and experienced Western Desert Air Force that included fighters and medium bombers of the United States Middle East Air Force (USMEAF), supplemented by medium bomber and coastal strike units further back under AHQ Egypt. In total the relevant Allied air forces included thirteen Hurricane, three Spitfire, seven Kittyhawk, one Tomahawk and two P-40F Warhawk fighter squadrons and two Boston, three Baltimore, four B-25 Mitchell and six Wellington bomber squadrons, plus two Beaufighter strike squadrons. Of the total forty-three squadrons, nine were South African, six American and two Australian.

Critical tactical reconnaissance duties were shared between the Hurricanes of 208 Sqn (XXX Corps) and 40 Sqn SAAF (XIII Corps). The ventral camera fitting is noteworthy in this line-up of Mk II aircraft of 208 Sqn. *Author's collection*

Countering the Allied air forces were *Luftwaffe* and *Regia Aeronautica* units in North Africa, Sicily, Crete and Greece. The fighter and ground attack units included the following (readers not familiar with German and Italian air force formations should consult Appendix 1):

Rommel attacked with three German and three Italian divisions as anticipated and was able to proceed while under attack from Allied fighter-bombers. His forces were delayed by having to cross a much denser minefield than had been expected and by the constant harassment of air strikes. The attackers were supported during the day by two waves of Ju 87 Stukas of StG 3, escorted by Bf 109s and Macchi C.202 fighters. Several raids were carried out by CR.42 fighters. Axis losses amounted to five 109s, three Ju 87s, two Ju 88s and an He 111 of the *Luftwaffe*, plus two C.202s, one C.200 and a CR.42 of the *Regia Aeronautica*. British losses were six Hurricanes, two Spitfires and three Baltimores.

Having bypassed the New Zealand Division situated to the north of the 'gate', the enemy turned north, anticipating a tank battle. However, British tank units were under instruction to work in a static, anti-tank, role so as to let German and Italian forces come up against well-prepared defences. By the end of 1 September the 15th *Panzer* Division was confronting the 10th Armoured Division on the Alam Halfa Ridge, with 7th Armoured Division to its right flank. Throughout that day Allied bombers with extensive escort flew at least seven major raids, losing three Baltimores brought down by flak. Fighters fared rather worse, especially at the hands of JG 27, whose *Oblt* Hans-Joachim Marseille claimed no less than seventeen destroyed or damaged during the day.

Short of fuel and under constant air attack from Allied air forces that had air superiority, Rommel had no option but to withdraw on the night of 2 September. Allied bombers were now flying in excess of 200 sorties a day with minimal loss; it was the escorting fighters that footed the bill. Wellingtons of 205 Group dropped 4,000lb GP bombs with devastating effect. Both Italian and German fighters tried to cover the retreating forces and protect them from attack, but with little success.

Although Montgomery was determined not to exploit victory by pursuing fleeing Axis troops so as to husband his resources for the impending assault from El Alamein, elements of the New Zealand Division did attack the retreating forces. Despite continuing air support, they suffered considerable casualties before the battle was eventually called off on 7 September.

Throughout the battle Hurricanes of 208 Sqn undertook tactical reconnaissance missions that were very heavily escorted, such were their importance. For example, on one critical sortie on 30 August, they were escorted by eight Hurricanes at low level and nine Spitfires flying top cover.[3] The price, though, was high: three Hurricanes and one Spitfire lost, two pilots killed. A constant stream of Boston and Baltimore bombers, together with USAAF B-25s, hit troop concentrations that were

Table 6.2 – Regia Aeronautica, Mediterranean, Autumn 1942

Regia Aeronautica			
2° Stormo			
8° Gruppo			
	92ª, 93ª, 94ª Squadriglia	C.200	Bu Amud
13° Gruppo			
	77ª, 78ª, 82ª Squadriglia	C.200	Bu Amud
3° Stormo			
18° Gruppo			
	83ª, 85ª, 95ª Squadriglia	C.200	Abu Haggag
23° Gruppo			
	70ª, 74ª, 75ª Squadriglia	C.202	Abu Haggag
4° Stormo			
9° Gruppo			
	73ª, 96ª, 97ª Squadriglia	C.202	El Daba, Fuka
10° Gruppo			
	84ª, 90ª, 91ª Squadriglia	C.202	El Daba, Fuka
5° Stormo			
101° Gruppo			
	208ª, 238ª Squadriglia	CR.42	Abu Nimeir
15° Stormo			
46° Gruppo			
	20ª, 21ª, Squadriglia	CR.42	Castel Benito
47° Gruppo			
	53ª, 54ª, nnª Squadriglia	CR.42	Castel Benito
Autonomous fighter units			
150° Gruppo			
	363ª, 364ª, 365ª Squadriglia	C.200	
160° Gruppo			
	375ª, 393ª, 394ª Squadriglia	CR.42	Benghazi

In addition, there were four squadriglia equipped with the Cant Z.1007*bis* bomber, some of which bombed Allied lines, and six squadriglia of Ca 311/313 light bombers that appear not to have participated.

Martin Baltimores of three squadrons were involved in tactical close support during the Alam Halfa battle, but they suffered heavy casualties. Mk IIIA FA204 hails from 55 Sqn. *Tinus le Roux*

obviously beyond the bomb line. As long as the enemy was advancing and the bombers had a very clear understanding of the location of temporarily static divisions, like those in the north, there was little risk of bombing friendly forces.

For all personnel, fighting in the desert brought its own special hazards. During the day it was very hot, at night freezing. Sandstorms could kick up with very little notice; dust got into every crevice. Disease was rife, including dysentery, as was jaundice and sores. Aircraft navigation could be very difficult, especially when flying over unfamiliar territory where tracks, ridges and outcrops looked pretty much the same as one another.

At the outset some units were based at permanent stations in the Delta area, but most fighter and light bomber formations were held at landing grounds carved out of the desert. One clutch of some eighteen landing grounds was created on a 20-mile stretch astride the Alexandria–Wadi Natrun road. At their meanest these were levelled 'fields' with a tent or two and an Aldis lamp. Pilots soon learned to take off in line abreast in order not to have to fly through the dust raised by preceding aircraft. All maintenance was undertaken in the open and, surprisingly given the conditions and the extent to which aircraft were being shot up by flak or enemy fighters, serviceability as high as 66%.

From 9 August pilots of two USAAF P-40 Warhawk squadrons had been distributed among RAF and SAAF units so that they might gain experience of desert war conditions generally and become familiar with flying bomber escort missions, in preparation for the battles ahead. In the online history of the 57th Fighter Group, the author presents an excellent picture of a typical Western Desert landing ground:[4]

> 'The procedure of building an airfield in this country was unique. One of the numerous level areas near a highway was simply marked off by gasoline drums at each of the four corners, a wind sock was erected, and the field was ready for business. The tent area covered a considerable amount of space due to the dispersal of the tents. To concentrate anything here – aircraft, gasoline, ammunition or personnel – was to invite disaster. Each tent had five occupants, two of whom maintained the aircraft parked close by it. At first a sentry mount of two score roving guards was tried but German reconnaissance aircraft overhead tended to make light sleepers of all the men so the plan was abandoned in favor of a guard post in the ration tent throughout the hours of darkness.'

Alam Halfa was to be the last Axis offensive in the Western Desert – and it failed. The RAF and the Royal Navy had dealt with the supply lines across the Mediterranean and Montgomery enjoyed the support of an air force twice the size of that of the Axis and more widely dispersed. Rommel had this to say:[5]

For the first time, aircraft of the USAAF were integrated within WDAF, mounting raids on forward Axis positions. This singular B-25 of the 12th Bombardment Group is obviously part of a close formation: note the RAF fin flash. ***Mark O'Boyle***

'We had learned one important lesson during this operation, a lesson which was to affect all subsequent planning and, in fact, our entire future conduct of the war. This was that the possibilities of ground action, operational and tactical, become very limited if one's adversary commands the air with a powerful air force and can fly mass air raids by heavy bomber formations unconcerned for their own safety.'

What Rommel could not know was the hugely important part that *Ultra* intercepts played in his defeat. In the application of air power in support of ground forces, Coningham described his priorities for success in the use of tactical air power:

'First, gain air superiority. Second, use the air superiority gained to interdict enemy reinforcements of men and materiel to isolate the battlefield. Third, combine air attacks with ground assaults on the front lines.'

Air supremacy, so essential in order to have clear skies within which close support aircraft could operate with impunity, was not at this stage achieved, but air superiority was. By strangling Axis forces' supply routes – whether by sea or air – the enemy simply lacked the fuel and ammunition to engage in widespread combat.

During the Battle of Alam Halfa, Allied losses in the air were three times those of the Axis air forces. Brief as it was, it was a battle in which, for the first time, Allied air forces were integrated into the overall battle plan. Allied losses were 1,730 men, sixty-seven tanks and at least 128 aircraft, although nearly half of these were recovered for eventual repair. Axis losses were 2,930 men, fifty-one tanks and forty-three aircraft. The Allies lost twenty-three pilots killed, fifteen wounded, plus five taken prisoner. Axis air forces suffered a similar loss in pilots. Some 400 trucks plus armoured cars and artillery pieces were also destroyed by roving Allied fighter-bombers.

Table 6.3 – Allied Air Force losses, 31 August–7 September 1942

Date	Type	s/d combat	s/d flak	Other
31/8	Tomahawk, Kittyhawk, P-40	5		
	Hurricane	7	1	2
	Spitfire	1		
	Bombers	1	4	
1/9	Tomahawk, Kittyhawk, P-40	9		
	Hurricane	8	1	2
	Spitfire	3		1
	Beaufighter			2
	Bombers		3	
2/9	Tomahawk, Kittyhawk, P-40	4		
	Hurricane	9		
	Spitfire	3		
	Bombers		1	
3/9	Tomahawk, Kittyhawk, P-40	7	1	1
	Hurricane	5		1
	Spitfire	2		
	Bombers		2	
4/9	Hurricane	1		2
	Bombers			1
5/9	Tomahawk, Kittyhawk, P-40	2		
	Hurricane	2		1
	Spitfire	2		
	Bombers			1
6/9	Tomahawk, Kittyhawk, P-40	8		
	Hurricane	7	1	3
	Spitfire	3		
7/9	Tomahawk, Kittyhawk, P-40	3		4
	Hurricane			1
	Spitfire			1
Total	Tomahawk, Kittyhawk, P-40	38	1	5
	Hurricane	39	3	12
	Spitfire	14	0	1
	Beaufighter	0	0	2
	Bombers	1	10	2
All		**92**	**14**	**22**

The Hurricane remained the mainstay for close support, although now supplemented by the Kittyhawk and with the first Spitfire Vs arriving as escorts to address the Bf 109F. Flying with the canopy open is Capt J. A. Gaynor in Hurricane IIC HL627/AX-X of 1 Sqn SAAF. *Author's collection*

Spitfire VB EP649/B of 92 Sqn which by November 1943 was one of three squadrons operating this welcome addition to the WDAF inventory. *Tinus le Roux*

The medium bombers were critical in containing Axis ability to wage war. The Wellingtons of several squadrons were adapted to carry 4,000lb 'cookies' including aircraft R of 104 Sqn. *Author's collection*

Allied aircraft losses, as shown in the accompanying table, were mainly to enemy fighters and illustrate vividly the cost of providing the Army with the effective support needed. In general, P-40 variants were used for ground attack or low cover for medium bombers and the Tac/R aircraft. Hurricanes were used in the same way, in addition to performing the Tac/R task. Hurricane losses were most numerous, but with P-40s they succeeded in protecting the all-important bombers which were attacking mainly troop, armour and artillery concentrations and dumps close to the front line.

Newly introduced Spitfires, flown mostly by pilots fresh to the type, provided top cover to escorting Hurricanes and Kittyhawks, their losses almost all to experienced pilots flying the Bf 109F or Macchi C.202. As a reminder of RAF flexibility, the two Beaufighters lost had been diverted from their normal anti-shipping role to strafing road convoys. Wellingtons bombing by night were similarly diverted from the norm of attacking Axis targets on Crete and in Greece.

Coningham's priorities for success were addressed – just. Air superiority was achieved through a combination of superior numbers and by suffocating the supply system, despite Allied pilots being less experienced. Interdiction worked well, the Army and Air Force co-ordinating effectively. Tactical reconnaissance, at the bidding of the Army commander, gave immediate updates on enemy activity behind the front line that enabled some limited direct, but not close, support to the Army as the battle progressed hour-by-hour. There was no mechanism in place to bring close support aircraft to bear in the immediacy of the battle. However, given the nature of the terrain, artillery could comfortably address the needs of forward troops with speedy reaction and accuracy.

The Second Battle of El Alamein, October 1942

By mid-October Montgomery was ready to attack the combined Italian-German Army, westwards from El Alamein through Libya to Tunisia. The Allies had been preparing for landings in Morocco and Algeria for several months in the planned Operation *Torch*, the aim of which was to establish a sound base in north-west Africa from which to squeeze Axis forces from the west and to provide bases from which to mount an assault on Sicily. At the outset the Allies had three Corps, totalling some 195,000 troops, organised as described at Table 6.4 below.[6] (Army Air Support Control tentacles are shown where attached.)

Some units were held under direct Army command to support mine clearance, HQ, and railway and anti-aircraft protection. Army troops were mainly engineers and signals.

In terms of equipment, the Eighth Army was better equipped than the Axis forces, fielding more than 1,000 tanks plus 200 in reserve. While some were older and outgunned by German tanks, the total included 252 newly delivered Shermans, 170 Grants and 119 Stuarts. Some of the older tanks had been converted for mine clearance. There were also 849 new 6-pounder (57mm) anti-tank guns, 554 of the older 2-pounder (40mm) AT gun and 830 25-pounder field guns, backed by 52 medium guns.[7]

A potent new weapon available from the summer of 1942 was the Hurricane IID armed with two 37mm anti-tank cannon (15 rounds apiece) and twin .303in machine guns for tracer aiming. Armour protected the pilot but the aircraft was slow and vulnerable in areas where there was effective AAA. *Author's collection*

Table 6.4 – Eighth Army order of battle

XXX Corps (Lt Gen Sir Oliver Leese) to the north, 15-mile front
9th (Australian) Division (tentacle)
20th Aus Brigade
24th Aus Brigade
26th Aus Brigade (tentacle)
51st (Highland) Division (tentacle)
152nd Brigade
153rd Brigade
154th Brigade
2nd (New Zealand) Division (tentacle)
5th NZ Brigade
6th NZ Brigade
9th Armoured Brigade (tentacle)
1st (South African) Division (tentacle)
1st SA Brigade
2nd SA Brigade
3rd SA Brigade
4th (Indian) Division
5th Ind Brigade
7th Ind Brigade
161st Ind Brigade
208 Sqn RAF Tac Recce
X Corps (Lt Gen Herbert Lumsden) behind XXX Corps
1st Armoured Division (tentacle)
2nd Armoured Brigade
7th Motorised Brigade
Hammerforce (ex 8th Armoured Division)
8th Armoured Division
Elements split between 1st and 10th divisions
10th Armoured Division (tentacle)
8th Armoured Brigade (tentacle)
24th Armoured Brigade (ex 8th Armoured Division)
133rd Lorried Infantry Brigade (ex 44th Division) (tentacle)
XIII Corps (Lt Gen Brian Horrocks) to the south, 25-mile front
50th Division (tentacle)
69th Infantry Brigade
151st Infantry Brigade
1st Greek Brigade
44th Division (tentacle)
131st Brigade
132nd Brigade
7th Armoured Division (tentacle)
4th Light Armoured Brigade (tentacle)
22nd Armoured Brigade (tentacle)
1st Free French Brigade Group
2nd Free French Brigade Group
40 Sqn SAAF Tac Recce

The WDAF had improved aircraft recovery and repair considerably, increasing the number of machines available. 31 Maintenance Unit provided mobile support for repair alongside 32 Air Stores Park, pilots were better trained and there was no shortage of fuel, bombs or ammunition. Additionally, the full resources of AHQ Egypt could be added to the equation, including bombers, workshops, signals and mobile radars.

The Axis line was held by 104,000 troops in thirteen divisions, five German and eight Italian, of which six were armoured. That gave Montgomery a near 2:1 superiority in manpower.[8] Formidable Axis minefields were between 1 and 2 miles deep and sown with 445,000 mines, 4% of them anti-personnel. Immediately behind the defences were anti-tank and machine guns, then heavier artillery and at the rear tanks, totalling around 550.

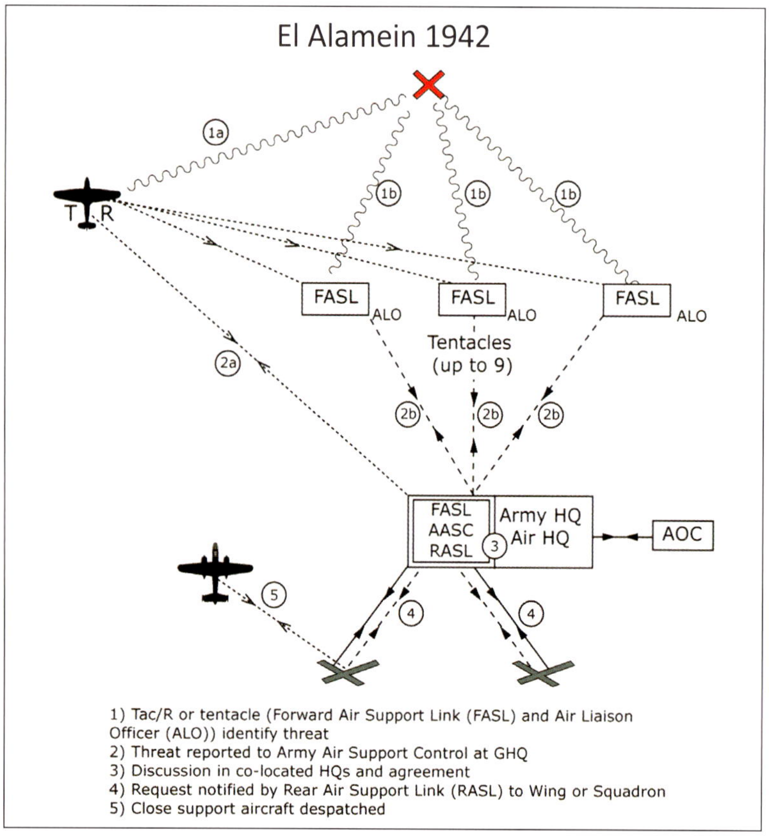

With just a 40-mile line over which to attack, Montgomery had few options. The plan for Operation *Lightfoot* was for a heavy attack by XXX Corps in the north, opening up the minefields for X Corps armour to pass through and creating their own cleared channels. At the same time XIII Corps would strike more conservatively in the south. Once bridgeheads were created armour and artillery would nibble away at resistance on the flanks. It was expected that this 'crumbling' would provoke an armoured assault, bringing the Axis tanks to battle on Allied terms.

Eighth Army staff were well prepared and had a clear understanding of enemy dispositions, supplies and limitations. The intelligence had come from a number of sources and by now was being analysed and communicated cohesively, effectively and speedily. There were three levels of intelligence: strategic, which gave commanders an overall appreciation of the enemy's situation and, perhaps, intent; operational, which provided information on dispositions, supply states and so on; and tactical, which was more immediate and enabled threats to be neutralised and opportunities embraced.

Sources included *Ultra* decrypts, prisoner-of-war interrogation, captured documents, 'Y' service wireless intercepts, strategic reconnaissance and tactical reconnaissance from the two allocated Tac/R squadrons and ground observation posts. The RAF was heavily involved not only in reconnaissance, but also in its own Y service (originally Wireless Interception – WI, hence 'Y'), for which it formed 276 Wing in August 1942. The Wing included ground units and 162 Sqn flying Blenheims and Wellingtons, the latter focusing on signals gathering and jamming.

Consequently, not only did Army commanders know what was where, but the WDAF was able to determine a precise support plan. However, this could not be guaranteed totally effective for two reasons. First, the Army had hitherto been slow to communicate the need for precise support and also had not demonstrated an understanding of the need to illustrate the bomb line – the line immediately in front of friendly troops. Would new arrangements now improve this consideration? Second, Allied air forces had air superiority, but not air supremacy. That meant that while Axis air forces were outnumbered, under-supplied and, in an attack, on the back foot, they could still field first-class fighters and dive-bombers flown by experienced pilots. This resulted in the Allied need for escorts for bombing and reconnaissance sorties at all times, added to which attacking aircraft were also vulnerable to very effective heavy and light anti-aircraft artillery.

Hurricane IIC AK-K of 213 Sqn undergoing first-line servicing at Misurata in a genuinely unposed photograph which shows a great deal of detail. *Alan Walton*

213 Sqn incorporated the central element of the squadron badge on to the middle of the fuselage roundel on its Hurricanes, but not repeated later on Spitfires or Mustangs. *Author's collection*

Introduced into RAF service in Spring 1942 the Curtiss Kittyhawk (US P-40E) was an improvement on the Tomahawk, employing a more powerful Allison engine. AL225/GA-T of 112 Sqn, pictured with the famous shark mouth marking, was a Mk I featuring four .50in machine guns and here carrying what appears to be a 250lb bomb. *Author's collection*

The Dominion squadrons were joined now by the first of the USAAF fighter units in theatre, flying the P-40F as seen here. *Author's collection*

Kittyhawk I
AL186/DB-G
2 SAAF Sqn.
Luca G. Canossa

Boston III SAAF W8376/C 12 Sqn. *Luca G. Canossa*

The light bombers played a crucial part in the attack from El Alamein. 24 Sqn SAAF, whose Boston III HK885/A is portrayed, was one of two Boston units in 3 SAAF Wing. ***Tinus le Roux***

Montgomery understood the potential of air power on the battlefield and implicitly the need for it to retain integrity. 'Air power is indivisible. If you split it up into compartments, you merely pull it to pieces and destroy its greatest asset, its flexibility.' Thus, apart from the two Tac/R squadrons allocated to Corps, the remainder of the WDAF was retained under centralised command by Coningham and organised in wings. Working adjacent to the Army Commander, he was in the best position to judge and agree with Montgomery where and when attacks should be made. New procedures eliminated delay and an agreed request for close support could be delivered within thirty minutes. One development which aided further the Allied air forces was the introduction of VHF radios with greater range than the earlier TR9 HF sets.

At this stage in the war the Army was still dependant on artillery for very close support; observation posts were very firmly on the ground, typically atop an appropriately equipped armoured car. Tac/R aircraft could identify potential targets and give a general indication of shooting effectiveness, but at speed and low level they struggled to conduct a shoot.

An important feature of WDAF was that it was, in effect, a composite Group. Indeed, to July 1941 it had been 204 Group. In totality it comprised aircraft of several types and functions that operated within wings that were able to be used in a coordinated manner. The squadrons within wings were located mostly on the same landing ground, typically some 30 miles behind the front. In addition, units under the command of AHQ Egypt could be called upon quickly, typically the Wellington bombers of 205 Group and Beaufighters of 235 Wing.

By the El Alamein battle only 5 Sqn SAAF remained operating the Tomahawk, typically AM196/GL-F ***AST collection***

One of the most important aircraft in providing support to the Army – while at the same time demonstrating almost total integration of air forces – was the Albacore of the Fleet Air Arm. Operated by 826 NAS from Dekheila, the type was used for target marking for the Wellington night bombers of 205 Group, as typified by N4424/4K. *Author's collection*

Air Support by November 1942

The key to air support was the Army Air Support Control (AASC) which, at this stage, had evolved from experience in the Western Desert and the theoretical models in Army Co-operation Command in the UK. By the time of El Alamein procedures were laid down clearly in the Middle East (Army and RAF) Directive of Direct Air Support.[9] Contained in seventy-two sections plus appendices, every detail was covered, including mechanisms for requesting air support; types of air support; good and poor target types; communications; and recognition symbols.

Mindful of criticisms on the part of the Army about air cover for troops on the front line, the point was made that if priority is to be given to attacking enemy forces on the ground the Army must look carefully to its own anti-aircraft provision. The Directive rejected the term 'close air support' and instead referred to 'indirect' and 'direct' air support. Indirect was, in effect, interdiction; direct was split between prearranged (easily organised) and impromptu, which was described as '...a far more difficult problem, especially in fluid operations and particularly in support of armoured formations.'

In Egypt a number of types was involved in less dramatic, but still essential tasks. Wellington Directional Wireless Installation (DWI) L4356 of 1 General Reconnaissance Unit (GRU) was fitted with a de-gaussing ring to explode magnetic mines dropped off Alexandria. *Author's collection*

To counter the threat posed by high-flying German Ju 86P reconnaissance aircraft 103 MU at Aboukir modified several Spitfires for high altitude flight. Armour was removed, the engine re-bored, extended wing tips added, a four-blade propeller fitted (later) and guns reduced to just two. Spitfire VC BR114 was one such modified aircraft, flown by the MU's staff pilots. *Author's collection*

From July 1942 a small number of USAAF B-24Ds was diverted to Egypt under the command of Col Harry Halverson. After a raid on the Rumanian oilfields in August the detachment, then supplemented by the 376th BG and based at Fayid, bombed ports in North Africa. *Alan Walton*

Direct support was further defined as being defensive (typically slowing an enemy ground advance) or offensive (in support of allied ground offensive). It was the former that created most problems and is where the tentacles came into their own. Either by direct observation or by monitoring Tac/R calls, Forward Air Support Links (FASLs) were able to pass requests directly to the AASC. One way of offering support was to intercept enemy dive-bombers, a task in which Allied air forces were helped by German rigidity. It was *Luftwaffe* standard practice to send off Stukas shortly after dawn, ergo standing patrols at this time proved very effective.

The Directive reflects well the situation at the time of its promulgation. It notes that the RAF had no dive-bombers and, referring to fighter in comparison with bomber attacks, has this to say:

> '...the fighter attack probably has the greater moral effect. But the fighter is the main weapon in the battle for air superiority, and to employ fighters against ground targets in a direct support role must inevitably be drawing them off from the main issue. Thus, though ... probably more effective ... this type of direct support ... cannot normally be expected until a considerable degree of air superiority has already been attained.'

By October 1942 there were sufficient fighters, and a degree of air superiority, to enable direct support.

By way of comparison with artillery, it is noted that aircraft can develop a considerable volume of fire speedily to assist formations which have outdistanced their artillery. But, the Directive asserts, aircraft should not be used when artillery and mortars are sufficient. Further, aircraft will not be able to sustain their attacks, and as they proceed, unlike artillery, they become less accurate due to enemy movement and up-to-the-minute intelligence. To succeed, air attack needs absence of opposition from the ground and in the air, good visibility and a clearly recognisable (from the air) target.

To aid the AASC staff there was clear guidance on suitable and unsuitable targets. Good targets, normally beyond ground visual observation, included: concentrations of troops, armour or M/T in close formation that can be surprised and which would have difficulty dispersing; unprotected HQs and signals centres; artillery positions in the open; supply columns, particularly petrol and rations; and crossing points. Among poor targets were: dispersed or sheltered troops and transport; troops and guns that are well protected; motor columns that are easily able to disperse.

In the event, the local 5 AASC, combined with 2 AASC (despatched from the UK), operating at Army level, was to be co-located with the joint Army/Air advanced HQ. It had nine mobile 'tentacles' attached to divisions or brigades, communicating by W/T; each divisional tentacle included a Forward Air Support Link and a trained (Army) Air Liaison Officer (ALO).

These tentacles were able to monitor Tac/R aircraft R/T (at the time described as Radio Telegraphy as opposed to the later Radio Telephony) and send back to the AASC requests for support based on observation and local intelligence. AASC included both Air Force and Army staff who between them sought approval and prioritised requests for missions. These were incorporated into, or in some circumstances replaced, programmed missions and were advised to the relevant wing by W/T or landline. It was then for local determination as to who would fly the sortie(s) and the precise weapons to be carried, depending on the targets and intended outcomes. There were also ALOs at landing grounds to brief and update pilots on the situation on the ground.

There remained some problems in defining and illustrating the bomb line. In the past it had been described by grid references, but this was changed to description by features. Various ground markers were tried with mixed success and to help identify transport on the move vehicles had RAF-style roundels applied to the roof. The Axis use of Allied vehicles created further significant problems for the WDAF attackers since, from August, no less than 85% of all Axis transport comprised captured trucks.[10]

In summary, the AASCs, which in schematic terms were located centrally, acted as a clearing-house for requests for air support initiated by forward army elements, organising sorties against targets selected as a result of information received from tactical reconnaissance and other sources of intelligence available at army headquarters. They were commanded by Army officers of Major rank.

The Organisation of Allied Air Forces

In preparation for the forthcoming battle WDAF fighters were organised into two groups in Plan *Buster*. Force A was 211 (Offensive Fighter) Group, which comprised various forms of P-40s, Spitfires and night intruder and anti-tank Hurricanes. From 5 November components of the Group would move west, keeping close behind the advanced troops and eventually operating from Tunisia. 212 (Fighter Control) Group was made up of Hurricane units and would in due course remain in the eastern Mediterranean. The Group was expected to provide cover for the Army base and shore up losses in 211 Group. Composition of the Groups is shown in the accompanying tables.

Prior to the deployment of the RAF Regiment squadron groundcrew were required to provide the defence of airfields. Here, personnel from 213 Sqn man a gun-pit armed with what appears to be a Bren light machine gun. *Alan Walton*

Spitfire VC EP455/UF-Y of 601 Sqn at LG 92. At this stage in the war the Spitfires were used to provide air defence and top cover to more vulnerable types. *Author's collection*

Squadrons within 211 Group each had advanced, main and base components and as the Army proceeded the advanced element was expected to move speedily to newly captured airfields. Airfield construction companies were also prepared to move forward swiftly and Royal Engineer units were allocated the task of clearing captured airfields of mines and other impediments. A total of forty Hudson transports of 216 Group was assigned to Amriya to meet any immediate demand for munitions or fuel near the front line.

The final part of the complicated mobile Group was the newly forming RAF Regiment. Although established in the UK in February 1942, it was only weeks before the battle that officers arrived in Egypt to assume command of the RAF gunners already working on airfield defence. Regiment flights were also tasked to move forward as part of the advanced element, to defend newly acquired aerodromes from ground or air attack.

Going into the decisive battle the arrangements for direct air support had the following key characteristics:

- WDAF units were held centrally, except the two Corps Tac/R squadrons
- Nine forward wireless tentacles with RAF and Army personnel – FASL
- FASL could listen to Tac/R and other WDAF flying units
- FASL did not control fighters
- FASL could pass back requests for support to AASC
- AASC filtered requests and submitted to AOC for approval
- When approved, AASC sent back requirement to available wing
- Wing despatched fighters/light bombers to meet need
- Wings had ALOs to keep aircrew briefed on land battle

Table 6.5 – 212 Group WDAF, September 1942

Wing	Squadron	Type	Base	Role
234	33, 213, 238,1 SAAF	Hurricane IIC	LG 172	FGA
7 SAAF	80, 127, 274, 335	Hurricane IIC	LG 37	GA
285	40 SAAF	Hurricane IIB	LG 39	Tac/R
285	208	Hurricane IIB	LG 202	Tac/R

Table 6.6 – 211 Group WDAF, September 1942

Wing	Squadron	Type	Base	Role
	6	Hurricane IID	LG 89	AT
	7 SAAF	Hurricane IID	LG 89	AT
244	73	Hurricane IIC	LG 89	Intruder
244	92,145	Spitfire VB, VC	LG 173	F
244	601	Spitfire VC	LG 92	F
233	5 SAAF	Tomahawk IIB	LG 97	GA
233	2 SAAF, 4 SAAF, 260	Kittyhawk I	LG 97	FGA
233	64th, 65th USAAF	P-40F	LG 174	FGA
239	66th USAAF	P-40F	LG 174	FGA
239	112, 250, 3 RAAF, 450 RAAF	Kittyhawk I, III	LG 91	FGA

Captured at Sirte was this 150mm SP gun based on a captured French Lorraine tractor. It was operated by 21st *Panzer* Division. *Alan Walton*

The two tactical reconnaissance squadrons, 40 SAAF and 208, were equipped with specially fitted Hurricane Mk IIs. These carried a vertical, 8in focal length F24 camera and a standard 4-channel TR1133 for communicating direct to the FASL, plus a TR9 HF set and a R3002 transponder. On sorties these aircraft would advise on air of any enemy movements or potential targets that were relevant, including immediate threats. On landing their film would be processed in the field and results analysed at two levels – initially by a detachment of the Army Air Photo Interpretation Unit (AAPIU) and subsequently by the Middle East Interpretation Unit (MEIU).

From July 1942 all reconnaissance assets in the eastern Mediterranean were absorbed into 285 (Reconnaissance) Wing. The Tac/R squadrons remained attached to their Corps, resulting in some

Table 6.7 – WDAF light bomber force, September 1942

Wing	Squadron	Type	Base	Role
3 SAAF	12, 24 SAAF	Boston III	LG Z	LB
3 SAAF	21 SAAF	Baltimore III, IV	LG 98	LB
232	55, 223	Baltimore II, III	LG 86	LB
12 BG USAAF	81st 82nd 83rd 434th	B-25	LG 88	LB

Table 6.8 – AHQ Egypt bomber and reconnaissance units, September 1942

Wing	Squadron	Type	Base	Role
231	37, 70	Wellington IC	Abu Sueir	Med B
236	108, 148	Wellington IC	Kabrit	Med B
238	40, 104	Wellington IC	Kabrit	Med B
242	160	Liberator II	Aqir	HB
245	14	Marauder I		Med B
245	462	Halifax II	Fayid	HB
201 Group	821 NAS	Albacore	Dekheila	PF
201 Group	826 NAS	Albacore	Dekheila	PF
285	2 PRU	Spitfire IV etc	Burgh al Arab	PR
285	1437 Flt	Baltimore II, III	LG 201	SR
285	60 SAAF	Maryland	LG 201	Survey
98 BG USAAF	343rd 345th 415th BS	B-24D	Lydda	HB

Table 6.9 – AHQ Egypt coastal and miscellaneous units, September 1942

Wing	Squadron	Type	Base	Role
201 Group	252, 272	Beaufighter VIC	Idku	AS
	39, 47	Beaufort I, II	Shallufa	AS
	38, 221, 458 RAAF	Wellington II, VIII	Shallufa	AS
	203	Baltimore I, II	LG227	AS
	459 RAAF	Hudson IIIA	LG Z	AS
	15 SAAF	Bisley	LG Z	AS
	13 Hellenic	Blenheim IV	St Jean	AS
	162	Wellington IC	Shallufa	EW
	417 RCAF	Hurricane IIC	Idku	AD
	46	Beaufighter IF	Idku	NF
	889 NAS	Hurricane IIC	Fayid	NF

friction, but at least there was scope for overall policy and allocation of resources. The photo reconnaissance service was provided by 2 Photographic Reconnaissance Unit (PRU) based at Heliopolis with the Spitfire Mk IV, a flight of which worked within WDAF under the aegis of 285 Wing and was for some time at Burgh al Arab. Strategic reconnaissance was the remit of 1437 Flight with Baltimores and 60 Sqn SAAF performed a survey and mapping function with Marylands.

The airfields mainly in use by both sides were between 30 and 50 miles from the front line, leaving them vulnerable to attack from the air. It also meant that in the event of a ground assault they would be quickly overrun, resulting in chaos, as had happened to forward elements of the WDAF during Rommel's assault on El Alamein in the summer. Fortunately, such was the strength of WDAF air defence that Allied landing grounds were rarely raided. One report[11] suggests that the *Luftwaffe* had stocks of crowsfeet, or caltrops, in North Africa. Between 1,000 and 1,500 were housed in 5ft 6in light metal containers carried by Ju 87, Ju 88 or He 111 bombers. Nasty and potentially disruptive as they were, no evidence was found of them causing problems on landing grounds.

Table 6.10 – AHQ Egypt Transport units, September 1942

Wing	Squadron	Type	Base	Role
283	117, 163, 267	Hudson IV, V	Amriya	Transport
	216	Hudson VI, Bombay	Amriya	Transport
	1 AAU	DH.86	Wadi Natrun	Ambulance

Caught by Hurricane tank-busters while retreating was this feared 88mm gun, equally valuable in the anti-tank or anti-aircraft role.

Both sides had effective mobile radars, so on occasion Allied air forces adopted decoy tactics when attacking forward Axis positions. The attackers flew low over the sea, past the target to avoid radar detection, before turning inland to strike from the rear. The outcome: surprise and confusion, especially for AA batteries. Immediately before the battle the RAF had set up a forward observation post on Ruweisat Ridge, between XIII and XXX Corps.

The WDAF had been flying constant reconnaissance sorties and bombing raids since the Alam Halfa battle. On 9 October heavy rain in the coastal area flooded Axis airfields around Fuka and El Daba, making them all but unusable. During the day some 500 sorties were launched against these airfields where a number of aircraft was destroyed on the ground. At twenty-eight aircraft Allied losses were high, but at least the RAF and SAAF could afford to lose numbers in a war of attrition. On 16 and 17 October the AASCs ran signals exercises, continuing poor weather restricting flying. However, even this late in the day precise plans were still being worked on that had the potential to impact significantly on the way in which ground forces might expect air support. The following notes are from the 2 AASC War Diary:[12]

> '18 Oct – Weather improved. RAF concentrated on serviceability. Army Cmdr[A] lecture on plan of Lightfoot. Reallocation of tentacles continues. Orders re employment of the limited supply of coloured smoke continue to be changed in high places.
>
> 19 Oct – Smoke laying exercise with 3 Wing and 7 Armd Div was successful from air point of view but ground organisation was not 100% effective.
>
> 20 Oct – The combined G Ops,[B] GS1[C] and Air Support Control layout is now established and has been adopted by two out of three of the corps. Much operational

[A] Commander

[B] General staff, operations

[C] General staff officer grade 1

Crashed Bf 109E-7 S9+DR of 7./ZG 1. *Author's collection*

work that was previously done by Air S.C. will now be accepted by G Ops in theory. In practice it remains to be seen how much of the air raids can be laid on by G Ops in addition to all the functioning of an Army HQ. All formations have now been brought up to scratch in air planning, air staff duties and signal procedure.

21 Oct – All ALOs met at 211 Gp[D] and were given the plan of operations. Any outstanding points of procedure were also discussed. 404 fighters were serviceable in the evening.

22 Oct – All tentacles now in battle positions but many of them on wireless silence. Very few enemy a/c have been reported over the battle area during the last few days. Major McNeill to DIKHEILA to put Albacore sqns in the picture.'

Severe sandstorms put a halt to flying for three days from 15 October, then on the 19th the WDAF began its offensive in the lead-up to the forthcoming battle. The main targets over the next few days were again the airfields around El Daba and Fuka, the key objective being destruction of Axis aircraft. Indeed, fighter-bombers were instructed to seek aerial combat as opposed to simply bombing. As an example of the commitment, in one mission on the 20th twenty-four Baltimores and B-25s bombing Fuka Main were escorted by a whole flock of Kittyhawks – twelve from 112 Sqn (top cover), ten from 3 Sqn RAAF (medium cover) and ten from 250 Sqn (close cover).[13]

By 22 October fifteen tentacles were in place (as noted in Table 6.4) and significantly there was a direct link from 2 AASC to 6 Sqn. Constant bombing of Axis airfields achieved results. On the eve of the impending battle the remaining Macchis of 4° Stormo were flown out from Abu Haggag to Abu Smeit. WDAF maintained the pressure during daylight hours on the 23rd with more escorted airfield strikes, but at a cost. Seven Kittyhawks, two Hurricanes, one Tomahawk and a Spitfire were shot down over two days, with more severely damaged and four pilots killed. On the eve of the impending battle some squadrons moved up to advanced landing grounds: 1,100 sorties were planned for the following day.

The El Alamein Battle

The land battle started with a 1,000-gun artillery barrage at 2140hrs on 23 October. The intensity of it was directed at enemy artillery, Bostons of 12 and 24 Sqns SAAF laying down smoke so as to add to the turmoil by reducing visibility. The location of Axis artillery had been painstakingly observed and noted and in the first instance the field artillery – now freed from the anti-tank role – was directed centrally on counter-battery fire. No fewer than 408 25-pounders and forty-eight medium guns were under the orders of the Commander Royal Artillery (CRA), XXX Corps.

[D] Group

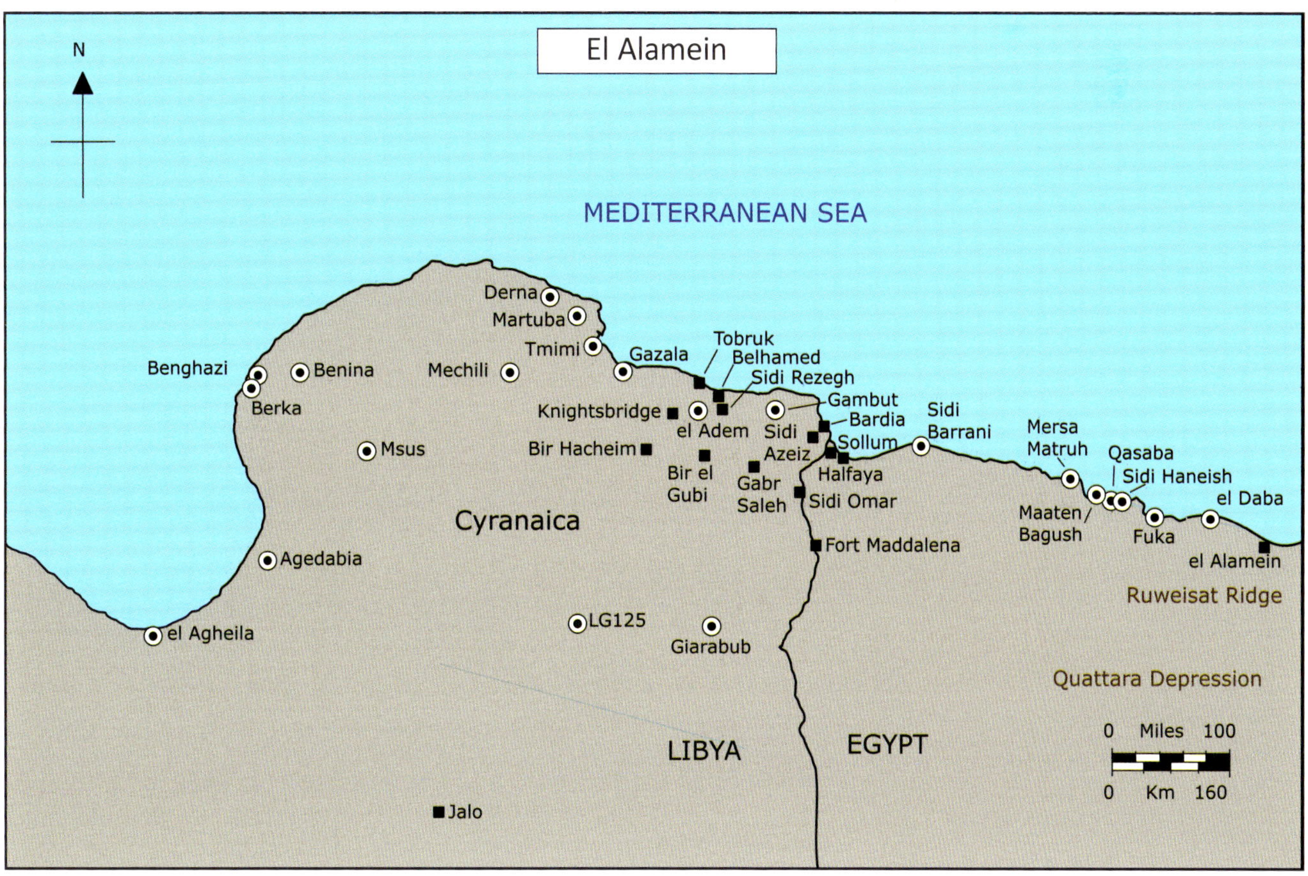

ZG 26 operated the Bf 110 twin-engined fighter. 3U+MS is a Bf 110D-2. *Author's collection*

Night fighters of NJG 2 were a particular problem for the Wellingtons of 205 Group. However, Ju 88C-2 R4+LH of NJG 2 is unlikely to fight another night. *Author's collection*

Axis forces operated a wide range of aircraft in the Western Desert including most bomber types. He 111H-6 5J+ER is from 7./KG 4.

Infantry then moved forward under a rolling barrage as RAF Wellingtons bombed troop concentrations and gun sites. Five other Wellingtons, of 162 Sqn, jammed Axis tank radio communications, causing considerable confusion. Elsewhere, Hurricanes of 73 Sqn strafed tank and M/T concentrations in the area occupied by 15 *Panzer* Division, flying twenty-six sorties.

From the outset there were delays in clearing the minefields, although considerable numbers of engineers and infantry had been allocated the task. They worked in conjunction with twenty-four Scorpion adaptations of Matilda tanks, converted for mine-clearing by the addition of flails. A problem, though, was that the Matilda Scorpions were slow and unreliable and created vast clouds of dust and rubble, adding to the difficulties of sappers who were clearing mines by hand. Despite these hiccups, the assault along the whole of the front line caused considerable mayhem. One unexpected outcome was the death of the German commander, General Stumme, deputising for Rommel who was ill. Stumme was at the front line to clarify the situation for himself when his staff car was shelled. (Some sources suggest that he died of a heart attack.)

The two armoured divisions of X Corps were slow to clear their minefield channels, so that by dawn the original objectives had not been met. In contrast, considerable progress had been made by the infantry divisions. However, not enough tanks had been able to move forward to start sorting out the flanks. Throughout the day Bostons and Baltimores flew escorted bombing missions ahead of the advancing Allied units while ground attack fighters maintained pressure. The AASC recorded sixteen raids, each of around eighteen bombers, nearly all against 15 *Panzer* Division opposing XXX Corps divisions in the north.

During the 24th the battle was going slowly for the British. X Corps had not opened the cleared

Ju 87B-2 S7+DK was brought down near El Alamein early in 1942. It displays the yellow griffon badge of 3./StG 3.

channels for tanks to flood through, those of 10th Division preparing for a defensive battle and refusing to move forward. The Germans now laid new minefields and resited anti-tank guns, hampering further the intended armoured breakthrough. Montgomery had to issue explicit instructions to get the tanks moving that night – which they did, but half-heartedly. The three divisions holding the Miteirya Ridge had suffered heavy casualties, so while Montgomery worked on changing his plans, the Air Force attacked continuously reforming Axis units.

Information coming back from tentacles gave specific targets for ground attack. In one such instance, according to the 6 Sqn ORB,[14] four aircraft took off at 1035hrs with two aircraft of 7 Sqn SAAF, escorted by 80 Sqn Hurricanes. Their task was to attack 'tanks & AMC 864249 and 868251'. The details state:

> 'The target could not be located at the given place but at 876243 Honeys and Crusaders being used by the enemy were located and attacked. W/Cdr Porteus hit 2 Honeys, Sgt Wilcox 1 Honey, F/Lt Morrison Bell 2 Honeys, P/O Carrick 1 Honey. 3 were left smoking after being on fire. The 7 SAAF pilots also hit 2 Honeys.'

What is remarkable about this (and further missions on the 24th and 26th), is that precise coordinates were given close to the bomb line and that the targets were captured British tanks being used by the Germans, so there was considerable room for error. ('Honey' was the British nickname for the US-supplied M3 Stuart light tank.) In the event, the Allied air forces flew 254 bomber, 625 fighter and seventy-four fighter bomber sorties on the 24th.

1st Armoured Division would now break through along the coast road, supported by the Australian Division. 10th Armoured Division was withdrawn. The fresh attack started on 25 October and by dawn the following day the Australians had reached their initial objective. During the day USAAF pilots of 64th FS claimed seven Bf 109s. The American units were integrated fully into the WDAF structure and their well-trained pilots were rapidly becoming acclimatised. Overnight, Wellington bombers had dropped 115 tons of bombs on forward positions, aided by the now customary illumination from naval Albacores.

Numbers of Ju 52/3m were used to bring supplies to Axis forces in North Africa, including petrol, from Italy and Crete. H4+AA of LLG 1 was seen at Derna late in 1942. Hardly recognisable as a three motor transport, the photo was wrongly labelled as being a Savoia! *Alan Walton*

This is believed to be the Ju 87B captured by 213 Sqn at LG 101, Sidi Haneish and later coded AK-?. It was used as a runabout from LG 10 at Mersa, especially for leave trips to Cairo... *Alan Walton*

Rommel, returned from convalescence at Hitler's command, counter-attacked without success and although tempted to bring reserves from the south, hesitated because he had not the fuel for them to return should there be the inevitable renewed assault by elements of XIII Corps. Over the next two days there was heavy and vicious fighting and eventually, by the 30th, the coast road had been taken. While there was close fighting on the ground the RAF was restricted to attacking troop concentrations and tanks behind the front line, so fluid was the battle.

On the 27th some forty-plus CR.42s acting as dive-bombers, along with seventeen Ju 87s, blitzed British positions around El Alamein. They were attacked by Allied fighters en route and again on their return despite a heavy escort of German and Italian fighters, nine of which were brought down. In excess of 700 Allied sorties were flown on both 26 and 27 October. As an example of the way in which air support was now functioning, bombers were switched from attacking Axis airfields to bombing concentrations of vehicles on the Rahman track. Allied fighter-bombers maintained attacks on armour of 15th and 21st *Panzer* Divisions which were confronting the 1st Armoured Division on Kidney Ridge.

There is some evidence that there was a rapid response system for close support not hitherto recorded. On 26 October, noting that air policy for the day was protection of the flanks of the Australian Division, the 2 AASC War Diary recorded: 'Early fighter-bomber sorties reported little and it had been agreed that the 'shuttle service' would not be undertaken unless good tgts[D] were seen from the air or requested from the ground.' The Australians reported Axis troops 'squaring up to attack' and these were hit in short order by eight RAF raids, the bombing being 'around forward troops.' The AASC was having a frustrating time and it was clear that some Army commanders remained incapable of using air resources properly.[15]

> '26 Oct – 6 Sqn had another successful sortie in the south but in spite of pressure were not allowed to fly again in the afternoon owing to alleged unsuitability of targets. Never again will they have a hunting ground as now exists between HIMEIMAT and KADIM, little flak, little chance of air interference and small parties of tanks employed in mobile defensive role. The ring is kept by the enemy minefield running due north...thus no own tanks or armd[E] cars can be in the area. Many valuable days may be wasted while waiting for an exactly suitable target to be submitted by 7 Armd Div who are in these peculiar circumstances, only too glad of any tank damage to enemy in that area.'

But it was not all rejection: the diary continues:

> 'This was a most successful day from the point of view of Air Support Control. The right target area was chosen from the beginning and good target indications were given in that area quickly and correctly by formations. Results were seen and reported by them and the weight of air attack in the right place undoubtedly gave 30 and 10 Corps a very valuable day for armoured attack.
>
> 27 Oct – [referring to targets in the Aqaqir area] Early fighter-bomber sorties found first good target and 11 raids were made of 18 light bombers on the same area, mostly within 3000 yds of our forward positions. 30 Corps asked for fighter cover for the move of 4 Ind Div to take over from SA Div! This although 6 divisions including 2 armd divs have been concentrated in an area 5 miles by 5 for 3 days with complete immunity from air attack.'

[D] targets
[E] Armoured cars

...and this is how they managed it. Three sergeant pilots in the rear gunner's cockpit of the squadron Stuka about to be flown off by Fg Off G. R. S. MacKay. *Alan Walton*

Such was the pressure on the *Luftwaffe* that some of its units were rotated. Several were withdrawn to Sicily, including III/JG 53 (replaced by I/JG 77 at Bir el Abd) and III/JG 77 at Tanyet Harum. III/ZG 1 was redesignated I/SchG 2, to operate Bf 109F-4s in the fighter-bomber role; I/JG 27 returned from its sojourn in Sicily. The Stukas were up as usual just after dawn on the 30th, to be met over the Allied front line by Hurricanes of 33 (low) and 238 (medium) Sqns. 33 Sqn aircraft braved friendly AA fire to get in among the Ju 87s, losing one aircraft and its pilot in the process. In a further development, USAAF P-40s were now flying unified missions, aircraft of the 64th and 65th fighter squadrons escorting RAF and SAAF Baltimores on a raid on the 31st.

601 Sqn Spitfires flew two missions on the 31st, the first a low-level squadron attack on Mersa Matruh in the morning, the second a loose offensive sweep at 1640hrs. Plt Off D. Llewellyn, flying Spitfire V BR132/E, recorded this about the afternoon sweep in his logbook:[16] 'Free lance offensive patrol; 1.20 [duration]; Shot up Panzer HQ in Wadi. Shot up by flak and crashed behind enemy lines. P/O Bryan Terry landed to pick me up.' On the next line the entry reads: '31 [Oct]; Spitfire M; Terry and Self; Dual; :30 [duration].' No other comment or description of how Terry landed the narrow track Spitfire on the unprepared desert floor, nor how two pilots managed to fit into the Spitfire's small cockpit and control the aircraft for thirty minutes. On 2 November Llewellyn was back flying two sweeps.

With initial success after seven hard days of battle and with a constant stream of relevant intelligence, Montgomery now planned his intended breakout, Operation *Supercharge*. The Army commander had regrouped his forces and with the Australians holding the line to the sea, the New Zealand Division immediately to its south was to attack across a 2½-mile front preceded by a rolling artillery barrage and supported by tanks. The new offensive was preceded by severe bombing raids on targets a mile or so ahead of the front line, to which sixty-eight Wellingtons and nineteen Albacores were committed. In the process the *Afrika Korps* signals system was destroyed.

The ground attack began at 0105hrs on 2 November, diversionary attacks along the coast by the Royal Navy and air raids continuing for more than seven hours. Despite difficulties in attacking anti-tank positions at Tell el Aqqaqir, overrun in a near suicidal attack by the 3rd King's Own Hussars, the Allied troops had achieved considerable inroads within twenty-four hours.

Fighters and fighter-bombers were in the air early to protect the Army against air attack and to mix it with Messerschmitts and Macchis in the continuing attritional battle. Despite losing two Tac/R Hurricanes in the day, the reconnaissance effort was maintained and with sound communications enabled a heavy raid by light bombers in the afternoon on the Abd el Rahman track, immediately in front of the bomb line. The absence of significant minefields now enabled armour to pass swiftly through territory gained by the infantry so that the tanks of X Corps could at last join battle.

The WDAF continued to apply enormous pressure on an Axis anti-tank screen that was holding up the armoured advance on the Abd el Rahman track. Each of the fighter-bomber wings conducted missions covered by Spitfires and two Stuka formations were broken up before they could attack British tanks. It proved an expensive day for WDAF: thirty-seven aircraft were either destroyed or seriously damaged, among them twenty-three Hurricanes. In personnel terms, ten airmen were killed, four missing, three wounded and three became prisoners of war.

Rommel had no choice but to withdraw, despite Hitler's order to stand firm. 51st (Highland) and 4th (Indian) divisions had destroyed the anti-tank screen, enabling 1st Armoured Division to break through and force a rout. The (mainly Italian) divisions to the south were now left to their own devices, short of fuel, ammunition and food. The retreating Axis forces were under constant attack by waves of Hurricanes, Kittyhawks and light bombers. 234 Wing, which conducted several sweeps, lost nine Hurricanes and four pilots. Ten Bf 109s were destroyed, six on the ground at Qotaifiya. In twenty-four hours WDAF and the bombers of 205 Group flew 1,208 sorties, dropping 396 tons of bombs.

By dawn on 4 November Axis forces were in full retreat along the coast road to Fuka. On the 5th air support was limited, due to the confused situation on the ground and the absence of any clear bomb line. For those reasons most bombing and strafing was conducted well ahead of what were presumed to be the British front lines. By now, though, the battle was won. The cost? 13,650 killed, wounded or missing. Despite armoured pursuit, much of the Axis remnants were able to make Tobruk, then Benghazi, but on the 8th faced another huge challenge when the *Torch* landings were made 1,500 miles to the west. So desperate for fuel were the Axis forces that thirteen Focke-Wulf Fw 200s of III/KG 40 and eleven He 111s of II/KG 4 flew in petrol to Tobruk on the 5th, followed by a further eight Fw 200 sorties on the 6th. Flying from and to Lecce, southern Italy, they all evaded WDAF fighters.[17]

In the two battles, one deliberately defensive, the second offensive, the air forces played a critical role in achieving success. Aircraft under the control of AHQ Egypt attacked shipping and bombed airfields in Crete and along the coast. Beaufighters strafed coastal roads. Wellington bombers maintained regular night sorties ahead of the front line, up to eighty at a time. So critical were the naval Albacore flare-ships that the two squadrons involved were routinely briefed personally by 2 AASC officers. All of these missions were coordinated with Army requirements against a wider tri-service plan. They combined to prevent supplies reaching the Libyan ports and then destroyed much of what did manage to get through.

The WDAF, comprising RAF, SAAF, USAAF, RAAF and Greek squadrons, managed to undertake numerous counter-air and interdiction missions with light bombers and fighter-bombers; there was very little loss to the bombers because of effective and systematic escort. Tac/R sorties were flown regularly and the product processed and analysed speedily. Fighter-bomber wings were then briefed on fresh targets to meet Army needs. That said, although there was a system in place to enable immediate and very close support to troops under pressure, it did not work effectively.

It appears that there were still misunderstandings as to the role and/or capabilities of the Air Force. Some years after the battle Montgomery's Chief-of-Staff, Major General Sir Francis de Guingand, had this to say in relation to the enemy's hasty retreat:[18]

> 'When on November 3 all information showed that the enemy was in full retreat it was hoped that the Desert Air Force [*sic*] would cause havoc among his transport; for reports described a scene of vehicles head to tail, four and sometimes eight deep moving westwards either on or just off the road. Indeed we had visions of the retreat being turned into a complete rout, bearing in mind the fact that we enjoyed virtual air superiority. In the event the results were very disappointing. When setting out along the road between the Alamein battlefield and Daba, I had expected to see a trail of devastation, but the visible signs of destroyed vehicles were few and far between.
>
> The fact is that at this period of the war we had not learned the technique of low strafing, for our fighter bombers had been employed in air fighting and bombing. I believe the attacks on the retreating columns were made mostly with bombs, and that the aircraft were not allowed to come down low; no doubt our pilots had not been trained in low-flying attacks with cannon. I feel, however, that an opportunity was lost, and that it should have been possible to have produced a form of paralysis in the enemy's rearward movement.'

Although written some twenty-five years after the event, not only is this disingenuous and unfair on the WDAF, it also demonstrates a real misunderstanding by a senior Army staff officer who was privy to the situation at all times.

First, it was clear that the Army did not follow up as quickly as it might have since the tanks soon ran ahead of their fuel supplies. Also, Montgomery exercised undue caution. The weather also slowed down the pursuit and an Army plan to cut off the retreat failed: the same weather slowed the retreating Axis forces, of course.

Second, a joint RAF/Army agreement of September 1941[19] defined targets that would be acceptable for attack. As noted earlier, these would include concentrations of troops, armour or M/T in close formation, all of which would have difficulty dispersing. Poor targets included dispersed or sheltered troops and transport or defended motor columns *easily able to disperse*.

Third, de Guingand would have known day by day the state of the Air Force, the capabilities of its squadrons and the nature of its frequent strafing attacks. One 213 Sqn armourer made these diary notes:[20]

> 'Tuesday, 3rd November – Our advance has really started, 213, 238 and 33 Squadrons have strafed enemy bases, aerodromes, aircraft, lorries and artillery...
>
> Wednesday, 4th November – ...the Germans are retreating on all fronts and sectors. Arrived early morning at el-Daba for a two-day stay. What a horrible sight: 87 Jerry aircraft left behind and bodies all over the place...
>
> Thursday, 5th November – We have never moved so quickly. I've counted 250 ammunition vehicles, every one full of explosives. At some places enemy aircraft had no time to take off, some were burnt out. Papers of all kinds, maps etc still burning...'

From 6 Sqn with its tank-busting Hurricanes, the following note on the afternoon of 3 November, when thirteen aircraft were despatched:[21] 'No escort was provided as no enemy aircraft were about at all. Any target at all was allowed and the operation was most successful.' The tally was logged precisely as thirty lorries, three half-tracks, two Crusaders, two M13 tanks, one Honey, one *Panzer* Mk IV Special, one armoured car and one tank transporter.

The ORB for 73 Squadron, the specialist night intruder outfit, records the following for the night of 5/6 November:[22]

> 'Gala night – all aircraft were fitted with long range tanks ready for a dusk and dawn straffing attack on the retreating enemy. Twelve aircraft operating in pairs arrived in the Garawla–Fuka area just before dusk and straffed hundreds of M.T. on the roads, many were carrying troops. Heavy and light A.A., also intense Breda fire was encountered – various gun positions were straffed and at least one Breda silenced. All aircraft returned to base but two were minus a long-range tank, another had been hit in the wing and another in the main tank. The dawn effort was not nearly so successful. Our army had pushed so rapidly that it was impossible to distinguish enemy troops near Garawla. Layer patrol was operated by two aircraft along the coast to Heneish but no hostiles were seen. The pilots reported everything quiet as far as Fuka.'

The logbook[23] of Plt Off M. Smyth of 73 Sqn for 5 November records: 'Dusk road straff; Road straffed at Qasaba road jammed with transport. Many hits seen, Green white explosion. Explosion among 3 M.T. Bags of flak. Tobruk in flames. Dropped bomb.'

Taken through the undercarriage struts of a resupply Bombay Hurricane IIC HL883/AK-W of 213 Sqn was one of thirty-six Hurricanes sent to LG 125 on 13 November. With aircraft of 238 Sqn their objective was to hit enemy formations from behind. *Author's collection*

Convoy MW13 was due to leave Alexandria on 16 November with urgent supplies for Malta, but it would be beyond the range of Allied fighters for part of the voyage, unless the Allies could take Martuba in time. In the event the Kittyhawks of 3 Sqn RAAF made it on the 15th. Illustrated is Kittyhawk 1A ET953/CV-V of 3 Sqn RAAF flown by Sqn Ldr Bobby Gibbes from LG 91.

In the retreat to El Alamein in the first part of 1942 the Army appeared uncoordinated and, arguably, only the actions of the WDAF prevented the *Afrika Korps* from reaching Alexandria. In the Second Battle of El Alamein success was achieved only as a result of a high level of coordination between Army and the complete Air Force, which included a system for direct support that worked.

There were tensions between Army and Air Force commanders post El Alamein, based around the way in which Montgomery took the credit for success.[24] The Air Force view was that, given the intelligence available to him, Montgomery should have pressed ahead faster and secured the clusters of airfields that would have enabled the WDAF to move forward and provide immediate cover, rather than having to operate from safe airfields that were now some way behind the front.

The airfield cluster at Martuba, behind Derna, was an explicitly stated mid-November target for ground forces because it was from here that most Axis air attacks on Malta-bound convoys were mounted. Malta, which had been a key naval and air base for attacking Axis convoys, was under siege and had received very limited supplies. On the verge of collapse, the island was due for resupply by convoy MW13, required to leave Port Said on 16 November in Operation *Stoneage*. Convoy protection was by naval flotillas and air cover from Egypt (departure) and Malta (arrival). For the middle part of the sailing it was essential that cover was provided from Libya.

Martuba was reached by ground forces on the 15th and within the following day the first Kittyhawks of 239 Wing (3 Sqn RAAF) moved in. However, it was a close-run affair. The convoy arrived at Malta on the 20th without loss to the freighters, although several warships were damaged by air attack.

Frustrated, on 13 November Coningham sent forward thirty-six Hurricanes of 213 and 238 Sqns to LG 125, some 120 miles SSW of Tobruk, to harass Axis transport from behind enemy lines. Ground personnel were airlifted in by Hudson. In three days the aircraft conducted 119 sorties, claiming 300 vehicles destroyed and many more damaged. German light AA remained effective, resulting in three Hurricanes being lost and four damaged.

The Air-Army tensions would no doubt have worsened had the war moved on incrementally. For the next year in the Mediterranean theatre it would shift through a number of discreet battles, during which Montgomery would fall out with American generals and by the end of 1943 return to the UK.

Between 23 October and 4 November the officially recorded[25] number of sorties and (in parentheses), the number of aircraft losses, were: RAF and Dominion 10,405 (77), USAAF 1,181 (20), *Luftwaffe* 1,550 (64) and *Regia Aeronautica* 1,570 (20). Maybe the final word should rest with the official military historian. Writing of high morale in the 8th Army,[26] he observed:

> 'Perhaps the most important factor which kept (morale) so high, and did much to lessen the enemy's, was the superiority of the Western Desert Air Force, which made it possible for the enemy to be attacked incessantly from the air, while the inevitably crowded areas behind the British lines were raided neither heavily nor often.'

German troops marching into captivity in November 1942, apparently escorted by French infantrymen. *Alan Walton*

[1] Purnell's *History of the Second World War*, vol 3, p1149
[2] For Luftwaffe structure see Appendix 1
[3] Shores et al, *History of the Mediterranean Air War Vol Two*, p317
[4] Wayne S Dodds, History of 57th Fighter Group at http://www.57thfightergroup.org/history.html
[5] Quoted in Purnell's *History of the Second World War* vol 3 p1152
[6] Ford, *El Alamein 1942*, p28
[7] Playfair, *History of the Second World War: Mediterranean and Middle East Vol IV*, p10
[8] Playfair, *History of the Second World War: Mediterranean and Middle East Vol IV*, p30
[9] TNA AIR23/6465
[10] Ehlers, *The Mediterranean Air War*, p236
[11] Higham, *Bases of Air Strategy*, p156
[12] TNA WO169/6638 *War Diary of 2 AASC*
[13] Shores et al, *History of the Mediterranean Air War Vol Two*, p376
[14] TNA AIR27/75
[15] TNA WO169/6638 2 AASC War Diary
[16] Logbook D E Llewellyn RAF Museum
[17] Shores et al, *History of the Mediterranean Air War Vol Two*, p433
[18] Purnell's *History of the Second World War*, vol 3 p1165
[19] TNA WO277/34
[20] Walton, *Desert War Diary*, p127
[21] TNA AIR27/75
[22] TNA AIR27/631
[23] Logbook of M W Smyth RAF Museum
[24] Terraine, *A Time for Courage*, p387
[25] Playfair, *History of the Second World War: Mediterranean and Middle East Vol IV*, p78
[26] Playfair, *History of the Second World War: Mediterranean and Middle East Vol IV*, p76

7 Operation *Torch* – the Allied Invasion of North Africa, November 1942

The Political Dimension

In early October 1942 the largest ever landing of troops – some 70,000 Allied soldiers carried in, or supported by, more than 400 ships – took place in North Africa. Out of range of land-based air support, cover was provided by the Royal and United States navies' flying arms. And, for the first time in nearly a quarter of a century, British soldiers would have support from Army pilots. While the landings embraced little that was new in respect of Army-Air collaboration, the invasion saw the low-key baptism of light, unarmed, artillery-spotting Austers.

Before the United States entered the war, senior staff officers had met secretly in Washington from January 1941. Their purpose was to agree a broad strategy for when the US was drawn into the conflict, looking to military coordination between America, Britain and Canada, hence the conference being known as ABC-1. That being so, when the United States entered the war in December 1941 Churchill and Roosevelt had already agreed that defeating Germany had priority over dealing with the Japanese, who would be held until there was sufficient men and materiel to fight on two hemispheres. Russia, once attacked by Germany in June 1941 in contravention of their non-aggression pact, pleaded with first Britain, then the United States, for arms and the opening of a second front. By the summer of 1942, with Stalingrad under siege, the situation was desperate.

From early 1942 there were meetings of British and US combined chiefs of staff in Washington to consider options. The Americans favoured an immediate, limited action on the Cherbourg peninsula, Operation *Sledgehammer*, followed by a full-scale invasion of France in September 1943, Operation *Round Up*. The British, though, favoured an attack on North Africa to squeeze Axis forces from east and west in Tunisia, leading to an invasion of Sicily, then mainland Italy, originally Operation *Gymnast*.

The African option was seen by the United States as being primarily in Britain's interest, so as to protect her oil supplies and Empire. However, Admiral Sir Andrew Cunningham, Commander of the British Mediterranean Fleet, was able to persuade the Americans that an assault on North Africa would relieve the shipping problem from the west to the Middle East, would relieve Malta, jeopardise Rommel's position in Libya, shake Italy and waken the occupied countries. The decision not to implement a French invasion too quickly was vindicated by Operation *Jubilee*, the disastrous Dieppe raid in August 1942.

The politics around the intended invasion were complex and impacted on the way in which ground forces could be protected. It was agreed that the United States would take the lead, General Dwight D. Eisenhower becoming Commander-in-Chief Allied Expeditionary Force. Cunningham was appointed Allied Naval Commander. Headquarters were established on Gibraltar. The Americans brought enthusiasm and many well-trained men and new equipment to the party but lacked experience. However, there was an overriding reason for making the invasion an apparently US affair: the countries along the north-west African coast were all French and occupied by Vichy forces, no friends of the British.

After the collapse of France in May 1940 the French agreed an armistice with Germany on 22 June. The north and west of the country were occupied by German troops, the centre and south-east administered by a collaborationist French government headed by Marshal Pétain and centred on Vichy. By way of contrast, the Free French government-in-exile was based in London. The French in Vichy ranged in their sympathies towards Germany from strong resistance to positive collaboration.

Most of the French colonies and overseas *départements* opted for government from Vichy. After the collapse of France, a major concern for the British was the powerful French fleet, elements of which were in UK naval bases, in Egypt (Alexandria), Algeria, French West Africa (modern Senegal) and Toulon. The Vichy government guaranteed that its Navy, under Admiral François Darlan, would remain neutral, but Churchill was anxious that it would be unable to resist German appropriation.

The British thus planned Operation *Catapult*, intended at least to neutralise the French fleet by requiring deactivation and transfer to distant 'neutral' ports, or destruction if negotiation or threat failed. In the event the Vichy Navy protested its independence, as a result of which the Royal Navy went into action. On 3 July 1940 vessels in Portsmouth were boarded but, more dramatically, British warships bombarded French ships in the port of Mers-el-Kebir, near Oran, with the loss of 1,297 killed and 350 wounded. The French retaliated by bombing Gibraltar with little effect.

There was thus a great deal of uncertainty as to how the French in North Africa might react to a British invasion, especially given that the naval commander, Admiral Darlan, was an Anglophobe. In an attempt to reduce friction, the invasion thus became ostensibly an American affair. The choice of landing locations was dictated by American concerns as to the part that Spain might play, either directly against the essential base in Gibraltar, or by virtue of losing its neutrality to Germany. Operation *Gymnast* now morphed into Operation *Torch*.

The Invasion Plan

There were to be three landings in French North Africa by a joint US–British force. General Eisenhower was in overall command with General Mark Clark as his deputy. Commander of British land forces was Lt Gen Kenneth Anderson. The Allied naval commander, Admiral Cunningham, was accountable for the western Mediterranean and the Atlantic sector while Admiral Sir Henry Harwood remained Commander-in-Chief Mediterranean. There were two subordinate air commanders. The American 12th Air Force was headed by Brig Gen James Doolittle, RAF elements being the responsibility of Air Marshal Sir William Welsh.

VGF-9 was one of the three F4F Wildcat units aboard USS *Santee*. Aircraft 4 appears to be prepared for take-off on a cover patrol. *USN Official*

The operation was conducted independently of the battles continuing in the Western Desert. Although some American units had been either integrated or worked in concert with the Western Desert Air Force (WDAF), there was little, if any, transfer of lessons learned in the concurrent fighting. Air cover to the invasion forces was thus less sophisticated than it might have been and during the landing phase provided solely by carrier-based aircraft.

There was agreement that two of the landings would be at Oran and Algiers, both in Algeria and about 220 miles apart. The choice for the third site was problematic, as the map illustrates. On the plus side, a landing in Tunisia (to the east of Algeria), would potentially shorten the fighting in North Africa by squeezing Axis forces retreating from Libya and the onslaught of the Eighth Army. On the debit side, the rainy season was about to start and this would delay Algeria–Tunisia overland progress. Other factors taken into consideration were that any convoys in Tunisian waters would be within range of bombers based in Sicily and Sardinia and should Gibraltar be occupied by Spanish and/or German forces, access to the Mediterranean would be cut. Thus, the decision was to mount the third landing in the vicinity of Casablanca, Morocco. In due course the North Africa landings date was set for 8 November.

A 13 August directive to Eisenhower from the combined chiefs of staff[1] described the objective clearly. 'The President and the Prime Minister have agreed that combined military operations be directed against Africa as early as practicable with a view to gaining, in conjunction with Allied forces in the Middle East, complete control of North Africa from the Atlantic to the Red Sea…' The objective was to be achieved in three stages – establish three 'lodgements'; connect them; move east to join the Eighth Army to squeeze Axis forces from North Africa.

For each of the invasion forces an initial and urgent objective was the capture of airfields. Once they were occupied, aircraft of two air forces would fly in from Gibraltar, whose airfield had been extended and where a massive fleet of more than 350 aircraft had been assembled by Britain and the United States. Western Air Command, under Brig Gen James Doolittle, was responsible for over-water operations to the west of Gibraltar and over-land to the west of Cape Tenes, between Oran and Algiers. Eastern Air Command, under Air Marshal Sir William Welsh, was given the Mediterranean and over-land to the east of Cape Tenes.

Vichy French forces had c56,000 troops in Morocco, c50,000 in Algeria and 15,000 in Tunisia, many of them colonial. The largest part of the French fleet was at Toulon, but there were destroyers and submarines at Bizerta, Oran and Casablanca. Coastal forts with heavy artillery were sited at strategic points. The composition of the Armée de l'Air and Aeronavale units in North Africa is shown in the table.

Table 7.1 – Vichy French Air units in North Africa, November 1942

Unit	Type	Base	Role
Morocco			
GC II/5	Hawk H-75A, D.520	Casablanca	F
GC I/4	Hawk H-75A	Rabat/Salè	F
1F	D.520	Port Lyautey	F
GB I/32	DB-7	Casablanca	B
GB I/23	LeO 451	Marrakech	B
GB II/32	Douglas DB-7	Agadir	B
GB II/23	LeO 451	Meknés	B
3F	Martin 167F	Port Lyautey	B
GR I/22	LeO 451	Rabat/Salè	R
GR I/52	Po.63	Marrakech	R
GT I/5	Po.29, Farman F.222	Rabat/Salè	T
GT III/15	Amiot 143, LeO 451	Oujda	T
Algeria			
GC III/3	D.520	La Senia	F
GC II/3	D.520	Maison Blanche	F
GC III/6	D.520	Maison Blanche	F
GB I/11	LeO 451	La Senia	B
GB I/19	Douglas DB-7	Blida	B
GB II/61	Douglas DB-7	Blida	B
4F	LeO 451	Tafaraoui	B
5F	Laté 298	Arzeu	TB
GR II/52	Bloch MB.174, 175	La Senia	R
GR I/36	Po.63	Setif	R
Esc 4BR	Po.63	Maison Blanche	R
GT II/15	Po.540, 650	Blida	T
Tunisia			
GC II/7	D.520	Sidi Ahmed	F
GB I/25	LeO 451	El Aouina	B
GB II/25	LeO 451	El Aouina	B
GR II/33	Bloch 174	El Aouina	R
Esc 1E	Bizerta, LeO 257bis	Karouba	U

The landings were preceded by a secret military mission on 22 October by Gen Clark to meet with French representatives at a location between Bône and Algiers. In summary, the envoys were assured that the French Army and Air Force were not likely to counter invasion, but that the Navy would probably remain loyal to Pétain and fight. Given that the French Navy manned port defences and coastal guns, this was not, perhaps, the news that had been hoped for. However, the decision was taken to refrain from Allied naval bombardment at the outset.

TBF1 Avengers with engines running on the flight deck of USS *Ranger*. *USN Official*

Action – Casablanca

The western, American, landings would actually be in three places in French Morocco – Mehedia/Port Lyautey (northern, codenamed Operation *Goalpost*); Fedala, near Casablanca (central, Operation *Brushwood*); and Safi (southern, Operation *Blackstone*). Troops, tanks and equipment embarked late October, convoy UGF-1 (United States–Gibraltar Fast) departing Hampton Roads, Virginia, on 24 October. In overall charge was Major General George Patton. Composition of the convoy is shown in the table.

Table 7.2 – Composition of Western Assault Force convoy and Task Groups (TG)

	TG 34.1 Cover	TG 34.8 Northern	TG 34.9 Central	TG 34.10 Southern	Total
Transports		8	15	8	31
Auxiliaries	1	5	7	6	19
Battleships	1	1		1	3
Cruisers	2	2	3	1	8
Destroyers	4	9	15	8	36
Submarines		1	2	1	4
Carriers		2	2	1	5
Aircraft		107*	111	31	249
Tanks		65	79	108	252
Men		9,099	18,783	6,423	34,305
Ships total	8	28	44	26	106

*Included seventy-seven P-40Fs of 33rd FG USAAF that were being ferried.

A priority for the assault forces was the capture of airfields at Casablanca, Fedala, Médiouna and Port Lyautey. The western assault had air cover provided by five carriers – four escort carriers of 11,400 tons and one light fleet carrier of 14,600 tons. Between them they embarked Grumman F4F-4 Wildcat fighters, Douglas SBD-3 Dauntless dive-bombers and Grumman TBF-1 Avenger torpedo-bombers. Overall, there were five infantry regimental combat teams (RCT), four armoured battalions and one engineer battalion.

SBD-3 Dauntlesses of VGS-26 and F4F-4 Wildcats of VGF-26 on the flight deck of USS *Sangamon* just prior to the *Torch* landings. *USN Official*

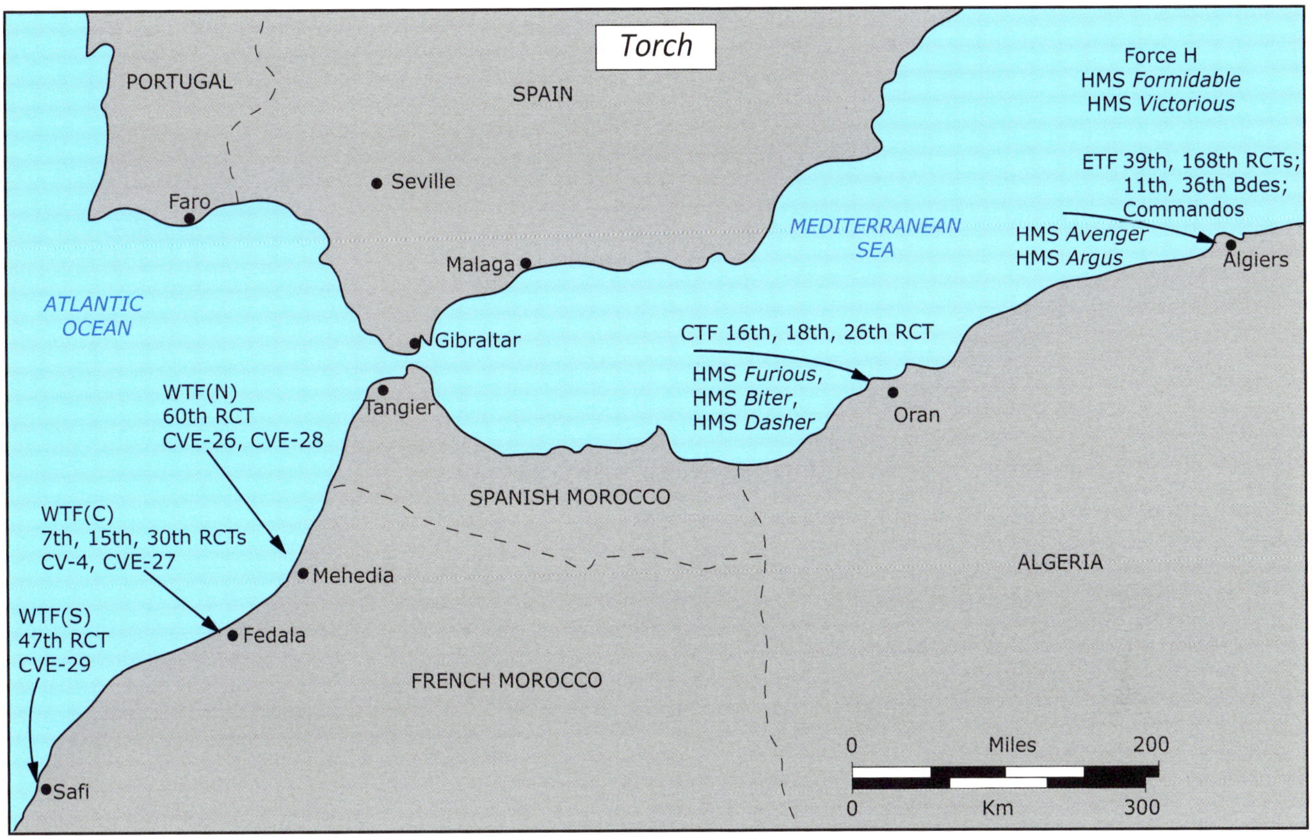

In addition to carrier-based units there were two others that were critically important to providing close support for landing soldiers. For naval gunfire spotting VO-7 provided Vought OS2U Kingfishers for the battleships and VCS-7 detached Curtiss SOC-3 Seagulls to the cruisers. The landing fleets were provided with deep cover by the battleship USS *Massachusetts*, cruisers USS *Wichita* and USS *Tuscaloosa*, and four destroyers, all of whose firepower could be added to any one of the landings if and when necessary.

The landings in Morocco did not go uncontested. There was heavy resistance from coastal batteries and warships, and the French Air Force (despite suggestions to the contrary) and Naval Air Arm flew offensive sorties. The landings themselves were poorly executed, with long delays and the loss of many landing craft. Yet at each of the three landing sites beachheads were established during 8 November. Close support for troops in the landing phase was provided by aircraft from the carriers or naval gunfire support (NGS) directed by spotter aircraft.

Dauntless dive bombers of VS-41 on USS *Ranger*. The aircraft appear to be in the process of being armed with 500lb bombs. *Author's collection*

Simple Air Observation Post
Operation *Torch*

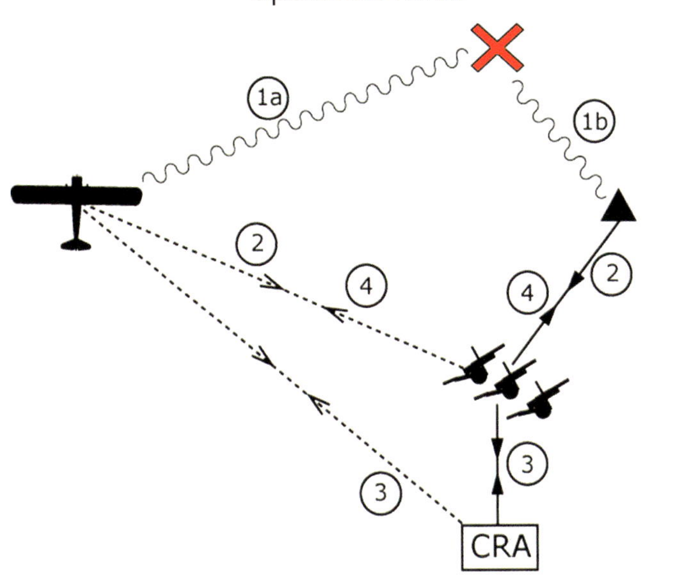

1) Spotter aircraft or artillery OP identifies threat
2) Details by R/T or landline to artillery battery
3) All monitored by Commander Royal Artillery (CRA)
4) Shot corrected by Spotter or artillery OP

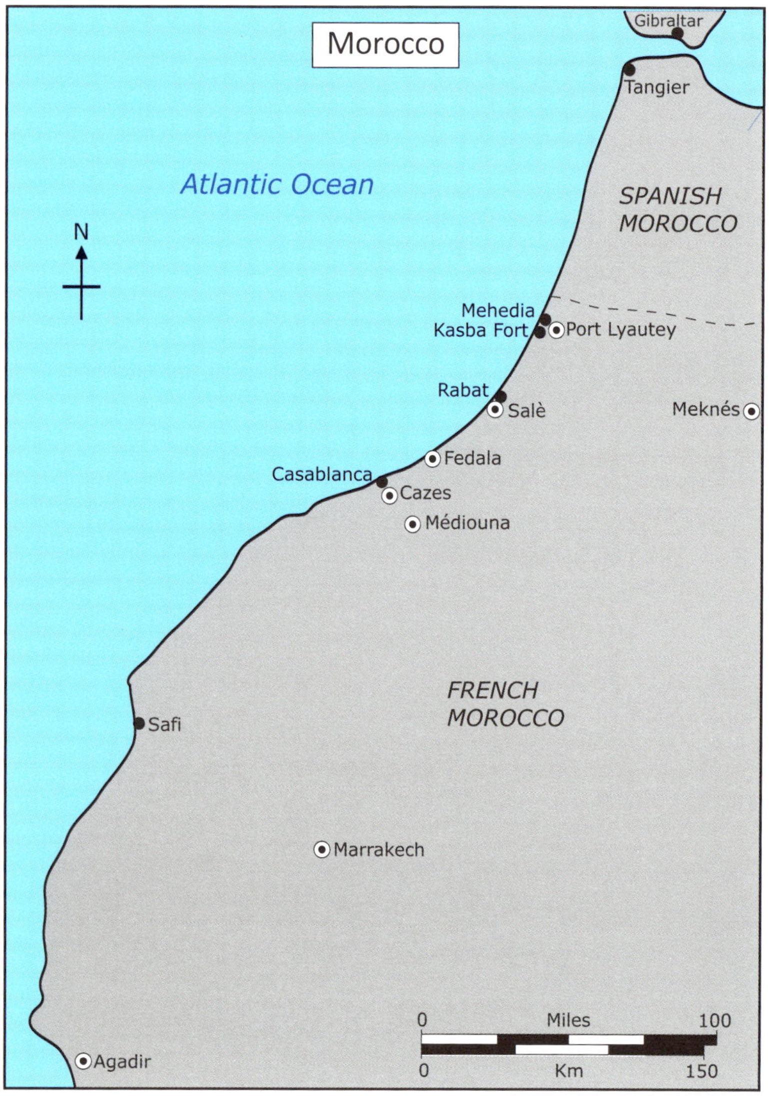

Curtiss P-40F Warhawks of the 33rd Fighter Group were brought in on board USS *Chenango* (CVE-28) utilised solely as a ferry carrier. The aircraft were flown off from 10 November for the large airfield at Port Lyautey. In the foreground is aircraft 41-14365. *USN Official*

There were many examples of friendly aircraft being shot down, both by AA fire from supporting warships and by USN Wildcats. These losses included British reconnaissance and anti-submarine aircraft as well as a number of Wildcats. There were local gains, but it was not until the 11th that the French surrendered, then to negotiate new roles for the Vichy forces.

The most southerly of the three landings, at Safi, commenced at 0440hrs on the 8th with two infantry groups landed by destroyer in the port and others on adjacent beaches. The force comprised:

47th RCT, two 67th Armoured Bns with air cover provided by

CVE-29 USS *Santee*

VGF-29 F4F Wildcat

VGS-29 SBD Dauntless, TBF Avenger

Capital ships with spotter aircraft were USS *New York* and USS *Philadelphia*

The destroyers came under heavy gunfire, answered by the US warships standing off. By dawn the SOC-3 Seagull and OS2U Kingfisher spotters from the cruiser *Philadelphia* and battleship *New York* respectively were airborne and directing NGS. The Wildcats of VGF-29 flew combat air patrol over the fleet; five were lost, mainly through errors in navigation. TBF Avengers of VGS-29 provided cover and reconnaissance for the landing. By early afternoon Safi was captured, but to ensure safety for the troops, aircraft from USS *Santee* bombed and strafed the aircraft of the French GB I/52 and GB II/32 squadrons at Marrakech on the 9th. On the 10th Wildcats from USS *Santee* flew close support for troops, attacking several machine-gun posts. French aircraft were active in the area, flying reconnaissance sorties. Fighting ceased on the morning of the 11th.

The Central Task Group went in at Fedala, 15 miles north of Casablanca. This was the most critical of the three landings since it would enable capture of the important port at Casablanca, which also housed French naval headquarters. The force comprised:

7th, 15th, 30th RCTs, 67th Armoured Bn, with air cover provided by

CV-4 USS *Ranger*

VF-9 F4F Wildcat

VF-41 F4F Wildcat

VS-41 SBD Dauntless, TBF Avenger

CVE-27 USS *Suwanee*

VGF-27 F4F Wildcat

VGF-28 F4F Wildcat

VGF-30 F4F Wildcat

VGS-27 TBF Avenger

Capital ships with spotter aircraft were USS *Brooklyn*, USS *Cleveland* and USS *Augusta*

The Fedala landings were a shambles. Many landing craft failed to reach their start lines, only a quarter making it to the right place – and an hour late. In due course more than half were lost and many soldiers drowned.

By first light the troops on the beach were vulnerable to enfilade fire from coastal guns while the French Navy put a number of destroyers to sea to attack the landing fleet. Aircraft from USS *Ranger* and USS *Suwannee* began sorties from 0610hrs, the targets for counter-air missions being the airfields at Rabat and Cazes, plus the coastal batteries. Dauntless dive-bombers of VS-41 targeted Casablanca harbour, specifically submarines – to prevent their escape to harry the US fleet – and the battleship *Jean Bart*, to prevent her from using her four 15in guns. At 0705hrs troops on the ground requested air cover to protect them from attacking French Dewoitine D.520s which, with Curtiss Hawk 75s, were now flying offensive as well as defensive sorties.

The French showed no signs of agreeing to an armistice, so a naval battle developed, US Navy fighters continuing to cover the beaches with numerous aerial engagements. During the course of the fighting a Spitfire IV of 544 Sqn made a run over the beachhead to feed back photo reconnaissance intelligence to Eisenhower in Gibraltar. Cover for the fleet against submarine attack rested in part with 233 Sqn RAF, based in Gibraltar. Sadly, four Hudsons went missing from a succession of standing patrols, brought down by USN fighters. In the afternoon, local forces in Fedala surrendered and on the 9th F-4 Lightnings of the 16th reconnaissance squadron moved into the local airfield.

During 9 October the fighting continued at sea, on land and in the air. The French launched air attacks on transport vessels, repulsed by American carrier-based aircraft. Notably, on this day, *Ranger* launched three L-4 (Piper Cub) airborne observation post aircraft to direct artillery of the 3rd Infantry Division. Flying over the cruiser USS *Brooklyn*, they were all shot at and destroyed. Not an auspicious start to AOP work.

On the 10th the guns of *Jean Bart* were in action against the headquarters cruiser USS *Augusta*. Within minutes the French vessel was put out of action by retaliatory attacks by Dauntless dive-bombers. As Casablanca was still holding out, and while waiting for Sherman tanks to come from Safi, Patton decided to launch a combined attack on the city at 0715hrs on 11 November. In the event it never happened because the French agreed terms. As the American fleet prepared for return to the United States, alternative American arms moved in, the 47th Bombardment Group (A-20) and 310th Bombardment Group (B-25) flying into Médiouna.

In the north the objective was Port Lyautey, which had a northwards rail link and was an important airfield. The assault force comprised:

60th RCT, 66th Armoured Bn, 540th Engineer Bn, all with air cover provided by

CVE-26 USS *Sangamon*

VGF-26 F4F Wildcat

VGS-26 SBD Dauntless, TBF Avenger

CVE-28 USS *Chenango*

33rd FG P-40F Warhawk (ferry)

Capital ships with spotter aircraft were USS *Texas* and USS *Savannah*

This assault, planned for 0400hrs on the 8th, was also delayed and compromised by a coastal convoy sailing through the fleet and alerting shore batteries. There were landings on four beaches, but ships soon came under fire from the Kasba fort battery, at the mouth of the Sebou river, causing them to retire 15 miles eventually. The cruiser *Savannah* and several destroyers opened fire on the battery, apparently unaware of orders to troops on the ground to take the fort by force, resulting in US casualties.

Curtiss SOC-3 Seagull of VCS-7 over USS *Augusta*. *USN Official*

While Wildcats of VGF-26 from USS *Sangamon* flew cover over the fleet, those from VF-9 from *Ranger* were sent to attack D.520s on the Port Lyautey airfield. Despite their best efforts to prevent it, US ground forces were nonetheless attacked by French aircraft. Wildcats of VF-41 had also been briefed to attack gun emplacements, but the Kasba guns continued to fire throughout the day. On the 9th, the situation for US ground forces became even more serious. They were short of ammunition, victuals, medical and other essentials and heavy seas made resupply hazardous. It was not until the 10th, with the airfield captured, that the destroyer USS *Dallas* with a seventy-five-man raiding party aboard, was able to force passage up the river past the fort, despite its guns remaining operational. They were silenced eventually at 0700hrs by air strikes from USS *Sangamon*.

After the initial friendly fire issue and with poor communications, the capital ships steered clear of giving NGS to targets very close to invasion forces. However, embarked spotters of the battleship USS *Texas* and cruiser *Savannah* reported a column coming up from Rabat, which was shelled effectively. P-40F Warhawks of the 33rd Fighter Group began flying off USS *Chenango* during the 10th for the airfield at Port Lyautey. Unfortunately, bombing and shelling had cratered the runway and after several aircraft had crashed on landing the remainder were flown off to Cazes on 12 November. (Of the total seventy-seven aircraft, two were lost and seventeen crash-landed. Thirty-five replacements were brought in by HMS *Archer* on the 13th, four of which also crash-landed!) As elsewhere in Morocco, fighting ended at 1100hrs on the 11th.

Losses of aircraft were high on both sides. The US Navy lost twenty-five Wildcats, nineteen dive-bombers and four spotters. The French air forces lost forty-one fighters, eighteen bombers and forty-seven other types, of which seventy-eight were destroyed on the ground.[2] The Western invasion demonstrated care in planning but inadequate thought given to the problems of landing in difficult seas, something to plague the Americans again in the 1944 Normandy landings. Another problem was aircraft identification. At this stage it had not occurred to planners to mark Allied aircraft in a distinctive way so as to avoid their falling victim to friendly fire.

Table 7.3 – Western Air Command, 8 November–31 December 1942

Group	Aircraft	Base	From	Role
Algeria				
IX Bomber Command 9th AF				
97th BG(H)	B-17F	Maison Blanche ex UK	13.11.42	HB
XII Bomber Command 12th AF				
301st BG(H)	B-17F	Tafaraoui, Biskra ex UK	24.11.42	HB
17th BG(M)	B-26	Telergma ex US	23.12.42	MB
319th BG(M)	B-26	Tafaraoui, Maison Blanche, Telergma ex UK	17.11.42	MB
XII Air Support Command 12th AF				
1st FG	P-38F	Tafaraoui ex UK	11.11.42	F
14th FG	P-38F	Tafaraoui ex UK	14.11.42	F
31st FG	Spitfire V	Tafaraoui, La Senia ex Gib	9.11.42	F
52nd FG	Spitfire V	La Senia, Tafaraoui, Bône ex Gibraltar	14.11.42	F
15th BS(L)	A-20	Tebessa, Tafaraoui ex UK	13.11.42	LB
3rd PG	F-4, F-5	La Senia, Tafaraoui, Algiers ex UK	12.11.42	PR
111st TRS	A-20	St Leu, Tafaraoui, Oujda ex UK	10.11.42	Tac/R
154 WRS	F-4, A-20	St Leu, Tafaraoui, Blida, Oujda ex UK	10.11.42	WR
51st Troop Carrier Wing				
60th TCG	C-47	Tafaraoui ex UK	8.11.42	C
62nd TCG	C-47	Tafaraoui ex UK	14.11.42	C
64th TCG	C-47	Tafaraoui, Casablanca ex UK	15.11.42	C
Morocco				
XII Bomber Command 12th AF				
310th BG(M)	B-25	Médiouna, Telergma ex US	19.11.42	MB
XII Air Support Command 12th AF				
33rd FG	P-40F	Port Lyautey ex USS *Chenango*	10.11.42	F
47th BG(L)	A-20	Médiouna ex UK	18.11.42	LB
16th RS	F-4, A-20	Fedala, Casablanca ex US	9.11.42	PR
United States Navy				
VP-73	PBY-5A	Port Lyautey ex UK	14.11.42	AS
VP-92	PBY-5A	Cazes ex Sierra Leone	14.11.42	AS

Convoys for Algeria

The Central and Eastern task forces both departed Scotland between 22 October and 1 November in four convoys, two slow and two fast. The merchant ships were of mixed type and national origin, some having been converted to carry smaller landing craft. Britain had been able to bring experience of landings in Madagascar and Dieppe to bear on the design of a variety of landing craft and on landing procedures. Various Royal Navy forces departed UK waters at the same time, eventually to form four units: a patrol in the Atlantic around the Azores to cover the convoys en route; a cover group for the Mediterranean; two groups in support of the landings.

In the broadest sense the convoys were protected at the outset by Coastal Command patrols out in the Atlantic and by the high security surrounding the operation. Thus, U-boats were down in the South Atlantic and when the convoys were spotted in the Straits of Gibraltar the German assumption was that they were headed for Malta or Cyrenaica, to cut off Rommel's retreat.

Troops ready to go ashore at H-Hour, 0100hrs on 8 November, would have cover provided initially by naval aircraft and NGS. It was hoped that the French would agree terms without a fight, so there was no naval bombardment initially. Naval gunfire worked generally at high velocity and a relatively flat trajectory, not always of great value to landing troops and with a high risk of friendly casualties. Spotting was undertaken by Walrus aircraft of 700 NAS carried by the capital ships. Once ashore, the troops were supported by Combined Operations Bombardment Units (COBU), Royal Artillery officers being in direct radio contact to direct gunfire support.

On 9 October USS *Ranger* launched three L-4 'Grasshoppers' to direct artillery fire for the 3rd Infantry Division. All were shot down by 'friendly' AAA fire from the cruiser USS *Brooklyn*. *USN Official*

If necessary, ground forces could also call on the two Royal Navy air wings embarked on the fleet carriers in Force H holding off to the north. However, like the escort carriers, their main concerns were to protect the assault fleets from air attack by Axis bombers based In Tunisia, Sardinia or Sicily. Force H comprised:

With the landings consolidated light bomber units flew into Algeria, including the 47th Bombardment Group. Based at Youks-les-Bains the A20 Havocs started operations early in December. A-20A 42-39639/18 *Princess Ruthie* appears to have flown rather low, probably over water, judging from the damage to the propeller blade tips. *Mark O'Boyle*

Another light bomber unit was the 310th Bombardment Group flying the B-25. First aircraft arrived in Morocco on 18 November, but by the time this photograph of aircraft 35 was taken the machine had flown twenty-seven bombing sorties.

HMS *Formidable*

885 NAS Seafire II

888 NAS Martlet II

893 NAS Wildcat IV

820 NAS Albacore

HMS *Victorious*

882 NAS Wildcat IV

884 NAS Seafire IIc

809 NAS Fulmar IIP

817 NAS Albacore

832 NAS Albacore

Note: Martlet was the Fleet Air Arm name for the Grumman F4F Wildcat fighter, up to the Mk III, after which mark the US name Wildcat was applied. The F4F was used widely by the US Navy in Operation *Torch*.

F4F-4 Wildcat '25' of VF-41 running up to take off from USS Ranger on a combat air patrol. Overhead may be seen two L-4 Cub spotters.
USN Official

Naval gunfire support was available from the battleship HMS *Duke of York*, battlecruiser HMS *Renown* and cruiser *Argonaut*.

Once the North African airfields were captured many of the air units based temporarily on Gibraltar would fly in to take over close support duties from naval aircraft. Others would deploy from more distant bases for transport, anti-shipping, bomber and defence tasks. The airfields around Oran were the destination for units of the USAAF XII Air Support Command; RAF fighter wings were to move directly further east to airfields around Algiers and beyond. Two new and significant military organisations supported the British in the east.

Servicing Commando Units (SCUs) came into being from 31 January 1942, each to comprise two officers and 148 other ranks with fifteen 3-ton lorries, a jeep and motorcycle. They were intended to land with forward troops and their function was to prepare airfields for immediate operational use once they had been captured. The men were trained to fight as well as to refuel, re-arm and service front-line aircraft. Each SCU was allocated either three fighter squadrons, two light bomber squadrons or one medium bomber squadron. They were totally self-sufficient, their equipment ranging from cookers (to ensure that aircrew were also fed) to more mundane but essential items like windsocks. The commando side of training also covered the use of, and disembarking from, landing craft. Numbers 3201 and 3202 SCUs were to land at Algiers, while 3203 SCU, aboard SS *Volendam*, was bound directly for Bône.

The other new organisation, deployed fully for the first time, was the RAF Regiment, formed in the UK in February 1942, almost coincidentally with that of the SCUs. Its role was to defend airfields from ground and air attack, and in this respect the RAF freed Army troops to concentrate on offensive duties. Once the initial landings had achieved their objectives the intention was to deploy Regiment units as shown.

As a further indication of the extent of preparation, 242 Group, which had formed in London in August to control two fighter wings and a light bomber wing, took with it five mobile radar sets, 381 Maintenance Unit (MU), six Repair and Salvage Units (RSUs), six Air Stores Parks (ASPs) and 301 Mobile Signals Servicing Unit (MSSU).

Seafire IIcs of 885 NAS on the deck of HMS *Formidable* in November 1942. Also on deck are a Martlet of 888 NAS and an Albacore of 820 NAS while the plane-guard destroyer has taken up station. *AST collection*

Five squadrons of Sea Hurricanes were committed to support during the *Torch* landings including 800 NAS, whose Mk IIb JS355 is seen on the deck of HMS *Biter*. *J. M. Bruen via AST*

Action Oran

The Central Task Force headed for Oran, Algeria. It comprised American troops carried in two British-led mixed convoys – KMS(Slow).1 and KMF(Fast).1. They departed the River Clyde in Scotland on 22 and 26 October respectively, to combine in the Mediterranean on 7 November. The convoys comprised eighty-nine transports or auxiliaries and fifty-three escorts, mainly sloops and corvettes. Between them they carried the 16th, 18th and 26th Regimental Combat Teams, a brigade-sized unit of the 1st Armoured Division (180 tanks) and the 1st Ranger Battalion. In total there were some 18,500 men to land on three sectors over a 50-mile stretch of beach. Key early objectives were the airfields at La Senia and Tafaraoui and a smaller one at Lourmel.

Table 7.4 – RAF Regiment wings

Wing	Role	Initial Location	RAF Regt ground defence	RAF Regt AA defence
322	F	Bône	2788 Sqn	4089 Flt
323	F	Maison Blanche	2825 Sqn	4088 Flt
324	F	Constantine	2744 Sqn	4091 Flt
325	F	Philippeville	2721 Sqn	4092 Flt
326	LB	Setif	2771 Sqn	4090 Flt
328	GR	Blida	None	None

F-4-F Wildcats of VF-9 (foreground) and VF-41 testing their machine guns on board USS Ranger prior to the landings. *USN*

Immediate air cover for this Central force was provided by three Royal Navy aircraft carriers. They stood back from the anchorages protected by the battleship HMS *Rodney*, cruisers HMS *Jamaica* and HMS *Aurora* (both to also provide supporting fire if necessary) and the AA cruiser HMS *Delhi*.

HMS *Furious*

- 801 NAS Seafire Ib
- 807 NAS Seafire IIc
- 822 NAS Albacore, Fulmar IIP

HMS *Biter*

- 800 NAS Sea Hurricane IIB, IIC

HMS *Dasher*

- 804 NAS Sea Hurricane IIC
- 891 NAS Sea Hurricane IIB

Soldiers on X sector, 25 miles to the west of Oran, could call on NGS from HMS *Aurora* and those on Z sector, 25 miles to the east, could look to HMS *Jamaica*, which carried a Walrus for spotting. HMS *Rodney* and the carriers stood off 25 miles to the north of Oran itself.

In general, there were few delays or problems with the landings that were largely unopposed on all three beaches. A key element of the assault was Operation *Reservist*, intended to place raiders in Oran harbour to capture the installations intact and prevent French warships from leaving. Two former US Coast Guard cutters, HMS *Hartland* and HMS *Walney*, were given the task of landing nearly 400 men of the 2nd Battalion, 6th Armoured Infantry Regiment, in the harbour, but after crashing the booms at 0310hrs both were fired upon by shore batteries and warships and sank with the loss of most of the crews and 189 US soldiers. The harbour installations were sabotaged.

Not only were airfields required for the early use of Allied squadrons, the aircraft on them were also primary targets so as to ensure that the landings were not subject to aerial attack. From 0600hrs Seafires of 807 NAS made for Tafaraoui while Albacores of 822 NAS, under the protection of Sea Hurricanes of 800 and 804 NAS, made for the slightly nearer La Senia. The Albacores achieved considerable success, reportedly damaging forty-seven aircraft on the ground,[3] but not before a number of Dewoitine D.520s had taken off to intercept them. Four Albacores were destroyed and four seriously damaged; three escorting Hurricanes and two Seafires were also lost. Seafires had attacked aircraft on the ground at Tafaraoui from 0640hrs, soon after which US tanks rolled in to capture the airfield. Around 1700hrs the first Spitfires of the 31st Fighter Group flew in from Gibraltar, one being shot down immediately by marauding D.520s from La Senia.

Sea Hurricane IIB JS327 of 804 NAS from HMS *Dasher* force-landed on a beach near Algiers on 8 November. All British Naval aircraft involved in Operation *Torch* were temporarily marked with the US star painted over the roundels given Vichy French antipathy towards British forces. *AST collection*

The naval pilots took their close support responsibilities most seriously. In doing so, one difficulty they had to overcome was lack of adequate radio links to ground forces, as demonstrated in the following note by Sub Lt Peter Twiss when recalling flying a Seafire of 807 NAS on a tactical recce sortie near La Senia.[4]

> 'I saw some tank movements, which I reported back to HMS Furious. At the same time, I noted an American group of tanks approaching the airfield. I could not communicate by radio to report the possible clash, so I decided to land near the US armoured column to warn them of the situation.
>
> I landed on what just seemed to be a runway-like surface and, leaving my engine ticking over, jumped out kicking a small stone in front of each wheel and rushed over to speak to the Americans. They were very pleased at the warning and asked a few questions about other local activities, which would help their next move. I remounted my Seafire and took off on a further reconnaissance reporting other tank movements two to three miles ahead.'

There were plans to capture both airfields by para-drop, but in the event things went somewhat awry. Thirty-nine C-47s of the USAAF 60th Troop Carrier Group departed Cornwall on the night of 7 November for which the options were either a 'war' drop at night or a 'peace' drop in daylight. It was the latter option that was taken, but with navigational consequences. Some aircraft had already become lost over neutral Spain; a covert radio beacon on the Algerian coast was off air, not having been told of the change to a later drop time; and a radio beacon on a vessel off Cap Figolo was broadcasting on the wrong frequency. As a consequence, several aircraft went missing and some landed in Spanish Morocco, the majority touching down on Srebka salt flats, just north of Tafaraoui.

The airfield at La Senia, though, remained in French hands and a thorn in the side of the attackers. At 0800hrs Sea Hurricanes of 891 NAS undertook a strafing mission with limited success; in the afternoon Tafaraoui was attacked by French bombers. The La Senia-based D.520s of GC III/3 were active, bringing down seven Albacores, a Hurricane, a USAAF Spitfire and forcing down four C-47s, all for the loss of eight of their own. A Seafire was shot down by AA over the airfield.

During the 9th, remaining Albacores of 822 NAS made precision dive-bombing attacks on several reported artillery emplacements. While there was otherwise little resistance, there was a need for NGS at Oran when shore batteries at Fort du Santon, above the port at Mers-el-Kebir, fired on Allied warships. Several responded with direct fire, among them HMS *Rodney* with her 16in guns, from 30,000 yards – the range of the guns in the fort having been assumed to be 28,500 yards. At this stage spotting for the guns was by *Rodney's* Walrus of 700 NAS, launched ten minutes before the first salvoes were

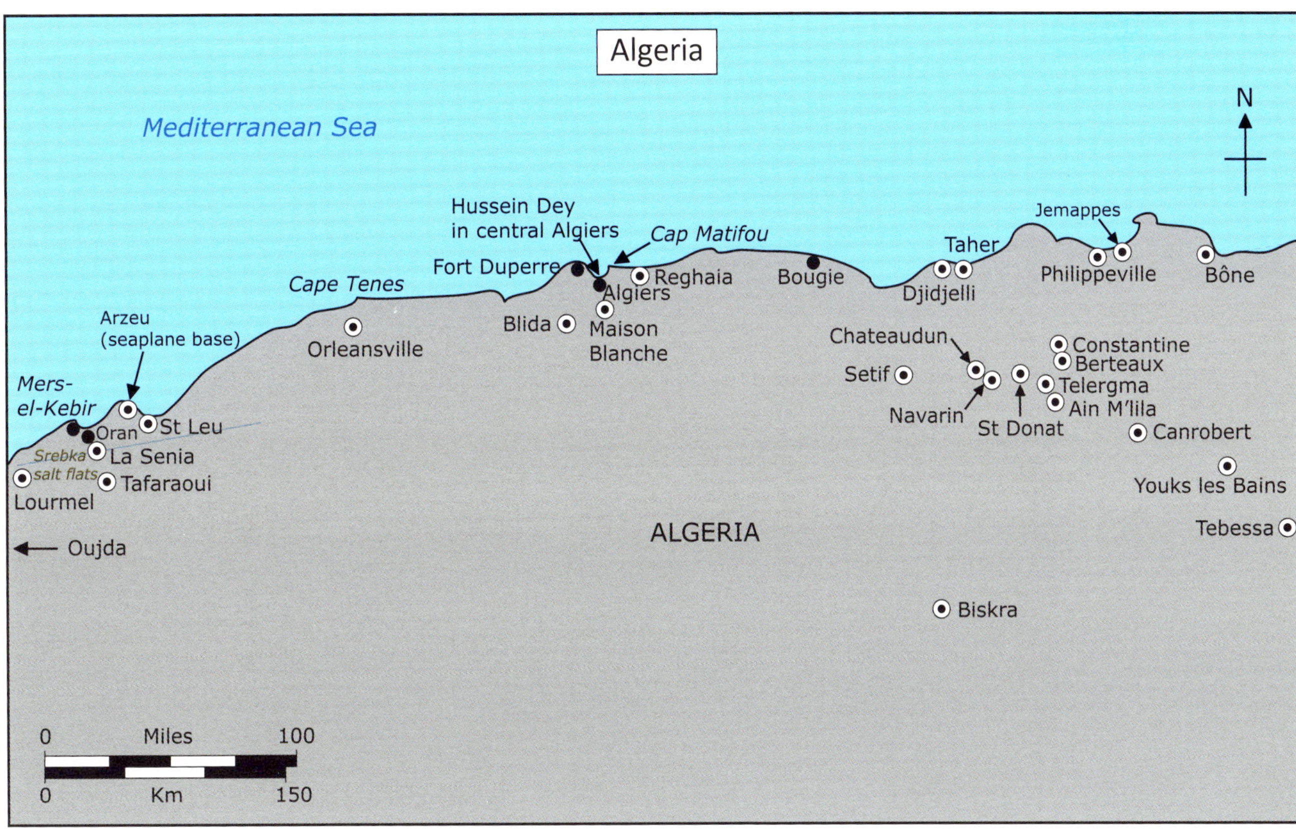

fired at midday. Initially there was no response, but later that evening the French guns fired on the battleship prompting further exchanges and loss of the Walrus to AA fire. The warship versus shore battery stand-off continued throughout the 9th, but on the 10th *Rodney* was successful in taking out the guns which had threatened the follow-up troops in their vulnerable landing craft.

With the American Spitfire Wing now in place at Tafaraoui the carriers began to withdraw, only for the airfield to come under French artillery fire. The Spitfires undertook reconnaissance sorties, also attacking a column threatening Arzeu. The remaining French aircraft at La Senia now departed for Morocco and the airfield was taken in the morning, after which a second Spitfire formation, the 52nd Fighter Group, flew in from Gibraltar. Allied fighters continued to support ground forces surrounding Oran, although at one stage they attacked in error a US light tank column. Oran was soon taken and an accommodation reached with the French.

In providing cover for the Central Task Force the Fleet Air Arm lost fifteen Sea Hurricanes, twelve Seafires, eight Martlets, eight Albacores and two Fulmars.[5]

Action Algiers

The Eastern task force of US and British troops was bound for Algiers, having departed Clydeside and Loch Ewe in two convoys. Seventeen transports and eleven escorts making up KMF.2 departed on 1 November. KMS.2, with fifty merchant ships and twenty-five escorts, left on 25 October. On board were the 39th and 168th RCTs of the US 34th Infantry Division; the 11th and 36th Brigade Groups of the British 78th Infantry Division; and the 1st and 6th Commandos, ad hoc units comprising both British and American troops. A most significant inclusion was eight Auster Mk Is of 651 Sqn, embarked on SS *Circassia*.

The speed with which the huge force was gathered is highlighted by one brief account from the logbook of a 225 Sqn pilot,[6] whose assembled aircraft were waiting at Gibraltar.

> *Oct 22 Left Macmerry by train for Padgate (near Warrington) 18 pilots plus CO*
>
> *Oct 24 Left Padgate and embarked MS* Leinster *(Irish Channel Boat) at Greenock*
>
> *Oct 26 Sailed*
>
> *Nov 8 Disembarked at Gibraltar – went to Governors Cottage rest camp*
>
> *Nov 14 Hurricane HV875 Gibraltar to Maison Blanche Force-landed wheels up. Lack of petrol. 3hrs 10mins*

The force overall totalled 20,000 men.[7] Key objectives were Blida and Maison Blanche airfields, followed by a rapid drive east via Bougie and capture of the airfields at Djidjelli, then Bône, before Axis forces in Tunisia had time to be strengthened. To give some idea of the complexity of the landing task, the structure of one of the two British infantry brigades is noted.

11th Brigade

- 1st Bn East Surrey Regt
- 5th Bn Northamptonshire Regt
- 2nd Bn Lancashire Fusiliers
- B Sqn 56th Reconnaissance Regt
- 132nd Field Regt RA
- 84th Light AA Battery
- 237th Field Coy RE
- 11th Field Ambulance
- 11th Brigade Coy RAOC
- Platoon 11th Brigade Coy RASC
- Coy 78th Div MP: Divisional Signals: Divisional Hygiene Section

Another view of the flight deck of HMS *Formidable* with Martlets and Seafires running up engines. *Crown copyright*

Air cover for the Eastern force was provided by two carriers, supported by the cruisers HMS *Charybdis*, HMS *Scylla* and HMS *Sheffield* and the monitor HMS *Roberts*. While the latter was slow, it was armed with two 15in guns and no less than forty AA guns of varying calibre. The carriers were:

HMS *Avenger*

802 NAS Sea Hurricane IIC

883 NAS Sea Hurricane IIC

HMS *Argus*

880 NAS Seafire IIc

As at Oran, H-Hour was 0100hrs on the 8th. The landings, in three sectors spread over some 40 miles, were successful despite some localised positional errors that were soon sorted. Heavy surf caused delays in the off-loading of some equipment, especially transport. On the ground, the French Army was generally passive and by 0630hrs the more northerly airfield at Maison Blanche was in Allied hands. Also, as at Oran, there was to be another heroic attempt to take Algiers harbour without damage, Operation *Terminal* involving the destroyers HMS *Broke* and HMS *Malcolm*. Both struggled to find the harbour entrance and, after eventually landing her troops from the US 135th Infantry, *Broke* was forced to withdraw.

From dawn aircraft from the two escort carriers flew cover over the landings and from 0600hrs the first troops arrived at Maison Blanche, which had been the civil airport for Algiers. The intention was to attack the airfield with air strikes from the fleet carriers in which 893 NAS Martlets and Seafires of 885 NAS were to take part. But a heavy mist prevented that from happening, also keeping grounded defending French D.520 fighters of GC II/3 and GC III/6. Meanwhile, sections of four Martlets of 882 NAS maintained a constant watch over Blida, strafing and destroying two bombers. Then, at 0830hrs, when the third relief Martlet section arrived overhead, the airfield was surrendered to Lt H. B. C. Nation who had landed to check on the status of the incumbents.

Despite there having been no confirmation of the capture of airfields, the first aircraft – eighteen Hurricanes of 43 Sqn – were despatched from Gibraltar at dawn, arriving at Maison Blanche at 1015hrs. Landing with the assault forces were 3201 and 3202 SCUs. After having been landed late from USS *Leedstown* and with little equipment, men of 3201 SCU marched 11 miles to Maison Blanche, arriving in time to refuel the newly arrived Hurricanes. For the first day or two there was much make do and mend and with no direct radio communications possible a Walrus was flown to Maison Blanche to provide contact with the HQ ship and Gibraltar. RAF Regt 4088 and 4089 AA Flts had also landed on the 8th, but with much equipment lost or misplaced it was several days before they could provide effective airfield defence.

Douglas SBD-3 Dauntless of VS-41 flying over the Western Task Force from USS *Ranger*. The dive-bombers later attacked the French battleship *Jean Bart* in Casablanca harbour. *USN*

The pace of operations is illustrated by entries in the logbook of 43 Sqn pilot Flt Lt J. Lister.[8]

Nov 8	*Hurricane IIC U407*	*Gib to Algiers*
Nov 8	*Hurricane IIC U407*	*Ops patrol over fleet*
Nov 8	*Hurricane IIC B403*	*Flap[A] (dusk)*
Nov 9	*Hurricane IIC U407*	*Patrol*
Nov 9	*Hurricane IIC U407*	*Dusk flap*
Nov 10	*Hurricane IIC D*	*Patrol*
Nov 10	*Hurricane IIC L*	*Dusk patrol*
Nov 11	*Hurricane IIC A*	*Patrol*
Nov 11	*Hurricane IIC A*	*Dusk patrol*
Nov 12	*Hurricane IIC L*	*Escort paratroopers Bône*
Nov 12	*Hurricane IIC U407*	*Dusk patrol over Bougie*

Next to arrive from Gibraltar were Spitfires of 81 and 242 Sqns, by noon on the 8th. The fighters soon established regular patrols to cover troops from air attack. Although the French Air Force was almost welcoming, the French Navy, as elsewhere, showed resistance, coastal batteries at Cap Matifou, Fort Duperre and Fort d'Estres firing at vessels in the harbour area. In response to calls for assistance, Albacores of 817, 820 and 832 NAS dive-bombed the forts, which were also shelled by HMS *Bermuda*, putting all out of action. HMS *Sheffield* and HMS *Bermuda* were attacked by Italian Savoia Marchetti SM.79 torpedo bombers in the afternoon and the destroyer HMS *Cowdray* was severely damaged by a bomb, resulting in it being beached the following day.

In Algiers a ceasefire was agreed at 1900hrs on the 8th. The assault had gone well, with minimum casualties. Had it been necessary, close support would have been provided by the warships while awaiting artillery observers and, indeed, artillery itself, to be off-loaded. But, whatever the French had decided, vessels still off-loading and airfields where the Allies had taken up residence, were now subject to air attack by Italian and German aircraft from Tunisia, Sardinia and Sicily. On the 9th HMS *Bulolo*, a converted armed merchant cruiser that served as flagship for the Eastern Naval Task Force, entered Algiers harbour.

[A] Panic, probably a scramble

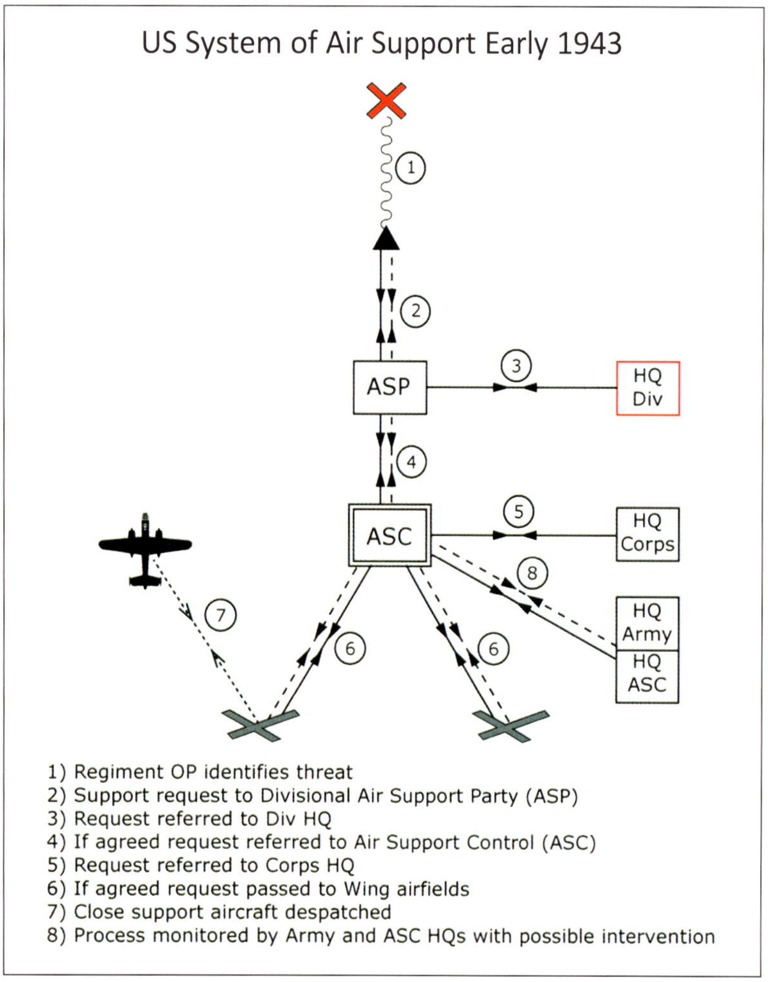

In the afternoon shipping, Algiers town and Maison Blanche airfield were attacked by up to thirty Ju 88s and He 111s. This attack coincided with the arrival of two B-17s, one with Eisenhower's deputy, Gen Mark Clark, aboard and escorted by Spitfires of 242 Sqn. As noted in Lister's log entry, the two events were the 'Flap (dusk)' in which Hurricanes of 43 Sqn and Spitfires of 81 Sqn were scrambled. In the resulting combat eleven Ju 88s and three He 111s were brought down at no loss to the RAF. Undeterred, at 1730hrs there was a follow-up raid by German and Italian torpedo bombers.

Also on the 9th, Axis forces occupied Tunisia via the airfield at El Aouina where twenty-seven Bf 109s of I/JG 53 and twenty-four Ju 87Ds of II/StG 3, plus a number of Ju 52/3m transports, were landed. On the 10th a reconnaissance Spitfire spotted 115 aircraft on the airfield and later in the day these were joined by twenty-one Italian Macchi C.202s of 155° Gr 51° St from Gela. Later in the day the airfield at Sidi Ahmed, Bizerta, was also occupied. In a demonstration of coordinated planning, a strike was undertaken by Beaufighters of 272 Sqn from Malta at 1605hrs, twenty-one aircraft being claimed destroyed or seriously damaged.

The Army now moved eastwards at a fast rate, with some of the follow-up convoys making for Bône. It was essential that the fighter squadrons were fully operational as soon as possible and on the morning of the 9th SCUs brought up 50,000 gallons of aviation fuel from the docks to Maison Blanche. Two companies of 3rd Battalion Parachute Regiment had flown from the UK to Maison Blanche on the 10th and at 0815hrs on the 12th they were dropped on Bône by C-47s of the 60th Troop Carrier Group (TCG) to capture the field. On 15 November it was the turn of the US 509th Parachute Battalion to drop on and capture the airfields at Youks-les-Bains and Tebessa, which they did without loss. The following day 1 Para was dropped on Souk el Arba in Tunisia, also captured without resistance.

A Lockheed Hudson of 233 Sqn flying off Gibraltar. The unit flew anti-submarine patrols protecting the US invasion fleets, but despite being an American type, no fewer than four were brought down by trigger-happy USN fighter pilots. *Author's collection*

Within days of the initial landings the three RAF fighter wings from Gibraltar were in Algeria with some units leapfrogging, so that Djidjelli airfield was in use on the 12th (154 Sqn), Bône by the 13th (81 and 111 Sqns) and Souk el Arba (72 Sqn) from the 20th. Most came in via Maison Blanche, 3203 SCU having been landed direct at Bône by SS *Volendam* for advanced servicing. Meanwhile, elements of 3202 SCU had moved forward on SS *Awatea*, its objective Djidjelli via Bougie, landing on the 11th shortly before the ship was sunk by German bombers. Cover was now limited to that provided by fighters based at Maison Blanche until Djidjelli was operational for the Allies. As the squadrons' own groundcrews arrived the SCUs packed their bags and moved forward. Aviation fuel was very limited at Bône, so stocks were flown in by C-47s escorted by 253 Sqn Hurricanes.

On 12 November SS *Circassia* landed its cargo on the beach at Hussein Dey, Algiers, which fortunately was also the small but central aerodrome occupied by the Sports Aérien d'Algiers flying club. Included were the eight Auster AOP Mk I artillery spotters with their Royal Artillery pilots and other ranks in company with RAF fitters and riggers. The first Auster was flown from Hussein Dey on the 16th, moving on to Bône on the 19th and directing fire (American by chance) from the 23rd. A new chapter in Army close support was about to be written. Just days before, on the 13th, the first B-17F Flying Fortresses of 97th BG(H) arrived at Maison Blanche from the UK, a clear sign that the Allies were now seriously intent on crushing the Axis forces concentrated in Tunisia.

Table 7.5 – Eastern Air Command, 8 November–31 December 1942

Sqn	Aircraft	Base(s)	From	Role
322 Wing Gibraltar				
81	Spitfire V	Maison Blanche, Bône	8.11.42	F
154	Spitfire V	Djidjelli	12.11.42	F
242	Spitfire V	Maison Blanche, Djidjelli, Bône	8.11.42	F
225	Hurricane IIC	Maison Blanche, Bône, Souk el Arba	13.11.42	Tac/R, FB
323 Wing UK via Gibraltar				
43	Hurricane IIC	Maison Blanche	8.11.42	F
253	Hurricane IIC	Maison Blanche, Philippeville	13.11.42	F
324 Wing UK via Gibraltar				
72	Spitfire VC	Maison Blanche, Bône, Souk el Arba	16.11.42	F
93	Spitfire VC	Maison Blanche, Souk el Arba	13.11.42	F
111	Spitfire VC	Maison Blanche, Bône, Souk el Arba	11.11.42	F
152	Spitfire VB	Maison Blanche, Bône, Souk el Arba	14.11.42	F
325 Wing UK via SS Antenor				
32	Hurricane IIC	Philippeville	7.12.42	F
87	Hurricane IIC	Philippeville, Djidjelli	7.12.42	F
232	Spitfire VB	Philippeville, Constantine	7.12.42	F
243	Spitfire VC	Philippeville, Constantine	7.12.42	F
326 Wing UK (Blenheims flew out)				
13	Blenheim V	Blida, Canrobert	18.11.42	LB
18	Blenheim V	Blida, Canrobert	11.11.42	LB
114	Blenheim V	Blida, Setif, Canrobert	15.11.42	LB
614	Blenheim V	Blida, Canrobert	18.11.42	LB
241	Hurricane IIC	Maison Blanche, Constantine, Souk el Arba	30.11.42	Tac/R, FB
255	Beaufighter VIF	Maison Blanche, Bône, Setif	15.11.42	NF
600	Beaufighter VIF	Blida, Maison Blanche	18.11.42	NF
Gibraltar based				
202	Catalina IB	Gibraltar	based	AS
233	Hudson III, V	Gibraltar	based	MR
500	Hudson III	Gibraltar ex St Eval	5.11.42	MR
608	Hudson III, V	Gibraltar ex Gosport	9.11.42	MR
813 NAS	Swordfish II	Gibraltar ex HMS *Eagle*	11.8.42	AS
833 NAS	Swordfish II	Gibraltar ex HMS *Avenger*	6.11.42	AS
544 B Flt	Spitfire IV	Gibraltar ex Benson	00.10.42	PR
4 PRU	Spitfire IV	Gibraltar	6.11.42	PR
Met Flt		Gibraltar		

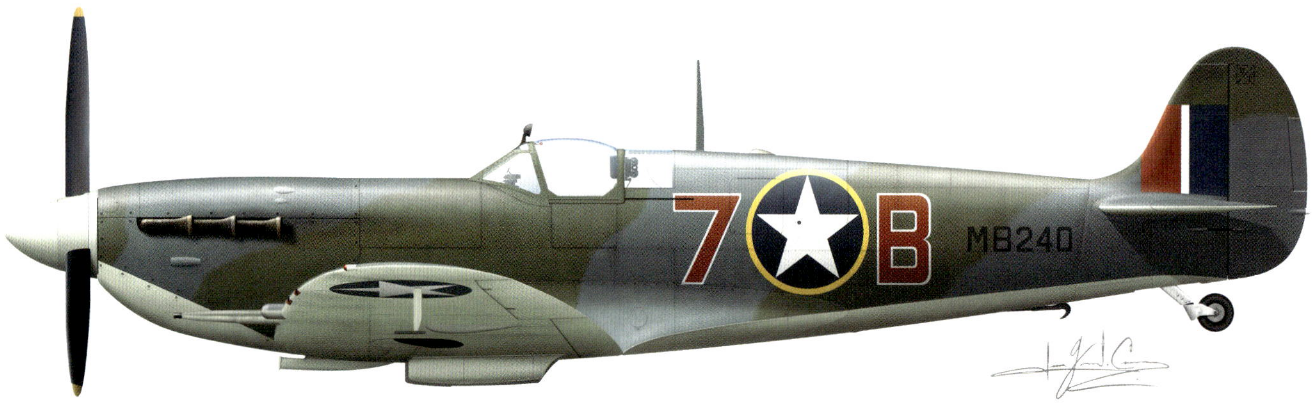

Seafire II MB240/7-B 880 NAS.
Luca G. Canossa

Summary

The invasion was far and away the biggest amphibious expedition of the war this far and was a combined operation in every sense. Security was such that the Germans were completely fooled as to the destinations of the huge convoys so that they arrived at their landing sites intact. With hindsight, it might have been better if the risk-averse Americans had agreed to a landing at Bizerta rather than Casablanca, but there was uncertainty about French reaction and some concern about possible Spanish intervention.

The French situation was highly complex, but suffice to say that there were so-called 'patriotic' elements in Algiers who prepared the way for the landings there. But equally, there was strong French naval resistance, resulting in the loss of ships and lives. The Germans ignored the armistice and invaded Tunisia as expected, but on the 11th they also occupied Vichy France in Operation *Anton*. When it became clear that there were German designs on the powerful French fleet at Toulon it was scuttled on the orders of Admiral Darlan. The occupation and hostility encouraged Darlan to co-operate with the Allies and from 23 December French forces in North Africa fought alongside them.

The British arrangements for direct air support had the following key characteristics:

- Initial support was by naval fighters
- Communications were poor and overloaded
- Land-based fighters available at earliest from Gibraltar
- Radar and related infrastructure shipped in
- SCUs speeded operational readiness
- RAF Regiment allowed RAF to concentrate on flying
- There was only one Divisional Tac/R squadron (225 Sqn)
- First AOP squadron in theatre

Another unit providing protection to the invasion fleets was 255 Squadron with its Beaufighter VIF based on Gibraltar. *Author's collection*

A significant development was the incorporation within the British invasion fleet of the Austers of 651 Sqn for artillery observation. Within days of landing at Algiers the aircraft were in action shooting US artillery units. Auster Mk I LB282, seen here in the UK, is indicative of the aircraft involved. *Author's collection*

| Sea Hurricane XII JS327 HMS Dasher 804 NAS. *Luca G. Canossa*

In respect of the actual landings, they demonstrated several weaknesses that would need addressing before further amphibious assaults were contemplated. The main problems seem to have been lack of training, especially in disembarking; inadequate appreciation of tide and sea states; inadequate reconnaissance of beaches; loss or stranding of much of the transport in vessels; unsystematic loading of stores; and disorganised landing of stores and equipment.

Despite near parity in air power at the time of landing, troops were more than adequately protected, but due in large part to French ambivalence. Within days the military was on the move eastwards with the infrastructure it needed to provide effective close support. However, the Germans under General Albert Kesselring, were quick to build up Axis air forces in Tunisia, Sardinia and Sicily on all-weather airfields, thereby proving a serious threat to Allied shipping and forward troop movements.

The Americans relied on Field Manual (FM) 31-35 for their air support system. This provided for a cumbersome and extended system of requesting and reporting that, in effect, gave each Corps its own mini air force. A request for support from the front would be communicated to the Air Support Party (ASP) at divisional level which would seek approval and, if given, forward the request to the Army Air Support Control (AASC) at Corps level for approval there. If that too was given, the request would move to Air Support Command HQ (being monitored on the way by Army HQ), from where it would be directed to the most appropriate air wing.

The Eastern Task Force took with it an Army Air Support Control and nine tentacles. As these tentacles moved forward they would make requests for either fighter protection or tactical reconnaissance. In the event, communications were extremely poor and for the first few days the fighters were able only to respond to incoming air raids.

No lessons had been transferred from the Western Desert experience. The key to supporting ground forces was first to take out enemy aircraft and airfields to help achieve air superiority, second to hit stores and lines of communications and third to provide immediate support over the battlefield. Understandably, the armies' idea of support was to see a constant stream of fighters overhead, which was both ineffective and wasteful.

Sadly few photographs of Vichy French aircraft confronting the *Torch* landings seem to exist. This wrecked Dewoitine D.520 394/4 of GC I/2 is at Meknés.

Once the British landings were consolidated a number of Blenheim light bomber squadrons flew into Blida. One of those units was 13 Sqn with its distinctive long-nosed Blenheim Vs. This variant was unpopular with crews and suffered heavy losses in North Africa. *Author's collection*

[1] Playfair, *History of the Second World War: Mediterranean and Middle East Vol IV*, p114

[2] Shores, *Mediterranean Air War Vol 3*

[3] Kemp, *Fleet Air Arm*, p193

[4] Twiss, *Faster Than the Sun*, p182

[5] Shores, *Mediterranean Air War Vol 3*, p83

[6] Logbook of Flt Lt Ian Stewart RAF Museum X003-2976/001

[7] Playfair, *History of the Second World War: Mediterranean and Middle East Vol IV*, p126

[8] Logbook of Flt Lt J Lister RAF Museum

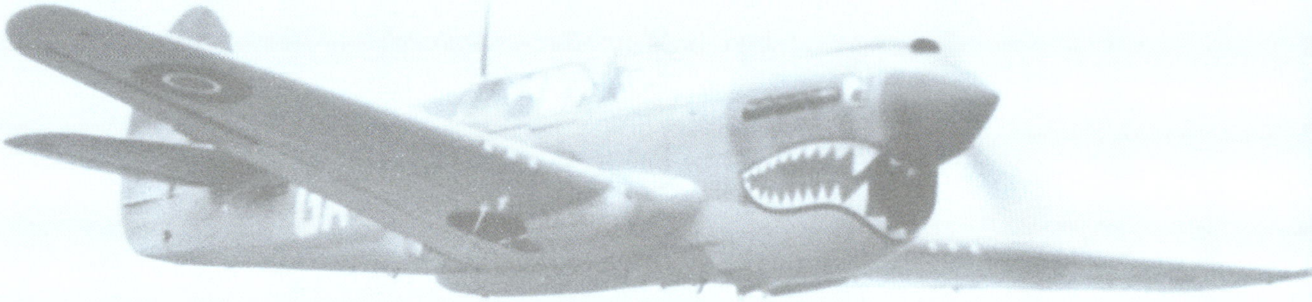

The Battle of El Hamma

Readying for the Knock-Out Blow in Africa

From the successful and largely uncontested *Torch* landings the Allied armies had moved steadily eastwards in an attempt to crush Axis forces on the anvil of the Eighth Army, supported by the Western Desert Air Force. Initially the advance to the Tunisian border had been swift, but as significant Axis reinforcements were flown into the country, and with the terrain favouring defence, the assault slowed. By 1 January 1943 the Allied (American, British and now Free French) First Army front line ran from a point about 30 miles west of Bizerta, due south to the Chott Djerid salt marsh.

On 23 January the Eighth Army took Tripoli and Rommel withdrew to the Mareth Line, a defensive fortification built by the French in southern Tunisia between the sea and the Matmata Hills, to defend against Italian incursion from Libya. From 25 January Axis forces attacked the First Army line at several points, determined to penetrate before the Allies had time to reinforce from Algeria. The most devastating attack was at the Kasserine Pass in mid-February, where inexperienced and poorly led American troops were beaten with huge losses. The Axis attack was helped by having air superiority that denied adequate reconnaissance to the RAF and USAAF.

The October blitz on Malta had ended and the blockade had been breached effectively by March 1943. From the island the RAF was in a strong position to disrupt enemy reinforcement and supply to Tunisia by sea and air. While the Allied armies in the west now regrouped, ineffective commanders being replaced, the Eighth Army prepared an offensive against the Mareth Line, to begin on 20 March. Codenamed Operation *Pugilist*, after a successful assault on the Mareth Line it was to continue as a left hook flanking movement four days later, as Operation *Supercharge II*. The scene was now set for the final major battle in North Africa at El Hamma.

The military organisation had been sharpened. The Supreme Allied Commander, General Dwight D. Eisenhower, appointed General Sir Harold Alexander as Deputy C-in-C and commander of the Eighteenth Army Group, comprising both the First and Eighth armies. The First Army, under Lt Gen Sir Kenneth Anderson, was composed of the British V Corps (Lt Gen Charles Allfrey), French XIX Corps (Lt Gen Marie-Louis Koëltz) and the US II Corps (Maj Gen George Patton). Montgomery retained command of the Eighth Army with Lt Gen Brian Horrocks commanding X Corps, Lt Gen Sir Oliver Leese XXX Corps and Gen Sir Bernard Freyberg the New Zealand Corps.

114 Sqn converted from the Blenheim Mk V to Boston III in March. Z2205, which had served with several squadrons in the UK, is here at Canrobert. *Crown copyright*

The Air Forces

As a prelude to describing the battle there needs to be an appraisal of the organisational changes made to achieve effective close support by the air forces of both sides. At the crucial Casablanca conference in January 1943 the continuing Allied (that is US/British – Stalin declined to attend) war strategy was agreed. The next stage in defeating Axis powers after removing them from Tunisia was to be the invasion of Sicily. In order to support the strategy a combined Mediterranean Air Command was formed from 18 February 1943 under Air Chief Marshal Sir Arthur Tedder, accountable to Eisenhower.

There was clearly a need to consolidate, coordinate and realign the various Air Components, especially as there was the prospect of operational differences between the Western Desert Air Force and the *Torch* air elements as they converged on Axis forces in Tunisia. All Allied air forces in the theatre were therefore brought together within Mediterranean Air Command, the principal elements of which were:

Northwest African Air Forces (Lt Gen Carl Spaatz)

Middle East Command (ACM Sir Sholto Douglas)

AHQ Malta (AVM Sir Keith Park)

RAF Gibraltar (AVM Sturley Simpson)

216 Group (transport) (Air Cdre Whitney Straight)

Tedder reported to Eisenhower in respect of his NAAF remit and to the British Chiefs of Staff for his other commands. For the Battle of El Hamma and the subsequent invasion of Sicily, it was to be NAAF and AHQ Malta that played the key roles. NAAF comprised the following:

Northwest African Strategic Air Force (Maj Gen James Doolittle)

Northwest African Coastal Air Force (AVM Hugh Lloyd)

Northwest African Tactical Air Force (AM Sir Arthur Coningham)

Northwest African Air Service Command (Maj Gen Delmar Dunton)

Northwest African Training Command (Brig Gen John Cannon)

Northwest African Troop Carrier Command (Brig Gen Paul Williams)

Northwest African Photographic Reconnaissance Wing (Col Elliott Roosevelt)

The Martin Baltimore served with eight Dominion squadrons in North Africa and continued flying through the Italian campaign. This Mk IV with Martin dorsal turret is FA463/U of 223 Sqn. *Crown copyright*

The first three of these were the combat commands that would be involved potentially in supporting ground forces. They were the cutting edge of a formidable Mediterranean Air Command, whose assets were distributed to meet all potential threats and to interdict Axis supply routes. All tables in this chapter reflect the situation as at 24 March 1943.

While the Northwest African Strategic Air Force was essentially a long-range, heavy bomber force, on occasion it nonetheless supported troops very close to the front line. The best example is probably the bombing of the monastery at Monte Cassino in 1944. It comprised seven USAAF bombardment groups plus three P-38 escort fighter groups, with an RAF contribution of six Wellington and one Halifax squadrons.

Table 8.1 – Northwest African Strategic Air Force

Northwest African Strategic Air Force			
Grp/Wing	**Squadrons**	**Type**	**Base**
5th Bombardment Wing USAAF			
97th BG	340, 341, 342, 414	B-17	Chateaudun, Alg
301st BG	32, 352, 353, 419	B-17	St Donat, Alg
99th BG	346, 347, 348, 416	B-17	Navarin, Alg
42nd Bombardment Wing USAAF			
17th BG	34, 37, 95, 432	B-26	Telergma, Alg
319th BG	437, 438, 439, 440	B-26	Oujda, Mor
1st FG	27, 71, 94	P-38G	Chateaudun, Alg
14th FG	37, 48, 49	P-38G	Medouina, Mor
47th Bombardment Wing USAAF			
310th BG	379, 380, 381, 428	B-25	Berteaux, Alg
321st BG	445, 446, 447, 448	B-25	Ain M'lila, Alg
82nd FG	95, 96, 97	P-38G	Telergma, Alg
205 Group RAF			
231 Wing	37, 40, 70	Wellington III	Gardabia W, Libya
236 Wing	104, 462 RAAF	Wellington III, Halifax II	Gardabia, Libya
330 Wing	142, 150	Wellington III	Blida, Alg

Table 8.2 – Northwest African Coastal Air Force

Squadron	Type	Base	Role
323 Wing 242 Group RAF			
43	Spitfire VC	Jemappes, Alg	AD
73	Hurricane IIC	Nefatia W, Tun	AD
32	Hurricane IIC	Maison Blanche, Alg	AD
87	Hurricane IIC	Taher, Alg	AD
253	Hurricane IIC, Spitfire VC	Maison Blanche, Alg	AD
GC II/5	P-40F	Maison Blanche, Alg	F
325 Wing 242 Group RAF			
153	Beaufighter VIF	Maison Blanche, Alg	NF
255	Beaufighter VIF	Setif, Alg	NF
600	Beaufighter VIF	Setif, Alg	NF
14	Marauder I	Blida, Alg	GR
820 NAS	Albacore	HMS *Formidable*	AS
821 NAS	Albacore	Nefatia W, Tun	AS
826 NAS	Albacore	Bône, Alg	AS
328 Wing 242 Group RAF			
500	Hudson V	Blida, Alg	GR
608	Hudson VI	Blida, Alg	GR
283	Walrus	Hussein Dey, Alg	ASR
238 Wing 205 Group RAF			
47	Beaufort I	Misurata W, Lib	AS
252	Beaufighter IC, VIC	El Magrun, Lib	AS
603	Beaufighter IC, VIC	Berka II, Lib	AS
274	Hurricane IIC	Mellaha, Lib	AD
52nd Fighter Group USAAF			
2nd FS	Spitfire VC	Youks-les-Bains, Alg	AD
4th FS	Spitfire VC	Youks-les-Bains, Alg	AD
5th FS	Spitfire VC	Youks-les-Bains, Alg	AD
81st Fighter Group USAAF			
91st FS	P-39L	Thelepte, Tun	AD
92nd FS	P-39L	Thelepte, Tun	AD
93rd FS	P-39L	Thelepte, Tun	AD
350th Fighter Group USAAF			
345th FS	P-39L	La Senia, Alg	AD
346th FS	P-39L	La Senia, Alg	AD
347th FS	P-39L	Orleansville, Alg	AD
480th Anti-submarine Group USAAF			
1st ASS	B-24	Port Lyautey, Mor	ASW
2nd ASS	B-24	Port Lyautey, Mor	ASW

The Coastal Air Force was not, as might be imagined, an essentially maritime outfit. Rather, it was a miscellany of tri-partite elements (RAF, USAAF and Free French) embracing air defence, general reconnaissance, anti-submarine, anti-shipping and air-sea rescue units, spread along the coast from Morocco to Libya.

In the anti-shipping role, the RAF fielded two Hudson GR squadrons, one of Beauforts and two of Beaufighters, the latter based in Libya. They were supported further by three versatile FAA Albacore squadrons. Two USAAF B-24 squadrons based in Morocco provided an anti-submarine force. For air defence the RAF contributed six squadrons – five of Hurricanes and one of Spitfires – while the newly expanded Free French Air Force provided one squadron of P-40s. For its part the USAAF deployed two fighter groups of P-39s (one in Tunisia) and one of Spitfires. For pilots ditching along the coast there was a Walrus air-sea rescue squadron based at Algiers.

The most critical of the new organisations was the Northwest African Tactical Air Force, itself split into three functional organisations – the US XII Air Support Command, the newly re-named Desert Air Force and a tactical bomber force committed primarily to interdiction, but also intended to have flexibility. The Tactical Air Force was responsible for close support for the British Army (through the DAF) and American Army (through XII ASC), but the expectation was that each would cover for the other when circumstance demanded.

Table 8.3 – NATAF: XII Air Support Command

Squadron	Type	Base	Role
111th TRS	F-6 Mustang	Oujda, Mor	FR
154th TRS	F-4 Lightning, F-6 Mustang	Thelepte, Tun	FR
27th Fighter-Bomber Group USAAF			
522nd FS	A-36 Invader	Nouvion, Alg	FB
523rd FS	A-36 Invader	Nouvion, Alg	FB
524th FS	A 36 Invader	Nouvion, Alg	FB
33rd Fighter Group USAAF			
58th FS	P-40F	Berteaux, Alg	FGA
59th FS	P-40F	Berteaux, Alg	FGA
60th FS	P-40F	Berteaux, Alg	FGA
31st Fighter Group USAAF			
307th FS	Spitfire VC	Thelepte, Tun	F
308th FS	Spitfire VC	Thelepte, Tun	F
309th FS	Spitfire VC	Thelepte, Tun	F

The Americans also played a significant part in the softening up, including 47th Bombardment Group with its A-20 Havocs as seen here flying over Tunisia. Of note is the British markings on aircraft 52, which, given the lack of US serial on the fin, could denote an aircraft destined for RAF service.

Operating independently, and at this stage working across First Army, was 651 Sqn. While the HQ Flight was at Souk el Arba, its Austers allocated to Army formations were as follows: A Flt – 46th Division, IX Corps; B Flt – 78th Division, V Corps; and C Flt – 6th Arm Division, IX Corps. They were joined by 654 Sqn in March and although neither took part in the El Hamma battle, they certainly played an important part in the assault from the west.

XII Air Support Command comprised three fighter groups, each of three squadrons, plus a tactical recce squadron with the camera-equipped F-6 version of the P-51 Mustang. In eastern Algeria were the A-36 Invader (the dive-bomber variant of the Mustang) and P-40F squadrons, while a Spitfire group operated in Tunisia.

Above: Another tactical bomber used by the USAAF was the B-25 Mitchell. Aircraft of the 12th Bombardment Group including 112863/33 accompany Baltimores of 55 or 223 Sqn on a mission.

Middle right: The USAAF 57th Fighter Group equipped with the P-40 was a key part of the Desert Air Force. P-40F, aircraft 62 of the 65th Fighter Squadron, is seen undergoing maintenance at Causeway LG in Tunisia. *Mark O'Boyle*

Right: P-40K of the 64th Fighter Squadron at Causeway LG with a single 500lb bomb and six 40lb munitions under the wings. *Mark O'Boyle*

Table 8.4 – NATAF: Desert Air Force

Squadron	Type	Base	Role
6	Hurricane IID	Senem, Tun	FGA
680 A Flt	Hurricane II, Spit IV	Senem, Tun	PR
682	Spitfire IV, XI	Maison Blanche, Alg	PR
40 SAAF	Hurricane IIB, Spit VB	Bu Grara, Tun	PR
60 SAAF	Baltimore II, III, Mosquito IV	Senem, Tun	PR
1437 Flt	Baltimore	Marble Arch, Lib	SR
239 Wing RAF 211 Group			
112	Kittyhawk III	Medanine, Tun	FGA
250	Kittyhawk III	Medanine, Tun	FGA
260	Kittyhawk III	Medanine, Tun	FGA
3 RAAF	Kittyhawk III	Medanine, Tun	FGA
450 RAAF	Kittyhawk III	Medanine, Tun	FGA
7 Wing SAAF 211 Group			
2 SAAF	Kittyhawk I	Hazbub, Tun	FGA
4 SAAF	Kittyhawk I	Hazbub, Tun	FGA
5 SAAF	Kittyhawk III	Hazbub, Tun	FGA
244 Wing RAF 211 Group			
92	Spitfire VB, VC	Bu Grara, Tun	F
145	Spitfire VB, IX	Bu Grara, Tun	F
601	Spitfire VC	Bu Grara, Tun	F
1 SAAF	Spitfire VC	Bu Grara, Tun	F
417 RCAF	Spitfire VB, VC	Ben Gardane, Tun	F
322 Wing RAF 211 Group			
81	Spitfire IX	Souk el Khemis, Tun	F
154	Spitfire VC	Souk el Khemis, Tun	F
232	Spitfire VB	Souk el Khemis, Tun	F
242	Spitfire VB	Tingley, Alg	F
324 Wing RAF 211 Group			
72	Spitfire IX	Souk el Khemis, Tun	F
93	Spitfire VC	Souk el Khemis, Tun	F
111	Spitfire VC	Souk el Khemis, Tun	F
152	Spitfire VC	Souk el Khemis, Tun	F
243	Spitfire VB, VC	Souk el Khemis, Tun	F
57th Fighter Group USAAF 211 Group			
64th FS	P-40F	Causeway LG, Tun	FGA
65th FS	P-40F	Causeway LG, Tun	FGA
66th FS	P-40F	Causeway LG, Tun	FGA
79th Fighter Group USAAF 211 Group			
85th FS	P-40F	Causeway LG, Tun	FGA
86th FS	P-40F	Causeway LG, Tun	FGA
87th FS	P-40F	Causeway LG, Tun	FGA

The battle-hardened RAF Desert Air Force, under Air Vice-Marshal Harry Broadhurst, now comprised eight squadrons of Kittyhawk fighter-bombers in two wings, fourteen squadrons of Spitfires in three wings and the experienced USAAF P-40F units (six squadrons in two groups). The latter had supported the Eighth Army thrust into Libya and were to remain proudly within DAF, which was actually an air force within an air force (NATAF) within an air force (NAAF) within Mediterranean Air Command! All combat units were based in Tunisia. The reconnaissance wing also lay within DAF, as did the sole Hurricane tank-buster squadron available to the Army commander.

(The Hurricane IID was a variant of the Mk II with just two .303in machine guns but with the addition of a pair of Vickers 40mm cannon. The machine guns were harmonised at 500 yards and fired tracer for ranging the cannon, confined to 15 rounds of 2½lb armour-piercing shells each. In order to compensate for the added weight, armour was reduced which, together with its slower speed (322mph compared to 340mph in the Mk IIb)[1] and relative lack of manoeuvrability, made it vulnerable both to air attack and flak.

The Tactical Bomber Force comprised nine Dominion squadrons of twin-engined bombers (four Blenheim, three Baltimore, two Boston)

Table 8.5 – NATAF: Tactical Bomber Force

Squadron	Type	Base	Role
225	Hurricane IIB, Spit VB	Souk el Arba, Tun	Tac/R
241	Hurricane IIB	Souk el Khemis, Tun	Tac/R/FB
55	Baltimore IIIA	Ben Gardane, Tun	LB
223	Baltimore IIIA	Ben Gardane, Tun	LB
326 Wing RAF 242 Group			
13	Blenheim V	Oulmene, Tun	LB
18	Blenheim V	Oulmene, Tun	LB
614	Blenheim V	Oulmene, Tun	LB
114	Blenheim V	Canrobert, Alg	LB
3 Wing SAAF			
12 SAAF	Boston III	Zuara, Lib	LB
21 SAAF	Baltimore III, IV	Zuara, Lib	LB
24 SAAF	Boston III	Zuara, Lib	LB
47th Light Bombardment Group USAAF			
84th BS	A-20	Youks-les-Bains, Alg	LB
85th BS	A-20	Canrobert, Alg	LB
86th BS	A-20	Canrobert, Alg	LB
97th BS	A-20	Canrobert, Alg	LB
12th Medium Bombardment Group USAAF			
81st BS	B-25	Canrobert, Alg	MB
82nd BS	B-25	Canrobert, Alg	MB
83rd BS	B-25	Canrobert, Alg	MB
434th BS	B-25	Canrobert, Alg	MB

in three wings and two USAAF bombardment groups (four each A-20 and B-25 squadrons). In addition, there were two RAF Hurricane Tac/R squadrons based in Tunisia. The bombers were distributed throughout Algeria, Tunisia and Libya.

Mention has already been made of the improving situation in Malta. The island base was now positioned crucially to interfere with shipping which, by early 1943, was concentrating on supplying the Axis base in Tunisia from Sicily and mainland Italy. The four airfields on the small island hosted no fewer than fifteen squadrons.

Both the Germans and Italians based aircraft of all types on the Italian mainland, Sardinia and Sicily. Their local functions were to defend against attacks from Malta, to attack Malta and to attack shipping. In North Africa, there were transport, escort, medium bomber, long-range reconnaissance, and air-sea rescue units.

In the Tunisian bridgehead there were seven *Gruppen* of Bf 109 fighters and one of newly arrived and potent Fw 190s. In addition, there were two Ju 87 dive-bomber units (one of them equipped to aero-tow DFS 230 troop-carrying gliders), two fighter-bomber (Bf 109F and Me 210) *Gruppen* and photo and Tac/R flights. In all there were around 250 aircraft. The *Regia Aeronautica*, with twenty fighter squadriglia in Tunisia, fielded around only seventy serviceable aircraft, mainly Macchi C.202s, despite the many units.

Table 8.6 – AHQ Malta

Squadron	Type	Base	Role
126	Spitfire VB, VC, IX	Luqa	F
185	Spitfire VC	Hal Far	F
229	Spitfire VC	Qrendi	F
249	Spitfire VC	Qrendi	F
1435 Sqn	Spitfire V	Luqa	F
23	Mosquito II	Luqa	Intruder
272	Beaufighter IC, VIC	Ta Kali	FGA/AS
40 det	Wellington IC	Luqa	MB
39	Beaufort II	Luqa	AS
221	Wellington VIII	Luqa	AS
458 RAAF	Wellington VIII	Luqa	AS
683	Spitfire IV, XI	Luqa	PR
69	Baltimore II	Luqa	PR
828 NAS	Albacore	Hal Far	TB
830 NAS	Swordfish I	Hal Far	AS

Table 8.7 – Luftwaffe in North Africa

Fliegerkorps II, Luftflotte 2, Luftwaffe			
Unit	**Type**	**Base**	**Role**
I/JG 53	Bf 109G-2	La Marsa	F
II/JG 53	Bf 109G-2	La Marsa	F
I/JG 77	Bf 109G-2	Fatnassa	F
II/JG 77	Bf 109G-2	Fatnassa	F
III/JG 77	Bf 109G-2	Fatnassa	F
I/JG 51	Bf 109G-2	Gabes	F
II/JG 51	Bf 109G-2	Gabes	F
III/SKG 10	Fw 190A-4	El Aouina	FB
I/SchG 2	Bf 109F-4	Gabes	FB
III/ZG 1	Me 210A-1	Sfax	FB
II/StG 3	Ju 87D-1	Mezzouanna	DB
III/StG 3	Ju 87D-1, DFS 230	Mezzouanna	DB
1.(F)/121	Ju 88D-1	Sfax	PR
2.(H)/14	Fw 189, Bf 109	Gabes	Tac/R
4.(H)/12	Bf 109G-2		Tac/R

Table 8.8 – Regia Aeronautica in North Africa

Regia Aeronautica 5 Squadra Aerea				
Gr	**Sqr**	**Type**	**Base**	**Role**
Settore Nord (Northern Sector)				
6	79, 81	C.202	Sfax	F
151	367, 368	G.50bis	Sfax	F
	384	C.200	El Aouina	F
Settore Sud (Southern Sector)				
7	76, 86, 98	C.202	El Hamma	F
13	77, 78, 82	C.202	El Hamma	F
16	167, 168, 169	C.202	LG K41	F
18	83, 85, 95	C.202	El Hamma	F
23	70, 74, 75	C.202	El Hamma	F

The Overall Plan

To recap, by early March – and after heavy fighting – the Allied First Army held a line running roughly due south from the coast, about 30 miles west of Bizerte. The Eighth Army had reached the defensive Mareth Line and captured a number of important airfields, enabling the DAF to establish its fighter-bomber wings within 20 miles of the front line. The weather throughout the winter had been appalling, unpaved airfields deep in mud, so access to hard runways was essential.

Montgomery was now under pressure to attack the Line and break through to secure Gabes, then Sfax, in the expectation that the First Army would simultaneously strike from the west, clearing Axis forces from North Africa. This was to be achieved by the end of April, ready for the planning of an invasion of Sicily during the summer.

Curtiss P-40 Kittyhawk Mk III of 450 Sqn RAAF: given the empty bomb shackles, the aircraft is running down after a sortie. The Dominion forces played a considerable part in the war in North Africa and Italy, both on the ground and in the air.

These GA-coded aircraft at Medanine are either off on a training mission or have just returned from dropping munitions. *Crown copyright*

Preparations for the assault took some time, given that it was now the Eighth Army that had extended supply lines that stretched some 1,800 miles from Cairo and 200 miles from the major port of Tripoli, which had been captured only on 21 January. Montgomery was fortunate in having as the new commander of DAF Harry Broadhurst who, at thirty-eight, was the youngest AVM in the RAF. DAF was, in effect, the Eighth Army's Air Force, although Broadhurst was accountable to Sir Arthur Coningham, who commanded all tactical air forces. Coningham's plan was for the US XII ASC and the tactical bomber force to bomb airfields relentlessly, assisted by the heavy bombers of NASAF. Fighter-bombers would meanwhile attack Axis ground forces and specific targets identified by the PR resources of DAF. It was intended that this approach would take pressure off the DAF, which would then be free to give maximum close support to the attacking troops.

Montgomery's plan was for a frontal assault on the Mareth Line in Operation *Pugilist*, set for 20 March. In the meantime, on 6 March, three German *Panzer* divisions had attacked his flank towards Medenine. Forewarned through air reconnaissance and *Ultra* decrypts, the British commander deployed hundreds of anti-tank guns in a trap for the *Panzers*. Though repulsed, they regrouped for a second attack, this time supported by newly deployed Me 210 and Fw 190 fighter-bombers. Nonetheless, the Germans were still heavily defeated, losing 25% of their 200 tanks, but the overcautious Montgomery was not tempted to exploit the local defeat and turn it into a rout. Rather, he preferred to stick to his plan.

Flt Lt D. E. Llewellyn of 601 Sqn was flying Spitfires at the rate of a sortie a day at this time.[2] On 6 March he records: 'Recce of Gabes and el Hamma: My No 2 tried flying under water – he failed.' This apparently callous observation referred to Flt Sgt J. E. Robinson,

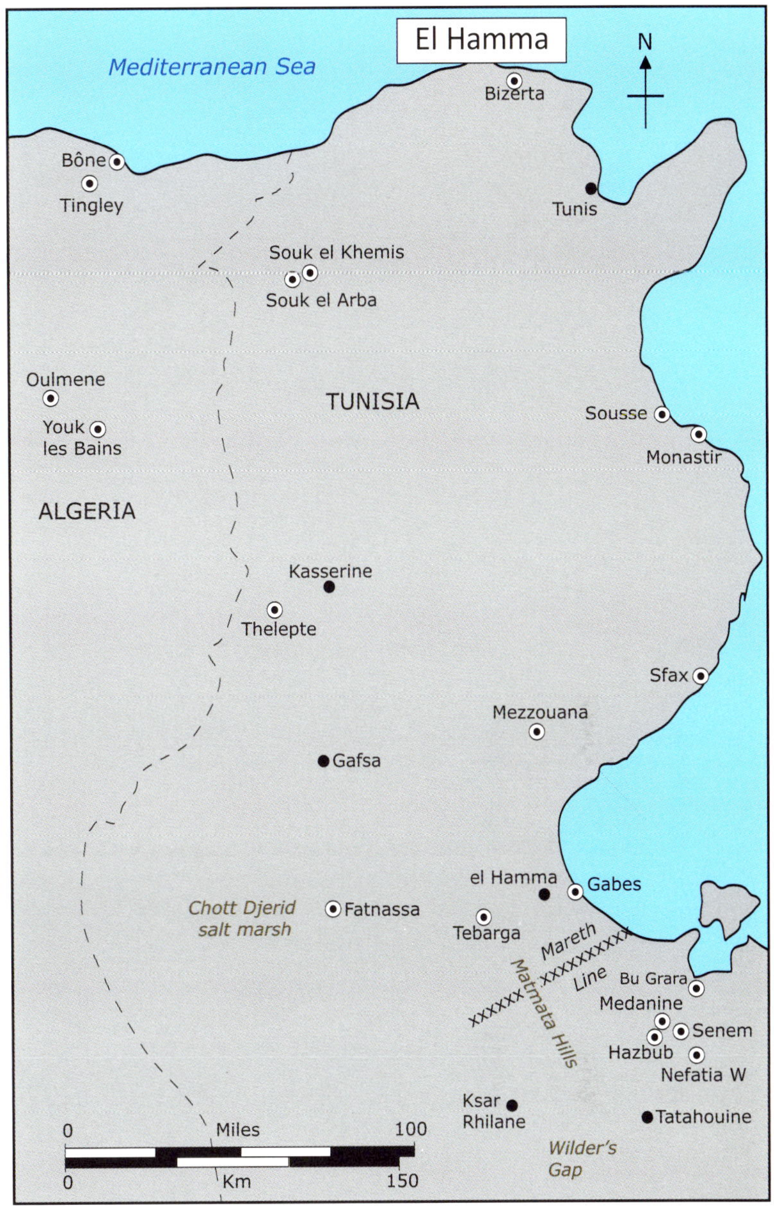

Kittyhawk Mk IV FX793 of 250 Sqn.
Author's collection

El Hamma March 1943

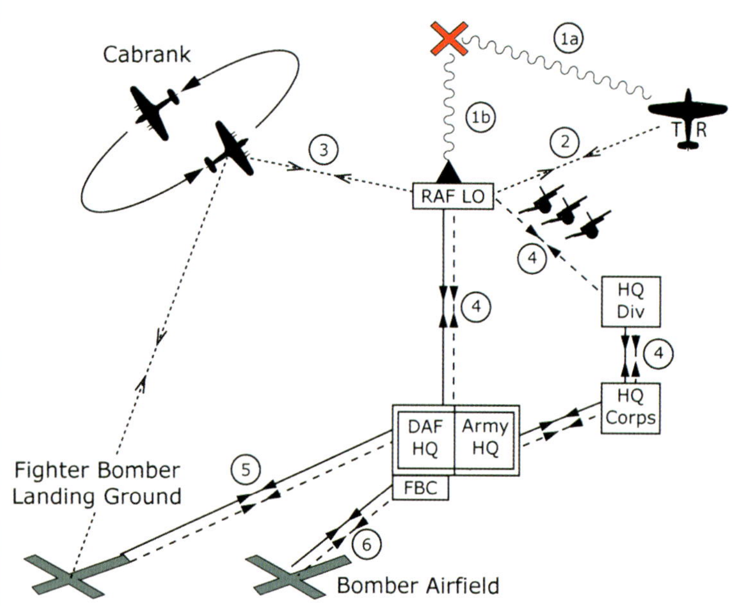

1) Tac/R aircraft and/or Forward OP identifies target
2) If within range artillery fires
3) If appropriate RAF Liaison Officer (RAFLO) calls in fighter-bombers in cabrank
4) Division, Corps and Army HQ monitor: Corps updates GHQ
5) Further fighter-bombers prepared to join cabrank
6) If necessary light bomber squadrons alerted and briefed by Forward Bomber Control (FBC)

flying Spitfire V ER317, who was shot down over the sea by a Bf 109 of JG 77. On the 10th Llewellyn records: 'Top cover to Tankbusters[A]: Split up in cloud, attacked by ME109E (Steele and Baxter destroyed it). Wizard show, bags of ground flames.'

The frontal assault was to be mounted by XXX Corps across Wadi Zigzaou with the 50th Division nearest the coast, the 51st Division to its left and the 4th Indian Division to the rear in reserve. X Corps was held behind, to come forward and exploit the hole punched in the Mareth Line by XXX Corps. This frontal attack was to be supplemented by a diversionary flanking movement through the Matmata Hills and north to the Tebaga Gap by the New Zealand Corps.

Arrayed behind the Line was a formidable Axis force. Four Italian infantry divisions spread across its 25-mile length, with two German divisions in support. Standing back were three *Panzer* divisions, but with only around 140 tanks between them. A serious problem with which Axis units lived was split command between the distant Italian supremo and the Germans on the spot.

With around 150 tanks, the New Zealanders had made good progress through Wilder's Gap, to the south of the Matmata Hills and had then turned north towards Tebaga. By the evening of 20 March they were about 20 miles south of the Gap, having mistakenly been bombed en route by US B-25s supporting a First Army assault on Gafsa, some 80 miles to the north-west.

Despite the New Zealand Corps, including the 8th Armoured Brigade, having moved up in apparent secrecy, Montgomery ordered that they were to throw caution to the wind and press on with great haste: this was in the belief that their movements had been compromised. In anticipation, the German commander began to withdraw 164th Light Division and 21st *Panzer* Division, ready for transfer to the Gap from the east to confront the New Zealanders. Whether Montgomery had received *Ultra* data confirming that the Germans were aware of movements towards the Gap, or the change was a cynical ploy to encourage the Germans to reduce the defensive force on the Line, is not clear from the official history, written prior to the existence of *Ultra* being made public. Certainly the Corps commander, General Sir Bernard Freyberg, was concerned that his troops would be sacrificed against superior German forces to enable Montgomery to break through the Line.

[A] Hurricane IID

Aircraft of 250 Sqn, coded LD, loaded with 250lb bombs ready for another mission against Axis positions. *Author's collection*

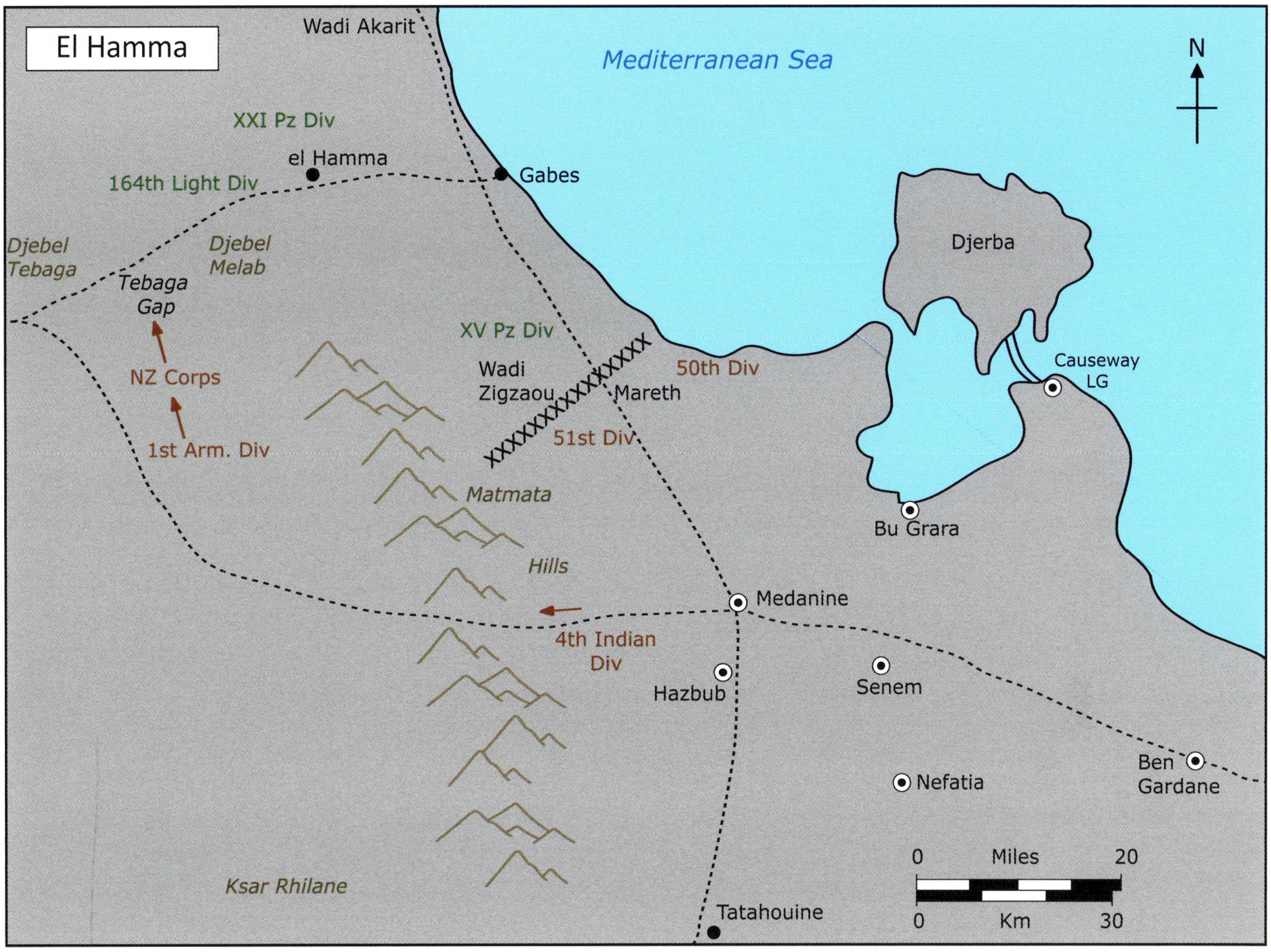

The RAF commitment to provision of cab-ranks for the first time was given to the Kittyhawk squadrons with Spitfire and Hurricane cover. 112 Sqn with its distinctive sharks-teeth nose was one of several involved. *Author's collection*

Failure and a Change of Plan

The attack on the Mareth Line by the 50th Division started at 2030hrs on the 20th and by the following morning a small bridgehead had been established. Little progress was made on the 21st and the following day, in appalling weather, 15 *Panzer* Division counter-attacked in strength. DAF fighters were unable to fly so, bereft of air support, the British withdrew, having lost almost forty tanks.

On 21 March Axis airfields were attacked at Mezzouana (by A-20s), Fatnassa, Gabes and Tebaga (by B-17s), escorts becoming involved in dogfights with defending Bf 109s. On the 22nd, despite heavy rain in Tunisia, there were further raids on Mezzouana, but for the most part Allied air attacks were concentrated on Palermo, Sicily, where ten vessels were destroyed in the harbour.

Montgomery now decided that his main attack would switch to the Tebaga Gap and El Hamma. The 4th Indian Division was sent from Medenine to force a shortened supply route through to the Tebaga road and the 1st Armoured Division was moved up hurriedly behind the New Zealanders, now held up at the Tebaga Gap. Poor Army HQ staff planning led to a considerable bottleneck at Medenine as the Indians converged with the 1st Armoured Division. By now the two German divisions were in place behind Italian units and for four days there was what was described in the official history[3] as 'sparring'; the reality was that the Allied units were effectively halted. Axis troops used the time to good effect by creating heavily defended posts along either side of the Gap, between Djebel Tebaga and Djebel Mela.

Up to this time the Allied air forces had been undertaking concerted and coordinated bombing against airfields, supply lines, MT and troop concentrations to keep Axis forces under pressure and to support the Army by securing air superiority. By the 24th the 1st Armoured Division was in place, together with X Corps HQ, encouraging Montgomery to decide on a transfer of leadership for the assault on the Gap and that on El Hamma. Having sensed that Freyberg was too cautious, he reassigned the responsibility to X Corps' Horrocks. In the event the generals worked unhappily, but effectively, together.

The Desert Air Force was now to play a crucial role, which makes it appropriate to quote a 112 Sqn Kittyhawk pilot describing the process of dive-bombing:[4]

> '...the formation to be flown was twelve 'Kittys' in two boxes of six with the second box flying a few hundred feet above, behind and slightly to one side of the first six, preferably between them and the sun. Dive bombing was from about 6,000–8,000 ft down to 1,000 ft. The target was approached until it disappeared under the centre of the port wing, count to three and then go into a dive down to the left until the target was in front of the aircraft nose. At about 2,000 ft pull up, count one, two and then release the bomb or bombs. Then we were to reform at about 5,000 ft in the same formation back to base. The dive was at about sixty degrees but felt like ninety!
>
> Strafing was, of course, from low level. We followed each other down onto the target or targets. Sometimes dive-bombing would be followed immediately by strafing at ground level before reforming.'

As the final preparations were made for the attack towards El Hamma, there was a remarkable development in the way in which the RAF would support the Army. RAF procedures had denied the use of standing patrols over front-line troops, deeming them wasteful and of limited value given the uncertainty of the position of the bomb line. However, Broadhurst now controversially agreed to send to the front several pilots to work with Army forward observation posts and to direct aircraft by radio on to targets holding up the advance. The New Zealanders had limited artillery and ammunition, so flying artillery was essential if success was to be achieved.

Montgomery decided formally on the 24th to issue his order for Operation *Supercharge II*, confirming that the Tunisian offensive would be undertaken by the NZ Corps and 1st Armoured Division. The plan was fully integrated with the air forces. The ground forces would secure several key high points and bring up infantry and artillery ready

7 Sqn SAAF was one of two flying the Hurricane IIB fitted with two 37mm anti-tank guns. HV663/U and HW313/S. *SAAF*

The first squadron to use the Hurricane IID with tank-busting gun was 6 Sqn. Due to its early success against tanks the unit subsequently informally applied a flying can-opener badge to its aircraft. BP188/JV-Z. *Author's collection*

for a drive through the Tebaga Gap, with H-Hour set for 1600hrs on D-Day, 26 March. The NASAF and elements of NACAF and NATAF would bomb airfields, but especially Axis forces immediately on the front line at Tebaga and around El Hamma. In this way it was expected that total air superiority would be achieved, that damage would be done to MT and telephone lines and, critically, that troops would be kept awake for forty-eight hours from being under constant night and day attack. This heavy bombing was to continue until 1530hrs on the 26th.

The Mk IIc Hurricane enjoyed superior performance to the Mk IId and its four 20mm cannon made it a formidable strafing aircraft. Auxiliary fuel tanks gave it a useful loiter time. *Author's collection*

Hurricane IID BP188/JV-Z 6 Sqn. *Luca G. Canossa*

At precisely 1530hrs there would be fifteen minutes of tactical bombing immediately ahead of the front line, followed by two and a quarter hours of non-stop fighter-bomber attacks on prepared positions. Thirty Kittyhawks (two and a half squadrons) would be overhead every fifteen minutes, dive-bombing and strafing. In addition, 6 Sqn tank-busters would be on hand. An elaborate plan involving coloured smoke had been formulated to ensure that the aircraft were always aware of the exact location of the bomb line.

The assault was to be driven by 2nd New Zealand Division and 8th Armoured Brigade to an initial objective 2,000 yards forward, moving at 100 yards a minute. Then at 1800hrs, after the fighter-bombers had withdrawn, the heavy armour of 1st Armoured Division would charge through towards a staging area, ready for a major thrust as the moon came up.

The military components of Operation *Supercharge II* were:

New Zealand Corps		
2nd NZ Division		
	Divisional Cavalry (left flank)	
	28th (Maori) Bn (right flank)	
	5th Brigade	
		21st Bn (right Point 184)
		22nd Bn (reserve)
		23rd Bn (centre right)
	6th Brigade	
		24th Bn (centre left)
		25th Bn (reserve)
		26th Bn (reserve)
	Artillery (three field regts, one AT regt, one light AA regt)	
	Engineers, MT, signals etc.	
8th Armoured Brigade		
	3rd Royal Tank Regt (covering 24th Bn left)	
	Staffordshire Yeomanry (covering 23rd Bn centre)	
	Nottinghamshire Yeomanry (covering 28th Bn right)	
	B, C and A coys of 1st Bn Buffs attached respectively	
Flying Free French column		
	Reconnaissance group	
	Spahi cavalry group	
X Corps		
1st Armoured Division		
	12th Royal Lancers	
	2nd Armoured Brigade	
		10th Royal Hussars
		2nd Dragoon Guards
		9th Queen's Royal Lancers
		Queen's Own Yorkshire Dragoons
	7th Motorised Brigade	
		7th Bn Rifle Brigade
		2nd Bn King's Royal Rifle Corps
		2nd Bn Rifle Brigade (mine clearance task force)
	Artillery (three field regts, one AT regt, one light AA regt)	
	Engineers, MT, signals etc.	

The Battle

The air battle for El Hamma had started almost a week earlier, on 20 March, during when there were raids by groups of eighteen Bostons or Baltimores throughout the day on airfields in the area, including that at Tebaga. Bombers from the Tactical Bomber Force were escorted by thirty fighters,

The Spitfires were used as cover for the ground attack and medium bomber units, including the Mk Vbs of 417 Sqn RCAF typified by BR4**/AN-V. *Crown copyright*

Kittyhawks mostly providing medium level cover and Spitfires top cover. In the afternoon Spitfires engaged C.202s of 3° Stormo escorting a Ju 88 reconnoitring NZ movements in the Ksar Rhilane area. The following day Kittyhawks and 6 Sqn Hurricane IId tank-busters were called in to break up a group of forty tanks. Again, throughout the day there were ten escorted missions, each by eighteen medium bombers, against transport especially.

The attacks continued on the 22nd, Kittyhawks of 112 Sqn bombing vehicles at El Hamma. At 1325hrs 6 Sqn Hurricanes were again called in to deal with tanks south of the town, nine of which were destroyed. However, as an indication that full air superiority was not yet achieved, they were set upon by Bf 109Gs of II/JG 77 and three were shot down with a fourth lost to flak on a later mission. Fortunately, there were no pilot fatalities.

The 23rd was an auspicious day as the first twelve Spitfire Mk IXs for DAF were collected from Algiers, by 92 and 145 Sqns which used them for top cover. The Kittyhawks continued their ground attack missions around El Hamma. Significantly, German losses were eight Bf 109s against an Allied deficit of one Baltimore, a Kittyhawk and a USAAF Spitfire of 52nd FG.

The air forces were required to apply even more pressure, resulting in constant activity until the breakthrough. Also on the 23rd B-17s of 97th Bomb Group attacked Bizerta, escorted by P-38s of 1st FG, a later B-17 attack on the same target being escorted by RAF Spitfires. Hurricanes of 241 and 253 sqns hit targets in the El Hamma area. Raids on the 24th included numerous USAAF-escorted B-25 attacks on airfields, including Tebaga North. Both on the 23rd and 25th P-39s of the 81st FG started the day's air activity by strafing trucks.

Hurricanes of the tactical bomber force and DAF Kittyhawks maintained constant pressure on Axis troops and strongpoints, Spitfires of 322 Wing providing cover. In two days fourteen Bf 109s and a Fw 190 were brought down at a cost of two USAAF P-40 Warhawks and a Spitfire. On the night of 25 March, 205 Group bombers flew 133 sorties against Axis forces in the Tebaga/el Hamma area and A-20s, B-25s and B-17s bombed throughout the 26th without loss.

By March 1943 there were thirteen Spitfire squadrons operating the Mk V in addition to the two Tac/R units. ER557/EF-D *Mustapha* of 232 Sqn is at Tingley, Algeria, about to escort USAAF light bombers on a mission. One of those of the 12th Bombardment Group is seen taking off.

Nearer the front, at 1445hrs, eleven Hurricanes of 6 Sqn set off to make a final search for Axis tanks, protected by Kittyhawks of 250 Sqn and 3 Sqn RAAF. No tanks were found, but two Hurricanes and three Kittyhawks were brought down by flak. As an indication of the intensity of the close support sorties, 6 Sqn lost seventeen Hurricane tank-busters in five days. Well protected from above, most succumbed to flak. However, the Hurricane was nothing if not robust; just one pilot was killed and two wounded. This mission, just before the ground offensive, was the final operation for the tank-busters, whose aircraft and crews were now rested.

There were three squadrons flying the more potent Mk IX Spitfire in Spring 1943 including C Flight of 145 Sqn operating as the Polish Fighting Team. EN315/ZX-6 was usually flown by Sqn Ldr Stanislaw Skalski. *Crown copyright*

Spitfire Vb JK112/WU-A 225 Sqn. *Luca G. Canossa*

The North American A-36 Invader (not to be confused with the later A-26 Invader) was the dive-bomber version of the P-51 Mustang. This aircraft of the 27th Fighter-Bomber Group is at Nouvion, Algeria, and is here loaded with two 500lb bombs. *Author's collection*

The P-39 was unusual in having the engine mounted in the fuselage behind the cockpit. Its performance was poor and despite heavy armament was unloved by pilots. These examples are believed to be from the 350th Fighter Group at La Senia, Algeria. Of interest is the French Amiot 143M bomber of GB I/38 lurking in the background. *Tinus le Roux*

Several pilots in armoured cars worked with Army forward observation posts using SCR-522 radios to direct fighter-bombers as required. An artillery creeping barrage marked the bomb line; along the start line large letters A, E and H marked where fighter-bombers were to orbit prior to attacking their targets. Squadrons were given primary and secondary targets but could, in addition, be directed to newly determined objectives that might be holding up the advance. The start line was also marked clearly by blue and red smoke, yellow being used from time to time to indicate the shifting bomb line.

In addition to tactical fighters, bombers were directed through the Forward Bomber Control (FBC) within Advance Air HQ. The FBC relied on landline communications to receive up-to-date target briefings based on Army requests and reconnaissance. From 17–26 March 205 Group alone flew nearly 500 tactical role sorties.[5]

As tanks and infantry of the NZ Corps readied for battle, sharp at 1530hrs, exactly as planned, three formations of light bombers from 12, 24 (both Boston) and 21 (Baltimore) Sqns SAAF, 55 Sqn RAF (Baltimore) and 83rd and 434th USAAF (B-25) swept in at low level and from a lowering sun on Axis defensive positions. As the infantry moved forward at 1600hrs, two plus hours of fighter-bomber raids began with thirty Kittyhawks, Warhawks or Spitfires attacking every fifteen minutes, overseen by Spitfire top cover. In the course of two and a half hours the Allies lost two Hurricanes, two Spitfires (plus two damaged), six Kittyhawks (fourteen damaged) and five American P-40Fs (nine damaged).[6] To create this awesome maelstrom the NATAF flew 412 sorties in this short period.[7]

Bert Horden, newly arrived at 112 Sqn from training in Egypt, recounted how his Kittyhawk was armed with two 250lb bombs under the fuselage with 12in rods on the weapons' nose cones for airburst, plus six 40lb anti-personnel bombs under the wing, in addition to the customary six .50in machine guns. He wrote:[8]

> '…it was not many minutes to our target area. On the way we could see other Kittyhawk squadrons moving towards the same area. It was all very well having a clear bomb-line on a map in the IO's[8] truck, but there was little on the ground to indicate where our lot ended and the Jerries began. This time, however, along the main road up to the valley to el Hamma we could see tanks and trucks

[8] Intelligence officer

The Martin B-26 Marauder served with just two RAF sqns, 14 and 39, the latter only from 1944, in addition to five SAAF squadrons. 14 Sqn was initially charged with maritime reconnaissance and shipping interdiction, for a short time using torpedoes as seen. *Author's collection*

moving up, while beyond, in enemy held territory, there was little to see.

Geoff Garton [CO] soon identified some German 88 mm gun emplacements for us to bomb. There was no ack-ack aimed at us at this stage as no doubt the German gunners were pointing their guns up the road at the New Zealanders' tanks instead of us. The CO went down. Then it was my turn. I clearly saw the emplacements disappear under my port wing before going down to the left. The dive felt like 90 degrees but was only about 60. I saw the CO's bombs burst on target just as I released mine. Others that followed also found the target so it was good accurate bombing.

Now we were to strafe any enemy targets that we could find. I saw some other guns at the side of the road and set about strafing. The six .5 inch guns all firing could be felt as a braking sensation on the flight of the Kitty and the destructive power at the receiving end was enormous. Most were explosive bullets mixed with a few tracers. As I went in to strafe, I noticed some objects shooting past the cockpit hood. At first I thought we were being attacked by enemy fighters but they were large objects. Then I realized they were artillery shells.

I continued strafing for a short time with tracers going into the enemy positions. Some small arms fire came up at me. Then I pulled up to orientate myself … I spotted some German trucks scurrying at high speed down the road – a rare sight – so set about them. I caught the rear truck, which burst into flames. I saw my bullets spraying the other two which crashed off the road into the scrub but didn't flame. I couldn't see any more targets…so pulled up and set off towards base.'

The Beaufighters of 252 and 272 Sqns also made a major contribution to denying Axis forces material and reserves and thus the means to fight effectively. 252 Sqn aircraft included Mk Ic T4877/BT-R. *Author's collection*

Protecting the Algerian bases was the Northwest African Coastal Air Force whose assets included night fighters. The nose aerial array gives away the role of Beaufighter Mk VIf of 255 Sqn, here at Souk el Arba in December 1942. *Author's collection*

By daybreak on Saturday 27 March the 1st Armoured Division and the New Zealanders had broken through the Gap, a feat that would have been impossible without the constant and concentrated firepower of the air forces. During the day DAF fighters continued offensive patrols to prevent reinforcements from reaching the front. El Hamma was secured later and within two days the Allied armies were confronting the withdrawn Axis forces on their new defensive line at Wadi Akarit. After further fighting the war in Africa came to an end on 13 May with the final surrender of the remaining Axis troops.

Blenheim V EH333/L 13 Sqn. *Luca G. Canossa*

Every little helps! The Fieseler Fi 156 *Storch* was captured in relatively large numbers in North Africa and put to good use by a number of Allied flying units.
Author's collection

Local Axis low-level air defence in the shape of the quadruple 20mm Flakvierling 38 on an 8-ton Zgkw Sd Kfz 7 truck.

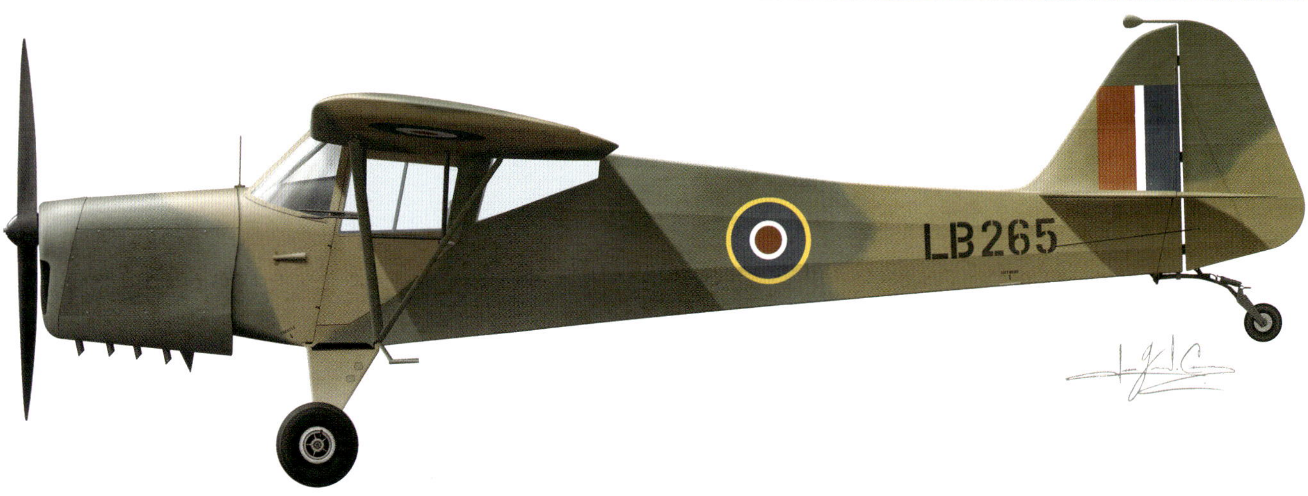

Auster I LB265
651 Sqn.
Luca G. Canossa

Supplies were brought in to Tunisia from Italy by sea and air. The six-engined Me 323 *Gigant* was one transport used to bring fuel and oil to the retreating German forces. On 22 April 1943 21 of 27 crossing from Sicily were shot down.

Another means of bringing in supplies from Sicily was the Gotha Go 242 glider, in the Mediterranean usually towed by a Ju 87D. In cargo form it could carry around 8,000lbs. *Author's collection*

The Ju 52/3m transport was also used routinely for bringing across much-needed supplies, but as with the Me 323 and shipping, losses were high. Having been attacked this aircraft is about to crash into the sea. *Author's collection*

The important changes in close support to the Army were recorded by a noted military historian thus:[9]

> 'For the first time the Royal Air Force had been persuaded to attack the enemy in the battle area from ground level with their cannons, instead of merely bombing an area from a higher level. In persuading Air Vice-Marshal Broadhurst to carry out this policy, de Guingand [Montgomery's CoS] did more than ensure a hitherto unheard of intimacy of air attack in support of British ground troops – he opened the way to tactical participation by aircraft such as the Royal Air Force had never countenanced before in any large-scale, set-piece battle, thus breaking the first link in the doctrine of separate air power which had partially chained the Royal Air Force for over two decades. The RAF pilots who drove up to the front line to direct fighter/bombers by radio from the

American airmen examine abandoned FW 190A-4 KM+EY of SKG 10 at El Aouiana, May 1943. The Butcher Bird was master of the skies until the Spitfire Mk IX was deployed.

The Bf 109G was the ultimate version of the iconic fighter to be deployed by the *Luftwaffe* in North Africa. This 109G-2/Trop appears to be an aircraft of JG 51. *Alan Walton*

The Italian contribution to the Axis air forces included the highly effective Macchi-Castoldi M.C.202 *Folgore*.

ground, were symbols of real joint-service co-operation, and the criticism later levelled at Broadhurst from above demonstrated how radical were his tactics – on the hard battlefield of experience, he overturned the dictates of the air power purists.'

The criticism of Broadhurst from the RAF hierarchy needs to be understood in context. As noted in an earlier chapter, through experience the Desert Air Force was evolving tactics and what would much later be termed doctrine, and in this it was ahead of the game. Even so, the ME (Army and RAF) Directive on Direct Air Support Issued by GHQ MEF and HQ RAF ME,[10] had the following to say:

'OFFENSIVE SUPPORT

12. It is in this sphere that the RAF are able mostly to assist ground operations, but it must be recognised that we do not possess suitable aircraft for dive bombing.

13. FIGHTER ATTACK. In this type of attack, something akin to dive attack on the German pattern is possible. Suitable targets and their relative positions on the battlefield are similar, with minor exceptions, to those for bombers considered below. The exceptions are that attack on AFVs by fighters with cannon are sometimes 'worth while', and fighters can attack by ground straffing methods targets nearer to our leading ground elements. It is difficult to assess the relative value of this type of attack as compared with bomber attack, but of the two, fighter attack probably has the greater moral effect. But the fighter is the main weapon in the battle for air superiority, and to employ fighters against ground targets in a direct support role must inevitably be drawing them off from the main issue. Thus, though direct support by fighter aircraft is probably more effective than that by bomber aircraft, this type of direct support, however desirable it may be, cannot normally be expected until a considerable degree of air superiority has already been attained.

16 THE CHARACTERISTICS OF DIRECT AIR SUPPORT BOMBING must be fully appreciated if maximum use is to be made of this type of support.

a) It is possible with Direct Air Support aircraft to develop suddenly a very considerable volume of fire to assist formations who have outdistanced their artillery.

b) As there will normally be targets in excess of the capacity of the available aircraft, the latter should not be used when other support, such as artillery and mortars, are sufficient for the purpose.

c) Unlike artillery, it will generally be impossible for Direct Air Support aircraft to sustain their attack for any length of time; neither does the attack tend to become more accurate as it proceeds.'

So, not only did Broadhurst apply his fighter-bombers over the troops and in very close direct support, contrary to Coningham's priorities of securing air superiority and then interdicting lines of supply and reinforcement, he also ignored a number of the detailed requirements of the Directive. Had he not, the ground forces would probably have been eliminated in the Tebaga Gap and the subsequent conquest of Tunisia and invasion of Sicily would have been delayed.

[1] Robertson, *Hawker Hurricane*, p67
[2] Flt Lt D E Llewellyn logbook. RAF Museum MF10070/7
[3] Playfair, *History of the Second World War: The Mediterranean and Middle East Vol IV*, p344
[4] Horden, *Shark squadron Pilot*, p51
[5] Playfair, *History of the Second World War: The Mediterranean and Middle East Vol IV*, p355
[6] Shores et al, *History of the Mediterranean Air War Vol 2*, p554
[7] Richards, *Royal Air Force 1939-1945 Vol II*, p266
[8] Horden, *Shark squadron Pilot*, p65
[9] Macksey, *Breaking the Mareth Line* , Purnell's History of the Second World War, p1341
[10] TNA AIR23/6465

Appendix 1
Army and Air Force Structures

Military Structures

This appendix describes the basic structure of the British Army in some detail and then goes on to outline those of the key air forces involved in the actions that are chronicled.

Trying to describe the evolution of close air support for the British Army is partial without also describing the basics of how armies work. (If the reader is familiar with the niceties of Army organisation and formations, they may comfortably skip this appendix.) The size of units, their weapons at each level and their command structures would all dictate how close air support might operate, whether for a handful of soldiers with rifles to a major armoured offensive, or from static positions under attack to fast mobile thrusts. The outline notional structure of the Royal Air Force is also included for completeness. The notes that follow relate to the second half of the Second World War.

The Military at the Highest Level

During the war the British Government, one of national unity and thus representative of the major political parties, determined overall strategy. It did this through the War Cabinet that oversaw five departments of state, three of which controlled the three services.

In order of seniority these were the Admiralty (Royal Navy), the War Office (Army), the Air Ministry (Royal Air Force) and the ministries of Supply and Aircraft Production. Each of these departments was headed by a politician (Secretary of State) with a senior military member. In the Admiralty this was the First Sea Lord in the person of Admiral of the Fleet Sir Dudley Pound to 15 October 1943, then Admiral of the Fleet Viscount Cunningham.

At the head of the Army was the Chief of the Imperial General Staff, from May 1940 to 25 December 1945, General, later Field Marshal, Sir Alan Brooke. Chief of the Air Staff to 31 December 1945 was Air Chief Marshal Sir Charles (later Lord) Portal. The Prime Minister, Winston Churchill, involved himself in the management of the war in some detail. He created the War Cabinet and took the role of Minister of Defence, dealing directly with the three service heads who then became the Chief of Staff's Committee.

The political heads of the services, the Secretaries of State, were A. V. Alexander (Admiralty), Sir P. J. Grigg (War) and Sir Archibald Sinclair Bt (Air). Each was supported by the respective departmental senior civil servant, the Permanent Under-Secretary of State.

At the highest level military strategy was determined through an iterative process whereby politicians attempted to set strategic goals, while the service heads advised on achievability based on available resources. Once strategies had been determined, it was for the service chiefs to make them work and to report back on setbacks and constraints. As noted earlier, accountable to the War Cabinet were the ministries of Aircraft Production and Supply. These ensured that the needs of the military, at least in terms of arms and *materiel*, were understood and commissioned. Or, of course, where supply could not conceivably meet demand, strategy, or certainly the tactics for delivery, was modified. The other key element in respect of opportunities or constraints on military action was manpower, managed throughout the war by the Ministry of Labour and National Service.

A key strategic objective was to deny the enemy the prospect of waging war through aerial bombardment of the means of production, delivery and operation. This was coupled with defence of the homeland against German assault and the maintenance of Egypt as the critical pivot in the Middle East. In the first two years of the war demands for properly armed forces elsewhere were forfeited against the needs for bombers, defence fighters and, for the Middle East, tanks and guns.

Overall Army Structure[1]

The demands of overall military strategy were effected through a flexible organisational structure. A notional or theoretical model would be adapted to suit the specific needs of the theatre, the assessed strength and capability of the enemy, available weaponry and so on.

At the forefront was the largest element, the Army, commanded by a General. Armies were numbered and might contain elements of several national subordinate units. In North Africa the British army involved was the Eighth, whereas Operation *Torch,* in late 1942, involved the First Army, comprising British, US and French elements. An Army could comprise up to one million men. The composition of the relevant armies and subordinate commands are detailed in the relevant chapters.

On occasions, when two armies were fighting in relatively close proximity, an Army Group could be created to co-ordinate command. In North Africa, Eighteenth Army Group was formed between 20 February and 15 May 1943. Commanded by General Sir Harold Alexander, its purpose was solely to direct the two armies in the fighting in Tunisia. For the invasion of Sicily,

Fifteenth Army Group was formed, embracing the British Eighth Army and the American Seventh, again under Alexander. When Italy was invaded, composition of the Fifteenth Army Group altered to that of the British Eighth Army and American Fifth Army. Subsequently it was redesignated Allied Forces in Italy in January 1944, then Allied Armies in Italy in March, reverting to Fifteenth Army Group when American General Mark Clark took over from Alexander in December 1944

Within the Army was the Corps, designated by nation and Roman numerals, as in *British V Corps*, one of four in the Eighth Army in 1944. Typically, there were three Corps within an Army and command of each was in the hands of a Lieutenant General. The Corps would comprise a number of divisions, perhaps between two and six. It would also control and deploy independently lower level units, typically specialised brigades.

Those Corps fighting in North Africa and Italy were V, IX, X, XIII, XXX (all British), I Canadian, II Polish and the unnumbered New Zealand Corps. The British Corps, although designated as such, included large numbers of Dominion troops. The Corps HQ or staff departments, each under a colonel, comprised the General (G) staff accountable for operations and intelligence; Adjutant General (A) staff, accountable for all personnel issues; and Quartermaster General (Q) staff, accountable for supplies, accommodation and movement. These roles were replicated at divisional and brigade level by officers of lower rank.

The Division was the lowest level of army formation that routinely was capable of independent operations and, typically in the wartime British Army, comprised around 18,000 men (in 1944). However, each division could be supported by up to 25,000 men operating within units directed or deployed from Corps or even Army level as the need arose. The Division was commanded by a Major General and comprised several brigades.

As an example of a division, the following is the construct of the 56th (London) Division at June 1944 when part of XIII Corps in Italy and commanded by Major General Gerald Templer.

56th (London) Infantry Division
- 167th (London) Infantry Brigade
  - 8th Bn Royal Fusiliers
  - 9th Bn Royal Fusiliers
  - 7th Bn Oxfordshire and Buckinghamshire Light Infantry
  - 167th Infantry Brigade Anti-tank Coy
- 168th (London) Infantry Brigade
  - 1st Bn London Scottish
  - 1st Bn London Irish Rifles
  - 1st Bn Welch Regiment
  - 2nd (London) Infantry Brigade Anti-tank Coy
- 169th (London) Infantry Brigade
  - 2/5th Bn Queen's Royal Regiment
  - 2/6th Bn Queen's Royal Regiment
  - 2/7th Bn Queen's Royal Regiment
- 169th Infantry Brigade Anti-tank Regiment

Divisional troops
- Machine gun
  - 6th Bn Cheshire Regiment
- Artillery
  - 64th Field Regiment, Royal Artillery
  - 65th Field Regiment, Royal Artillery
  - 113th Field Regiment, Royal Artillery
  - 67th Anti-tank Regiment, Royal Artillery (16x6pdrs, 32x17pdrs)
  - 100th Light Anti-aircraft Regiment, Royal Artillery (54x40mm Bofors)
- Engineers
  - 220th Field Company, Royal Engineers
  - 221st Field Company, Royal Engineers
  - 501st Field Company, Royal Engineers
  - 563rd Field Park Company, Royal Engineers
- Signals
  - 1st London Divisional Signals Regiment, Royal Corps of Signals

In addition, there would be specialists from across most of the service branches. Thus, in this instance, there were three brigades, each including three infantry battalions. Divisions were either infantry, as in the case of the 56th detailed above, or armoured. The latter comprised at least one armoured brigade equipped with light and heavy tanks, one or two infantry brigades, perhaps motorised or mechanised, and relevant divisional support.

Brigades came below divisions, were commanded by a brigadier and comprised a HQ, three battalions, detached divisional assets and, in an armoured brigade group, a tank regiment of around twenty tanks. The structure of the battalion will be described in the next section: divisional assets included a reconnaissance squadron, field, anti-tank and anti-aircraft artillery, machine-gun company, engineers, transport company, field ambulance and a Royal Electrical and Mechanical Engineer (REME) workshop.

The Fighting Arms: The Teeth of the Army

Infantry

The infantry battalion is best viewed from the bottom up, starting with the private foot soldier. Wars are ultimately won by feet on the ground, the 'poor bloody infantry'. The typical British infantryman of the Second World War was armed with a .303in calibre Lee-Enfield Rifle with an effective range of 400yds (but up to 2,800yds against large targets in volley), carried fifty rounds of ammunition and two hand grenades the range of which was as far as he could throw it (c25yds)! In addition, he carried 20–40lbs of personal kit and, subject to role, specialised equipment, like a radio or mortar parts.

The infantryman was part of a battalion, typically around 800 men. The battalion was organised in companies, usually four (lettered A–D), plus support and HQ companies, each commanded by a major. Rifle companies were further divided into platoons, usually three (numbered 1–12 overall) and each commanded by a Lieutenant. In turn, the platoon was subdivided into sections of ten men, headed by a corporal. The battalion was led by a Lieutenant Colonel and at each level down to platoon there was a small HQ managing specialised arms and equipment.

The ten men of a section comprised the corporal in charge, six riflemen and a Bren light machine gun crew of three. The three sections within the platoon could look to the platoon HQ to provide both a light mortar and light anti-tank gun. At company level were several tracked carriers and trucks, plus administration. The battalion support company included a mortar platoon, anti-tank platoon, pioneer platoon, medium or heavy machine guns and a carrier platoon. Thus, the commanders at each level were able to deploy a wider range of weapons and men to support individual sections as and when the need arose.

The battalions might be termed light, essentially operating and moving on foot; motorised, moving forward in 'soft-skinned' – and therefore vulnerable – lorries; or mechanised, when transport was in armoured personnel carriers.

Battalions were formed within regiments which, at the start of the Second World War, were still largely geographically-based. A regiment might have one regular army battalion serving in the UK, one serving abroad and possibly a HQ battalion acting as the training core for one or more territorial (reserve) battalions.

While the battalion owed its allegiance to the monarch and the regiment, it was deployed within a quite separate operational construct. Thus, different battalions of the same regiment might serve in quite separate theatres of war. It was also a possibility that a battalion might be disbanded and its men transferred to make up numbers in battalions that had suffered serious losses in action, thus diluting any regional affiliation. Within battalions there were also attached soldiers from other specialised arms or services.

Armour

The Royal Armoured Corps was formed in April 1939 by the merger of eighteen cavalry regiments with eight regular and seven territorial battalions of the Royal Tank Corps, thereafter the Royal Tank Regiment. During the first years of the Second World War there were changes in structure of the British armoured units, but by late 1943 a pattern had emerged.

The *raison d'être* for an armoured division was mobility and the exploitation of weaknesses in enemy dispositions, subject to the nature of the terrain. Static, tanks were, in effect, artillery and extremely vulnerable. By 1943 they were of two main types – cruisers that were lightly armed and fast so as to thrust forward and create havoc, or slower-moving, heavily armoured, infantry tanks. If they were on the charge, they needed an efficient supply line and infantry to take and consolidate territory. They also needed to work in tandem with fast-moving artillery, some in the form of self-propelled guns, reconnaissance units equipped with light tanks and scout cars and specialised engineers.

An armoured division was composed of two brigades, one of tanks and the other of motorised or mechanised infantry. Typically, an armoured brigade comprised three tank regiments, either of the same or a mixture of types, each commanded by a Lieutenant Colonel. A regiment comprised a HQ with four-six tanks, anti-aircraft and light reconnaissance tanks, and three squadrons, each commanded by a major. In turn, squadrons were operated in troops of three to six, each under the leadership of a Lieutenant.

Some armoured brigades operated independently within a Corps and were intended to do so alongside other armoured formations or infantry. By mid-1944 the typical armoured brigade deployed a total of 342 tanks, made up of 223 cruisers, twenty-four close support, sixty-three light, twenty-four anti-aircraft and eight observation. The supporting vehicle fleet included tank transporters.

As an example of an armoured division, the following is the structure of the 6th Armoured Division when part of XIII Corps in Italy in June 1944.

6th Armoured Division
- 26th Armoured Brigade
  - 16th/5th Lancers (M4 Sherman)
  - 17th/21st Lancers (M4 Sherman)
  - 2nd Lothians and Border Horse (M4 Sherman)
- 61st Infantry Brigade
  - 2nd Bn Rifle Brigade
  - 7th Bn Rifle Brigade
  - 10th Bn Rifle Brigade

Divisional troops
- Reconnaissance
  - 1st Derbyshire Yeomanry (Dingo, Humber AC, Sherman)
- Artillery
  - 12th Regiment, Royal Horse Artillery (24xSPGs)
  - 152nd (Ayrshire Yeomanry) Field Regt, Royal Artillery (24x25-pdrs)
  - 72nd Anti-tank Regiment, Royal Artillery (48x17-pdrs)
  - 51st Light Anti-aircraft Regiment, Royal Artillery (54x40mm Bofors)
- Engineers
  - 8th Field Squadron, Royal Engineers
  - 625th Field Squadron, Royal Engineers
  - 144th Field Park Squadron, Royal Engineers
  - 6th Bridging Troop, Royal Engineers
- Signals
  - 6th Armoured Division Signals Regiment, Royal Corps of Signals

Artillery

The Army used a range, of 'guns', from mortars to howitzers. The mortars and some 6-pdr anti-tank guns were organic and operated within companies and battalions; larger weapons were deployed by the Royal Artillery. Smaller and very mobile guns, like the ubiquitous 25-pdr, were operated by field regiments, as were self-propelled guns; larger and usually less mobile guns and howitzers were operated by medium and heavy RA regiments.

Heavier artillery regiments were deployed under the designation Army Groups Royal Artillery (AGRA), controlled by the Army but allocated to Corps with one in reserve. Those serving in Italy were 1, 2, 5 (to May 1944), 6, 7 (from 1944) and 10. A typical AGRA would comprise one heavy and three medium regiments, occasionally with a field regiment added. The medium (4.5in and 5.5in) and heavy (7.2in and 9.2in) regiments comprised sixteen guns or howitzers in batteries of four.

Field regiments were allocated generally to divisions on a one per brigade basis. Mainly they used the 25-pdr, organised in three batteries of eight guns and each subdivided into two troops of four. As already noted, Divisions were also allocated an anti-tank regiment and an anti-aircraft regiment. The former comprised forty-eight guns in four batteries, each with one troop (four guns) of 6-pdrs and two troops (also four guns) of 17-pdrs. The light AA regiments comprised fifty-four 40mm Bofors guns in three batteries of three troops, each with six guns.

There were, in addition, heavy anti-aircraft regiments deployed statically to cover vital installations, like ports and airfields. Regiments were commanded by a Lieutenant Colonel, batteries by a Major and troops by a Lieutenant.

An important part of the Royal Artillery was the air observation post (AOP) squadrons, the work of which was fundamental to the subject matter of this book. The need for eyes in the sky had long been understood, but after the First World War and the separation of the Army from its air arm, the Royal Air Force had concentrated on priorities other than Army co-operation. After considerable pressure the RAF agreed reluctantly to the Army having its own aircraft, it being demonstrably easier to learn to fly a light aircraft than to manage the wizardry of gunnery.

The aircraft eventually selected for the role was the Auster, initially a British development of the American-designed Taylorcraft. The first squadron was 651 which was operational in Tunisia in early 1943 and in due course there were five squadrons in Italy. The squadrons were commanded by a Major and included eighteen artillery officers, all Captains. There was a headquarters flight of three aircraft and three flights (A, B and C) of four aircraft each. Each aircraft within a flight was a section, normally numbered from 1 upwards through all of the operational flights. Each squadron was assigned to a Corps and each flight to a Division or AGRA. Individual pilots would typically control the shooting of local batteries or elements of an AGRA. On at least one occasion in Italy a single pilot of 657 Sqn directed a whole Army shoot of around 300 guns on a single target.

The following table shows indicative numbers and levels, but by no means the actual distribution of artillery. This would vary depending on topography, enemy positions and the type and nature (and even morale) of the supported Divisions.

Signals

The Royal Corps of Signals was responsible for Army communications and those of RAF formations operating directly in support of the Army – telephone, radio, teleprinter and telegraph. It was an extremely demanding role, especially in rapidly moving warfare. Using both telephone line and radio links, communications were vertically through command levels and laterally connecting the arms.

Where possible lines were laid for telephone communications, reckoned more secure than radio. However, lines needed maintenance, in areas where there was bombing or shelling especially. Signals were also responsible for codes and ciphers. Whereas telephone was speech only, radios were used for speech (radio telephony (R/T)) or Morse (Army – continuous wave (CW); RAF - wireless telegraphy (W/T)).

Radios in army service operated in the high frequency (HF) range, whereas aircraft radios (except AOP aircraft) operated in the very high frequency (VHF) range. That simply resulted in the Army and Air Force being unable to talk to one another!

Army level	Artillery	Role	Number of guns	AOP
Army	AA Regt	Base protection	16 each	
Corps	AGRA	Heavy and medium	64	Sqn
Division	AT Regt	Anti-tank	48	
Division	LAA Regt	Mobile AA	54	Flt
Brigade	Field Regt	Field artillery	24	Section (pilot)
Battalion	Battery	Field artillery	8	

To be effective, good communications were essential between troops/batteries, the artillery command chain, battalions or regiments supported, observation posts and HQs. These networks, a combination of telephone line and wireless, evolved over time from core principles and are described in the relevant chapters.

Engineers

The Corps of Royal Engineers was responsible for a wide range of support tasks in or around the front line. Specialised units were held at Army and Corps level and as noted elsewhere, each Division had several field units and a field park unit allocated. These were designated companies in infantry divisions and squadrons in armoured divisions, working usually alongside brigades. A bridging platoon was retained at divisional level.

Among key engineer duties were the construction of defences; mine-laying and clearing; bomb and shell disposal; bridge-building; demolition; construction or repair of roads, camps, ammunition dumps, railways and ports; water supply; and management of the postal system.

At divisional level was the Commander, Royal Engineers, a Lieutenant Colonel who advised the division commander, directing engineer assets within the formation. Field companies/squadrons were commanded by a major. Companies were split into platoons commanded by a subaltern and these in turn operated as sections, each managed by an NCO and with twelve sappers (engineers) in total. Sappers were armed with rifles and a Bren gun per section and could and did fight as infantry when required.

The divisional field park companies/squadrons provided workshops, stores and heavy equipment. Like their field counterparts, they were commanded by a Major.

At Army, Corps and Divisional levels there was a signals regiment of battalion strength commanded by a Lieutenant Colonel. This was split into companies (later squadrons) commanded by a Major, in turn divided into troops commanded by subalterns. The army HQ had three squadrons, one for line laying and maintenance and two for operations and maintenance of communications and equipment. Messenger services were also provided.

At Corps level individual squadrons were assigned to construction and maintenance, operations and meeting the needs of the attached AGRA. At Divisional level the signals regiment also comprised three squadrons, in turn broken down into troops. Some of the latter were specialised and functional while others were similar in structure, providing services to brigades or artillery regiments within the division. By late 1944 the three squadrons within the divisional regiment had the following responsibilities:

1 Sqn – Main HQ wireless, line and despatch riders between HQ, upwards, down to brigades and flank units, and the operations of the signals office at HQ.

2 Sqn – Provision of comms for the artillery regiments, commander Royal Artillery net, link to AOP and detachments to the anti-tank and light anti-aircraft regiments.

3 Sqn – Brigade signals, forward comms for Commander Royal Engineers, maintenance of radios.

In respect of any system for close support, whether to infantry or armour, ground-based artillery or to air support by fighter-bombers, it follows that signals were at the core. Over time the net with its tentacles became more and more complex to ensure that the relevant arms could be brought to bear on enemy targets quickly and precisely.

The Services

There were numerous support services essential to the prosecution of the war and supporting the arms. While all were essential to the proper management of the Army, some were of more relevance to close support than others.

The **Royal Army Service Corps** (RASC) moved people and things, operating lorries of all sorts, boats and railways; it also provided air despatch units to work with RAF transport aircraft. Key responsibilities were the short-term storage and distribution of supplies, including food, weapons and ordnance, and fuel. In Italy forward delivery relied heavily on mule or packhorse, of which some 45,000 were used. While most units had their own vehicles for immediate use, the RASC undertook delivery to battalion level. The **Royal Army Veterinary Corps** (RAVC) was on hand to ensure that animals were properly cared for.

Maintenance of vehicles and, for example, radar equipment, was the responsibility of the **Royal Electrical and Mechanical Engineers** (REME), formed in 1942 as the need for more specialised personnel became evident. It also had the task of recovery and repair of damaged vehicles and equipment, maintaining workshops at each level.

The **Royal Army Ordnance Corps** (RAOC) was accountable for the procurement, storage and allocation of all weapons, including armoured fighting vehicles, munitions including RAF bombs, radios and similar equipment, clothing and general stores, apart from consumable material.

An important adjunct of the Royal Engineers was the **Pioneer Corps** whose members, while trained as infantry, undertook the hard graft involved in building and maintaining the whole range of infrastructure. Towards the end of the war it comprised nearly half a million men worldwide, also employing a million civilians locally.

Treating the sick and wounded was the **Royal Army Medical Corps** (RAMC) which in battle had medical officers employed from battalion upwards. Medical services were complemented by staff of the **Dental Corps**.

There were numerous branches committed to the soldier's further wellbeing. Physical fitness was the job of the **Army Physical Training Corps** (APTC), sustenance was provided by the **Army Catering Corps** (ACC), spiritual support by the **Royal Army Chaplain's Department** (RAChD) and intellectual stimulation by the **Army Education Corps** (AEC). Pay and personnel records were managed by the **Royal Army Pay Corps** (RAPC) – a huge task given the large number of dependants of conscripted soldiers. Discipline was the job of the **Corps of Military Police** (CMP), the 'Redcaps', highly visible when signposting routes and preventing congestion by directing traffic.

This brief catalogue would not be complete without mention of the postal services run by the **Royal Engineers** (RE) and baths and washhouses, part of the duties of the RAOC. The civilian-run **Navy, Army & Air Force Institute** (NAAFI) provided canteens close to the front line while the **Entertainments National Service Association** (ENSA) put on a range of shows for servicemen (otherwise known as 'Every Night Something Awful'!).

RAF Organisation

The outline structure of the Royal Air Force, emulated by the Dominion air arms during the Second World War, is relatively simple to describe after the complexity of that of the Army and its various interpretations of corps, division, regiment, battalion, troop and squadron. However, in the Middle East, when British units were fighting alongside those of Allies, the structure could be confusing.

At the head of the RAF, and accountable for all policy and the means for its implementation, was the **Air Council** whose President was the Secretary of State for Air and which included the Chief of the Air Staff and a number of senior officers. Immediately below the Air Council was the Air Staff that oversaw **RAF commands** under the direction of a Marshall of the Royal Air Force as Chief of the Air Staff. Subject to scale and nature, commands were variously under the direction of an Air Vice-Marshal, as Air Officer Commanding (AOC), or by an Air Marshal as Air Officer Commanding-in-Chief (AOC-in-C). Bomber Command and Fighter Command were examples of the latter. Some commands were geographical and if small commanded by an Air Commodore.

Within commands were usually, but not invariably, **groups** (with an Air Vice-Marshal typically as officer commanding). Usually they were organised around a specific function and varied considerably in size. The teeth of the operational groups and of the commands of which they were part were the **squadrons**, commanded in the Second World War either by a Squadron Leader or later in war often by a Wing Commander. (In the South African Air Force a Major since the SAAF used Army ranks.)

Squadrons were hosted by aerodromes, the more permanent of which were **stations** commanded by a Group Captain or sometimes a Wing Commander. The station would provide the infrastructure necessary for the squadrons to operate effectively, having its own engineering, motor transport, accommodation, medical services, emergency services, catering and so on. Although squadrons were self-contained, it was to a limited extent. While they handled operations, administration, intelligence and first-line engineering – squadron ground personnel included fitters (engine), riggers (airframe) and armourers – they needed the umbrella support of the larger station infrastructure. In some cases, in Fighter and Bomber commands in particular, stations were grouped as clusters, one or more satellite airfields being attached to the main base and squadrons dispersed between them.

Where several squadrons with similar aircraft types and operational function were working together for common purpose they might be organised within **wings**. These squadrons could be operated together as and when appropriate and led in action by one of the squadron leaders (for example the Duxford Wing during the Battle of Britain), or more formally designated as such and commanded by a Wing Commander. Throughout the period covered close support and tactical reconnaissance units were organised in numbered wings and frequently operated from the same airfield.

In the United Kingdom there were numerous support commands, among them maintenance, flying training and technical training, and units to handle works, bomb disposal and embarkation. A key component of the Service was the **RAF Regiment**, formed in 1942 from the original RAF armoured car companies and accountable primarily for the defence of RAF bases. The regiment comprised 280 squadrons eventually, each of 185 officers and men, and many being used either as infantry or transferred to infantry regiments late in the war.

In Egypt and India there was considerable infrastructure built up over time, including workshops, stores parks and permanent stations. Supplementing the RAF as it moved forward were maintenance, communications, radar, transport and stores units, and to provide immediate support to squadrons on the move, **Servicing Commando Units** that were also an invention of the Second World War.

The Royal Air Force in the Mediterranean Region

In 1941 the Royal Air Force in the Middle East was reformed as a command under Air Chief Marshal Sir Arthur Tedder. The numerous subordinate command formations were mainly at the eastern end of the Mediterranean and included AHQ Egypt, Western Desert Air Force and AHQ Malta. With the Allied invasion of Morocco and Algeria in November 1942, two temporary air forces were formed – Eastern Air Command (RAF) and XII Air Force (USAAF).

Because of the need for greater co-ordination and to support squeezing Axis forces out of Tunisia from both directions, a completely new structure was created on 15 February 1943 under the overall command of Tedder. This was Mediterranean Air Command, which subsumed Northwest African Air Forces, Middle East Command, AHQ Malta, RAF Gibraltar and 216 Group RAF.

The powerful Northwest African Air Forces, providing the air power for the forthcoming invasion of Sicily, then Italy, comprised Northwest African Strategic Air Force (mainly USAAF and commanded by Major General James Doolittle), Northwest African Tactical Air Force (Air Marshal Sir Arthur Coningham) and Northwest African Coastal Air Force (Air Vice-Marshal Sir Hugh Lloyd). The renamed Desert Air Force (DAF) was one component of the Tactical Air Force, resulting in the peculiarity of an air force (DAF) within an air force (NATAF) within an air force (NAAF) within a Command (MAC)!

With the invasion of Italy there was further restructuring with the creation of Mediterranean Allied Air Forces (MAAF), directing all Allied Air Forces in the Western Mediterranean and still with Tedder as Commander in Chief. (When he returned to the UK as General Eisenhower's deputy for the forthcoming invasion of France he was succeeded by Gen Ira Eaker.)

MAAF controlled the three air forces (Strategic, Tactical and Coastal) plus XII Troop Carrier Command, a PR Wing and servicing and engineer commands. In due course a further command, the Balkan Air Force, was added. The need for integration was essential given that the overall structure included formations from the RAF, South African Air Force, Royal Australian Air Force, Royal Canadian Air Force, USAAF, Free French Air Force, Italian Co-Belligerent Air Force plus Brazilian, Greek, Jugoslav and Polish squadrons. MAAF was disbanded in May 1945.

United States Army Air Force

The USAAF was formed in March 1942 from the United States Army Air Corps. It accounted to the Army Chief of Staff and comprised a number of air forces and several support commands. The air forces, formally described by Roman numerals, were constructed both geographically and to some extent functionally. Thus VIII Air Force (commonly referred to as 8th Air Force) was a bomber organisation in the United Kingdom, with both bomber and escort fighter components, while IX Air Force, also in the UK in 1944, comprised transport and tactical combat elements to support the invasion of Normandy.

Within the **Air Force** (General) were **wings** or **divisions** (Major General) which in turn comprised a number of groups. The **group** (Colonel) had three or four **squadrons** (Major), each having on charge between eight (heavy bomber) and twenty-four (some fighter) aircraft. Usually the squadrons of a group operated from the same airfield, but would often be assigned separate missions.

Certain types of squadrons were operated directly by either a wing or air force, for example reconnaissance and rescue. Some squadron designations changed over time; thus observation became reconnaissance and pursuit became fighter. Whereas the RAF would refer simply to 67 Sqn, the USAAF form of identification would be 67th Bombardment Squadron.

Armée de l'Air

With the fall of France a few aircraft and rather more airmen evacuated to the United Kingdom. The bulk of the air force, however, was retained by the Vichy government and despatched to North Africa.

The structure downwards at operational level was *Escadres* (Wings), then *Groupement* (Squadrons) that were split into Escadrilles (Flights). In reality *groupementes* were larger than RAF squadrons, the *escadrilles* within them being identified by Arabic (later Roman) numerals and often by a name. As an example, the second *escadrille* of *Groupe de Bombardement 20* is shown as – 'GB II/20 *Lorraine*'.

Groupements were designated by role in the following way:

GB – Groupe de Bombardement (Bomber squadron)

GC – Groupe de Chasse (Fighter squadron)

Comparative ranks

Royal Navy	Army	Royal Air Force
Admiral of the Fleet	Field Marshal	Marshal of the Royal AF
Admiral	General	Air Chief Marshal
Vice-Admiral	Lieutenant General	Air Marshal
Rear Admiral	Major General	Air Vice-Marshal
Commodore	Brigadier	Air Commodore
Captain	Colonel	Group Captain
Commander	Lieutenant Colonel	Wing Commander
Lieutenant Commander	Major	Squadron Leader
Lieutenant	Captain	Flight Lieutenant
Sub-Lieutenant	Lieutenant	Flying Officer
Midshipman	Second Lieutenant	Pilot Officer

GR – Groupe de Reconnaissance (Reconnaissance squadron)

GT – Groupe de Transport (Transport squadron)

In the course of the occupation of North Africa by Allied forces from late 1942, many notionally-neutral Vichy units transferred to the Allied side and acquired RAF squadron numbers, for example GC II/7 *Nice* also became 326 Sqn. The Free French Air Force was the *Forces Aériennes Françaises Libre* (FAFL).

Luftwaffe[2]

Organisationally, the lowest level of flying unit in the German Air Force with a designation was the ***Staffel***. This had nine aircraft initially, increasing to sixteen by the war's end. The *Staffelkapitaen* held the rank of *Oberleutnant* or *Hauptmann*.

Staffeln usually operated within a ***Gruppe***, commanded by a *Kommandeur* with the rank of Major or *Hauptmann*. The *Gruppe* comprised a headquarters flight (***Stab***) with three aircraft, and three *staffeln*, although this number increased to four as the war progressed. A three *staffeln gruppe* would total thirty aircraft.

The largest flying unit was the ***Geschwader***, normally made up of three *gruppen* plus a *stab* of four aircraft and commanded by a *Kommodore*, he being a Major, *Oberstleutnant* or *Oberst*. The *geschwader* had a prefix that denoted its role. Although some managed to operate with all *gruppen* co-located, the latter were often spread across several battlefronts. In this respect the *geschwader* may be likened to a British Army regiment deploying battalions as required. However, some specialised *gruppen* were formed to operate as such and not within a *geschwader*.

The designations of *Luftwaffe* units by role was as follows, noting that reconnaissance units formed at *gruppe* rather than *geschwader* level:

Fighter	*Jagdgeschwader* JG
Night fighter	*Nachtjagdgeschwader* NJG
Destroyer	*Zerstörer* ZG (twin engine fighters)
Bomber	*Kampfgeschwader* KG
Dive-bomber	*Stukageschwader* StG
Ground attack	*Schlachtgeschwader* SG
Transport	*Transportgeschwader* TG
Reconnaissance	*Aufklärungsgruppe* Aufk.Gr

The identity of units was straightforward, *geschwader* and *staffel* numbering in Arabic and *gruppen* in Roman, usually followed by a stop. A typical fighter *geschwader*, flying Messerschmidt Bf 109s throughout the war, was JG 27. When operating as such the immediate subordinate units were Stab/JG 27 or, for example II./JG 27. The *staffeln* were numbered sequentially from 1 to 9, 1–3 in I Gruppe, 4–6 in II Gruppe and 7–9 in III Gruppe. (There was sometimes a 10th *staffel* in fighter units, usually a fighter-bomber *staffel*.) So when a *staffel* was described as such it would be 7./JG 27.

Regia Aeronautica

The Italian Air Force too is best understood from the bottom up. The basic unit was the ***squadriglia*** of sixteen (fighter) or twelve (bomber) aircraft. Two (bomber) or three (fighter) *squadrigli* formed a ***Gruppo***. Above the *gruppi* was the ***Stormo***, commanded by a Colonel.

Some *gruppi* were autonomous, but those operating within a *Stormo* were usually co-located. In a broad sense the structure is comparable with the RAF squadron, wing and group organisation.

[1] Much of the Army structure is noted from Forty's *Companion to the British Army 1939–1945*

[2] From Price, *Luftwaffe Handbook 1939–1945*

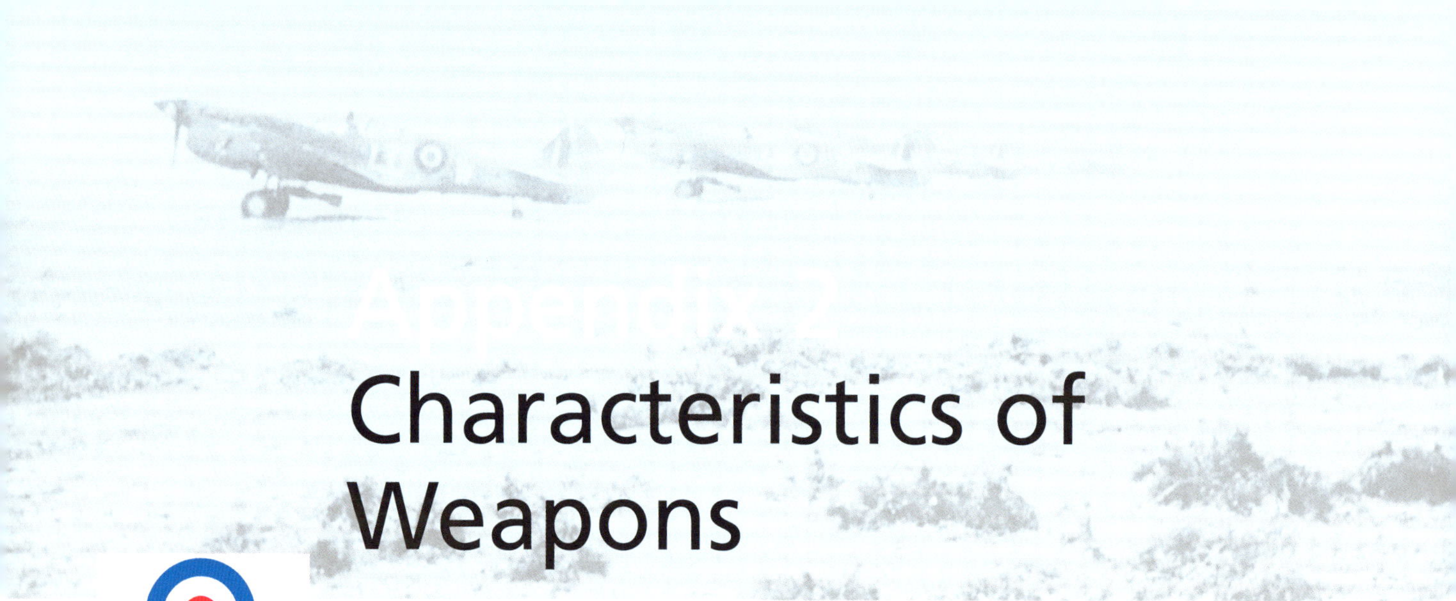

Characteristics of Weapons

What follows are the key characteristics of close support-related weapons referred to in the main text. For aircraft, these extend to light bombers. For guns, they do not include side-arms or mortars. Principle types of tank are included, but not warships.

Aircraft

Performance figures for aircraft are those pertinent to their operating in support roles for land and amphibious forces which, being low-level, is why service ceiling is not included. Those for speed and range depend very much on payload, made up primarily of fuel and ordnance carried, but also including the weight of the pilot! There is a three-way trade-off between payload, speed and range: increase any one to the maximum and one or both of the other functions decrease. Entry into service dates are for the specific aircraft mark with the air arm(s) of the country under which it is listed.

Fighters: Army Co-operation: Dive-Bombers

British service

Beaufighter Ic, Bristol Strike fighter.
Service from December 1940.
Two 1,400hp Bristol Hercules III engines.
Loaded weight 21,000lbs.
Cruise 280mph, max speed 330mph.
Range 1,300mls.
Four 20mm cannon, six .303in machine guns.
Beaufighter VIF Night fighter.
Service from March 1942.
Two 1,670hp Bristol Mercury VI/VIII engines.
Loaded weight 21,600lbs.
Cruise 280mph, max speed 333mph.
Range 1,470mls.
Four .303in machine guns.

Gladiator II, Gloster Last biplane fighter used by the RAF and first with an enclosed cockpit.
Service from February 1937.
840hp Bristol Mercury engine.
Loaded weight 4,750lbs.
Cruise 210mph, max speed 250mph.
Range 400mls.
Four .303in machine guns.

Hurricane I, Hawker First monoplane fighter for the RAF.
Service from December 1937.
1,030hp Rolls-Royce Merlin II/III engine.
Loaded weight 6,600lbs.
Cruise 260mph, max speed 316mph.
Range 460mls.
Eight .303in machine guns.
Hurricane II More powerful and heavily armed version used extensively in North Africa.
Service from September 1940.
1,280hp Rolls-Royce Merlin XX.
Loaded weight 7,800lbs.
Max speed 340mph.
Four 20mm cannon and two 250lb or 500lb bombs (IIc); two .303in machine guns, two 40mm cannon (IId).

Kittyhawk I, Curtiss Development of the Tomahawk as P-40D/E, serving only in Middle East and Pacific.
Service from January 1942.
1,150hp Allison V-1710 engine.
Loaded weight 8,515lbs.
Cruise 308mph, max speed 334mph.
Range 716mls.
Six 0.5in machine guns.
Kittyhawk II Equivalent to P-40F.
1,300hp Packard V-1650 (Rolls-Royce Merlin 28) engine.
Service from June 1942.
Loaded weight 8.720lbs.
Cruise 300mph, max speed 370mph.
Armament supplemented to include 500lb bomb.
Kittyhawk III Equivalent to P-40-K/M.
Service from September 1942
1,600hp Allison V-1710 engine.
Loaded weight 8,500lbs.
Cruise 300mph, max speed 362mph.
Six 0.5in machine guns and up to 1,000lb bombs.

Lysander, Westland Army co-operation aircraft that soon become obsolescent in this role.
Service from May 1938.
890hp Bristol Mercury XII engine.
Loaded weight 5,920lbs.
Cruise 120mph, max speed 220mph.
Range 600mls.
Three .303in machine guns, six light bombs.

Martlet II, Grumman Carrier-based fighter, equivalent to US Navy F4F-3 Wildcat.
Service with Royal Navy from March 1941.
1,200hp Pratt and Whitney Twin Wasp engine.
Loaded weight 6,100lbs.
Cruise 260mph, max speed 315mph.
Range 1,150mls.
Six 0.5in machine guns.

Seafire LIIc, Supermarine Carrier-based version of Spitfire Mk V.
Service from June 1942.
1,640hp Rolls-Royce Merlin 32 engine.
Loaded weight 7,000lbs.
Cruise 280mph, max speed 333mph.
Range 490mls.
Two 20mm cannon, four .303in machine guns, one 500lb or two 250lb bombs.

Spitfire I, Supermarine More versatile, longer-lived but less robust than the Hurricane.
Service from August 1938.
1,030hp Rolls-Royce Merlin II engine.
Loaded weight 5,784lbs.
Cruise 300mph, max speed 355mph.
Range 500mls.
Eight .303in machine guns.
Spitfire V First version to fulfil fighter-bomber role.
Service from February 1941.
1,440hp Rolls-Royce Merlin 45 engine.
Loaded weight 6,417lbs.
Max speed 374mph.
Range 470mls.
Various armament options, e.g. two 20mm cannon plus four .303 machine guns or four 20mm cannon plus one 500lb bomb.
Spitfire IX built to combat Fw 190.
Service from July 1942.
1,560hp Rolls-Royce Merlin 61 engine.
Loaded weight 7,500lbs.
Max speed 408mph.
Range 435mls.
Two 20mm cannon plus four .303 machine guns and up to 1,000lb bombs.

Tomahawk IIB, Curtiss Initial deliveries of Mk I ex-French order: Mk.IIb equivalent of US P-40C. Low-level army support because of poor high-level performance.
Service from February 1941.
1,040hp Allison V-1710 engine.
Loaded weight 7,459lbs.
Cruise 270mph, max speed 345mph.
Range 730mls.
Six .303in machine guns.

United States service

A-36A Apache/Invader, North American Dive-bomber version of the P-51 Mustang.
Service from April 1943.
1,325hp Allison V-1700 engine.
Loaded weight 10,000lbs.
Cruise 250mph, max speed 310mph.
Range 550mls.
Six 0.5in machine guns, 1,000lb bombs.

F4F-4 Wildcat, Grumman Carrier-based single-seat fighter.
Service from March 1942.
1,200hp Pratt and Whitney R-1830 Twin Wasp engine.
Loaded weight 7,952lbs.
Cruise 155mph, max speed 320mph.
Range 770mls.
Six 0.5in machine guns.

P-38G Lightning, Lockheed Twin engine, twin boom fighter.
Service from September 1941.
Two 1,325hp Allison V1710 engines.
Loaded weight 15,482lbs.
Cruise 305mph, max speed 395mph.
Range 450 mls.
One 20mm cannon, four 0.5in machine guns.

P-39L Airacobra, Bell Single-seat fighter with engine mid-fuselage and tricycle undercarriage.
Service from April 1941.
1,325hp Allison V-1710 engine.
Loaded weight 8,400lbs.
Cruise 210mph, max speed 365mph.
Range 800mls.
One 37mm cannon, two 0.5in and four 0.3in machine guns, 500lb bombs.

P-40 Warhawk, Curtiss *See* Kittyhawk

German service

Bf 109E, Messerschmitt Single-seat day fighter, blooded in the Spanish Civil War.
Service from February 1939.
1,050hp Daimler-Benz DB601A engine.
Loaded weight 5,875lbs.
Cruise 300mph, max speed 348mph.
Range 210mls.
One 20mm cannon, four 7.9mm machine guns.
Bf 109F Improved performance to counter Spitfire V.
Service from January 1941.
1,350hp Daimler-Benz DB601E engine.
Loaded weight 6,390lbs.
Cruise 355mph, max speed 390mph.
Range 250mls.
One 20mm cannon, two 7.9mm machine guns, but some fitted with extra cannon for anti-bomber role at expense of performance.
Bf 110C, Messerschmitt Two-seat day and night fighter.
Service from January 1939.
Two 1,100hp Daimler-Benz DB601A engines.
Loaded weight 14,880lbs.
Cruise 260mph, max speed 336mph.
Range 500mls.
Two 20mm cannon, five 7.9mm machine guns.

Fw 190A, Focke-Wulf Single-seat day fighter/fighter-bomber.
Service from July 1941.
1,700hp BMW 801 engine.
Loaded weight 9.660lbs.
Cruise 295mph, max speed 402mph. Range 490mls.
Two 20mm cannon, two 7.9mm machine guns.

Ju 87D, Junkers Dive-bomber.
Service from February 1942.
1,400hp Jumo 211J engine.
Loaded weight 14,550lbs.
Cruise 183mph, max speed 240mph.
Range 370mls.
Four 7.9mm machine guns, 2,200lb bombs.

Hs 126, Henschel Army co-operation; superficial resemblance to British Lysander.
Service from November 1938.
610hp Jumo 210 engine.
Loaded weight 6,810lbs.
Cruise 160mph, max speed 220mph.
Range 360mls.
Two 7.9mm machine guns, 110lb bombs.

Italian service

CR.42, Fiat Biplane day fighter, similar to British Gladiator.
Service from May 1939.
840hp Fiat A74R1C engine.
Loaded weight 5,060lbs.
Cruise 245mph, max speed 270mph.
Range 480mls.
Two 12.7mm machine guns.

C.200 Saetta, Macchi Single-seat day fighter.
Service from August 1939.
870hp Fiat A74RC radial engine.
Loaded weight 4,850lbs.
Cruise 270mph, max speed 310mph.
Range 350mls.
Two 12.7mm machine guns.

C.202 Folgore Development of C.200 with in-line engine.
Service from July 1941.
1,160hp Alfa Romeo RA1000 engine (licence-built DB601A).
Loaded weight 6,460lbs.
Cruise 315mph, max speed 370mph.
Range 475mls.
Two 12.7mm, two 7.7mm machine guns.

French service

D.520, Dewoitine Single-seat day fighter.
Service from January 1940.
950hp Hispano-Suiza 12Y-49 engine.
Loaded weight 5,900lbs.
Cruise 295mph, max speed 350mph.
Range 780mls.
One 20mm cannon, four 7.5mm machine guns.

Light bombers

British service

Blenheim IV, Bristol Twin engine light bomber, crew three.
Service from March 1939.
Two 905hp Bristol Mercury XV engines.
Loaded weight 14,400lbs.
Cruise 210mph, max speed 265mph.
Range 1,460mls.
Three .303in machine guns, 1,320lb bombs.
Blenheim V New nose, more armour.
Service from June 1942.
Two 950hp Bristol Mercury 30 engines.
Loaded weight 17,000lbs.
Cruise 210mph, max speed 265mph.
Range 1,600mls.
Four .303in machine guns, 1,000lb bombs

Maryland, Martin Four-seat recce-bomber.
Service from October 1940.
Two 1,200hp Pratt and Whitney Twin Wasp engines.
Loaded weight 16,800lbs.
Cruise 220mph, max speed 275mph.
Range 1,800mls.
Five .303in machine guns, 2,000lb bombs.

Baltimore Four-seat light bomber.
Service from January 1942.
Two 1,660hp Wright Cyclone GR-2600 engines.
Loaded weight 23,000lbs.
Cruise 220mph, max speed 300mph.
Range 950mls.
Eight .303in machine guns, 2,000lb bombs.

Boston III, Douglas Four-seat light bomber.
Service from July 1941.
Two Wright Cyclone GR-2600 engines.
Loaded weight 25,000lbs.
Cruise 250mph, max speed 300mph.
Range 1,020mls.
Eight .303in machine guns, 2,000lb bombs.

United States service

A-20C, Douglas *See* entry for Boston

B-25C Mitchell, North American Five-place light bomber.
Service from January 1942.
Two 1,700hp Wright Cyclone GR2600 engines.
Loaded weight 24,000lbs.
Cruise 230mph, max speed 284mph.
Range 1,500mls.
Six 0.5in machine guns, 3,000lb bombs.

Guns

Rate of fire is shown as rounds per minute, representative muzzle velocity as feet per second. Range is in yards, except in the case of anti-aircraft weapons where it is shown in feet. While most German guns had a primary function, many were used in dual anti-aircraft and ground combat roles. In these instances range is given in feet in the anti-aircraft role and yards in ground combat role.

British

2-pdr anti-tank gun
Crew – 4-5
Weight – 1,795lbs
Bore – 40mm
Rate of Fire – 22rpm
Muzzle Velocity – 2,600fps
Range – 1,000yds

6-pdr anti-tank gun
Crew – 6
Weight – 2,520lbs
Bore – 57mm
Rate of Fire – 15rpm
Muzzle Velocity – 2,600fps
Range – 5,000 yds

17-pdr anti-tank gun
Crew – 5-6
Weight – 4,624lbs
Bore – 76.2mm
Rate of Fire – 10rpm
Muzzle Velocity – 3,950fps
Range – 2,000yds effective

25-pdr field gun
Crew – 6
Weight – 3,600lbs
Bore – 87.6mm
Rate of Fire – 5rpm
Muzzle Velocity – 1,750fps
Range – 13,400yds

4.5in counter-battery gun
Crew – 10
Weight – 12,635lbs
Bore – 4.5in
Rate of Fire – 2–3rpm
Muzzle Velocity – 2,250fps
Range – 20,500yds

5.5in medium gun
Crew – 10
Weight – 13,650lbs
Bore – 5.5in
Rate of Fire – 2rpm
Muzzle Velocity – 1,675fps
Range – 16,200yds

20mm Oerlikon anti-aircraft gun
Crew – 1
Weight – 400lbs
Bore – 20mm
Rate of Fire – 320rpm
Muzzle Velocity – 2,700fps
Range – 2,500ft

40mm Bofors anti-aircraft gun
Crew – 4
Weight – 4,370lbs
Bore – 40mm
Rate of Fire – 120rpm
Muzzle Velocity – 2,890fps
Range – 23,490ft

3.7in anti-aircraft gun
Crew – 7
Weight – 20,540lbs
Bore – 3.7in
Rate of Fire – 10–20rpm
Muzzle Velocity – 2,600fps
Range – 30,000ft

German

Flak 30 anti-aircraft gun
Crew – 5
Weight – 992lbs
Bore – 20mm
Rate of Fire – 180rpm
Muzzle Velocity – 2,950fps
Range – 7,200ft/5,230yds

Flak 18/36 anti-aircraft gun
Crew – 6-7
Weight – 3,420lbs
Bore – 37mm
Rate of Fire – 160rpm
Muzzle Velocity – 2,500–2,800fps
Range – 13,800ft/8,750yds

Pak 38 anti-tank gun
Crew – 5
Weight – 2,200lbs
Bore – 50mm
Rate of Fire – 13rpm
Muzzle Velocity – 1,800–3,700fps
Range – 3,000yds

Pak 40 anti-tank gun
Crew – 6
Weight – 3,140lbs
Bore – 75mm
Rate of Fire – 14rpm
Muzzle Velocity – 2,500fps
Range – 2,000yds effective

Flak 18/36 anti-aircraft gun
Crew – 10
Weight – 16,325lbs
Bore – 88mm
Rate of Fire – 13rpm
Muzzle velocity – 2,690fps
Range – 26,240ft/16,250yds

Tanks and Self-Propelled Guns

Tanks and self-propelled guns tended to be developed extensively, predominantly with changes to armour and armament. The data shown are representative of models in action in North Africa to early 1943.

British service

Cruiser Mk II
Crew – 4
Engine – 150hp
Weight – 13.75tons
Speed – 16mph
Range – 100mls
Main armour – 30mm
Armament – One 2-pdr gun, one .303in machine gun

Cruiser Mk IV
Crew – 4
Engine –340hp
Weight – 14.75tons
Speed – 30mph
Range – 90mls
Main armour – 30mm
Armament – One 2-pdr gun, one .303in machine gun

Cruiser Mk VI Crusader
Crew – 5
Engine – 340hp
Weight – 19tons
Speed – 27mph
Range – 100mls
Main armour – 50mm
Armament – One 2-pdr gun, one 7.92mm machine gun

Tank Infantry Mk II Matilda
Crew – 4
Engine – 190hp
Weight – 26.5tons
Speed – 15mph
Range – 70mls
Main armour – 78mm
Armament – One 2-pdr gun, one .303in machine gun

M3A5 Grant
Crew – 6
Engine – 400hp
Weight – 29tons
Speed – 25mph
Range – 115mls
Main armour – 57mm
Armament – One 75mm gun, two-four .30in machine guns

M4A1 Sherman
Crew – 5
Engine – 400hp
Weight – 33tons
Speed – 28mph
Range – 110mls
Main armour – 76mm
Armament – One 75mm gun, two 7.62mm machine guns

Panzer IV
Crew – 5
Engine – 300hp
Weight – 25.4tons
Speed – 25mph
Range – 120mls
Main armour – 50mm
Armament – One 75mm gun, two 7.92mm machine guns

StuG III Assault gun (based on Panzer III hull)
Crew – 4
Engine – 196hp
Weight – 26.35tons
Speed – 25mph
Range – 95mls
Main armour – 30mm
Armament – One 75mm gun, one 7.92mm machine gun

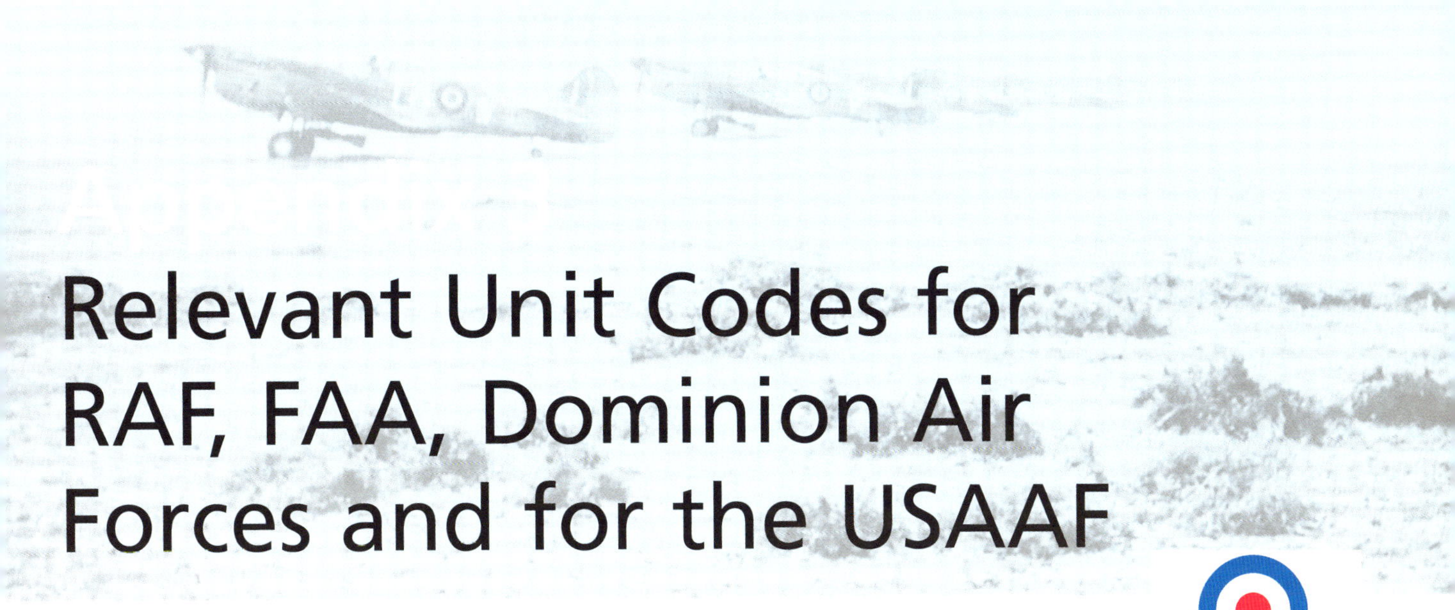

Relevant Unit Codes for RAF, FAA, Dominion Air Forces and for the USAAF

Codes are shown by unit and then alphabetically to aid identification of unit. In the latter table, USAAF units are identified by being in the form '123 FS'. (USAAF codes are shown only where they comprise two characters, in line with RAF practice: most US units carried a single letter or two-digit codes.)

By unit

Sqn	Code
RAF	
2	KO
3	QO
4	TV
6	JV
8	HV
11	YH
12	PH
13	OO
15	LS
16	EE
17	YB
18	WV
21	YH
22	OA
23	YP
26	RM
32	GZ
33	NW, RS
37	LF
38	HD
39	AV, XZ
40	BL
43	FT
45	OB
53	PZ
55	KQ
56	US
57	DX
59	TR
70	SJ
72	RN
73	TP
79	NV
80	EY
81	FL
82	UX
85	VY
87	LK
88	RH
92	QJ
93	HN
94	GO
98	VO
101	SR
103	PM
104	EP
105	GB
107	OM
111	JU
112	RT, GA
113	AD
114	RT
117	LD
126	MK
127	EJ
139	XD
142	QT
145	SO, ZX
150	JN
151	DZ
152	UM
154	HT
206	VX
208	RG
213	AK
216	SH, LO
218	HA
220	NR
221	DF
225	WU
226	MQ
228	DQ
229	RE, HB
230	DX
232	EF
233	ZS
235	LA
238	KC
241	RZ
242	LE
243	SN
245	DX
249	GN
250	LD
252	BT
253	SW
254	QY
255	XD
260	HS
267	KW
272	TJ
274	YK, NH
283	FG
335	FG
500	MK
501	SD
601	UF
607	AF
608	UL
614	LJ
615	KW
1435	V*
Fleet Air Arm	
801 NAS	A3
806 NAS	L6
812 NAS	G3
815 NAS	L3
820 NAS	A4
821 NAS	A5
825 NAS	G5
826 NAS	S4
828 NAS	S5
RAAF	
3	NW, CV
450	OK
458	MD
459	GK
RCAF	
417	AN
SAAF	
1	AX
2	DB
4	KJ
5	GL
12	VL
15	ZP
24	OZ
40	WR
USAAF	
2 FS	QP
4 FS	WD
5 FS	VF
27 FS	HV
48 FS	ES
49 FS	QU
71 FS	LM
94 FS	UN
111 TRS	N5
307 FS	MX
308 FS	HL
309 FS	WZ

By code

Code	Unit
A3	801 NAS
A4	820 NAS
A5	821 NAS
AD	113
AF	607
AK	213
AN	417 RCAF
AV	39
AX	1 SAAF
BL	40
BT	252
CV	3 RAAF
DB	2 SAAF
DF	221
DQ	228
DX	57
DX	230
DX	245
DZ	151
EE	16
EF	232
EJ	127
EP	104
ES	48 FS
EY	80
FG	283
FG	335
FL	81
FT	43
G3	812 NAS
G5	825 NAS
GA	112
GB	105
GK	459 RAAF
GL	5 SAAF
GN	249

Code	Unit
GO	94
GZ	32
HA	218
HB	229
HD	38
HL	308 FS
HN	93
HS	260
HT	154
HV	8
HV	27 FS
JN	150
JU	111
JV	6
KC	238
KJ	4 SAAF
KO	2
KQ	55
KW	267
KW	615
L3	815 NAS
L6	806 NAS
LA	235
LD	117
LD	250
LE	242
LF	37
LJ	614
LK	87
LM	71 FS
LO	216
LS	15
MD	458 RAAF
MK	126
MK	500
MQ	226

Code	Unit
MX	307 FS
N5	111 TRS
NH	274
NR	220
NV	79
NW	33
NW	3 RAAF
OA	22
OB	45
OK	450 RAAF
OM	107
OO	13
OZ	24 SAAF
PH	12
PM	103
PZ	53
QJ	92
QO	3
QP	2 FS
QT	142
QU	49 FS
QY	254
RE	229
RG	208
RH	88
RM	26
RN	72
RS	33
RT	112
RT	114
RZ	241
S4	826 NAS
S5	828 NAS
SD	501
SH	216
SJ	70

Code	Unit
SN	243
SO	145
SR	101
SW	253
TJ	272
TP	73
TR	59
TV	4
UF	601
UL	608
UM	152
UN	94 FS
US	56
UX	82
V*	1435
VF	5 FS
VL	12 SAAF
VO	98
VX	206
VY	85
WD	4 FS
WR	40 SAAF
WU	225
WV	18
WZ	309 FS
XD	139
XD	255
XZ	39
YB	17
YH	11
YH	21
YK	274
YP	23
ZP	15 SAAF
ZS	233
ZX	145

Glossary

AAPIU	Army Air Photo Interpretation Unit
AASC	Army Air Support Control
AASF	Advanced Air Striking Force
AASG	Army Air Support Group
ACAB	Allied Central Air Bureau
ACM	Air Chief Marshal
ADG	Air Defence Group
ADGB	Air Defence of Great Britain
AFE	Airborne Forces Establishment
AIL	Air Intelligence Liaison
Air Cdre	Air Commodore
ALO	Air Liaison Officer (Army)
AM	Air Marshal
AMES	Air Ministry Experimental Station (radar set or station)
AOC-in-C	Air Officer Commanding–in-Chief
AOP	Air Observation Post
Arty/R	Artillery Reconnaissance
AS	Anti-Ship(ping) or Anti-Submarine
ASC	Air Support Control
ASP	Air Stores Park
ASSU	Air Support Signals Unit
AT	Anti-Tank
AuxAF	Auxiliary Air Force
AVM	Air Vice-Marshal
BAFF	British Air Forces in France
Bde	Brigade
BEF	British Expeditionary Force
Btn	Battalion
CIB	Central Information Bureau
CLS/E	Central Landing School/Establishment
CO	Commanding Officer (in the RAF of a station or equivalent or above)
COBU	Combined Operations Bombardment Unit
COL	Chain Overseas Low (radar)
CRA	Commander Royal Artillery
CSBC	Close Support Bomber Control
CSG	Close Support Group
CU	Camouflage Unit
CW	Continuous Wave (radio)
Div	Division
FAA	Fleet Air Arm
FASL	Forward Air Support Link
FBC	Forward Bomber Control
FFBF	Free French Bomber Flight
Fg Off	Flying Officer
Flt Lt	Flight Lieutenant
GCCS	Government Code & Cipher School
GNF	Gun(s) Now Firing
Gp Capt	Group Captain
GRU	General Reconnaissance Unit
HF	High Frequency
HQ	Headquarters
JIC	Joint Intelligence Committee
JIC(S)	Joint Intelligence Committee sub-committee
LAA	Light Anti-Aircraft
LB	Light Bomber
LRDG	Long Range Desert Group
LT Col	Lieutenant Colonel
M/T	Motor Transport
MEIU	Middle East Interpretation Unit
MORU	Mobile Operations Room Unit
MRAF	Marshal of the Royal Air Force
MSSU	Mobile Signals Servicing Unit
MU	Maintenance Unit
NAS	Naval Air Squadron
NF	Now Firing
NGS	Naval Gunfire Support
NRO	No Results Observed
OC	Officer Commanding (in the RAF of a squadron or wing)
OP	Observation Post
OR	Other Ranks
ORB	Operations Record Book
OTU	Operational Training Unit
PDU	Photographic Development Unit
PES	Parachute Exercise Squadron
Photo/R	Photo Reconnaissance (tactical)
Plt Off	Pilot Officer
PR	Photo Reconnaissance
PRU	Photographic Reconnaissance Unit
PTC	Parachute Training Centre
R/T	Radio Telegraphy (later Radio Telephony)
RA	Royal Artillery
RAF	Royal Air Force
RAFC	Royal Artillery Flying Club
RASC	Royal Army Service Corps
RASL	Rear Air Support Link
RCT	Regimental Combat Teams
RE	Royal Engineers
RFC	Royal Flying Corps
RNAS	Royal Naval Air Service
RNFS	Royal Navy Fighter Squadron
RSU	Repair and Salvage Unit
RUO	Result unobserved
SAAF	South African Air Force,
SAC	School of Army Co-operation
SASO	Senior Air Staff Officer
SCU	Servicing Commando Units
SPG	Self-Propelled Gun
Sqn Ldr	Squadron Leader
SRAF	Southern Rhodesian Air Force
SSF	Special Survey Flight
Tac/R	Tactical Reconnaissance (visual)
TAF	Tactical Air Force
TCG	Troop Carrier Group
VHF	Very High Frequency
W/T	Wireless Telegraphy (later Wireless Telephony)
WDAF	Western Desert Air Force
Wg Cdr	Wing Commander
WI	Wireless Interception (Y Service)

Bibliography

— *The Attack of Ground Targets by Fighters, Air Staff Operational Monograph No 3* (Air Ministry, London, 1945)

— Air Publication 3235 *AHB Narrative Air Support* (Air Ministry, London, 1955)

— *Allied Landings in Sicily Museum* (Provincia Regionale Catania, Palermo, 2002)

— *RAF Middle East: The Official Story of Air Operations Feb.1942 – Jan.1943* (HMSO, London, 1945)

Ashworth, C., *RAF Bomber Command 1936–1968* (PSL, Yeovil, 1995)

Ashworth, C., *RAF Coastal Command 1936–1969* (PSL, Yeovil, 1992)

Azaola, J. R., (ed.), *Spitfires over the Mediterranean & North Africa* (Osprey, London, 2000)

Bachelor, L., *Supermarine Seafire (Merlins): Profile 221* (Profile Publications, Windsor, 1971)

Ballance, T., et al., *The Squadrons and Units of the Fleet Air Arm* (Air-Britain, Staplefield, 2016)

Baughen, G., *The RAF in the Battle of France and the Battle of Britain* (Fonthill, 2016)

Baughen, G., *The Rise of the Bomber: RAF-Army Planning 1919 to Munich 1938* (Fonthill, 2016)

Bazeley H. C., *The Air Observation Post* (AAC, Middle Wallop, 2012)

Beedle, J., *The Fighting Cocks: 43 (Fighter) Squadron* (Pen & Sword, Barnsley, 2011)

Bickers, R. T., *Air War over Normandy* (Leo Cooper, Barnsley, 1994)

Bickers, R. T., *The Desert Air War 1939–1945* (Leo Cooper, Barnsley, 1991)

Bowyer, C. & Shores, C., *Desert Air Force at War* (Ian Allan, London, 1981)

Bowyer, C., *Airmen of World War 1* (Arms and Armour Press, London, 1975)

Bowyer, M. J. F., *2 Group RAF: A Complete History 1936–1945* (Faber, London, 1974)

Brown, D., *Carrier Operations in World War II: Volume I The Royal Navy* (Ian Allan, London, 1968)

Brown, E. M., *Duels in the Sky: World War II Naval Aircraft in Combat* (Airlife, Shrewsbury, 1989)

Brown, L., *A Radar History of World War II: Technical and Military Imperatives* (Institute of Physics Publishing, Bristol, 1999)

Carrington, C. E., *Soldier at Bomber Command* (Leo Cooper, London, 1987)

Cooling, B. F. (ed.), *Case Studies in the Development of Close Air Support* (Office of Air Force History, Washington 1990)

Cornwell, P. D., *The Battle of France Then and Now* (After the Battle, Old Harlow, 2007)

Cross, Sir Kenneth, *Straight and Level* (Grub Street, London, 1993)

Cull, B. & Lander, B., *Twelve Days in May* (Grub Street, London, 1995)

Darling, K., *Vicker Supermarine Merlin Seafire: Warpaint 72* (Warpaint Books, Bucks, 2008)

Duke, N., *Test Pilot* (Grub Street, London, 1992)

Dunning, C., *Courage Alone: The Italian Air Force 1940–1943* (Hikoki, Manchester, 2009)

Ehlers R. S., *The Mediterranean Air War: Airpower and Allied Victory in World War II* (University Press of Kansas, Lawrence, 2015)

Embry, Sir Basil, *Mission Completed* (Methuen, London, 1957)

Evans, B., *The Decisive Campaigns of the Desert Air Force 1942–1945* (Pen & Sword, Barnsley 2014)

Flintham, V. and Thomas, A., *Combat Codes: A Full Explanation and Listing of British, Commonwealth and Allied Air Force Unit Codes since 1938* (2nd edition) (Pen & Sword, Barnsley, 2008)

Ford, K., *Battles of World War II: El Alamein 1942 The Turning of the Tide* (Osprey, Oxford, 2005)

Ford, K., *Gazala: Rommel's Greatest Victory* (Osprey, Oxford, 2008)

Ford, K., *Operation Crusader: Rommel in Retreat* (Osprey, Oxford, 2010)

Ford, K., *The Mareth Line 1943: The End in Africa* (Osprey, Oxford, 2012)

Forty, G., *Companion to the British Army 1939–1945* (The History Press, Stroud, 1998)

Franks, N., *Air Battle of Dunkirk: 26 May – 3 June 1940* (Grub Street, London, 1983)

Franks, N., RAF *Fighter Command 1936–1968* (PSL, Sparkford, 1992)

Gladman, B. W., *Intelligence and Anglo-American Air Support in World War Two: The Western Desert and Tunisia, 1940–43* (Palgrave Macmillan, Basingstoke, 2009)

Granfield, A., *Bombers Over Sand and Snow: 205 Group RAF in World War II* (Pen & Sword, Barnsley, 2011)

Grice, F., *War's Nomads: A Mobile Radar Unit in Pursuit of Rommel* (Casemate, Oxford, 2015)

Guedalla, P., *Middle East 1940-–1942: A Study in Air Power* (Hodder & Stoughton, London, 1944)

Hall, D. I., *Strategy for Victory: The Development of British Tactical Air Power, 1919–1943* (Praeger Security, Westport, 2008)

Halley, J. J., The *Squadrons of the Royal Air Force and Commonwealth 1918–1988* (Air-Britain, Tonbridge, 1988)

Hallion, R., *Strike from the Sky: The History of Battlefield Air Attack 1911–1945* (Airlife, Shrewsbury, 1989)

Hallows, I. S., *Regiments and Corp of the British Army* (Arms and Armour Press, London, 1991)

Hart, P., *Aces Falling: War Above The Trenches, 1918* (Weidenfeld & Nicolson, London, 2007)

Hezlet, A., *Aircraft and Sea Power* (Peter Davies, London, 1970)

Hickey, S. M. W., *The Army Air Corps Past and Present* (AAC Centre, Middle Wallop, 1980)

Higham, R., *Bases of Air Strategy: Building Airfields for the RAF 1914–1945* (Airlife, Shrewsbury, 1998)

Horden, H. A., *Shark Squadron Pilot* (Independent Books, Bromley, 2002)

Jefford, C. G., *RAF Squadrons* (2nd edition) (Airlife, Shrewsbury, 2001)

Jefford, C. G., *The Flying Camels: The History of 45 Sqn RAF* (Jefford, High Wycombe, 1995)

Johnson, P., *Royal Artillery Glossary of Terms and Abbreviations* (The History Press, Stroud, 2008)

Judd, D., *Avenger from the Sky* (William Kimber, London, 1985)

Kemp, P. K., *Fleet Air Arm* (Herbert Jenkins, London, 1954)

Kersaudy, F., *Norway 1940* (Collins, London, 1990)

Ketley, B., *Auster: A Brief History of the Auster Aircraft in British Military Service* (Flight Recorder Pubs, Ottringham, 2005)

Leaf, E., *Above All Unseen: The Royal Air Force's Photographic Units 1939–1945* (Patrick Stevens, Somerset, 1997)

Leeson, F. M., *The Hornet Strikes: The Story of No. 213 Squadron Royal Air Force* (Air-Britain, Tunbridge Wells, 1998)

Lenton, H. T. & Colledge, J. J., *(British and Dominion) Warships of World War II* (Ian Allan, London, 1964)

Lenton, H. T. & Colledge, J. J., *British Warship Losses of World War II* (Ian Allan, London, 1964)

Lind, R. G. (ed.), *The Falcon: Combat History of the 79th Fighter Group USAAF 1942–1945* (79th FG, Munich, 1946)

Lowe, M. V., *North American Aviation P-51 Mustang: Part 1 Allison Powered* (SAM Publications, Bedford, 2013)

Lucas, J., *War in the Desert: The Eighth Army at El Alamein* (Arms and Armour Press, London, 1982)

Macksey, K., *Military Errors of World War Two* (Arms and Armour Press, London, 1987)

Macksey, K. & Batchelor, J. H., *Tank: A History of the Armoured Fighting Vehicle* (Ballantine, New York, 1971)

Marr, D. S. B., *208 Squadron History* (Privately published, c1968)

Mason, F. K., *The Gloster Gladiator* (Macdonald, London, 1964)

Mason, F. K., *The Hawker Hurricane* (Aston, Bourne End, 1987)

McGuirk, D., *Rommel's Army in Africa* (Airlife, Shrewsbury, 1987)

McNab, C., *Order of Battle: German Luftwaffe in WWII* (Amber Books, London, 2009)

Mead, P., *The Eye in the Air* (HMSO, London, 1983)

Middlebrook, M. & Everitt, C., *The Bomber Command War Diaries: An Operational Reference Book 1939–1945* (Midland Publishing, Earl Shilton, 1996)

Molony, C. J. C. et al., *History of the Second World War: The Mediterranean and Middle East Volume IV* (HMSO, London, 1966)

Montgomery, B. L. Viscount, *El Alamein to the River Sangro: Normandy to the Baltic* (BCA, London, 1973)

Moorehead. A., *The Desert War* (Hamish Hamilton, London, 1965)

Morley-Mower, G., *Messerschmitt Roulette: The Western Desert 1941–42* (Phalanx, St Paul, 1993)

Mortensen, D. R., *A Pattern for Joint Operations: World War II Close Air Support in North Africa* (Office of Air Force History, Washington DC, 1987)

Moyes, P., *Bomber Squadrons of the RAF* (Macdonald, London, 1964)

Napier, M., *Winged Crusaders: The Exploits of 14 Squadron RFC and RAF 1915–1945* (Pen & Sword, Barnsley, 2012)

Neate, D., *Scorpions Sting: The Story of No. 84 Squadron Royal Air Force* (Air-Britain, Tonbridge, 1994)

Oliver, K., *Through Adversity: The History of the Royal Air Force Regiment* (Forces and Corporate Publishing, Rushden, 1997)

Orange, V. et al., *Winged Promises: A History of No. 14 Squadron RAF 1915–1945* (Royal Air Force Benevolent Fund, Fairford, 1996)

Owen, R. *The Desert Air Force* (Hutchinson, London, 195?)

Parham, H. J. & Belfield, E. M. G., *Unarmed into Battle* (Picton Publishing, Chippenham, 1956)

Partridge, E., *A Dictionary of RAF Slang* (Michael Joseph, London, 1945)

Philpott, B., *German Fighters over the Med* (Patrick Stevens, Cambridge, 1979)

Pitchfork, G., *The Sowreys* (Grub Street, London, 2012)

Playfair, I. S. O., *History of the Second World War: The Mediterranean and Middle East Volume IV* (HMSO, London, 1966)

Popham, H., *Into Wind: A History of British Naval Flying* (Hamish Hamilton, London, 1969)

Powell, M., *The Development of British Tactical Air Power 1940–1943: A History of Army Co-operation Command* (Macmillan, London, 2016)

Price, A., *Late Marque Spitfire Aces 1941–45* (Osprey, London, 1997)

Price, A., *Luftwaffe Handbook 1939–1945* (Ian Allan, London, 1977)

Price, A., *Spitfire Mk V Aces 1942–45* (Osprey, London, 1995)

Quarrie, B., *Airborne Assault: Parachute Forces in Action 1940–91* (PSL, Sparkford, 1991)

Raines, E. F., *Eyes of Artillery* (University Press of the Pacific, Honolulu, 2002)

Rawlings, J. D. R., *Coastal, Support and Special Squadrons of the RAF* (Janes, London, 1982)

Rawlings, J. D. R., *Fighter Squadrons of the RAF* (Macdonald, London, 1969)

Richards, D. and Saunders, H. St G., *Royal Air Force 1939–1945: Volume II The Fight Avails* (HMSO, London, 1954)

Ries, K., *The Luftwaffe: A Photographic Record 1919–1945* (Batsford, London, 1987)

Robertson, B., *Aircraft Camouflage and Markings 1907–1954* (Harleyford Publications, Marlow, 1956)

Robertson, B., *The Army and Aviation: A Pictorial History* (Robert Hale, London, 1981)

Robertson, B., *The RAF: A Pictorial History* (Robert Hale, London, 1978)

Robertson, B. and Scarborough, G., *Hawker Hurricane* (PSL, Cambridge, 1974)

Rosier, Sir Frederick, *Be Bold* (Grub Street, London, 2011)

Shores, C. F., *Air War for Yugoslavia, Greece and Crete 1940–41* (Grub Street, London, 1987)

Shores, C. F., *Dust Clouds in the Middle East: The Air War for East Africa, Iraq, Syria, Iran and Madagascar, 1940–42* (Grub Street, London, 1996)

Shores, C. F., *Fledgling Eagles: The Complete Account of Air Operations During the 'Phoney War' and Norwegian Campaign, 1940* (Grub Street, London, 1991)

Shores, C. F., *Mediterranean Air War Volume One* (Ian Allan, London, 1972)

Shores, C. F., *Mediterranean Air War Volume Two* (Ian Allan, London, 1973)

Shores, C. F., *Mediterranean Air War Volume Three* (Ian Allan, London, 1974)

Shores, C. F. & Massimello, G., *A History of the Mediterranean Air War 1940–1945 Volume One June 1940 – January 1942* (Grub Street, London, 2012)

Shores, C. F. & Massimello, G., *A History of the Mediterranean Air War 1940–1945 Volume Two February 1942 – March 1943* (Grub Street, London, 2012)

Shores, C. F. & Massimello, G., *A History of the Mediterranean Air War 1940–1945 Volume Three November 1942 – May 1943* (Grub Street, London, 2016)

Shores, C. F. & Massimello, G., *A History of the Mediterranean Air War 1940–1945 Volume Four May 1943 – June 1944* (Grub Street, London, 2018)

Short, N., *German Defences in Italy in World War II* (Osprey, Oxford, 2006)

Silverstone, P. H., *U.S. Warships of World War II* (Ian Allan, London, 1965)

Slessor, Sir John, *The Central Blue* (Cassell, London, 1956)

Smith, J. R. & Kay, A., *German Aircraft of the Second World War* (Putnam, London, 1972)

Smith, P. C., *Dive Bomber: Aircraft, Techniques and Tactics in World War II* (Casemate, Newbury, 2008)

Smith, P. C., *Stukas over the Mediterranean* (Greenhill, London, 1999)

Spires, D. N., *Patton's Air Force: Forging a Legendary Air-Ground Team* (Smithsonian, Washington, 2002)

Sturtivant, R., *Fleet Air Arm Aircraft 1939 to 1945* (Air-Britain, Tunbridge Wells, 1995)

Sturtivant, R., *RAF Flying Training and Support Units since 1912* (2nd edition) (Air-Britain, Tonbridge, 2007)

Terraine, J., *A Time for Courage: The Royal Air Force in the European War, 1939–1945* (Macmillan, New York, 1985) (published in the UK as *The Right of the Line*)

Thomas, A., *Tomahawk and Kittyhawk Aces of the RAF and Commonwealth* (Osprey, London, 2002)

Twiss, P., *Faster Than The Sun* (2nd revised edition) (Grub Street, London, 2005)

Wakefield, K., *Lightplanes at War: US Liaison Aircraft in Europe 1942–1947* (Tempus, Stroud, 1999)

Walton, J., *Desert War Diary: An RAF Armourer Remembers 213 Squadron 1941–1945* (Woodfield, Bognor Regis, 2000)

Warner, G., *First in the Field: 651 Sqn Army Air Corps* (Pen & Sword, Barnsley, 2011)

Weller, D. M., *Naval Gunfire Support of Amphibious Operations* (Naval Sea Systems Command, Washington, 1977)

Wenham, T. et al., Auster: The Company and the Aircraft (Air Britain, Staplefield, 2018)

White, B. T., *British Tanks and Fighting Vehicles 1914–1945* (Ian Allan, London, 1970)

The Putnam series of books is an extremely useful guide to aircraft operated by British, American and German forces and also to the products of specific British and American manufacturers.

Websites

There are some extremely useful and reliable websites. Wikipedia is a good starting point for many searches if used with care.

British Artillery in WW2:
http://nigelef.tripod.com/directory.htm
Luftwaffe Units:
https://www.asisbiz.com/Luftwaffe-Units.html
Naval Battles and Warships: http://www.naval-history.net/index.htm
USAAF in WW2 Aug 42–Dec 43:
https://www.ibiblio.org/hyperwar/AAF/II/AAF-II-14.html#cn27

Index

AIRCRAFT

Allied & British

PEOPLE

PLACES